ASSESSING STUDY ABROAD

Published by Stylus Publishing, LLC.
22883 Quicksilver Drive
Sterling, Virginia 20166-2102

Library of Congress Cataloging-in-Publication Data
Assessing study abroad : theory, tools, and practice / edited by
Victor Savicki and Elizabeth Brewer. -- First Edition.
    pages cm
  Includes bibliographical references and index.
  ISBN 978-1-62036-213-6 (cloth : acid-free paper)
  ISBN (invalid) 978-1-62036-214-3 (paperback : acid-free paper)
  ISBN 978-1-62036-215-0 (library networkable e-edition)
  ISBN 978-1-62036-216-7 (consumer e-edition)
  1. Foreign study--Administration--Handbooks, manuals, etc.
  2. International education--Handbooks, manuals, etc.   3. College
  administrators--Handbooks, manuals, etc.   I. Savicki, Victor.
  II. Brewer, Elizabeth.
   LB2376.A68 2015
   370.116'2--dc23
                                                    2015010468
  13-digit ISBN: 978-1-62036-213-6 (cloth)
  13-digit ISBN: 978-1-62036-214-3 (paperback)
  13-digit ISBN: 978-1-62036-215-0 (library networkable e-edition)
  13-digit ISBN: 978-1-62036-216-7 (consumer e-edition)

Printed in the United States of America

All first editions printed on acid-free paper
that meets the American National Standards Institute
Z39-48 Standard.

Bulk Purchases

Quantity discounts are available for use in workshops and for
staff development.
Call 1-800-232-0223

First Edition, 2015

10 9 8 7 6 5 4 3 2 1

ASSESSING STUDY

Theory, Tool

Edited by Victor

Eliza

Foreword

To all those working to make study abroad a high-impact learning experience for students, in faith and belief that the process of assessing will improve the study abroad profession, enhance student growth, and benefit both sending and host institutions and communities.

CONTENTS

PART THREE: CASE STUDIES OF PRACTICE IN ASSESSING STUDY ABROAD

FOREWORD

This is an interesting and challenging time for higher education globally. In the United States, the cost of providing a university education continues to rise, and, with it, the price that students and their families must pay. At the same time, universities and colleges are being asked to provide better education and training to serve a wide range of personal, societal, national, and global needs.

In this environment it is more important than ever for a higher education institution to create and sustain an effective culture and practice of assessment in order to improve continuously, be accountable to its many constituents, and demonstrate the value that it claims to deliver.

In the United States, the promise of education abroad is being promoted more now than ever before, and the benefits of education abroad have been voiced at the highest level of the U.S. government. President Obama has supported the U.S. government's 100,000 Strong initiatives and, on a number of occasions, has spoken about the ways in which education abroad can benefit students and, with them, U.S. society and our increasingly globalized world as a whole.

Together, these influences make this book on assessment of study abroad timely and relevant. This book's framework promotes an *institutional* approach to assessing study abroad, with advice on and examples of how to embed effective assessment strategies into the workings of a college, university, or education abroad organization. As with study abroad programming itself, study abroad assessment is bound to fail if it stands apart from the missions, goals, cultures, and shared practices of an institution or organization, a lesson that this book's authors know and understand firsthand. Each chapter presents practical guidance on the many aspects of study abroad assessment, which can be approached through a collaborative model of shared responsibility and commitment to benefit all constituents.

This book is distinctive in that it includes both theoretical perspectives from assessment experts and concrete examples from practitioners who have been involved in different aspects of study abroad assessment. The fact that most of these practitioners are not experts in assessment should inspire other study abroad professionals to develop and sustain their own assessment efforts at their institutions in order to make study abroad a more robust vehicle for student learning and development.

This book outlines important reasons to assess study abroad programs, and these are developed by assessment and education abroad leaders who have learned the lessons of what it takes to be successful. The contributors' strength is to approach their topics with a critical perspective. Each has accumulated substantial experience in assessment, in not only achieving success but also encountering difficulties and not always being successful.

This type of wisdom and experience informs the guidance offered in this book and leads to several qualities that readers will appreciate. First, it is written by colleagues at multiple levels of experience and expertise in study abroad assessment, and, therefore, relevant for everyone in the field. Second, the theory and methodology are aimed specifically at study abroad and require no translation from an academic discipline to the study abroad field. Third, by discussing and analyzing both successful projects and the many bumps and pitfalls along the way, this book demonstrates many different approaches to tackling the real challenges and problems that assessment brings. Finally, this book, unlike other books on assessment, is approachable to practitioners in the field because it explains ideas and methods in clear, jargon-free language and with plenty of concrete examples to elucidate its points.

Study abroad has a long past but a short history. Educational travel to other countries and cultures has been important to world history for thousands of years. But the organized field and profession of education abroad is but a blip on this historical timeline, and the assessment of programs and student outcomes has been considered an important part of the field for only the past 10 years or so.

During this time, study abroad has made significant progress in enhancing its reputation as an academically serious and valuable educational endeavor. However, education abroad still needs more and better data to support what we believe overall to be true. This book will contribute significantly to this effort.

Brian Whalen
President and CEO
The Forum on Education Abroad

INTRODUCTION

Issues in Assessing Study Abroad

Victor Savicki and Elizabeth Brewer

F or many years, it was assumed that placing students into another culture would lead to positive results; such an assumption illustrated "beliefs in the inherent goodness of study abroad, although the assumption might be wrong" (Twombly, Salisbury, Tumanut, & Klute, 2012). In the past 20 years, study abroad participation rates have quadrupled in the United States, and more than 90% of colleges and universities now offer study abroad options (Hoffa & DePaul, 2010). Has the increase been warranted? What does study abroad achieve?[1]

These questions are raised in the wider context of higher education, where accreditation requires that the effectiveness of academic programs be assessed. "Are colleges and universities achieving the results they claim?" Although study abroad and international education more broadly are often marginalized within academia (e.g., Bringle & Hatcher, 2011), the field of study abroad is increasingly driven by accountability and interest in student learning to engage with outcomes assessment.

The following principles for navigating the tension between assessing for accountability and assessing for student learning can guide those embarking on study abroad assessment (Ewell, 2009). Applied to study abroad, these are as follows: (a) take concerns expressed by stakeholders seriously; (b) use findings to make changes that will improve outcomes; (c) assess study abroad outcomes *and* link these to students' ongoing educations; (d) embed assessment in ongoing processes, be this predeparture (advising, orientation), during (courses, programming), and/or post-study abroad (reflective activities, course work, capstones); and (e) consider the impacts on host communities and partners. In other words, anything related to study abroad is fair game for assessment.

How can we describe, in specific, concrete, and meaningful terms, the difference study abroad makes in the lives of students, the work of institutions, and the lives of community members? The returning student's enthusiastic "It was awesome" is not sufficient. This volume seeks to serve as a guide to understand the outcomes of study abroad and to use this information to strengthen its positive impacts.

An Informal Poll of the State of the Field Regarding Assessment

Over the past few years, we have had conversations with international educators in workshops, round table discussions, presentation breakout groups, and various informal settings to discuss assessing study abroad learning. Several impressions emerged. First, assessment is burgeoning and becoming expected if not required in study abroad. Second, knowledge, experience, and expertise with study abroad assessment vary dramatically. Some professionals have yet to get started, others have begun but wonder about next steps, and some are well underway. This book seeks to speak to each of these groups. Third, anxiety around assessment can be high. Do I have the skills? Is there a right way? In fact, there is not a single right way or an exclusive set of prerequisite skills. Instead, we need to draw on what we know, identify unanswered questions, and tailor assessment to both our questions and our capacities. Fourth, although assessment findings are often expressed using numbers, outcomes can be measured, and results can be derived without using complicated statistics. Should statistical analysis prove necessary, colleagues can be asked to help. Fifth, time and money must be considered. Where will these come from? The case studies in this book demonstrate that money need not be a barrier. A plethora of assessment resources are nonmonetary. And although assessment requires time, it brings both direct and indirect benefits. In simple language, assessing means finding evidence to answer important questions, tasks that speak to the talents and values of those engaged with study abroad.

Unpacking "Assessing Study Abroad"

The term *assessing* raises a number of questions. Who will assess what, when, where, why, and how? What will be done with the findings? This book hopes to offer answers to such questions. Let us now begin to address them.

Who Will Assess What?

Those involved in study abroad increasingly are called on to demonstrate its value. They may be faculty members, study abroad advisors, international education administrators, study abroad organizations, on-site program faculty and staff, or host partners and community members. Students also have a stake and can be enlisted in assessment (Blaich & Wise, 2011), as several institutions represented in this book are doing. The "who" responsible for assessing study abroad are thus those who touch, shape, engage with, and are impacted by study abroad, a broad swath of people influencing and influenced by study abroad.

What Should Be Assessed?

In the United States, student learning outcomes receive the most attention, although this focus can be critiqued as too narrow. After all, partners and host communities are also impacted. But the impact of study abroad on sending institutions should not be neglected (e.g., Brewer & Cunningham, 2009). The "what" has also evolved over time; the academic, disciplinary learning that was of central importance in study abroad several decades ago has not disappeared but has been eclipsed in the literature by intercultural learning (e.g., Deardorff, 2009; Savicki, 2008; Vande Berg, Paige, & Lou, 2012).

Three clarifications of the "what" of assessment are needed. First, outputs (the number of students studying abroad, the proportion of males to females, countries of sojourn) should not be confused with outcomes, which in higher education involve students developing "knowledge, skills, attitudes, competencies, and habits of mind" (National Institute for Learning Outcomes Assessment, n.d.). Sending male student B to country Y for a semester counts as one student abroad, one male abroad, and a semester of study in country Y. The outcome is what B learns and how B changes. Second, what B learns and how B changes is different from B's level of satisfaction with his experiences. Third, the purpose of assessment is not to "grade" student performance but to measure the effectiveness of a particular activity in which students participate (e.g., study abroad program, institutional approach to study abroad, community engagement within study abroad, independent study projects). The scope of what to assess is quite wide and inclusive. In essence, we can question all aspects of study abroad in terms of their effects on learning outcomes.

To What End?

Assessment does not exist in a vacuum, and the tension between accountability and improvement remains after more than 30 years of assessment in higher education (Ewell, 2013). Trustees may want to know if the tuition spent on study abroad could be better used elsewhere. A college president may ask if alumni who studied abroad are more or less likely to become donors. Study abroad advisors may be interested in intercultural development. A language department might ask if language and cultural competency increase through study abroad, whereas political scientists might be more interested in students' abilities to understand complex social problems. Pre-study abroad, many students hope to grow personally by leaving their comfort zones. How can this growth be measured? In addition, a university may be interested in augmenting its educational offerings through partnerships.

Stakeholders thus are differently invested in assessment findings. Paying attention to these differences can strengthen the impacts of assessment, and identifying assessment goals and aligning them with measurement and other components of the assessment process is a key driver. However, less may be more; feasible, narrow focus is better than collecting data that cannot be analyzed or paralyzing one's self by imagining an overwhelming, virtually impossibly large task. An incremental, step-by-step approach to assessment may be more feasible than the ideal, multimeasure approach.

When, Where, and How?

Assessment can occur at different times and places. However, experts on assessment advise that "authentic, information-rich" assessment is preferable to scores from "single-sitting, snapshot measures of learning" (Banta, Griffin, Flateby, & Kahn, 2009). Furthermore, as already noted, assessment is, if possible, best embedded in existing processes and, ideally, should also benefit the student (e.g., by facilitating reflection and meaning-making).

A psychologist from the early 1900s, E. L. Thorndike, famously said, "If something exists, it exists in some quantity. If it exists in some quantity, it can be measured." In contrast, a quote attributed to Albert Einstein reads, "Not everything that can be counted counts, and not everything that counts can be counted." The key to selecting an assessment methodology is to focus on the desired outcome. The chapters in this book discuss assessment questions, methods, and findings. Their authors would all agree that identifying what you want to know and why is the place to start. Methodology flows from these questions, not vice versa.

Tests or Texts?

"Psychology majors like tests; literature majors like texts." Thus, the psychology major will be more inclined toward quantitative measures, and the literature major will prefer qualitative measures. Ultimately, a mix of methods works best, and both approaches can be used effectively in tandem in study abroad assessment. The concept of "triangulation" looms large here. Multiple views of study abroad outcomes lead to a deeper understanding of not only what has occurred but also why and how. The methods chapters in part two of this book and the case studies in part three illustrate ways to approach assessment from either starting point.

How to Operationalize Generalizations?

Assessment requires creativity: How can concrete indicators for somewhat ambiguous study abroad goals be identified? Consider, for example, measuring developing empathy toward the host culture or expanding cultural self-knowledge? Perhaps a well-documented questionnaire in the literature will help, or well-constructed rubrics can be used for content analysis. In either case, creativity can help capture the information "that counts" in ways that can be counted.

Measures, Metaphors, and Links

The concept of *measurement* seems to be a sticking point for many approaching the task of assessing study abroad. Measurement may be expressed through well-constructed surveys that can be analyzed with inferential statistics that use probability statements to demonstrate that the effects of study abroad are real and not by chance alone. Many professionals use bar graphs, pie charts, and other visual depictions of measurement findings. And, in the qualitative approach, assessors can use language terms to describe how students fair on study abroad tasks. In all of these approaches, the goal is to indicate how study abroad student learning, and all of the other aspects of the study abroad process (accommodation, activities, orientation, reentry, etc.), can be evaluated so that these measures can be available to compare against other measures (e.g., level of language competence in relation to intercultural sensitivity). Measurement is at the heart of assessment, but it is only one component of assessment. Assessment projects that ask students to take one survey instrument and report only those scores may satisfy the powers that be in an organization, but they ignore the broader context of assessment and the power of assessment findings to drive program improvement. After all, a number on a survey inventory has no meaning unless it is given context. A more useful approach might be to reconceptualize how the survey's data might align with the goals for study abroad or to adapt or construct measures specifically aimed at those goals (see the case studies in chapters 7, 11, 12, 13, and 14).

Measurement occurs in the middle of the process. There are important components to consider both before and after measurement occurs. When a study abroad advisor asks, "What instrument or survey should I use?" the question is fraught with presuppositions. The question is impossible to answer without backtracking to discover what contextual factors (both before and after measurement) need to be considered and what questions about study abroad the advisor is trying to answer. Though study abroad professionals may start with the question of measurement, it is important to fill in the context in order to design a more effective project.

Several metaphors regarding the assessment process will appeal to different people in accordance with their habits of mind. Some like to think of assessment as a checklist in which specific tasks are ordered in a fixed sequence, and no deviation is allowed. There is some comfort in this thought pattern, because the process is very definitive, and one always knows what is supposed to happen next. Another metaphor that may appeal to others is that of assessment as telling a story. In a good story, there is a beginning, middle, and end. Setting the stage in the beginning helps the reader understand the action (measurement) in the middle and how the story turns out at the end. This approach is a bit less constraining, but the author or assessor needs to understand and appeal to his or her audience, as well as spin a good tale. Last, although other metaphors surely exist, assessment can be seen as an organic process, akin to cultivating a garden. In this case, the assessors have the seed of an idea and need to think about how to prepare the ground so that the seed will sprout. They need to consider how to determine how well the seed flourishes. They need to think about what to do with the blooms or fruit. The important point here is that no matter how assessment is conceptualized, the assessor needs to put thought into all of its various components, and measurement is only one. This does not mean that everything needs to be settled before beginning the process. Learning about assessment happens along the way. Most of the case studies in part three demonstrate how assessment efforts morph over time based on emerging findings and changing external conditions. Nevertheless, it pays to keep in mind that the measurement component is not the whole of assessment and that assessment gains meaning through the context in which it occurs, both before and after measurement. For a full discussion of assessment components, see chapter 3.

Another key feature of effective assessment projects is making linkages among components. Study abroad assessment goals gain legitimacy to the degree that they reflect the goals and mission of the larger organization of which the study abroad program is a part. Selection of measurement instruments and methods can be guided by their linkages to stated assessment goals and desired learning outcomes. Future adjustments to program design can be suggested and supported by measurement results. Communication of assessment findings can intensify their impact when linked to goals and measurement as indicators of study abroad goals and institutional mission. In the best of circumstances, the links between components show an alignment of components; the parts of the assessment process support and amplify each other. In the real world, this is a difficult aspiration. The perfect assessment project has not yet been, and probably will not ever be, designed. In an uncontrolled, naturalistic environment, there are too many variables to account for. Assessors are likely to find answers to some of their questions and find even more questions based on those answers. We advocate an approach that values repeated assessment over time, each building on the information gathered by previous projects. Many of the case studies in this volume take this approach.

Overview of Chapters

This book has three parts. Part one introduces the subsequent discussions and focuses on questions raised about study abroad and learning outcomes, frameworks employed, and theories related to study abroad and its assessment. Chapters in part two explore strategies and tools to expedite assessment activities: quantitative and qualitative methods and institutional decision making relating to assessment. Part three is then devoted to nine case studies of study abroad assessment covering a wide span of goals, methods, and results, and a concluding chapter discusses building capacity to assemble resources useful in assessing study abroad.

In chapter 1, Mark Salisbury critiques claims about the impact and value of study abroad; some may be exaggerated or not entirely attributable to study abroad. He then looks at the broader history of assessment in higher education and suggests ways that study abroad professionals and higher education institutions might most effectively and efficiently assess the impact and value of study abroad.

What is the contribution of study abroad to academic disciplines? What do disciplines think about study abroad? In chapter 2, Rachel Shively discusses questions, methods, and findings from nearly 40 years of research on language acquisition. Although language skills *can* improve during study abroad, improvement is not guaranteed. Victor Savicki then discusses perspectives from psychology (reactions to cross-cultural encounters, acculturation challenges and strategies, student well-being, contact theory, and prejudice reduction). In contrast, Nick Gozik shows that professional fields (nursing, social work, teacher education) look to study abroad as preparation for practice with diverse populations. Business, however, focuses more on the potential of study abroad to provide advantages in the job market. Finally, Elizabeth Brewer and Dennis M. Doyle examine agendas for study abroad being set in anthropology, communication studies, political science, sociology, student development, and service-learning. Some are focused on student well-being, others on the value of experience abroad, and still others on pedagogies that in themselves both further learning and document it.

Chapter 3 seeks to demystify assessment, and many of the themes discussed by Nick Gozik (tying goals and desired outcomes to institutional mission, consulting with stakeholders and experts, matching methods and tools to questions, communicating and acting on findings) reemerge in the case studies that constitute part three. Whether assessment is driven externally (e.g., for accreditation purposes) or internally (with questions such as "Are we being effective?"), student learning should be central. Furthermore, as this chapter and subsequent case studies make clear, assessment is collaborative and iterative.

Part two begins with an elaboration of context setting in assessment. In chapter 4, Kevin P. Saunders, Jen Hogan, and Christa Lee Olson offer practical ways to place assessment in a broader context, to determine the purpose of the assessment, and to identify evidence needed to answer specific questions. They suggest finding and using existing data and aligning assessment with institutional culture, and they discuss approaches for data collection. Finally, as is recommended in chapters 3, 5, and 6, they recommend forming partnerships to conceptualize and undertake the work. Case vignettes from Drake University illustrate how partnerships can ensure that study abroad assessment is both manageable and fruitful not only in terms of answering specific assessment questions but also in terms of positioning study abroad in a larger political context of a university and community.

In chapter 5, Tasha Bleistein and Mary Shepard Wong distinguish between quantitative methods (What did a large sample of study abroad students learn?) and qualitative methods (Which conditions shaped unique learning and students' understanding of it?) and note an increase in mixed methods. Qualitative research invites collaboration in data collection and analysis, including with students, as seen in chapters 7, 11, and 13. Bleistein and Wong use study abroad research scenarios to illustrate application of a variety of methods (interviews, focus groups, observations, student artifacts, open-ended questionnaires, case studies) and underline the importance of matching the method to the purpose of the assessment, resources, and supports. Qualitative methods forefront discussions in chapters 7, 10, and 14.

In chapter 6, Mark E. Engberg and Lisa M. Davidson discuss quantitative methods and offer examples using SPSS software for statistical analysis of survey data. As in chapters 3, 5, and 10, they emphasize the importance of carefully formulating and prioritizing assessment questions before getting started. Any research design involves trade-offs (What is the purpose? Is the design feasible? Are the findings accurate?), and the advantages and drawbacks of different instruments, whether locally or commercially produced, need consideration. They illustrate how quantitative approaches can answer fine-grained assessment questions. Finally, they encourage study abroad practitioners to not go it alone; reaching out for additional resources and colleagues with expertise in quantitative analysis is not only acceptable but also recommended. Applications of quantitative methods in study abroad assessment can be found in chapters 9, 11, 12, and 13.

The chapters in part three illustrate various approaches to planning, experimentation, application of findings, and preparation for next steps. False starts and lessons learned are discussed in chapters 7, 10, 12, and 14 and suggest both how to avoid wrong turns and errors and how better alternatives can be found. Although initial efforts may not have succeeded, they led to clarifications of the purpose of the assessment and selection of methods better suiting office and institution capacities and cultures.

In chapter 7, Elizabeth Brewer and Joshua Moore discuss the application of rubrics to analyze post-study abroad essays. Questions about the development of lifelong learning skills and intercultural competency are related to the mission of Beloit College, where they work. Teams of faculty, students, and staff analyzed the essays; this achieved a secondary goal of educating the larger campus about study abroad. Beloit's assessment emphasizes student ownership of study abroad, a theme that repeats in chapter 10. When examined by program type, Beloit's data indicated that outcomes associated with direct enrollment were no less strong than those associated with provider programs.

Institutional mission is also featured in chapter 8. Nick Gozik offers Duke University as an example of assessment evolving in response to changes in organizational needs. Although accreditation was the initial driver, over time more fully formed assessment plans developed as Duke's Global Education Office for Undergraduates took ownership of the process. When internationalization expanded across the institution, assessment activities were rearticulated accordingly. As is seen elsewhere in this volume, assessment replaced satisfaction surveys, and at Duke it focused on leadership development and ethics.

In chapter 9, Dennis M. Doyle reports on a global perspectives requirement at Central College that emerged from a three-year curriculum review. Implementation required adjustments to the core curriculum, study abroad goals, and on-site programming abroad, as well as extensive faculty development. To determine the contribution of study abroad to meeting the requirement, the Central College Abroad Office used the Global Perspective Inventory (GPI). Next steps include gathering assessment data from other sources within Central College.

Like Central College, Yale College (as Kelly McLaughlin writes in chapter 10) experimented with pre- and posttesting of the GPI. However, its Center for International and Professional Experience (CIPE) lacked the capacity to disaggregate the data and, for reporting purposes, wanted to capture student voices. CIPE therefore turned to self-reports in surveys to examine the development of knowledge and skills (important to Yale) and attitudes (important to CIPE). CIPE has now developed tools and principles to guide its work, recommitted to avoiding negative impacts on host communities, and taken steps to encourage student ownership of international experiences. Yale has now established a committee to do similar assessment across the college.

Trained in psychology, Elaine Meyer-Lee and Karen Chambers (chapter 11) want to understand student growth. At Saint Mary's College, they use multiple methods (GPI, American Identity Measure, intercultural engagement measures, student self-reported goals) and program variables to study intercultural development during study abroad. To make assessment more manageable, they enlisted student researchers, and Chambers, a faculty member, has been assigned part-time to Meyer-Lee's office. Findings have been used to improve programs (e.g., to better suit particular majors), change policies (e.g., GPA requirement), and advocate for study abroad (e.g., it improves retention and alumnae giving).

Initially driven by accreditation needs, Victor Savicki, an emeritus professor, helped Michele V. Price (chapter 12) develop an in-house survey at Western Oregon University. When the results failed to capture significant personal growth and development as a result of study abroad, a staff-undergraduate student team then examined reentry essays from a study abroad course. Predeparture individual student characteristics affected reentry goal attainment but did not suggest concrete ideas for program design. Still examining student reentry essays, a graduate student team then identified and analyzed sentences discussing cultural differences; predeparture openness and an ability and willingness to process experiences critically and creatively corresponded to intercultural sensitivity development. Finally, computer-based content analysis examining critical thinking in journal assignments saved time and labor, and now analysis of computer blogs during study abroad is taking place.

Steven E. Stemler and Carolyn K. Sorkin (chapter 13) created the Wesleyan Intercultural Competence Scale (WICS) to understand intercultural development during study abroad. WICS involves 16 scenarios likely encountered in study abroad. Six possible responses to each align with Milton Bennett's levels of intercultural competence. Undergraduate students were enlisted and scored responses from 30 students to beta test WICS. The more scenarios encountered abroad, the higher the scores; language usage also related to scores. As has been found elsewhere, women scored higher than men. WICS is available at no cost, can be adapted and expanded, provides direct measures, is easily administered and scored, and can examine the relationships between student and program characteristics and outcomes.

Chapter 14 focuses on student learning in programs administered by the Associated Colleges of the Midwest (ACM). When findings from a pre- and posttest of student learning proved inconclusive, the ACM focused on writing assignments. Faculty-staff teams examined these for evidence of new knowledge or insight at the end of students' programs and application of academic work to interpret the host culture and society. The chapter authors, Joan Gillespie, Elizabeth Ciner, and David Schodt, describe the assignments and scoring rubric. In the future, assignments will be tailored to the context of each program. However, scoring the essays proved informative for the teams, and the data yielded are being used to improve program elements.

Chapter 15 addresses a question raised in chapter 10 about the impacts on host communities. Mary F. Price, Julie A. Hatcher, Dawn Michele Whitehead, and Gil Latz argue that a partnership lens can position study abroad to contribute to social good and has enabled Indiana University–Purdue University Indianapolis to shift from transactional to transformative partnerships, particularly where service-learning is involved. Desired outcomes and how these will be measured should be clarified before proceeding to program conceptualization and design. Furthermore, community engagement theory can result in programs that positively impact institutions and community. A case study within a long-term, multifaceted partnership in Kenya illustrates the principles discussed.

This book concludes with a discussion of capacity building for assessing study abroad outcomes. Drawing on the experiences of the authors of the book's case studies, Elizabeth Brewer (chapter 16) discusses resources, methods, collaborations, and trial and error processes that have led to fertile assessment practices in the institutions and organizations represented in this book. Although there were initial struggles (to find the right methods and instruments and to make assessment feasible), assessment led to clarifications of study abroad's purpose and improvements in practice.

Note

1. A note on terminology: Study abroad is the most common international experience discussed in this book, although this volume also includes assessment of some non-credit-bearing international experiences. Also discussed are intersections between learning abroad and learning on the home campus, and how their outcomes are measured. The intended audience is the range of individuals (study abroad advisors, administrators, faculty members, program staff) taking responsibility for study abroad and its assessment. As students are primary stakeholders, they may also be interested.

References

Banta, T. W., Griffin, M., Flateby, T. L., & Kahn, S. (2009, December). Three promising alternatives for assessing college students' knowledge and skills (NILOA Occasional Paper No. 2). Urbana, IL: University of Illinois and Indiana University, National Institute for Learning Outcomes Assessment.

Blaich, C. F., & Wise, K. S. (2011, January). *From gathering to using assessment results: Lessons from the Wabash national study* (NILOA Occasional Paper No. 8). Urbana, IL: University of Illinois and Indiana University, National Institute for Learning Outcomes Assessment.

Brewer, E., & Cunningham, K. (Eds.). (2009). *Integrating study abroad into the curriculum: Theory and practice across the disciplines.* Sterling, VA: Stylus.

Bringle, R. G., & Hatcher, J. A. (2011). International service learning. In R. G. Bringle, J. A. Hatcher, & S. J. Jones (Eds.), *International service learning: Conceptual frameworks and research* (pp. 3–28). Sterling, VA: Stylus.

Deardorff, D. K. (Ed.). (2009). *The Sage handbook of intercultural competence.* Thousand Oaks, CA: Sage.

Ewell, P. T. (2009, November). *Assessment, accountability, and improvement: Revisiting the tension* (NILOA Occasional Paper No. 1). Urbana, IL: University of Illinois and Indiana University, National Institute for Learning Outcomes Assessment.

Ewell, P. T. (2013). *Assessing assessment: Successes, failures, and the future.* IUPUI 2013 Assessment Institute. Retrieved December 2, 2014, from http://planning.iupui .edu/1017.html

Hoffa, W. W., & DePaul, S. C. (2010). *A history of U.S. study abroad: 1965–present.* Carlisle, PA: Forum on Education Abroad.

National Institute for Learning Outcomes Assessment. (n.d.). *Making learning outcomes usable and transparent.* Retrieved from http://www.learningoutcomeas sessment.org/TFComponentSLOS.htm

Savicki, V. (Ed.). (2008). *Developing intercultural competence and transformation: Theory, research and application in international education.* Sterling, VA: Stylus.

Twombly, S., Salisbury, M., Tumanut, S., & Klute, P. (2012). *Study abroad in a new global century: Renewing the promise, refining the purpose* (ASHE Higher Education Report). Hoboken, NJ: Wiley.

Vande Berg, M., Paige, R. M., & Lou, K. H. (Eds.). (2012). *Student learning abroad: What our students are learning, what they're not, and what we can do about it.* Sterling, VA: Stylus.

PART ONE

THEORY AND BACKGROUND ON ASSESSING STUDY ABROAD

I

HOW WE GOT TO WHERE WE ARE (AND AREN'T) IN ASSESSING STUDY ABROAD LEARNING

Mark Salisbury

The increased emphasis on assessing study abroad learning might seem to be relatively recent. However, the assessment of postsecondary student learning has a long and complicated history, and efforts to research the educational or developmental effects of study abroad date back to at least the 1920s. Similar to learning assessment in higher education, study abroad assessment has experienced twists and turns that continue to influence the degree to which current assessment practices produce useful, or even valid, results or contribute to the educational improvement of study abroad. This chapter endeavors to weave together a historical view of learning assessment in higher education, the research frameworks developed by higher education scholars for studying the educational impact of college experiences, and our developing understanding of the challenges, pitfalls, and possibilities for study abroad assessment. Finally, this chapter discusses ways that institutions and study abroad professionals can leverage assessment to better achieve study abroad's desired student learning outcomes.

A Brief History of Learning Assessment in Higher Education

The history of assessment in higher education is quite long: Culminating measures of acquired knowledge or achievement (e.g., exams, research papers, or final projects) have been around in one form or another since the Middle Ages (Wilbrink, 1997). However, scholars of assessment in higher education tend to situate the origins of learning outcomes assessment amidst the early twentieth-century emergence of the social sciences, the evolution of cognitive psychology as a unique academic discipline, and early efforts to quantify intelligence and discipline-specific content knowledge (Shavelson, 2007). The Pennsylvania Study, conducted between 1928 and 1932, was the most prominent of these early assessment efforts, with 12 hours of testing that covered content knowledge in numerous disciplines, as well as a test of general intelligence. The project's immediate contribution was to demonstrate that it was indeed possible to measure student learning by testing the same cohort of students during their senior year in high school, their sophomore year in college, and their senior year in college. However, as Shavelson (2007) suggested, the employment of a longitudinal design also helped solidify the belief that a college experience uniquely contributed to learning and that such learning could be quantified.

This might seem an obvious assertion; the content knowledge tested by the Pennsylvania Study would almost assuredly have been learned through college course work. However, as the effort to measure learning gained steam, the assumption about a college education's unique contribution to learning held firm even as educational testing instruments turned away from discipline-specific content toward broader conceptions of cognitive abilities not directly related to college course work. In addition to varying approaches to measuring intelligence, postsecondary assessment efforts increasingly began to tackle some combination of reading comprehension, interpretation, and critical reasoning, with the best-known example of this approach encapsulated in the Graduate Record Exam (GRE) (Shavelson, 2007). Although individual subject tests continued to be available, within several decades the overarching conception of a college education's learning outcomes—at least as measured by large-scale efforts to assess postsecondary learning—had shifted to a generalized set of cognitive skills and abilities perceived to be applicable across a range of settings. Parallel to the shift to a more general set of cognitive skills and abilities was a general acceptance of a common conception of the cognitive outcomes of a college education.

When content was king, control over the curriculum allowed institutions and, especially, individual academic departments to shape the nature of the content knowledge conveyed to students. By contrast, once the outcome of a college education became a more abstract concept involving a range of cognitive skills, control and responsibility for defining the nature and scope of cognitive outcomes shifted to the psychometricians and educational researchers constructing assessment instruments. As a result, even though institutional conceptions of broader outcomes may not have been explicitly or thoroughly shared, the broad acceptance of large-scale quantitative instruments cultivated an implicit consensus regarding the nature and scope of learning outcomes.

At the same time, the meaning of "assessment" evolved at institutions and among educational researchers. Traditionally, assessment and evaluation were considered synonymous with the testing and grading that occurred in a course or, in some cases, at the end of a program. But as the range of measurement instruments grew in quality and usage, assessment in higher education began to be understood as a process of determining the overall educational effectiveness of a program. Thus, a faculty member might evaluate a student's work in order to assign a grade, whereas a graduate school admissions officer might review the work to determine eligibility for admission. Furthermore, an accrediting body might look at the work to evaluate the quality of the student's academic department or college or university. Assessment thus differed from measuring student performance in specific courses.

Higher education leaders and researchers soon began to suggest an expanded range of plausible outcomes of a college education; institutions should accept some responsibility for the variety of psychosocial attitudes, beliefs, and values long assumed to develop in students during college. This expanded view is evident in both the range of measurement instruments developed to assess postsecondary learning (Pellegrino, 2004) and the growing body of social science research in the 1960s and 1970s investigating the impact of college on a host of psychosocial outcomes (Feldman & Newcomb, 1969; Pascarella & Terenzini, 1991). As this body of research filtered up to higher education leaders and policymakers, colleges and universities (likely simultaneously influenced by broader cultural shifts among American college students) began to more explicitly accept the notion that a college experience should produce gains across a holistic body of cognitive, psychosocial constructs and interpersonal outcomes. In recent decades there has been substantial growth in the number and quality of measurement instruments intended for postsecondary learning outcomes assessments. The basic premise that a college experience should uniquely impact student learning and growth across a holistic range of complex outcomes has also become pervasive, and with it, the pressure to document learning and prove the cost-benefit of a college education has intensified.

One benefit of this extensive growth in college impact research is the development of a variety of theoretical frameworks for understanding the way that specific college experiences, such as study abroad, impact student learning. By far the most prominent of these frameworks is Astin's input-environment-output (I-E-O) model (Astin, 1977). The I-E-O model argues that accurately assessing the impact of any given college experience or set of college experiences requires an analytic model organized into three groups. First, the analysis needs to account for the reality that students come to college with a wealth of characteristics or inputs (I) from their precollege lives. In addition to academic preparation, these characteristics would include race, gender, socioeconomic status, and attitudes or values formed prior to college. Second, the model needs to account for the environment (E) within which students interact and engage their college experience; this environment shapes the nature and extent of their learning and growth. This category of potentially influential factors would include in-class learning (e.g., in a major or a minor) and out-of-class college experiences (e.g., study abroad, student clubs and athletics, community engagement). Third, it is the combination of precollege inputs (I) and experiences within the college environment (E) that most thoroughly explains the learning or change on any particular outcome (O).

Pascarella's (1985) expansion of the I-E-O model perceptively parsed the environment category of Astin's model to account for the iterative way that an environment can prove influential. Rather than assuming the environment to be largely static, Pascarella recognized the need to account for the unique impact of the institution (e.g., the college's or university's structure, organization, size, values, etc.) and individual (e.g., the nature of the student's interactions with faculty and staff, the extent of the student's involvement with campus activities, etc.) on the educational effectiveness of the environment. By independently categorizing these two aspects of an undergraduate environment, Pascarella's model further emphasized the basic conception of the I-E-O model as a crucial mechanism for assessing the educational impact of specific experiences. Since their introduction, Astin's I-E-O model and Pascarella's General Model for Assessing the Effects of Differential Environments on Student Learning and Cognitive Outcomes have become the pervasive frameworks for assessing student learning in college and identifying the experiences that impact that learning.

Although learning outcomes assessment in higher education has clearly evolved over time, placing study abroad learning assessment within this broader historical context helps to highlight gaps. For the purposes of this chapter, these gaps can be organized into two groups. First, because the impetus for assessing student learning has primarily focused on identifying or proving the cumulative outcome(s) of a college education, efforts to measure postsecondary learning have historically focused on capturing a measurement of those outcomes in their most comprehensive form. As a result, the instruments that were developed, as well as the ones now commonly available (thanks to the testing industry that has emerged to take advantage of heightened interest in assessment), are "achievement" measures (Shavelson, 2007) meant to measure what is hypothesized to be demonstrable at the end of a college education. Unfortunately, there is little evidence to suggest that these instruments are equally useful (if they are useful at all) in teasing out incremental gains on complex outcomes at any given point in a college education, and few, if any, were designed or validated to do so. Further complicating the problem, there is little research on the degree to which any of the broad constructs addressed by the instruments are realistically achievable by the time a student is 22 years old, when a traditional undergraduate would complete college, or over 4 to 5 years, the time span traditionally set aside for an undergraduate education. In short, although these instruments might capture the breadth of the outcomes for which they are intended, and may be appropriate for assessing learning gains in college, there is little reason to believe that they are appropriate for assessing learning that might result from much shorter, finite experiences within college, such as study abroad.

Second, although the development of empirically vetted theoretical frameworks for studying learning in college has helped to clarify the importance of students' individual experiences, these models, and the subsequent body of research demonstrating their validity, do little to explain the nature of the contribution of experiences. Substantive, transformational learning requires three types of learning: (a) *content knowledge*: the facts, theories, and principles specific to one or more field of study; (b) *applied knowledge*: the skills that come from applying content knowledge to practice; and (c) *integrative knowledge*: the internalization of learning that comes from putting knowledge from distinct experiences together for a specific purpose in a new context. Progress toward achieving the broad learning outcomes that institutions claim, and multiple instruments now aspire to assess, requires a hefty dose of all three types of learning, particularly integrative learning. Yet even the most rigorous analyses of the relationship between an individual experience (e.g., study abroad) and a complex learning outcome (e.g., intercultural competence) produce a statistical effect that merely explains the relative proportion of the experience's impact on the outcome. The findings do not tell us anything about how complex learning might emerge over the course of a series of singular experiences. Thus, despite a range of instruments, some of which address outcomes long associated with study abroad, there is a largely uncharted chasm between the appropriate application of these instruments, the usefulness of their results, and the identification of the potential learning that results from study abroad.

Fortunately, alternative means of gathering evidence and assessing learning are emerging to address the limitations of quantitative assessment and survey data. Although survey instruments still dominate the assessment landscape, some institutions have found success with the use of rubrics that establish thresholds across various aspects of a given outcome. Rubrics provide a distinct advantage in comparison to standardized tests by requiring student work for their application. This weaves assessment into the learning context. By contrast, standardized tests by their nature necessitate abstraction and disregard of any unique learning experience. The Association of American Colleges and Universities (AAC&U, 2010) has developed a series of rubrics (see www.aacu.org/value/rubrics) that have found a growing body of assessment advocates. At the same time, AAC&U has successfully promoted the use of electronic portfolios; work stored by students in the portfolios can be scored with the rubrics to gauge competence on corresponding learning outcomes.

A Brief History of Assessing Study Abroad

Reviewing the history of study abroad assessment in light of the larger history of learning outcomes assessment helps to provide some important context for understanding how and why study abroad assessment has evolved as it has. This context also provides a more stable starting point for using the assessment process to strengthen the way that we identify, articulate, and improve learning and development from study abroad.

Unlike higher education assessment, grades (or other summative assessment) and credits have not always been integral to study abroad. Although some early study abroad involved courses designed for American study abroad students, study abroad initially largely entailed taking courses at local universities. Differences in course structure, instructional style, language proficiency, library resources, and the metrics for assessing student performance made American institutions reticent to award home institution credit for this course work. Moreover, for many years "no university in Europe would permit an American student to take an examination" (Murray, 1965), making it exceedingly difficult to produce more than cursory evidence of student learning. Bowman (1987) described the early rationales for assessment of study abroad learning in terms of (a) the challenges students experienced when trying to navigate the stark differences between American and European universities and (b) the concern that American students might—and apparently sometimes did—find the local culture far more intriguing than their university classes. Thus, the supposition that study abroad is rarely as rigorous as course work at the home institution emerged right along with study abroad itself.

This set in motion a long-standing demand for academic rigor in study abroad. In turn, study abroad professionals developed criteria for quality in study abroad, whether for faculty-led tours, direct enrollment in foreign universities, or programs conducted by outside providers. A given study abroad experience needed to be educationally similar to taking classes on the home campus, and leadership, administration, housing, transportation, facilities, and finances also were considered. Interestingly, although study abroad directors uniformly agreed that programs of dubious quality were hurting the general reputation of study abroad, they were less certain about the identity of those programs. Academic differences between foreign (largely European) universities and American institutions made it difficult to equate what was learned abroad with what might have been learned at home. Faculty-led study tours were sometimes suspected of emphasizing the tour at the expense of study, and third-party providers were suspected of succumbing to the desire of their student customers for ample free time to partake of the locale fare. The assessment of study abroad learning and student growth remained vulnerable to suspicions of dubious quality.

Efforts to assess study abroad learning did not, however, result immediately in the development of measurement instruments that could be utilized by all or most programs equally. Instead, the focus was on finding more satisfactory ways to translate students' academic performance at foreign institutions into American-style credits and grades. This made sense: Students expected their study abroad course work to count toward their studies and graduation requirements. Progress made to recognize course work completed abroad toward home institution degrees encouraged study abroad professionals to equate learning assessment with grades and credits. What students should learn abroad remained largely framed in terms of content knowledge, particularly in arts, humanities, and foreign languages.

Concerns over inconsistencies in educational quality only grew as study abroad opportunities began to grow in the decades immediately following World War II. In response, the Council on Student Travel (1965) developed *A Guidebook to Institutional Self-Study and Evaluation of Educational Programs Abroad* to assist institutions in evaluating the quality of a study abroad experience, regardless of program type. This document provided guiding principles, points of inquiry, and opportunities to rate a program on each of the requisite criteria. Course grades remained the primary measure of student learning. Indeed, the chapter addressing testing and evaluation pushed to ensure that courses be designed and administered just as they might be on an American institution's home campus. Reflecting the depth of the concern over potential relaxed academic rigor, "systematic comparison of grades before and after the period of study abroad" (1965, p. 27) was recommended as a second check of academic quality. Some went beyond the codification of study abroad educational quality characteristics to call for regional accrediting organizations, then growing in authority, to set and ensure expectations for academic rigor (Pfnister, 1970).

The degree to which both study abroad professionals and home institution faculty members equated academic rigor with student learning cannot be overemphasized. Furthermore, learning was entirely in the hands of the student. Hard work and persistence were what counted, not the instructor's approach or teaching abilities. Academic rigor was therefore the primary institutional mechanism for ensuring student learning. Policing study abroad academic rigor also related to concern for academic reputation:

> The reputations in (the director's) own programs were endangered by laxness in the programs of other institutions. The presence of any American students in Paris who spent an undue portion of their time in sidewalk cafes tended to reflect on the quality of all the study abroad programs in the city. Rumors of such sybaritic behavior dogged directors' efforts to give assurances to the deans at home that their students were studying assiduously. (Bowman, 1987, p. 39)

Students' readiness for study abroad made up the other half of the equation. To account for this variable, American colleges and universities focused on selecting the right students for study abroad (third-party programs may have been less exacting). If only students who were ready to study abroad actually did so, and the courses they took were academically rigorous, grades would suffice as evidence of learning. GPA to date and the "rigor" of courses already taken determined study abroad readiness. This approach seemed largely unquestioned as long as the primary learning outcome aligned with academic course work. Most study abroad offices, no matter what kinds of study abroad opportunities they offer, still maintain a set of selection criteria that include applicants' academics. However, some have reduced minimum academic preparation criteria in response to pressures to increase participation, as well as in recognition that academic rigor is not the only measure of study abroad quality. Nonetheless, too often other criteria—the student's goals, intentions, and promise to benefit more holistically—are not considered, perhaps because these are less easily quantified.

Although it was not uncommon for study abroad literature to discuss the educational benefits of a cross-cultural or "foreign" experience and interactions with individuals from host countries, much of the early language addressing this issue suggests that students be "introduced" to a different culture (Murray, 1965), a goal that no other college experience at the time could achieve. However, study abroad professionals had little grounding to determine how such introduction might change students. In fact, tracing a history of intercultural learning, Milton Bennett (2010) pointed out that no mature language existed to describe the learning that might come from cross-cultural interactions, and "students did not seem to have any technical jargon with which to refer to this aspect of their experience" (p. 419). Efforts to capture evidence of cross-cultural learning were limited to asking students how they thought their attitudes toward other countries and cultures had changed. The single question about cross-cultural learning in the Council on Student Travel's (1965) guidebook seems intended more to inspire reflection than to isolate a precise measure of change. Furthermore, emphasis was on "the importance of the individual American traveling abroad (and) 'creating' an image of ourselves among citizens of other countries" (p. 2), with the cross-cultural encounter helping the study abroad student better understand "his national identity within the context of his international experience" (p. 43). However, as cross-cultural encounters fell almost entirely outside course work and, therefore, could not be graded, the frequency, quality, and outcomes of the interactions largely went unexamined.

As perceptions of the range of expected outcomes of a college education expanded to include a more holistic picture of cognitive and psychosocial outcomes in the 1960s and 1970s, study abroad assessment also began to focus on the educational impact of cross-cultural interaction. Having found ways to recognize study abroad course work, perhaps the field was now sufficiently mature to focus assessment on other areas. Later reviews of research on study abroad (Sell, 1983) argued that one obstacle to identifying a consistent set of findings across an increasingly diffuse body of research was the lack of agreement on a common outcome or on an instrument for measuring that outcome. Seemingly unwilling to question the foundational hypothesis that study abroad produces a measurable degree of attitudinal change, researchers often opined that the outcome instruments utilized in their studies were simply not sensitive enough to pick up the change that had occurred in students. Future researchers, therefore, were encouraged to design instruments more capable of capturing the effect of studying abroad.

Today, a variety of new survey instruments, developed over the past several decades, claim to better capture the increasingly complex conceptualizations of change hypothesized to result from study abroad (see Deardorff, 2004, and Salisbury, 2011, for extended reviews of such instruments). Although the instruments differ, all attempt to capture the full scope of the construct they address, and many include subscales representing different elements of their particular overall construct. Yet, as with the findings of Hull and Lemke (1975) almost 40 years ago, the results of this new body of research provide only tepid support for study abroad's alleged transformational impact (see Twombly, Salisbury, Tumanut, & Klute, 2012, for a thorough review of the research on study abroad). Crucially, although higher education has strengthened its commitment to a broad range of expected learning outcomes and matched this with a body of assessment research, study abroad assessment has largely remained focused on aspects of the cross-cultural interaction. Although a small number of research studies are exploring the impact of study abroad on other aspects of psychosocial development, this broader focus is uncommon in institutional assessment efforts.

Learning From the Past to Improve in the Future

Assessment is a process that should situate improvement as its primary intended outcome. Organizations and institutions that fail to introduce changes based on assessment findings have not really assessed. Unfortunately, higher education generally and study abroad specifically have often fallen into the trap of assessing for the purpose of proving what is already believed to be so. The consequences of such endeavors have left both fields with a mountain of research and little improvement to show for it. Yet, prior efforts to demonstrate the nature of student learning in study abroad can inform and substantially improve current and future efforts to assess study abroad's impact.

Choosing the Outcome

Although the study abroad community has always known that students can grow in a variety of ways because of their experiences abroad, the field's focus on attitudinal or dispositional change resulting from cross-cultural interaction has resulted in a tendency to narrow the focus of assessment to some version of intercultural competence or intercultural learning. This is not to say that engagement with difference should not be an emphasis in study abroad. Rather, expectations for substantial growth on such a complex learning outcome should be tempered by the reality that legitimate intercultural learning takes much more time than the length of even the longest study abroad experience. Moreover, much of the literature on study abroad seems to overstate the magnitude of direct impact on intercultural competence (Twombly et al., 2012). Instead, study abroad professionals should more confidently assert that the learning outcomes of study abroad extend beyond cross-cultural outcomes.

When higher education began to expand its range of expected learning outcomes of an undergraduate college experience, the study abroad community did not follow suit and may instead have focused even more keenly on cross-cultural outcomes. This is likely due to a subtle coercion that comes from the preponderance of literature, conference presentations, and promotional brochures that tout the importance of cross-cultural learning. Many institutions also place much of the responsibility for intercultural learning on the international exchange of students and scholars (Twombly et al., 2012). In light of the expansive range of study abroad options now available to students, it seems particularly appropriate to first expand the range of available and "acceptable" learning outcomes and then find ways to measure their achievement.

Defining the Outcome

As discussed previously, a common response to finding no significant differences in pre- and post-study abroad outcome scores is to blame the instrument; it must not be sufficiently sensitive to capture the change. New measurement instruments are thus produced to better do the job.

This variety of instruments and the almost blinding array of underlying definitions point to one of the primary difficulties in determining with confidence the nature of study abroad's impact. Even if a mountainous body of research findings all pointed in the same direction, if the outcome measures used in the research differed, distilling the findings to a single and generalizable conclusion would be difficult. This problem is exacerbated if the measurement instrument does not take into account any aspects of the learning context. In addition, if the assessment depends on a standardized instrument that, by its very design, only tracks respondents' perceptions of their attitudes, the resulting scores do not demonstrate the degree to which respondents might have actually exercised those attitudes while abroad.

In contrast, some of the most encouraging findings in research on study abroad suggest a move away from the continuing effort to develop a more comprehensive, more nuanced, more complete instrument. Instead, these findings note the existence of notable change on specific (and often more tangible) elements of the larger construct. For example, one recent analysis of the impact of study abroad on intercultural competence (Salisbury, 2011) found that although the overall effect of studying abroad on intercultural competence was not particularly large, the effect of studying abroad on students' tendencies to engage in diverse interactions was substantial. Although this finding does not support the rhetoric of transformation through study abroad, it suggests that students are on a trajectory toward longer term intercultural development. This is more in line with what we know about the length of time it takes to develop complex skills. To borrow a sports analogy, if the results of study abroad assessment on a particular campus repeatedly demonstrate that the experience has a high batting average of hitting singles and moving base runners into scoring positions, this seems preferable to assessment results in which sometimes study abroad hits a home run and sometimes study abroad strikes out woefully. There is some suggestion that study abroad may help students become more invested in learning. If this is so, study abroad then helps move students along the trajectory toward the lifelong learning desired by most institutions.

Situating the Outcome

In addition to better defining the outcome to be assessed, study abroad professionals can increase the effectiveness of their assessment initiatives by applying theoretical frameworks developed by college impact researchers to situate the outcome within the broader learning development expected of a college experience. Just as these frameworks situate individual student experiences as singular pieces of a larger learning puzzle, so too should study abroad professionals limit their expectations of the learning that might come from studying abroad to a single element of the more complex learning outcomes expected from the entirety of a college experience. For example, numerous institutional learning outcomes (e.g., intercultural competence or collaborative leadership) require the individual to have developed a nuanced sense of identity and self-awareness. This disposition is critical to effective communication with others in situations where the topic of conversation involves difficult or complicated issues. Some research has suggested that studying abroad contributes to a deepening of an individual's understanding of self (Twombly et al., 2012). Although it makes little sense to suggest that a single study abroad experience could develop an individual into a masterful collaborative leader, it would be entirely realistic to focus on the development of sense of self in study abroad; longer term, this would contribute to the development of collaborative leadership skills. Likewise, if a study abroad experience is particularly effective at increasing the propensity of individuals to engage with diversity (e.g., attend or participate in activities or experiences that feature or derive from cultural origins other than one's own), then study abroad offices might well focus more precisely on fostering that outcome and linking it to post-study abroad experiences.

When higher education generally and study abroad specifically began to expand their anticipated outcomes to include attitudinal change resulting from interactions with difference, both described the scope of their educational impact in similar terms. Yet, a study abroad experience is only a part of an undergraduate experience. As such, different study abroad experiences and learning outcomes should be linked to broader institutional learning outcomes. This means that although two study abroad experiences might well contribute to intercultural learning, they might do so in different ways and at varying levels of complexity. A study abroad program designed for first-year students at an institution where most students have little or no experience with travel and difference might simply introduce students to difference and its cultural implications. By contrast, another program designed for seniors within a particular major might strive for keen sensitivities to the nuances of difference gained in an applied, collaborative setting (see Salisbury, 2015, for a detailed model for off-campus program design that applies a situated notion of learning outcomes). Of course, this may present a challenge if study abroad offerings have been designed for the widest range of students. In such situations, reframing to more closely align and achieve particular learning outcomes may require rearticulating of study abroad goals and enrollment criteria.

Integrating the Outcome

While situating the intended outcome of a given study abroad program in terms of its contribution to more complex learning outcomes, the likelihood of gleaning actionable guidance for improving study abroad's educational impact can be increased by anticipating how what was learned abroad might be integrated into broader college learning. Study abroad directors have long understood the potentially negative impact of reverse culture shock (sometimes called "reentry"). Yet, far too often we assess the learning that students might acquire from studying abroad right at the end of the experience. Thus, the field learns little about how (and whether) students internalize their study abroad learning over the longer term.

Research on the phases necessary for deeper learning can help. Articulated most clearly in Baxter Magolda's (2001) work on the developmental theory of self-authorship, students need a period of meaning-making in order to make sense of and internalize the learning that might come from a substantive disequilibrating experience. As study abroad can make for a prime example of a disequilibrating experience, the most important learning may well most likely occur after a student returns to the home campus.

This presents a particularly difficult challenge to study abroad administrators if they alone are expected to be responsible for assessing study abroad learning. However, the learning outcomes of study abroad should be articulated in a way that not only recognizes but also explicitly applies what we already know about the nature of substantive learning. The assessment of study abroad then becomes a shared responsibility between the institution and the study abroad office or program. Study abroad directors can assess the more concrete learning and growth that can realistically happen during a study abroad experience (in terms of both content-related knowledge and setting the conditions for future change), whereas the institution can assess the degree to which study abroad is integrated with other learning and experiences that help move students toward the institution's more complex institutional learning outcomes.

Capturing the Outcome

The recent development of rubrics and portfolios as plausible means for assessing student learning seems to be particularly applicable to assessing study abroad. Portfolio work lends itself well to reflective writing and the kinds of assignments that seem to be most productive in fostering cross-cultural learning. In addition, the broader categories of attainment that are characteristic of strong rubrics allow some flexibility in describing learning that seems to align more closely to the complex nature of cross-cultural learning than some of the other developmental outcomes that have long been associated with study abroad. By contrast, survey instruments that have been designed and validated by psychometric standards of measurement can sometimes seem excessively constraining.

Improving the Outcome

With all of the aforementioned focus on measuring the intended outcomes of study abroad, turning the findings of that measurement into improvements that can be confidently applied to current programming requires an additional set of data that captures the nature of students' experience and connects that data to the outcomes in question. In essence, approaching assessment in this way simply mirrors the theoretical models for assessing learning in higher education where researchers take into account students' precollege characteristics, the nature of their within-college experiences, and the scores on the intended outcome. Applied to assessing study abroad, this means designing an assessment instrument to gather both outcomes data and experience data; this allows for analyses that can test the relationships between the experiences and the outcomes. Even if the number of participants is too small for complex statistical analysis, the combination of outcome and experience data allows for some simple comparisons that may suggest implications for either taking fuller advantage of experiences that are already proving successful or reducing experiences that seem to inhibit learning.

Implications and Some Suggestions for Practice

One of the more practical benefits of approaching assessment primarily through a lens of improvement (as opposed to a lens of obtaining proof or validation) is that it allows those saddled with the responsibility of conducting the assessment to simplify the nature of their approach to measurement, thereby freeing them to dedicate more time and effort to identifying and implementing changes that might result in demonstrable improvement. One way to simplify assessment is to approach the design of the outcome in a way that emphasizes accessibility over comprehensiveness. Another way to simplify assessment is to more explicitly share the responsibility of spurring student learning with all of the campus actors who might contribute to the iterative process of learning, assessing, and improving the educational effectiveness of the institution. This final section will provide a few suggestions for how study abroad professionals and higher education institutions might recalibrate their assessment efforts to improve student learning from study abroad.

First, study abroad administrators can simplify their assessment efforts by reducing the amount of data they collect. As with many things in life, it's not what you do but how you do it. Higher education institutions are often (and rightly) criticized for being data rich and decision poor. Although the intercultural competence instruments familiar to most study abroad practitioners (e.g., Intercultural Development Inventory; Global Perspectives Inventory; Beliefs, Events, and Values Inventory; etc.) are by all measures valid operationalizations of the constructs they endeavor to capture, they each (a) require substantive time, effort, and resources to administer and analyze and (b) seem a better match for measuring the complex learning outcomes resulting from a complete college experience than the more modest gains to be made through studying abroad. By contrast, there are other ways to capture some of the key intended outcomes of study abroad that are not only much shorter but also available publicly and at no cost.

Two short instruments used by the Wabash National Study of Liberal Arts Education (2014) can serve as examples and are equally useful in capturing various elements of intercultural competence. The Miville-Guzman Universality-Diversity Scale (M-GUDS) tracks three relevant subscales: a tendency toward diverse contact, comfort in the midst of diverse contact, and relativistic appreciation of difference. Although there is a 45-item version of this instrument, the Wabash National Study used an equally valid 15-item version. Another short instrument used by the Wabash National Study, the Openness to Diversity and Challenge scale, is a 7-item scale that assesses students' "interest in exploring diversity in culture, ethnicity, perspectives, values, and ideas." Extensive information on both instruments and numerous research studies that have used them is also available on the Wabash study website (www.liberalarts.wabash.edu/study-instruments).

Another way to assess change in student learning is to gather data on behaviors that would be legitimate proxies for intercultural learning. For example, a question from the National Survey of Student Engagement (NSSE) asks students to indicate how often they have serious conversations with people who are very different from them in race or ethnicity. NSSE asks this question of both freshmen and seniors and uses those responses to represent any change that has occurred during a college experience. Ideally, seniors would indicate that they have these kinds of conversations more frequently than freshmen. This question could be adapted to better fit an institution's particular context or to fit the nature of the intended outcome of a particular study abroad program. For example, for a study abroad program designed around cross-cultural experiences in a country whose political philosophy differs from that of the United States, such as China or Cuba, the question might be rephrased to focus on difference across political spectrum.

Second, if student learning across all of an institution's intended learning outcomes is expected to occur as a result of the entire college experience, then it makes little sense to relegate the assessment of changes in student learning to an office that administers only a small piece of that overall learning experience. This is particularly true in the case of study abroad and its expected contribution to the development of intercultural competence. We already know that (a) intercultural competence takes years to develop effectively and (b) the educational effectiveness of study abroad is crucially influenced by both the degree to which students are prepared to take advantage of their experience through predeparture programming and the degree to which they are able to make useful meaning of their experience post-study abroad. Assessing the intercultural outcomes of studying abroad at a level anywhere but at the institutional level, therefore, makes little sense. This does not absolve those involved with delivering study abroad (faculty, site directors, administrators) of the responsibility for assessing aspects of study abroad. It does mean, however, that the assessment of study abroad should not fall to the study abroad office or program alone. Rather, the responsibility to conduct, analyze, and implement change in study abroad should be shared across the institution, and the influence of all of those who contribute to student learning pre- and post-study abroad should be brought to bear as well. One way to make this effort more explicit might be to organize institution-wide committees that focus on how students, throughout the course of their experience at that institution, make gains on each institutional learning outcome. This kind of a committee takes the focus away from individual offices as sole purveyors of specific learning outcomes and transfers it in a way that matches how students learn during college.

Third, the fields of college impact research and study abroad would benefit greatly from additional research on the ways in which study abroad experiences contribute to student learning. In addition to the long-standing call for more research on how learning and experiences might vary across student types (e.g., men, women, minority students, first generation, etc.), much more research needs to be done on the way that study abroad learning might combine with the learning that comes from other college curricular or cocurricular experiences to ultimately influence gains on broad, complex institutional learning outcomes. Furthermore, because assessment is best framed as a process intended to produce improvement, the field is in desperate need of research that demonstrates ways in which study abroad assessment can lead to improvements that in turn contribute to more complex student learning.

All educational endeavors are most likely to improve when information is collected to assess the endeavors' effectiveness in meeting their articulated learning goals. For study abroad to improve and meet its intended goals for student learning and development, everyone involved with delivering high-quality study abroad experiences can learn from the lessons of past efforts to measure study abroad's educational effectiveness. Moreover, engaging this process efficiently will allow all of us who are busily swept up in designing or selecting study abroad options, attracting participants, advising students, and ensuring their safety to meet our own calling as educators.

References

Association of American Colleges and Universities. (2010). *VALUE rubrics*. Retrieved from www.aacu.org/value/rubrics/index_p.cfm?CFID=6634177&CFTOKEN=40351583

Astin, A. (1977). *Four critical years: Effects of college on beliefs, attitudes, and knowledge*. San Francisco, CA: Jossey-Bass.

Baxter Magolda, M. (2001). *Making their own way: Narratives for transforming higher education to promote self-development*. Sterling, VA: Stylus.

Bennett, M. (2010). A short conceptual history of intercultural learning in study abroad. In W. Hoffa & S. Depaul (Eds.), *A short history of U.S. study abroad: 1965–present*. Special publication of *Frontiers: The Interdisciplinary Journal of Study Abroad*, pp. 419–449.

Bowman, J. E. (1987). *Educating American undergraduates abroad: The development of study abroad programs by American colleges and universities*. Council on International Educational Exchange (CIEE) Occasional Paper Series No. 24. Retrieved from www.ciee.org/images/uploaded/pdf/occasional24.pdf

Council on Student Travel. (1965). *A guide to institutional self-study and evaluation of educational programs abroad*. New York, NY: Author. Retrieved from www.ciee.org/images/uploaded/pdf/occasional_appendix.pdf

Deardorff, D. K. (2004). *The identification and assessment of intercultural competence as a student outcome of internationalization at institutions of higher education in the United States* (Doctoral dissertation). North Carolina State University, Raleigh, NC.

Feldman, K. A., & Newcomb, T. M. (1969). *The impact of college on students.* Piscataway, NJ: Transaction.

Hull, W. F., & Lemke, W. H., Jr. (1975). The assessment of off-campus higher education. *International Review of Education, 21*, 195–206.

Murray, J. R. (1965). *Academic study abroad: Its present status.* Council on International Educational Exchange (CIEE) Occasional Paper Series No. 5. Retrieved from www.ciee.org/images/uploaded/pdf/occasional05.pdf

Pascarella, E. T. (1985). College environmental influences on learning and cognitive development: A critical review and synthesis. In J. Smart (Ed.), *Higher education: Handbook of theory and research* (Vol. 1, pp. 1–64). New York, NY: Agathon.

Pascarella, E. T., & Terenzini, P. T. (1991). *How college affects students.* San Francisco, CA: Jossey-Bass.

Pellegrino, J. W. (2004). *The evolution of educational assessment: Considering the past and imagining the future.* Princeton, NJ: Educational Testing Service Policy and Evaluation Center.

Pfnister, A. O. (1970). *Improving the educational quality of study abroad programs.* Council on International Educational Exchange (CIEE) Occasional Paper Series No. 16. Retrieved from www.ciee.org/images/uploaded/pdf/occasional16.pdf

Salisbury, M. H. (2011). *The effect of study abroad on intercultural competence among undergraduate college students* (Doctoral dissertation). University of Iowa, Iowa City, IA.

Salisbury, M. H. (2015). Matching program and student characteristics with learning outcomes: A framework for study away curriculum development. In N. W. Sobania (Ed.), *Putting the local in global education: Models for transforming learning through domestic off-campus programs.* Sterling, VA: Stylus.

Sell, D. K. (1983). Research on attitude change in U.S. students who participate in foreign study experiences: Past findings and suggestions for future research. *International Journal of Intercultural Relations, 7*, 131–147.

Shavelson, R. J. (2007). *A brief history of student learning assessment: How we got where we are and a proposal for where to go next.* Washington, DC: Association of American Colleges and Universities.

Twombly, S., Salisbury, M., Tumanut, S., & Klute, P. (2012). *Study abroad in a new global century: Renewing the promise, refining the purpose* (ASHE Higher Education Report). Hoboken, NJ: Wiley.

Wabash National Study of Liberal Arts Education. (2014). *Overview.* Retrieved from www.liberalarts.wabash.edu/study-overview/

Wilbrink, B. (1997). Assessment in historical perspective. *Studies in Educational Evaluation, 23*, 31–48.

2

BEYOND THE STUDY ABROAD INDUSTRY

Perspectives From Other Disciplines on Assessing Study Abroad Learning Outcomes

Elizabeth Brewer, Rachel Shively, Nick Gozik, Dennis M. Doyle, and Victor Savicki

An important axiom of any research endeavor is to first understand what research already exists. Which questions are raised? What methods are used? What are their advantages and disadvantages? To what extent do the findings answer the original questions? And what do they suggest for future research? Asking such questions can both help take research in new directions and ensure its timeliness and validity. Furthermore, an examination of research in other disciplines can bring new questions and modes of inquiry to researchers' home fields.

The bulk of the chapters in this book examine study abroad learning outcomes from the viewpoint of the growing field of study abroad and research on higher education assessment more broadly. Although fewer than 10% of American undergraduates study abroad as part of their education, at 289,408 students in 2012–2013, the number has more than doubled over the past 15 years (Institute of International Education, 2014), and the Generation Study Abroad initiative seeks to double study abroad participation over the next five years (Institute of International Education, n.d.). Participation in study abroad is increasing and expectations about the experience are changing. Three things stand out. First, whether driven by accreditation and questions of accountability or interest in effective educational experiences, there is greater interest in understanding study abroad's learning outcomes. Second, there are calls to pay attention to study abroad's integration into the home campus curriculum (Brewer & Cunningham, 2009), as well as to students' overall educational trajectories (Twombly, Salisbury, Tumanut, & Klute, 2012). Third, although study abroad has professionalized in the past decades, and certification of one's knowledge and expertise is possible through the Forum on Education Abroad (Forum on Education Abroad, n.d.), the role of faculty in study abroad is a regular topic of discussion at study abroad conferences, while the number of faculty leading short-term study abroad programs is increasing.

It thus seems natural to ask how academic disciplines think about study abroad and its contributions to students' learning and preparation for life and careers. As this chapter will show, however, excepting language acquisition, study abroad is not a robust focus of inquiry for most disciplines. Nonetheless, there is work being done to better understand how and what students in specific disciplines learn abroad and to experiment with program design, pedagogies, and assessment methods to strengthen study abroad as a component of students' educations.

The discussion begins with research on language acquisition, where despite the decline in the percentage of language majors represented in U.S. study abroad (4.9% in 2012–2013) (Institute of International Education, 2014), research is most robust, perhaps because of its early association with study abroad. This chapter then moves to perspectives from other disciplines, particularly social sciences, and professional programs. What are students learning abroad? The short answer: It depends. Learning in study abroad is shaped by a host of factors and conditions, including but not limited to students' prior preparation, program design, pedagogy, opportunities to engage with host nationals, student willingness to take advantage of learning opportunities, and supports for meaning-making. Read on.

Research on Second Language Acquisition in Study Abroad

Study abroad where the second language is spoken has long been viewed as crucial to gaining linguistic competence. The assumption is that language skills will improve abroad through informal, out-of-class language use and regular interactions in real-life situations. In turn, it is assumed that this immersion will lead to gains in vocabulary, pronunciation, grammar, fluency, and communicative competence, among other things.

This assumption has been examined by research in applied linguistics that investigates the language-learning outcomes of study abroad. Among the many questions addressed by researchers in the United States are variations of the following "utilitarian" questions (Kinginger, 2009, p. 29): (a) Do students' linguistic abilities improve during study abroad? (b) What factors influence this? (c) How do foreign language study at home and abroad compare?

More than two decades of quantitative and qualitative research confirms that study abroad has the *potential* to greatly benefit language learning. However, some students make impressive gains, others modest gains, and some no gains, and study abroad may not be more advantageous than intensive study at home, despite advantages over regular classroom learning (e.g., Freed, Segalowitz, & Dewey, 2004; Martinsen, Baker, Dewey, Bown, & Johnson, 2010). This section explores research methods and results and the implications for study abroad assessment practices.

Second Language Learning Outcomes From Study Abroad

Research on language learning abroad has examined global proficiency; listening; speaking; reading; writing; and grammatical, sociolinguistic, and pragmatic competence. The Oral Proficiency Interview (OPI) and the C-Test (Coleman, 1996) have been used to measure global proficiency; the OPI measures holistic oral proficiency, and the C-Test measures overall language ability. Both large- and small-scale studies have reported gains in global proficiency after individuals spend time abroad (e.g., Brecht, Davidson, & Ginsberg, 1995; Coleman, 1996; Hernández, 2010). However, some found considerable individual differences, including no measureable gains (e.g., Freed, 1990).

Holistic measures such as the OPI also have disadvantages, as they cannot pinpoint specific ways language skills are developed (Freed, 1990). The OPI score, for example, only distinguishes between broadly defined proficiency levels ("Intermediate High," "Advanced Low"). Particularly in short-term study abroad, OPI scores may not increase, although students may show greater skill in verbal interaction (appropriate greetings, pause fillers, discourse markers, closings) than peers at home (Lafford, 1995). Thus, research that goes beyond global proficiency scores can provide important insights into learning outcomes.

Studies of speaking have focused on fluency and pronunciation. *Fluency*—often "a major goal and expected outcome of language learning abroad" (Kinginger, 2009, p. 49)—has been variously defined and measured. Study abroad students improve in rate of speech (Freed, 1995), length of continuous speech (Segalowitz & Freed, 2004), complexity of turns (Towell, Hawkins, & Bazergui, 1996), and use of conventional or formulaic expressions (Bardovi-Harlig & Bastos, 2011; Juan-Garau & Pérez-Vidal,

2007), as well as decrease in hesitation and interrupted speech (Freed et al., 2004). Similarly, pronunciation improves (e.g., Díaz-Campos, 2006; Simões, 1996), although not always more than at home (e.g., Díaz-Campos, 2004; Mora, 2008). Individual students' gains also vary (Martinsen & Alvord, 2012). Teaching pronunciation before study abroad may improve gains (Lord, 2000).

Fewer studies have assessed the development of listening, writing, and reading. Many students believe their listening skills improve greatly (Kinginger, 2009), and pre- and post-listening tests largely confirm this perception (e.g., Allen & Herron, 2003; Kinginger, 2008). Expressing ideas in writing may improve abroad (Sasaki, 2004), although not necessarily more than at home (Freed, So, & Lazar, 2003). Reading can also improve abroad (e.g., Brecht et al., 1995; Dewey, 2004).

Vocabulary and grammar abilities underlie all four skill areas but may be affected differently abroad. More vocabulary is generally acquired abroad than at home (e.g., Milton & Meara, 1995; Serrano, Llanes, & Tragant, 2011), but grammatical correctness is not (e.g., Allen & Herron, 2003; Freed et al., 2003). Furthermore, accuracy with specific structures can improve abroad (e.g., Howard, 2005; Isabelli, 2004; Lafford & Ryan, 1995), but peers at home make equal or *greater* gains in grammar (e.g., DeKeyser, 1991), and some evidence suggests that the stronger the grammar ability *before* study abroad, the greater the gains in grammar and oral proficiency *during* study abroad (e.g., Brecht et al., 1995; Segalowitz & Freed, 2004).

Finally, sociolinguistic and pragmatic competence (second language use in socially and contextually appropriate ways) has been examined: speech acts of requesting (e.g., Shively, 2011) and apologizing (e.g., Cohen & Shively, 2007), terms of address (e.g., Kinginger, 2008), listener behaviors (e.g., Masuda, 2011), and vague expressions and humor (Shively, 2013a). Most data have been gathered through questionnaires or role-plays, with naturalistic and ethnographic recordings increasingly used.

Social interactions abroad may teach students to use language in social contexts through observation and practice, something generally not taught at home (e.g., Regan, Howard, & Lemée, 2009). However, learning in uninstructed contexts proceeds slowly; even advanced learners tend to make only modest improvements speaking appropriately in different social contexts (e.g., Barron, 2003; Félix-Brasdefer, 2004). The pace of learning also relates to specific sociolinguistic or pragmatic features. Greetings and leave-takings are acquired earlier (e.g., Hassell, 2006) than refusing an invitation (Félix-Brasdefer, 2004) or deploying nuanced terms of address to index social relationships and identities (e.g., Kinginger, 2008).

In summary, language abilities may improve abroad, particularly oral fluency, acquisition of vocabulary and formulaic expressions, and sociolinguistic and pragmatic competence. Grammar, however, may be taught equally or more effectively at home. Factors influencing language learning abroad are discussed next.

Factors Influencing Language Learning Abroad

Variation in study abroad learning outcomes has been linked to a variety of factors: individual characteristics (e.g., motivation, gender, age, proficiency, dispositions, intercultural competence), living situation, program type, length of stay, and quantity and quality of social interaction. Some students are more motivated to interact with the language outside of class (Hernández, 2010). Gender may predict second language gains (e.g., Brecht et al., 1995) or not (e.g., Rees & Klapper, 2007). Older students tend to outperform younger students abroad in certain skills in the short term, but the reverse occurs in the long term (Llanes & Muñoz, 2012; Muñoz, 2006). Greater proficiency before study abroad tends to lead to greater linguistic gains, for example, in sentence complexity (Isabelli & Nishida, 2005). Finally, dispositions, histories, and social situations and experiences abroad can all impact individual learning outcomes (e.g., Kinginger, 2004, 2009).

Intercultural competence and linguistic ability have long been viewed as interconnected (e.g., Byram, 1997; Citron, 1995), and the link during study abroad is being studied. In an early qualitative study, greater acceptance of cultural differences led to more social interaction with native speakers and language acquisition (Wilkinson, 1998). Quantitative studies have also reported that cultural sensitivity predicts language learning: Predeparture focus in programming on culture leads to more gains in oral proficiency (Vande Berg, Connor-Linton, & Paige, 2009), whereas the predeparture level of cultural sensitivity predicts gains in oral proficiency (Martinsen, 2010) and pronunciation (Martinsen & Alvord, 2012). The reverse relationship is not found; cultural sensitivity does not grow with language skill (Martinsen, 2011). Furthermore, there may be no statistical correlation between gains in pragmatic ability abroad and gains in intercultural competence (Shively & Cohen, 2008). In sum, research suggests that the higher the cultural sensitivity beforehand, the greater the language learning during study abroad. However, this relationship is not fully understood.

Accommodation abroad can influence language learning. Although homestays are generally perceived as the sine qua non of immersion, the linguistic benefits are mixed; experiences with host families differ (Kinginger, 2009). Although students often consider their host families to be key to learning (e.g., Magnan & Back, 2007; Shively, 2013b), some have negative experiences, and interaction with host families may be less than expected (e.g., Isabelli-García, 2006; Rivers, 1998; Wilkinson, 1998). Thus, linguistic gains may correlate with a homestay (e.g., Hernández, 2010) or not (e.g., Martinsen, 2010; Rivers, 1998). Furthermore, it is the amount of language used with the host family that counts, not living with a host family per se (Vande Berg et al., 2009).

The impact of program type (e.g., direct enrollment, faculty led) on language learning has been little studied, although service-learning students benefit from chances to use language with community members (Martinsen et al., 2010). Length of stay matters; large-scale studies (Coleman, 1996; Vande Berg et al., 2009) have found the longer the students' sojourns abroad, the greater the gains in their language proficiency scores. Length abroad also impacts pragmatic abilities (Félix-Brasdefer, 2004), fluency (Llanes & Muñoz, 2009), and writing skills (Sasaki, 2009). Study abroad of eight weeks or less may result in modest linguistic gains (e.g., Freed, 1990) but greater motivation (e.g., Castañeda & Zirger, 2011).

Quality and quantity of contact with the language abroad may trump length of stay (e.g., Bardovi-Harlig & Bastos, 2011). Some studies have indicated that the quantity of out-of-class interaction predicts gains (e.g., Freed et al., 2003; Hernández, 2010); others have found no correlation (e.g., Ginsburg & Miller, 2000; Magnan & Back, 2007). Qualitative research has indicated that access to and social interaction with members of the host culture abroad varies considerably (e.g., Knight & Schmidt-Rinehart, 2010; Wilkinson, 2002). Some students develop large social networks with native speakers, others spend most of their time alone or with home-country peers (e.g., Isabelli-García, 2006; Kinginger, 2004, 2008), and some may be motivated but unsuccessful at meeting host nationals.

In conclusion, language and cultural learning abroad are affected by the characteristics, backgrounds, and experiences of individual students, as well as housing, program format and duration, and degree of participation in social interaction.

Conclusions

Applied linguistics research indicates that study abroad can benefit second language acquisition by providing opportunities for social interaction in host communities. However, increased language proficiency is not guaranteed; linguistic gains vary considerably by student. What specific types of and how language acquisition is assessed also matters. Indeed, a variety of quantitative and qualitative assessment instruments is crucial to understanding the learning outcomes and lived experiences of language learners. Despite limitations to assessment practices found in the existing research (the variety of assessments and small number of participants in some make generalizations difficult), the literature continues to grow and offer new insights into language learning in study abroad.

Study Abroad: Views From Psychology

Although the literature on study abroad is less robust in fields beyond language acquisition (e.g., Twombly et al., 2012), psychologists have begun to conduct research on study abroad's learning outcomes. This section discusses some of the questions, research methods, and findings psychologists pose for study abroad.

Although anthropology and sociology have long claimed "culture" as their preserve, psychology researches the person–culture interaction as it impacts reactions to cross-cultural encounters. Acculturation psychology (Sam & Berry, 2006) emphasizes a highly prized feature of study abroad: the impact of culture on student sojourners. Strategies to deal with "acculturative stress" (Berry, 2005) caused by adapting to a different culture include marginalization, separation, assimilation, and integration. Integration strategy (identification with both host and home cultures) may be most beneficial but is also complex (Savicki, Cooley, & Donnely, 2008).

At the individual level, affect, behavior, and cognition (the ABCs of acculturation) (Ward, Bochner, & Furnham, 2001) connect acculturation challenges to well-researched psychological processes. At the affect level, study abroad students' psychological adjustment and well-being are of most interest. According to the cognitive mediational model of stress (Lazarus, 1999), individual reactions to stress are dependent on appraisal (how the individual views the stressor) and coping (what the individual does about the stressor). Although study abroad students may experience significant stress, they also are likely to increase their psychological well-being (Savicki, Downing-Burnette, Heller, Binder, & Suntinger, 2004). Positive well-being is more likely when acculturative stressors are appraised as challenges rather than threats and responded to with positive coping skills (e.g., positive reinterpretation) rather than negative ones (e.g., behavioral disengagement) (Savicki et al., 2004).

At the behavioral level, Masgoret and Ward (2006) advanced a cultural learning approach to acculturation, including sojourners' learning of a new and refined behavioral repertoire to "fit in" with the host culture. Although this approach supersedes the more traditional U-curve explanation of cultural adjustment, recent research has found that cultural adaptation seems to follow different patterns for different cultural challenges (Savicki, Adams, & Binder, 2008). Early ease of behavioral, sociocultural adjustment is associated with more positive well-being across a study abroad sojourn. However, students facing more difficult adjustment seem eventually to catch up with those whose adjustment was easier (Savicki, 2010). Language proficiency helps with early sociocultural adjustment, but its effects dwindle over time (Savicki, 2011).

At the cognitive level, research focuses on social identity broadly, and cultural identity more explicitly (Ward et al., 2001). National identity, and specifically American identity, has been measured along two factors: commitment to one's nation, and exploration of one's national identity (see Meyer-Lee & Chambers, chapter 11, this volume). Students who chose to remain at home had high commitment and low exploration (identity foreclosure), whereas students choosing to study abroad had both high commitment and high exploration (achieved identity) (Savicki & Cooley, 2011). Only study abroad students' identities were disrupted, and this disruption may be what students mean when they say that study abroad changed their life. Higher levels of predeparture commitment to American culture may make it more difficult for students to identify with the host culture (Savicki & Cooley, 2011). The ABCs of acculturation framework has spurred a growing body of research on how students respond to their study abroad experience.

The "contact hypothesis" (e.g., Pettigrew & Tropp, 2006) proposes that contact between people of differing characteristics, including culture, may lead to decreased prejudice when the right conditions are met, and an axiom in study abroad is that the more cultural contact, the better. Although prejudice may decrease in study abroad, the effect is small to moderate, even under the best of conditions. And when anxiety or threat exists, prejudice and avoidance can actually increase significantly in relation to contact with other cultures (Voci, 2006). Thus, cultural contacts may have positive, negative, or no change.

Study Abroad and Professional Fields

Licensing and accreditation have encouraged assessment in professional disciplines more so than in others. Study abroad has also increased in professional education out of desires to prepare graduates to work with diverse populations or be competitive in the marketplace. Although published data by individual discipline are not available, the percentage of health professions in study abroad rose from 3.2% in 2000–2001 to 6.4% in 2012–2013 and, over the same period, from 18.1% to 20.4% in business (Institute of International Education, 2014). Although much of the literature on outcomes assessment in the professional fields is still quite nascent and does not lend itself easily to generalizations, here we provide examples of study abroad outcomes assessment in four professional areas where a body of literature is emerging: nursing, teacher education, business, and social work.

Nursing

Nursing is a professional field with one of the longest traditions of both sending students abroad and tracking their progress. Nurses need to be equipped to attend to patients from diverse backgrounds, whether new immigrants or inner-city residents. Study abroad can help them gain "a different perspective on life in the United States" and "realize what it [feels] like to be a minority" (DeDee & Stewart, 2003, p. 242), become aware of divergent approaches to health care, and become more comfortable working with diverse populations (Bentley & Ellison, 2007; Nash, 2008).

In the 1950s, Madeline Leininger coined the term *transcultural nursing* (Leininger, 1991). Impacts of a semester abroad on nursing students' cognitive levels have been studied (Frisch, 1990), as well as longer term impacts on nursing graduates (Zorn, 1996). Additional studies (e.g., Rolls, Inlis, & Kristy, 1997; St. Clair & McKenry, 1999) helped launch a broader conversation on the benefits of study abroad; questions about preparation for practice dominate.

Most studies in nursing establish clear learning outcomes and focus on programs run by the authors' own institutions (Bentley & Ellison, 2007; Rolls et al., 1997; Zorn, 1996). Studies of baccalaureate students predominate, although some focus on community college students. Beyond the United States, there is research from Finland (e.g., Koskinen & Tossavainen, 2004) and Australia (Rolls et al., 1997). Most studies are small scale, involving as few as 10 students, and rely on interviews, learning documents, journals, or surveys such as the International Education Survey (DeDee & Stewart, 2003; Zorn, 1996). Some capture alumni views.

Teacher Education

Teacher education shares nursing's concern with preparing students to engage with diversity as professionals. In the United States, public school students are increasingly diverse (DeVillar & Jiang, 2009; Sharma, Phillion, & Malewski, 2011), and the percentage of minority students is expected to rise to 55% by 2023 (U.S. Department of Education, 2014). At the same time, 85% to 90% of U.S. teachers are White (Sharma et al., 2011). Thus, the need to prepare future teachers to be effective in diverse classrooms is thus great.

Teacher education began to be internationalized as early as the 1950s, when teaching exchanges were established (Baker & Giacchino-Baker, 2000), and continued in 1960, when the Peace Corps was launched. By 1972, 27 of 170 institutions surveyed by the National Center for Education Communication reported that they offered overseas teaching opportunities (Kuschman, 1972). The earliest of these began in the Midwest, with short-term programs in English-speaking countries; today individual institutions and consortia offer options. The latter include the Consortium for Overseas Teaching (see Cushner, 2007; Cushner & Mahon, 2002; Doppen, 2010) and the Pacific Region Student Teaching Program and Bilingual Cross-Cultural Language and Academic Development certificate program (see Quezada, 2004).

Using international experience to prepare future teachers to engage with diversity emerged in the 1990s (Baker & Giacchino-Baker, 2000). Markers of preparation include foreign language proficiency (Marx & Moss, 2011; Quezada, 2004; Stachowski & Visconti, 1997), adaptability (Mahon & Stachowski, 1990), broadened worldviews, and cross-cultural competency (Deardorff, 2006; Quezada, 2004).

Examples of research on teaching abroad from beyond the United States come from Canada (Trilokekar & Kukar, 2011) and Hong Kong (Lee, 2009; Tang, 2003; Tang & Choi, 2004), among other countries. Teaching abroad is also critiqued; although there is agreement that experience abroad should be an option in teacher preparation, the quality of the experience is more important than quantity (Doppen, 2010; Mahon, 2010; Trilokekar & Kukar, 2011).

Studies of teacher education abroad tend to be small scale and focused on a subset of 2 to 20 participants in a given program (e.g., Lee, 2009) or a similarly sized cohort of returnees (e.g., DeVillar & Jiang, 2009). Data are gathered from interviews, journal entries, reflection papers, and surveys. Interviews permit in-depth case studies and yield deeper and more nuanced understandings of how students begin to interpret their host countries and their roles as overseas teachers. However, small numbers make it difficult to generalize findings; additional studies are needed that include a larger array of respondents from multiple institutions.

Business

Compared to nursing and teacher education, in business the outcomes assessment literature is significantly more varied; multiple subfields have their own theoretical underpinnings and approaches to research. Research in marketing, for example, draws from psychology, whereas accounting and finance align more easily with mathematics and statistics. Furthermore, there is far more research on study abroad learning outcomes in marketing, business administration, and tourism than in accounting and finance.

As in other fields, research questions often focus on the impact of study abroad on student development. However, given increasing integration and mobility throughout the world (Douglas & Jones-Rikkers, 2001), there is interest in the role of study abroad in making students more marketable in a competitive workforce. However, study abroad's role in preparing students for the business world is not clear (Gullekson, Tucker, Coombs, & Wright, 2011; Orahood, Woolf, Kruze, & Pearson, 2004), and unless hiring for positions that explicitly require cross-cultural skills, employers do not necessarily seek out candidates who have studied abroad (Thompson, 2004). The skills they seek may or may not be fostered abroad (Orahood, Woolf, & Kruze, 2008). Human resource professionals and others responsible for hiring are more likely to value study abroad than CEOs and presidents (Trooboff, Vande Berg, & Rayman, 2008). Those who value study abroad recognize that U.S. business students are competing for jobs with candidates from around the world.

Borrowing from tourism studies, some ask if more effective program development and marketing can lead to higher participation rates among business students (Cardon, Marshall, & Poddar, 2011; He & Chen, 2010). Can theories such as planned behavior (Goel, de Jong, & Schnusenberg, 2010; Presley, Damron-Martineza, & Zhanga, 2010), conjoint analysis (Garver & Divine, 2008), and risk propensity (Payan, Svensson, & Høgevold, 2012; Relyea, Cocchiara, & Studdard, 2008) provide answers? Although student decision making around study abroad is studied in other fields (Salisbury, Umbach, Paulsen, & Pascarella, 2009), business scholars are unique in paying more attention to what students want, as customers, and how to deliver corresponding services.

In contrast to the small-scale, qualitative studies that predominate in nursing and education, quantitative research with larger pools of respondents is more typical in business. The instruments employed depend on the learning outcomes being assessed. Studies measuring cross-cultural awareness use tools employed in other disciplines, such as the Cross-Cultural Adaptability Inventory (Black & Duhon, 2006; Kelly & Meyers, 1992) and the Scale to Measure World-Minded Attitudes (Douglas & Jones-Rikkers, 2001; Sampson & Smith, 1957). Some use multiple instruments to examine different aspects of student development. Gullekson et al. (2011), for example, integrated scales for ethnocentrism (Neuliep & McCroskey, 1997a), intercultural communication apprehension (Neuliep & McCroskey, 1997b), and international awareness and activities (Chieffo & Griffiths, 2004). Researchers have also created surveys to examine particular questions.

Social Work

Those in "helping professions" (e.g., social work, nursing, education) are argued to need a skill set that includes a deeper understanding of other cultures (Merrill & Frost, 2011). Given a tendency toward ethnocentrism in the United States, "it is particularly valuable for U.S. social work students to see there are alternative ways of thinking, governing, and meeting the needs of citizens" (Lindsey, 2005, p. 247). Indeed, the Council of Social Work Education (2008) has advanced a core educational value by training social workers to recognize the global interconnections of their work and to increase their awareness and understanding of cultures different from their own. Study abroad has the potential to promote these competencies through high-impact, experiential learning, but more research is needed to assess its outcomes for social work students (Lindsey, 2005).

Study abroad can also increase cognitive learning goals, such as understanding and awareness of how social issues are addressed in other cultures (Poole & Davis, 2006), using coping strategies, developing cultural adaptations skills, and reflecting on changes in self-concept (Cordero & Rodriguez, 2009; Gammonley, Rotabi, & Gamble, 2007). As is the case for other study abroad students, predeparture programming (focused on identifying learning goals, anticipating personal challenges, and clarifying personal value systems) may positively impact learning outcomes, and host language and culture competency may positively influence social work students' degree of engagement in cultural immersion when they feel competent in the host language.

As observed in the prior discussion of study abroad in other professional programs, many of the studies conducted in social work are limited by the demographics (gender, ethnicity, age, etc.) and the short length (three to five weeks) of most study abroad experiences. Most studies also rely on qualitative data gathered from observations, interviews, and journal entries. A broader range of qualitative and quantitative instruments is needed to assess an equally broader range of social work students' study abroad experiences.

Emerging Agendas for Study Abroad in Other Disciplines

Despite the long history of study abroad in a number of other disciplines, attention is only beginning to be paid to study abroad's relationship to them. Nevertheless, the integration of study abroad with the curriculum warrants such attention. How can study abroad benefit disciplinary learning? What can it add to traditional classroom learning? What can it teach disciplines about student learning and development beyond content that nonetheless enhances content mastery? This section looks at research agendas emerging in several disciplines.

First, communication studies tends to look at how students adapt their communication strategies while abroad (Peterson, Milstein, Chen, & Nakazawa, 2011; Pitts, 2009); how students build support networks to help cope with stressful situations abroad (Peterson et al., 2011); and the extent to which study abroad students can assess and adapt communication strategies (introductory talk, information sharing, storytelling, gossiping, use of humor, and expressing complaints) (Pitts, 2009). Other research looks at the relationship between ethnocentrism and communication apprehension (Neuliep & McCroskey, 1997b) and between ambiguity and uncertainty and communication competency (Neuliep & McCroskey, 1997b).

Student development looks at study abroad's influence on self-concept and cultural identity (Braskamp, Braskamp, & Merrill, 2009; Savicki & Cooley, 2011); management of interpersonal relationships, particularly post-study abroad (e.g., Wielkiewicz & Turkowski, 2010); deliberation concerning lifestyle choices (Jones, Niehaus, Rowen-Kenyon, Cilente Skindall, & Ireland, 2012); and coping skills (Lindsey, 2005). Preprogramming and staff training can help students set goals (Kitsantas, 2004), whereas pre-, during, and post-study abroad data gathering will best shed light on student development (Jones et al., 2012).

Political scientists believe they can play a unique role in arguing for resources to support global learning (Ingebritsen, 2007), and both faculty and students need the transcultural competence to "decipher political speech across cultural boundaries" (Leslie, 2007, p. 108). Nonetheless, political scientists face challenges in assessing study abroad for credit (Ellett, Kiwuwa, & Roberts, 2009); paying more attention to global perspectives within the curriculum could help elevate the value of cross-cultural experiences (p. 582). For study abroad to be of value in international relations, the focus needs to be on disciplinary learning at universities abroad, not abstract global citizenship development in study abroad programs (Gordon, 2014).

Sociology seeks to "increase students' exposure to multicultural, cross-cultural, and cross-national content relevant to sociology" (McKinney, Howery, Strand, Kain, & Berheide, 2004, p. 19). However, study abroad's unique challenges (e.g., language barriers, experiential learning) make it more difficult to assess progress toward disciplinary learning goals (Fobes, 2005).

The introduction to a collection of essays argues that anthropology can contribute to making experiential learning in international and intercultural developments be "meaningful and significant" (Cunningham, Howell, & Loewe, 2010, p. 2). Ethnographic projects, structured reflection, visual thinking and acting, and ordinary conversations can all promote learning, and anthropologists would do well to pay attention to conversations about intercultural competence, self-authorship, and transformative learning taking place in other fields.

Finally, service-learning pedagogy can be employed in many disciplines, and the structured reflection it emphasizes can generate, document, and provide a basis for assessment (Hatcher & Bringle, 2012). Lessons from service-learning can inform study abroad more broadly. Who benefits? Only students? Or host communities and partners? How can challenges involved in developing reciprocal partnerships (communication over distance and issues of power, privilege, and institutional agendas) be addressed? How can these issues be applied to study abroad? The potential for losers and winners, positive and negative impacts, must be recognized.

Lessons for Study Abroad Practitioners

Perhaps unsurprisingly, this chapter's review of views from beyond study abroad indicates that research on study abroad is greater in disciplines with obvious stakes in study abroad. The stakes may involve study abroad's potential for adding value to disciplinary learning (e.g., language acquisition) or helping students acquire skills related to practicing the discipline (e.g., engaging with difference as teachers, social workers, or nurses). In disciplines where it can be argued that disciplinary content and methods could just as well be learned at home, there has been less interest in research on study abroad. In part, this may be because commonly understood potential outcomes of study abroad (e.g., understanding of self) seem peripheral to disciplinary goals.

Is this view too limited? When Barbara Burn and her coprincipal investigators were working on their landmark investigation of study abroad's impacts on American students (Carlson, Burn, Useem, & Yachimowicz, 1990), one of the international educators recruited to help with the project came to the University of Massachusetts to conduct interviews. Speaking with the head of the studio art program, he asked about studio art students who had studied abroad. "They come back behind in terms of technique," was the reply, "but are more mature." "So they shouldn't study abroad. It doesn't advance their art," replied the researcher. "No, we want them to study abroad. We can catch them up on technique. But we can't offer them the experiences that make them into better artists because they have more questions to ask and more to say." Similarly, a discussion of study abroad's contribution to senior theses in international relations (Toral, 2009) indicates that because students had witnessed the impacts of poverty and disease on people's lives while abroad or the struggles of those internally displaced, they were both more committed and more able to understand, apply, and synthesize international relations theory and methodology. They could also better imagine their futures.

As authors of this chapter, we therefore encourage collaborations with colleagues in the academic departments on our campuses to examine study abroad's potential to help students become both better students of their disciplines and more self-aware and capable humans, who after graduation will be in a better position to contribute positively to society.

We also offer a caveat and plea. Many of the studies represented in this review focus on outcomes from programs designed specifically for study abroad students; program design is therefore pivotal. Yet the majority of students who study abroad in the world do so by enrolling in universities. What kinds of teaching and learning strategies should we be deploying on our campuses to help these students master the "self-authorship" (Baxter-Magolda & King, 2008) that can enable them to identify and achieve learning goals for study abroad, learn from them, and link what they learn abroad to their next endeavors? If this means inventing more opportunities for applying learning beyond the classroom, engaging with difference, and using structured reflection and other strategies to make meaning, might this benefit more of our students, including those who do not study abroad?

References

Allen, H., & Herron, C. (2003). A mixed-methodology investigation of the linguistic and affective outcomes of summer study abroad. *Foreign Language Annals, 36,* 370–385.

Baker, F., & Giacchino-Baker, R. (2000). *Building an international student teaching program: A California/Mexico experience.* Washington, DC: U.S. Department of Education.

Bardovi-Harlig, K., & Bastos, M. (2011). Proficiency, length of stay, and intensity of interaction, and the acquisition of conventional expressions in L2 pragmatics. *Intercultural Pragmatics, 8,* 347–384.

Barron, A. (2003). *Acquisition in interlanguage pragmatics: Learning how to do things with words in a study abroad context.* Amsterdam, the Netherlands: John Benjamins.

Baxter-Magolda, M. B., & King, P. M. (2008). Toward reflective conversations: An advising approach that promotes self-authorship. *Peer Review, 10*(1). Retrieved from www.aacu.org/publications-research/periodicals/toward-reflective-conversations-advising-approach-promotes-self

Bentley, R., & Ellison, K. (2007). Increasing cultural competence in nursing through international service-learning experiences. *Nurse Educator, 32*(5), 207–211.

Berry, J. W. (2005). Acculturation. In W. Friedlmeier, P. Chakkarath, & B. Schwarz (Eds.), *Culture and human development* (pp. 291–302). New York, NY: Psychology Press.

Black, H., & Duhon, D. (2006). Assessing the impact of business study abroad programs on cultural awareness and personal development. *Journal of Education for Business, 81*(3), 140–144.

Braskamp, L. A., Braskamp, D. C., & Merrill, K. (2009). Assessing progression in global learning and development of students with study abroad experiences. *Frontiers: The Interdisciplinary Journal of Study Abroad, 18,* 101–118.

Brecht, R. D., Davidson, D., & Ginsberg, R. (1995). Predictors of foreign language gain during study abroad. In B. F. Freed (Ed.), *Second language acquisition in a study abroad context* (pp. 37–66). Philadelphia, PA: John Benjamins.

Brewer, E., & Cunningham, K. (2009). *Integrating study abroad into the curriculum: Theory and practice across the disciplines.* Sterling, VA: Stylus.

Byram, M. (1997). *Teaching and assessing intercultural communicative competence.* Clevedon, UK: Multilingual Matters.

Cardon, P., Marshall, B., & Poddar, A. (2011). Using typologies to interpret study abroad preferences of American business students: Applying a tourism framework to international education. *Journal of Education for Business, 86*(2), 111–118.

Carlson, J. S., Burn, B. B., Useem, J., & Yachimowicz, D. (1990). *Study abroad: The experience of American undergraduates.* Westport, CT: Greenwood.

Castañeda, M., & Zirger, M. (2011). Making the most of the "new" study abroad: Social capital and the short-term sojourn. *Foreign Language Annals, 44,* 544–564.

Chieffo, L., & Griffiths, L. (2004). Large-scale assessment of student attitudes after a short-term study abroad program. *Frontiers: The Interdisciplinary Journal of Study Abroad, 10,* 165–177.

Citron, J. L. (1995). Can cross-cultural understanding aid second language acquisition? Toward a theory of ethno-lingual relativity. *Hispania, 78,* 105–113.

Cohen, A. D., & Shively, R. L. (2007). Acquisition of requests and apologies in Spanish and French: Impact of study abroad and strategy-building intervention. *The Modern Language Journal, 91,* 189–212.

Coleman, J. (1996). *Studying languages: A survey of British and European students: The proficiency, background, attitudes and motivations of students of foreign languages in the United Kingdom and Europe.* London, UK: Centre for Information on Language Teaching and Research.

Cordero, A., & Rodriguez, L. N. (2009). Fostering cross-cultural learning and advocacy for social justice through an immersion experience in Puerto Rico. *Journal of Teaching in Social Work, 29,* 134–152.

Council of Social Work Education. (2008). *2008 education policy and accreditation handbook.* Retrieved from www.cswe.org/File.aspx?id=13780

Cunningham, K., Howell, J., & Loewe, R. (2010). Anthropological contributions to experiential learning in international and intercultural contexts. *Practicing Anthropology, 32*(3), 1–3.

Cushner, K. (2007). The role of experience in the making of internationally-minded teachers. *Teacher Education Quarterly, 34*(1), 27–39.

Cushner, K., & Mahon, J. (2002). Overseas student teaching: Affecting personal, professional, and global competencies in an age of globalization. *Journal of Studies in International Education, 6*(1), 44–58.

Deardorff, D. (2006). Identification and assessment of intercultural competence as a student outcome of internationalization. *Journal of Studies in International Education, 10*(3), 241–266.

DeDee, L., & Stewart, S. (2003). The effect of student participation in international study. *Journal of Professional Nursing, 19*(4), 237–242.

DeKeyser, R. (1991). Foreign language development during a semester abroad. In B. F. Freed (Ed.), *Foreign language acquisition research and the classroom* (pp. 104–119). Lexington, MA: D. C. Heath.

DeVillar, R., & Jiang, B. (2009). U.S. student teachers in Belize, China, and Mexico: Patterns of cultural, professional, and character development. *Journal of Emerging Knowledge on Emerging Markets, 1,* 153–169.

Dewey, D. (2004). A comparison of reading development by learners of Japanese in intensive and domestic immersion and study abroad contexts. *Studies in Second Language Acquisition, 26,* 303–327.

Díaz-Campos, M. (2004). Context of learning in the acquisition of Spanish second language phonology. *Studies in Second Language Acquisition, 26*, 249–273.

Díaz-Campos, M. (2006). The effect of style in second language phonology: An analysis of segmental acquisition in study abroad and regular-classroom students. In C. A. Klee & T. L. Face (Eds.), *Selected proceedings of the 7th conference on the acquisition of Spanish and Portuguese as first and second languages* (pp. 26–39). Somerville, MA: Cascadilla Proceedings Project.

Doppen, F. (2010). Overseas student teaching and national identity: Why go somewhere you feel completely comfortable? *Journal of International Social Studies, 1*(1), 3–19.

Douglas, C., & Jones-Rikkers, C. (2001). Study abroad programs and American student worldmindedness: An empirical analysis. *Journal of Teaching in International Business, 13*(1), 55–66.

Ellett, R., Kiwuwa, D., & Roberts, J. W. (2009). Internationalizing the curriculum. *PS: Political Science and Politics, 42*, 581–582.

Félix-Brasdefer, C. (2004). Interlanguage refusals: Linguistic politeness and length of residence in the target community. *Language Learning, 54*, 587–653.

Fobes, C. (2005). Taking a critical pedagogical look at travel-study abroad: "A classroom with a view" in Cusco, Peru. *Teaching Sociology, 33*, 181–194.

Forum on Education Abroad. (n.d.). *Professional certification in education abroad.* Retrieved from www.forumea.org/training-events/professional-certification-in-education-abroad

Freed, B. F. (1990). Language learning in a study abroad context: The effects of interactive and noninteractive out-of-class contact on grammatical achievement and oral proficiency. In J. Alatis (Ed.), *Linguistics, language teaching, and language acquisition: The interdependence of theory, practice, and research* (pp. 459–477). Washington, DC: Georgetown University Press.

Freed, B. F. (1995). What makes us think that students who study abroad become fluent? In B. F. Freed (Ed.), *Second language acquisition in a study abroad context* (pp. 123–148). Philadelphia, PA: John Benjamins.

Freed, B. F., Segalowitz, N., & Dewey, D. (2004). Contexts of learning and second language fluency in French: Comparing regular classrooms, study abroad, and intensive domestic programs. *Studies in Second Language Acquisition, 26*, 275–301.

Freed, B. F., So, S., & Lazar, N. A. (2003). Language learning abroad: How do gains in written fluency compare with gains in oral fluency in French as a second language? *ADFL Bulletin, 34*, 34–40.

Frisch, N. (1990). An international nursing student exchange program: An educational experience that enhanced student cognitive development. *Journal of Nursing Education, 29*(1), 10–12.

Gammonley, D., Rotabi, K. S., & Gamble, D. M. (2007). Enhancing global understanding with study abroad: Ethically grounded approaches to international learning. *Journal of Teaching in Social Work, 27*, 115–135.

Garver, M., & Divine, R. (2008). Conjoint analysis of study abroad preferences: Key attributes, segments and implications for increasing student participation. *Journal of Marketing for Higher Education, 17*(2), 189–215.

Ginsburg, R. B., & Miller, L. (2000). What do they do? Activities of students during study abroad. In R. D. Lambert & E. Shohamy (Eds.), *Language policy and pedagogy: Essays in honor of A. Ronald Walton* (pp. 237–261). Philadelphia, PA: John Benjamins.

Goel, L., de Jong, P., & Schnusenberg, O. (2010). Toward a comprehensive framework of study abroad intentions and behaviors. *Journal of Teaching in International Business, 21*(4), 248–265.

Gordon, D. (2014). Curriculum integration versus educating for global citizenship: A (disciplinary) view from the international relations classroom. *Frontiers: Interdisciplinary Journal of Study Abroad, 24*. Retrieved from www.frontiersjournal.com/volxxivfall2014.htm

Gullekson, N., Tucker, M., Coombs, G., & Wright, S. (2011). Examining intercultural growth for business students in short-term study abroad programs: Too good to be true? *Journal of Teaching in International Business, 22*(2), 91–106.

Hassell, T. (2006). Learning to take leave in social conversations: A diary study. In M. A. DuFon & E. Churchill (Eds.), *Language learners in study abroad contexts* (pp. 31–58). Clevedon, UK: Multilingual Matters.

Hatcher, J. A., & Bringle, R. G. (Eds.). (2012). *Understanding service-learning and community engagement: Crossing boundaries through research.* Charlotte, NC: Information Age Publishing.

He, N., & Chen, R. (2010). College students' perceptions and attitudes toward the selection of study abroad programs. *International Journal of Hospitality and Tourism Administration, 11*(4), 347–359.

Hernández, T. A. (2010). The relationship among motivation, interaction, and the development of second language oral proficiency in a study-abroad context. *The Modern Language Journal, 94*, 600–617.

Howard, M. (2005). On the role of context in the development of learner language: Insights from study abroad research. *ITL Review of Applied Linguistics, 147–148*, 1–20.

Ingebritsen, C. (2007). Global APSA: An institutional perspective. *PS: Political Science and Politics, 40*, 117–118.

Institute of International Education. (n.d.). *Generation study abroad.* Retrieved from www.iie.org/Programs/Generation-Study-Abroad/About

Institute of International Education. (2014). Fields of study of U.S. study abroad students, 2000/01–2012/13. In *Open doors report on international educational exchange.* Retrieved from www.iie.org/opendoors

Isabelli, C. A. (2004). The acquisition of null subject parameter properties in SLA: Some effects of positive evidence in a natural learning context. *Hispania, 87*, 150–162.

Isabelli, C. A., & Nishida, C. (2005). Development of the Spanish subjunctive in a nine-month study abroad setting. In D. Eddington (Ed.), *Selected proceedings of the 6th conference on the acquisition of Spanish as first and second languages* (pp. 78–91). Somerville, MA: Cascadilla Press.

Isabelli-García, C. L. (2006). Study abroad social networks, motivation, and attitudes: Implications for SLA. In M. A. DuFon & E. Churchill (Eds.), *Language learners in study abroad contexts* (pp. 231–258). Clevedon, UK: Multilingual Matters.

Jones, S. R., Niehaus, E., Rowen-Kenyon, H. T., Cilente Skindall, K., & Ireland, M. S. (2012). The meaning students make as participants in short-term immersion programs. *Journal of College Student Development, 53,* 201–220.

Juan-Garau, M., & Pérez-Vidal, C. (2007). The effect of context and contact on oral performance in students who go on a stay abroad. *Vigo International Journal of Applied Linguistics, 4,* 117–134.

Kelly, K., & Meyers, J. (1992). *Cross-cultural adaptability inventory, action-planning guide.* Chicago, IL: NCS Pearson.

Kinginger, C. (2004). Alice doesn't live here anymore: Foreign language learning as identity (re)construction. In A. Pavlenko & A. Blackledge (Eds.), *Negotiation of identities in multilingual contexts* (pp. 219–242). Clevedon, UK: Multilingual Matters.

Kinginger, C. (2008). Language learning in study abroad: Case studies of Americans in France. In *Modern Language Journal monograph, Volume 1.* Oxford, UK: Blackwell.

Kinginger, C. (2009). *Language learning and study abroad: A critical reading of research.* New York, NY: Palgrave Macmillan.

Kitsantas, A. (2004). Study abroad: The role of college students' goals on the development of cross-cultural skills and global understanding. *College Student Journal, 38,* 441–452.

Knight, S. M., & Schmidt-Rinehart, B. C. (2010). Exploring conditions to enhance student/host family interaction abroad. *Foreign Language Annals, 43,* 64–79.

Koskinen, L., & Tossavainen, K. (2004). Study abroad as a process of learning intercultural competence in nursing. *International Journal of Nursing, 10*(3), 111–120.

Kuschman, W. (1972). *Overseas student teaching programs: A study of American collegiate participation.* Washington, DC: National Center for Educational Communication.

Lafford, B. (1995). Getting into, through, and out of a survival situation: A comparison of communicative strategies used by students studying Spanish abroad and "at home." In B. F. Freed (Ed.), *Second language acquisition in a study abroad context* (pp. 97–121). Philadelphia, PA: John Benjamins.

Lafford, B., & Ryan, J. (1995). The acquisition of lexical meaning in a study abroad context: The Spanish prepositions *por* and *para. Hispania, 75,* 528–547.

Lazarus, R. S. (1999). *Stress and emotion: A new synthesis.* New York, NY: Springer.

Lee, J. (2009). ESL student teachers' perceptions of a short-term overseas immersion program. *Teaching and Teacher Education, 25*(3), 1095–1104.

Leininger, M. (1991). *Culture care diversity and universality: A theory of nursing.* Washington, DC: National League for Nursing.

Leslie, I. (2007). Internationalizing political theory courses. *PS: Political Science and Politics, 40,* 108–110.

Lindsey, E. W. (2005). Study abroad and values development in social work students. *Journal of Social Work Education, 40,* 229–250.

Llanes, À., & Muñoz, C. (2009). A short stay abroad: Does it make a difference? *System, 37*(3), 353–365.

Llanes, À., & Muñoz, C. (2012). Age effects in a study abroad context: Children and adults studying abroad and at home. *Language Learning, 63*(1), 63–90.

Lord, G. (2000). *The combined effects of instruction and immersion on L2 pronunciation.* Unpublished manuscript, University of Florida, Gainesville.

Magnan, S. S., & Back, M. (2007). Social interaction and linguistic gain during study abroad. *Foreign Language Annals, 40,* 43–61.

Mahon, J. (2010). Fact or fiction? Analyzing institutional barriers and individual responsibility to advance the internationalization of teacher education. *Teaching Education, 21*(1), 7–18.

Mahon, J., & Stachowski, L. (1990). New horizons: Student teaching abroad to enrich understanding of diversity. *Action in Teacher Education, 12*(3), 13–21.

Martinsen, R. A. (2010). Short-term study abroad: Predicting changes in oral skills. *Foreign Language Annals, 43,* 504–530.

Martinsen, R. A. (2011). Predicting changes in cultural sensitivity among students of Spanish during short-term study abroad. *Hispania, 94,* 121–141.

Martinsen, R. A., & Alvord, S. M. (2012). On the relationship between L2 pronunciation and culture. *Spanish in Context, 9,* 443–465.

Martinsen, R. A., Baker, W., Dewey, D., Bown, J., & Johnson, C. (2010). Exploring diverse settings for language acquisition and use: Comparing study abroad, service learning abroad, and foreign language housing. *Applied Language Learning, 20,* 45–69.

Marx, H., & Moss, D. (2011). Please mind the culture gap: Intercultural development during a teacher education study abroad program. *Journal of Teacher Education, 62*(1), 35–47.

Masgoret, A.-M., & Ward, C. (2006). Cultural learning approach to acculturation. In D. L. Sam & J. W. Berry (Eds.), *The Cambridge handbook of acculturation psychology* (pp. 58–77). Cambridge, UK: Cambridge University Press.

Masuda, K. (2011). Acquiring interactional competence in a study abroad context: Japanese language learners' use of the interactional particle *ne. The Modern Language Journal, 95,* 519–540.

McKinney, K., Howery, C. B., Strand, K. J., Kain, E. L., & Berheide, C. W. (2004). *Liberal learning and the sociology major updated: Meeting the challenge of teaching sociology in the twenty-first century.* Washington, DC: American Sociological Association.

Merrill, M. C., & Frost, C. J. (2011). Internationalizing social work education: Models, methods and meanings. *Frontiers: The International Journal of Study Abroad Education, 21,* 189–210.

Milton, J., & Meara, P. (1995). How periods abroad affect vocabulary growth in a foreign language. *ITL Review of Applied Linguistics, 107–108,* 17–34.

Mora, J. C. (2008). Learning context effects on the acquisition of a second language phonology. In C. Pérez-Vidal, M. Juan-Garau, & A. Bel (Eds.), *A portrait of the young in the new multilingual Spain* (pp. 241–263). Clevedon, UK: Multilingual Matters.

Muñoz, C. (2006). *Age and the rate of foreign language learning.* Clevedon, UK: Multilingual Matters.

Nash, K. (2008). Interprofessional, cross-cultural immersion in Nicaragua. *Sigma Theta Tau international reflections on nursing leadership.* Retrieved from www.nursingsociety.org

Neuliep, J., & McCroskey, J. (1997a). The development of a U.S. and generalized ethnocentrism scale. *Communication Research Reports, 14*(4), 385–398.

Neuliep, J., & McCroskey, J. (1997b). The development of intercultural and interethnic communication apprehension scales. *Communication Research Reports, 14*(2), 145–156.

Orahood, T., Woolf, J., & Kruze, L. (2008). Study abroad and career paths of business students. *Frontiers: The Interdisciplinary Journal of Study Abroad, 17,* 133–141.

Orahood, T., Woolf, J., Kruze, L., & Pearson, D. (2004). The impact of study abroad on business students' career goals. *Frontiers: The Interdisciplinary Journal of Study Abroad, 10,* 117–130.

Payan, J., Svensson, G., & Høgevold, N. (2012). The effect of attributes of study abroad and risk aversion on the future likelihood to study abroad: A study of U.S. and Norwegian undergraduate marketing students. *Journal for Advancement of Marketing Education, 20*(3), 70–81.

Peterson, J. C., Milstein, T., Chen, Y., & Nakazawa, M. (2011). Self-efficacy in intercultural communication: The development and validation of a sojourners' scale. *Journal of International and Intercultural Communication, 4,* 290–309.

Pettigrew, R. F., & Tropp, L. R. (2006). A meta-analytic test of intergroup contact theory. *Journal of Personality and Social Psychology, 90,* 751–783.

Pitts, M. J. (2009). Identity and the role of expectations, stress, and talk in short-term student sojourner adjustment: An application of the integrative theory of communication and cross-cultural adaptation. *International Journal of Intercultural Relations, 33*(6), 450–462.

Poole, D. L., & Davis, T. S. (2006). Concept mapping to measure outcomes in study abroad programs. *Social Work Education, 25*(1), 61–77.

Presley, A., Damron-Martineza, D., & Zhanga, L. (2010). A study of business student choice to study abroad: A test of the theory of planned behavior. *Journal of Teaching in International Business, 21*(4), 227–247.

Quezada, R. (2004). Beyond educational tourism: Lessons learned while student teaching abroad. *International Education Journal, 5*(4), 458–465.

Rees, J., & Klapper, J. (2007). Analysing and evaluating the linguistic benefit of residence abroad for UK foreign language students. *Assessment and Evaluation in Education, 32,* 331–353.

Regan, V., Howard, M., & Lemée, I. (2009). *The acquisition of sociolinguistic competence in a study abroad context.* Clevedon, UK: Multilingual Matters.

Relyea, C., Cocchiara, F., & Studdard, F. (2008). The effect of perceived value in the decision to participate in study abroad programs. *Journal of Teaching in International Business, 19*(4), 346–361.

Rivers, W. P. (1998). Is being there enough? The effects of homestay placements on language gain during study abroad. *Foreign Language Annals, 31,* 492–500.

Rolls, C., Inlis, A., & Kristy, A. (1997). Study abroad programs: Creating awareness of and changing attitudes to nursing, health and ways of living in other cultures. *Contemporary Nurse, 6*(3–4), 152–156.

Salisbury, M., Umbach, P., Paulsen, M., & Pascarella, E. (2009). Going global: Understanding the choice process of the intent to study abroad. *Research in Higher Education, 50*(2), 119–143.

Sam, D. L., & Berry, J. W. (2006). *The Cambridge handbook of acculturation psychology.* Cambridge, UK: Cambridge University Press.

Sampson, D., & Smith, H. (1957). A scale to measure world-minded attitudes. *Journal of Social Psychology, 45*(1), 99–106.

Sasaki, M. (2004). A multiple-data analysis of the 3.5-year development of EFL student writers. *Language Learning, 54,* 525–582.

Sasaki, M. (2009). Changes in English as a foreign language students' writing over 3.5 years: A sociocognitive account. In R. M. Manchón (Ed.), *Writing in foreign language contexts: Learning, teaching, and research* (pp. 49–76). Clevedon, UK: Multilingual Matters.

Savicki, V. (2010). Implications of early sociocultural adaptation for study abroad students. *Frontiers: The Interdisciplinary Journal of Study Abroad, 19,* 205–223.

Savicki, V. (2011). Relationship of foreign language proficiency to study abroad outcomes and inputs. *Frontiers: The Interdisciplinary Journal of Study Abroad, 21,* 63–85.

Savicki, V., Adams, I., & Binder, F. (2008). Intercultural development: Topics and sequences. In V. Savicki (Ed.), *Developing intercultural competence and transformation: Theory, research, and application in international education* (pp. 154–172). Sterling, VA: Stylus.

Savicki, V., & Cooley, E. (2011). American identity in study abroad students: Contrasts and changes. *Journal of College Student Development, 52,* 339–349.

Savicki, V., Cooley, E., & Donnelly, R. (2008). Acculturative stress, appraisal, coping and intercultural adjustment. In V. Savicki (Ed.), *Developing intercultural competence and transformation: Theory, research, and application in international education* (pp. 173–192). Sterling, VA: Stylus.

Savicki, V., Downing-Burnette, R., Heller, L., Binder, F., & Suntinger, W. (2004). Contrasts, changes, and correlates in actual and potential intercultural adjustment. *International Journal of Intercultural Relations, 28,* 311–329.

Segalowitz, N., & Freed, B. F. (2004). Context, contact, and cognition in oral fluency acquisition: Learning Spanish in at home and study abroad contexts. *Studies in Second Language Acquisition, 26,* 173–199.

Serrano, R., Llanes, À., & Tragant, E. (2011). Analyzing the effect of context of second language learning: Domestic intensive and semi-intensive courses vs. study abroad in Europe. *System, 39,* 133–143.

Sharma, S., Phillion, J., & Malewski, E. (2011). Examining the practice of critical reflection for developing pre-service teachers' multicultural competencies: Findings from a study abroad program in Honduras. *Issues in Teacher Education, 20*(2), 9–22.

Shively, R. L. (2011). L2 pragmatic development in study abroad: A longitudinal study of Spanish service encounters. *Journal of Pragmatics, 43*, 1818–1835.

Shively, R. L. (2013a). Learning to be funny in Spanish during study abroad: L2 humor development. *The Modern Language Journal, 97*, 930–946.

Shively, R. L. (2013b). Out-of-class interaction during study abroad: Service encounters in Spain. *Spanish in Context, 10*, 53–91.

Shively, R. L., & Cohen, A. D. (2008). Development of Spanish requests and apologies during study abroad. Íkala, Revista de Lenguaje y Cultura, *13*, 57–118.

Simões, A. (1996). Phonetics in second language acquisition: An acoustic study of fluency in adult learners of Spanish. *Hispania, 79*, 87–95.

St. Clair, A., & McKenry, L. (1999). Preparing culturally competent practitioners. *Journal of Nursing Education, 38*(5), 228–234.

Stachowski, L., & Visconti, V. (1997). Adaptations for success: U.S. student teachers living and teaching abroad. *International Education, 26*, 5–20.

Tang, S. (2003). Challenge and support: The dynamics of student teachers' professional learning in the field experience. *Teaching and Teacher Education, 19*(5), 483–498.

Tang, S., & Choi, P. (2004). The development of personal, intercultural and professional competence in international field experience in initial teacher education. *Asia Pacific Education Review, 5*(1), 50–63.

Thompson, J. W. (2004). *An exploration of the demand for study overseas from American students and employers.* A report prepared for the Institute of International Education, the German Academic Exchange Service (DAAD), the British Council, and the Australian Education Office. Retrieved from www.iienetwork.org/file_depot/0–10000000/0–10000/1710/folder/10528/JWT+Study.doc

Toral, P. (2009). Synthesis and career preparation: The international relations senior thesis. In E. Brewer & K. Cunningham (Eds.), *Integrating study abroad into the curriculum: Theory and practice across the disciplines* (pp. 191–208). Sterling, VA: Stylus.

Towell, R., Hawkins, R., & Bazergui, N. (1996). The development of fluency in advanced learners of French. *Applied Linguistics, 17*, 84–119.

Trilokekar, R., & Kukar, P. (2011). Disorienting experiences during study abroad: Reflections of pre-service teacher candidates. *Teaching and Teacher Education, 27*(7), 1141–1150.

Trooboff, S., Vande Berg, M., & Rayman, J. (2008). Employer attitudes toward study abroad. *Frontiers: The Interdisciplinary Journal of Study Abroad, 15*, 17–33.

Twombly, S., Salisbury, M., Tumanut, S., & Klute, P. (2012). *Study abroad in a new global century: Renewing the promise, refining the purpose* (ASHE Higher Education Report). Hoboken, NJ: Wiley.

U.S. Department of Education. (2014). *Condition of education 2014.* Washington, DC: Author.

Vande Berg, M., Connor-Linton, J., & Paige, R. M. (2009, Fall). The Georgetown Consortium project: Intervening in student learning abroad. *Frontiers: The Interdisciplinary Journal of Study Abroad, 18,* 1–75.

Voci, A. (2006). The link between identification and in-group favouritism: Effects of threat to social identity and trust-related emotions. *British Journal of Social Psychology, 45,* 265–284.

Ward, C., Bochner, S., & Furnham, A. (2001). *The psychology of culture shock* (2nd ed.). London, UK: Routledge.

Wielkiewicz, R. M., & Turkowski, L. W. (2010). Reentry issues upon returning from study abroad programs. *Journal of College Student Development, 51,* 649–664.

Wilkinson, S. (1998). On the nature of immersion during study abroad: Some participants' perspectives. *Frontiers: The Interdisciplinary Journal of Study Abroad, 4,* 121–138.

Wilkinson, S. (2002). The omnipresent classroom during summer study abroad: American students in conversation with their French hosts. *The Modern Language Journal, 86,* 157–173.

Zorn, C. (1996). The long-term impact on nursing students participating in international education. *Journal of Professional Nursing, 12*(2), 106–110.

3

CLOSING THE LOOP

Linking Stages of the Assessment Cycle

Nick Gozik

For many of us in education abroad, the assessment of student learning outcomes is an aspiration, something that we hope to do in the future when time permits. Assessment is often considered an ancillary task, added on top of all of the other duties that must be carried out to ensure that students will get something out of study abroad. The more pressing day-to-day concerns of preparation—advising, predeparture orientations, visas, and processing forms, among others—take precedence. It is also understandable that education abroad advisors focus on preparation; it is in this period that they have the most contact with students and when students are most likely to see advisors as a logical resource.

More recently, assessment has become unavoidable, and arguably for good reason. First, because education abroad activities, in most cases, count toward students' degrees, they fall under institutional accreditation practices calling for the assessment of learning outcomes. Second, with the number of students studying, working, interning, volunteering, and engaging in service abroad increasing at a nearly exponential rate (Institute for International Education, 2013), more attention is being paid to who goes abroad and what students gain from their time off campus (Twombly, Salisbury, Tumanut, & Klute, 2012). Furthermore, education abroad involves an allocation of resources—personal, public, and private—and, thus, there is a need to evaluate whether the allocation is merited in terms of return on investment.

Resource limitations, moreover, force offices to justify the funding devoted to education abroad. Data collection can help demonstrate student success.

Recognizing the need to assess, education abroad professionals may be tempted to simply borrow the practices of another office or employ an instrument as is. If initially easier, such practices never quite get at the fundamental goals of assessing. These include outlining clear outcomes specific to an organizational, institutional, or program context; determining if the outcomes are being met; then communicating and acting on the findings to better facilitate attainment of the outcomes (Deardorff, 2009). Absent a plan to link these steps, one risks asking the wrong questions and wasting valuable time and resources.

Other authors have traced the steps toward creating an assessment plan for education abroad activities (Deardorff, 2009). Rather than duplicating these efforts, the aim of this chapter is to demystify the process. This chapter also sets the stage for later case studies in this volume, which explore the approach taken by individual institutions and organizations at various stages of the assessment cycle. The terminology and examples used here are oriented toward education abroad offices and professionals on U.S. college and university campuses. That said, the framework may be employed in a variety of contexts. Finally, by the end of this chapter, the title of this chapter should be clear: Assessment is an iterative process. Our discussion begins with the question "Why assess?"

Why Assess?

Before turning to the development of the assessment plan, we need to consider why and for whom we are assessing. In carrying out assessment, some education abroad offices are responding to external demands (from an accrediting agency or senior-level administrator), whereas others are looking internally to gauge the value and effectiveness of study abroad, such as whether the college or university offers its own programs or uses other options. It is also quite possible to be driven by both external and internal factors or to begin by fulfilling external requirements and later adapt processes to meet office needs, or vice versa. As a plan matures, it is quite often the case that external factors will take a backseat to internal ones, as an office takes ownership of the process. Whatever the motivation, identifying the primary objectives for assessment allows for a more tailored approach and the most effective use of limited resources. A clear strategy ensures, moreover, that the spotlight remains on student learning, a point that is not always obvious in discussions of assessment.

Institutional Demands

Institutional stakeholders—senior-level administrators, an assessment office, academic departments, or governing boards—may expect education abroad offices to assess. There may be a need to demonstrate that programming actually leads to the types of outcomes that are frequently used to promote education abroad, including cross-cultural competency, an increased sense of independence, adaptability, greater disciplinary knowledge and skills, and improved language proficiency. Questions about outcomes are common for most campus units, perhaps most so in public institutions and systems. With pressure mounting from policymakers, state universities and colleges have been increasingly forced to demonstrate that higher education leads to the development of a more qualified and skilled workforce.

It can be challenging to translate the value of what is gained during education abroad into demonstrable skills; arguably, education abroad students' true learning is long term and may not be noticeable immediately upon return. Longitudinal studies, such as one produced by the Institute for the International Education of Students as part of its Model Assessment program (Dwyer & Peters, 2004), can be costly and difficult; alumni disperse and may be difficult to track. Longitudinal studies nevertheless provide a rich illustration of the impacts of education abroad.

Accreditation

Accreditation is another impetus for assessment. For those in professional fields, this is not new or surprising. The Accreditation Board for Engineering and Technology requires engineering schools to collect data on student learning outcomes related to specific standards (DiBiasio & Mello, 2004; Hornfeck & Jouny, 2010). Fields such as nursing and teacher education must meet similar certification requirements.

In the United States, the integration of assessment into accreditation has varied from one region to another (Gozik, 2014). A nongovernmental organization, the Council for Higher Education Accreditation (CHEA), regulates accreditation at the postsecondary level, with reviews of individual colleges and universities handled by regional accrediting bodies. These accrediting bodies follow standards outlined by the CHEA and the U.S. Department of Education but set their own requirements. The Southern Association of Colleges and Schools has focused heavily on outcomes assessment (see chapter 8 in this volume) within the past decade; other regions are following suit.

At some institutions, education abroad offices have not yet been directly involved in accreditation. Even so, accreditation can have ripple effects on a campus, creating an overall culture of assessment. In regions where assessment has not been linked to accreditation, education abroad offices have followed the example of counterparts in regions where it is. In these cases, the education abroad offices may lead the way for other campus units to begin assessing. Accreditation thus may be having an unexpected impact on the field of education abroad.

Program Satisfaction

External pressures notwithstanding, one of the primary reasons that education abroad offices have long engaged in assessment is to gauge student satisfaction, notably through postprogram evaluations and reentry debriefing sessions. Evaluations typically ask participants to rate their contentment with on-site support, orientation, classroom facilities, housing, and activities, among other aspects. Responses may lead to changes to ensure students' comfort and safety in a program or to the removal of a problematic program from an approved list. At the same time, there is growing recognition that measuring customer satisfaction and assessing learning outcomes are not the same (Vande Berg, Conner-Linton, & Paige, 2009). Accordingly, many in education abroad have begun to focus on the latter.

Advising

Assessment results can similarly influence advising. Former participants' perceptions of a program can be drawn on to manage expectations and to direct prospective students to options appropriate for their needs. Thus, if evaluations suggest minimal on-site support in a given location, an advisor may direct less independent students toward other options. More formatively, advising can help students determine their own learning goals. At Boston College, for instance, students are asked to identify three to five goals for going abroad. Although initial responses may rest at the surface level (e.g., to travel, take time off, or have fun), understanding students' motivations is a first step in helping students become more intentional about their choices. As students articulate more specific academic and personal growth goals, advisors can match them with programs designed to achieve related outcomes.

Advocacy

Assessment results can help education abroad offices increase their visibility. Duke University, for example, developed a fact sheet aimed at students and parents with participants' demographic data, figures for scholarships and grants, and percentages of students in disciplines with unusually high participation rates in comparison to national figures. To complement the statistics, quotes from evaluations, with the necessary permissions in place, add a student voice. Similarly, Duke has provided in-depth reports on findings from evaluations and the Global Perspective Inventory (Global Perspective Institute, n.d.) to senior-level administrators to demonstrate success in programming efforts. In addition, assessment results can become powerful tools for advocating for increases in resources.

What Is Being Assessed?

Having considered reasons for assessing, we turn to the visualization and creation of an assessment plan. The term *assessment plan* may have different meanings. The scope of the plan is one consideration: Some plans are straightforward, focusing on one outcome and one measure, whereas others are more elaborate and include a long-term and possibly multistage implementation approach. Thus, the scope of the analysis must be appropriate to the needs and capacities of the particular education abroad office.

In this chapter, an assessment plan is understood to focus on student learning outcomes. Figure 3.1 depicts the relationship of learning outcomes to programs, offices, and institutions.

Institution

Many colleges and universities have developed internationalization plans with comprehensive strategies across all campus units. The ideal is for institutions to

Figure 3.1 Levels of assessment in an education abroad office

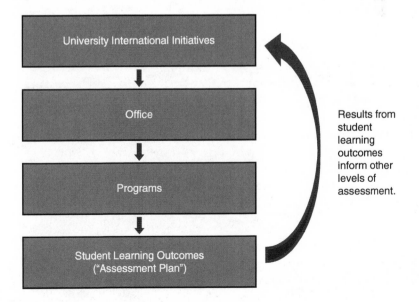

move beyond oft-touted statistics (e.g., numbers of study abroad participants, international students, and language learners) and to consider the ways in which campuses may become fully and seamlessly international. The American Council on Education's model for comprehensive internationalization (Olson, Green, & Hill, 2005) is intended to help institutions engage faculty, students, and staff in such efforts. Even if a comprehensive internationalization strategy has not been entirely articulated, education abroad offices should be aware of overarching institutional priorities, either explicit or implied.

Office

A longer term office plan can avoid the risk of becoming reactive rather than proactive (Gozik, 2014). A plan should start with a review of the office mission statement to ensure that it aligns with institutional aims and reflects what the office hopes to accomplish. An office-wide assessment may also encompass a review of the office's structure and operations, ranging from staffing and reporting lines to program offerings, budgeting, marketing and outreach, health and safety, predeparture and reentry training, and assessment. Self-reporting may take place on an annual basis and with results disseminated to campus leaders and other key stakeholders. At other times, it is useful for an office to be reviewed by an external team, whose members come from on or off campus. Indeed, many institutions have standardized the process by including education abroad offices in the regular cycle of academic program reviews. In addition to allowing an office to function more effectively and strategically, office reviews can be used to advocate for additional space, staffing, and funding or otherwise receive recognition.

Program

Education abroad offices must also evaluate individual education abroad programs, whether these are administered by the institution and another entity, such as another U.S. university or college, an exchange partner, or a third-party organization. Program type determines the extent to which an office can make changes to a program. In the case of external offerings, the choices might be limited to removing a program from an approved list or, more proactively, offering with the hope that the stated concerns be addressed. Programs administered directly by the institution require greater attention to ensure that they are aligned with the institutional and office mission and goals, are cost-effective and run efficiently, meet desired outcomes, and comply with standards of good practice such as those issued by the Forum on Education Abroad (2011).

One of the most common tools for assessing programs is the postprogram evaluation. As noted previously, some evaluations focus primarily on customer satisfaction with logistics, housing, academics, and activities. To be a true assessment tool, evaluations must include mechanisms to measure the extent to which stated goals are being met in study abroad in general or in particular program options. As there are weaknesses to data collected through postprogram evaluations, results should be supplemented with data from other measures.

Reviews can be valuable in evaluating a program's effectiveness. As with office reviews, evaluating teams may be composed of internal and/or external members. Reviewers should receive background materials: program history, staffing, budget, marketing and publications, course syllabi, and evaluation tools and findings. Ideally, one or more members of the team will have an opportunity to visit the program site to make observations and conduct interviews with students, faculty, and others involved in the program. Program reviews can thus range from a relatively short visit by an office staff member to much more involved stays. Furthermore, site visits need to be distinguished from reviews, and in the latter case, those on the ground must be made aware that a review is being conducted. Reviewers should receive clear instructions and/or instruments (e.g., rubrics) for evaluating the program and submit a report with comments and recommendations for improvements.

Student Learning Outcomes

Although these levels of analysis are relevant to education abroad, in the end the learning outcomes (knowledge, skills, abilities, attitudes) identified as important by the institution (and/or the students) are paramount. These, in turn, are shaped by institutional and unit designs to foster student learning and development. At the same time, assessment plans need to be outlined expressly to evaluate student success in education abroad, aside from other logistical and structural frames. Furthermore, outcomes need to be established and measured as part of a holistic assessment cycle, from mission to goals and learning outcomes, instruments and methods, and means of conveying results to stakeholders.

In the remainder of this chapter, we focus on designing plans to assess student learning outcomes. The logic employed may be adapted to other levels of analysis, though here the examples will center on how to gauge the extent to which students have met specified objectives. We begin by considering what we already know.

What Do We Already Know?

Assessment planning can be daunting, so much so that it may be one of the reasons for not beginning at all. The fact is we have much more experience, data, and knowledge at our fingertips than we imagine. Knowledge may come through anecdotal means, such as conversations with students, faculty, and colleagues. Such informal feedback can lead to questions that drive a more rigorous and systematic assessment process. Tapping existing sources and then looking to see where the gaps might lie is a smart and efficient way to start the planning process.

Students

Talking to students can be one of the most valuable sources of information, whether this is within the context of advising, orientations, site visits, or elsewhere. Students often want to share their perceptions of study abroad, including why they are going, what they expect to accomplish, their fears and hopes in living and studying abroad, and their plans for applying skills gained abroad to future careers. They can also provide valuable insights into why peers may or may not go abroad, as well as strategies for reaching under-represented populations within education abroad, including males, students in certain disciplines, minorities, and first-generation students. Although input given by students should be filtered and contextualized, understanding how students view their own development can be an excellent place to start thinking about what we want to assess.

Existing Data

One common fallacy is that it is necessary to start from point zero in collecting data. In fact, just as students are already providing information relevant to our assessment of education abroad outcomes, most of us are also sitting on a mountain of data that can be mined and analyzed. The most typical data collected within an office are in the form of postprogram evaluations. Although the quality and depth of responses from students vary greatly, evaluations can reveal much about students' growth while abroad. In addition, offices may house reports from site visits and on-site staff and have access to students' journals, blog entries, and projects, all of which can provide clues to student learning.

Beyond the education abroad office, sources of information can come in many forms. Large-scale surveys administered to incoming first-year students and outgoing seniors are generally not oriented specifically to education abroad yet may still include relevant questions. Data from the National Survey of Student Engagement (NSSE, n.d.) can illuminate questions about study abroad (Ogden, 2014). One question on the 2012 NSSE asked about intention to study abroad. When correlated with responses to other questions, findings can suggest differences between study abroad and non-study abroad students in terms of background and activities. Institutions can also add campus-specific questions to the Cooperative Institutional Research Program (CIRP) (Higher Education Research Group, n.d.) first-year and senior surveys. To do so requires the support of campus leaders, who determine which questions are included; with a variety of demands from offices across campus, the decisions are strategic and sometimes political.

Transcripts can likewise be mined in a multitude of ways. At Boston College, the study abroad office checks the courses students intend to take abroad to see if these align with the students' majors and/or minors. Although students may benefit from expanding their interests outside narrow domains (a possible goal on its own), if they are not taking any courses in their chosen fields, the students may envision study abroad as a vacation rather than as something integrated into their ongoing studies. Grades may similarly be analyzed to evaluate academic success. If students are performing well in courses related to their majors or minors, one might conclude that they are on track to benefit from their studies abroad and bring the study abroad experience to bear on their studies upon returning to the home campus. Grades should be evaluated judiciously, however: Study abroad participants may be more likely to be high achievers in the first place and thus apt to perform well abroad. Nonetheless, grade analysis within the University of Georgia system (Sutton & Rubin, 2004) showed positive impacts of study abroad on post-study abroad academic success.

Our Own Experience

Finally, one of the reasons many of us enter the field of education abroad is the personal impact from having worked, volunteered, studied, and/or traveled abroad, and we continue to have experiences that influence who we are professionally and personally. However, much may have changed since we lived abroad. The role of technology, and especially the rise of social media, is shocking to those who remember being almost entirely disconnected from friends and family, with perhaps only a phone call home every few weeks. Furthermore, when we travel now, we may spend only a couple of days at a site rather than live abroad for a summer, semester, or academic year, as is the case with students. These caveats aside, our own experiences can guide the formation of assessment strategies and instruments. If a plan does not intuitively feel as if it will yield useful and grounded results, the plan may need to be recalibrated.

These are a few illustrations of the knowledge education abroad practitioners bring to assessment. It is hoped these will diffuse some of the anxiety or fear that may come along with "Assessment" with a capital "A" by highlighting the fact that we have a rich font of knowledge and experience from which to start.

Designing an Assessment Plan

Having explored reasons for assembling an assessment plan, what a plan might constitute, and what types of knowledge can aid in formulating a plan, we now turn to designing a plan. Individual offices may approach the planning process differently. The following steps are not intended to be prescriptive; rather, they provide a rough road map that can and should be altered to an individual institution's needs.

Regardless of where one begins, it is critical that each of the components of a plan—the mission statement, learning goals and outcomes, assessment tools, and distribution of results to key constituents—link together within a cohesive cycle (see figure 3.2). This ordering ensures that learning outcomes align with the office and institutional mission and priorities and that there is a method for measuring each of the stated goals and outcomes. Once data have been collected, there should be a system for sharing findings and using the data to improve programs and activities. A holistic plan allows for continual reflection and monitoring at each stage of the process, so that assessment measures can be modified as warranted.

Mission Statement

It can be all too tempting to draft and perfect an office mission statement and then set it aside without further thought. For the purposes of establishing student learning outcomes, an office nevertheless needs to agree on a common vision, a task that can be accomplished through the formation of a new statement or revision of an existing one. In doing so, at least two

Figure 3.2 Assessment cycle

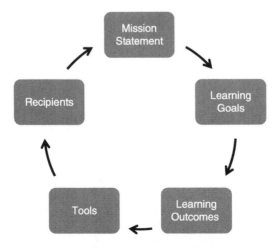

questions should be asked: Does the current or proposed mission statement align with the institutional mission? Does the statement accurately reflect what the office hopes to accomplish?

One can begin by surveying the ways in which campus decision makers have articulated the college's or university's core principles and goals. The most obvious place to start is with the institutional mission statement. In revising its mission, for example, Boston College's Office of International Programs (OIP) looked to the college's mission:

> [Boston College] seeks both to advance its place among the nation's finest universities and to bring to the company of its distinguished peers and to contemporary society the richness of the Catholic intellectual ideal of a mutually illuminating relationship between religious faith and free intellectual inquiry. (Boston College Board of Trustees, n.d.)

Emphasis on Catholic ideals was not surprising; the Society of Jesus founded Boston College in 1863. Even so, the clear expression of the institution's commitment was a valuable reminder of the institution's identity, which in turn led the OIP to open its mission statement with, "In accordance with Boston College's tradition and values." Although Boston College students, faculty, and staff represent a wide variety of faiths, and not all are Catholic, the values referenced in the statement and elsewhere on campus are largely universal and applicable to a host of cultural contexts, perhaps because the Jesuit order is global in scope. The OIP also found many of the ideals to be well suited for education abroad, including the commitment to social justice with the notion of "men and women for others" and the need for personal reflection in the "here and now."

Other institutions send altogether different signals through their mission statements. New York University (NYU, n.d.), for example, pledges to become "the first global network university" and highlights the connections between its Washington Square campus and NYU satellite locations around the world. NYU underscores the fact that its campuses are located in "great cities," beginning with New York City, that are "magnets for talented, ambitious people." And last, there is a commitment to being "a top quality international center of scholarship, teaching and research." Each of these themes is reiterated, in both language and spirit, in the descriptions and missions of international offices and study away programs throughout NYU. From an assessment perspective, the repetition ensures that the goals and learning outcomes of individual units reinforce those of the institution.

In addition to official mission statements, an environmental scan can identify other priorities to be conveyed across campus, either explicitly or implicitly. A scan entails a survey of institutional websites, publications, and other forms of communication to trace patterns. University website search engines can capture the frequency with which a term is employed. Yale (see chapter 10) and Duke (see chapter 8) found that the term *leadership* recurred repeatedly and in a variety of contexts. Although not unexpected—both institutions are competitive and attract top students who also tend to be leaders—the repetition of *leadership* speaks to a core value on the two campuses. Knowing what matters to faculty, students, and staff is critical for developing programs and initiatives that fit the ethos of the institution and in turn receive support and interest.

Having completed a scan, one can, when sitting down to write a mission statement, struggle to find words that accurately convey what the office hopes to accomplish. Many have an initial attack of writer's block while searching for formal and precise language that sounds impressive and befitting of a mission. It can be more productive to capture core concepts by using plain and straightforward language. Mission statements are best drafted by an individual or small team, after which they can be shared to elicit additional input. Although initial drafts may need refining, the final product should remain clear and representative of both what the office aims to do and what it does on a regular basis.

Developing a mission statement takes time. However, the process offers an excellent opportunity for an office to evaluate its role vis-à-vis other units on campus, as well as to engage in strategic planning beyond assessment.

Goals and Learning Outcomes

With a mission statement in place, the next step is to develop learning goals and outcomes. Goals are intended to be broad, with learning outcomes specific and measurable. Some prefer to merge the two; this is not problematic, but it is essential to ensure that each of the goals and outcomes can be measured (Gozik, 2014).

Goals typically result in multiple desired outcomes. If a language immersion program in Spain endeavors to have all students attain a certain level of fluency, for instance, the goal might be "increased proficiency in Spanish-language comprehension and skills." To operationalize this goal, programs can ask any number of questions, each corresponding to a learning outcome: Are we looking to see whether students can carry out daily tasks such as using public transportation, making purchases at the grocery store, or dealing with transactions at the bank? Do we want to know whether students can follow and contribute to a college-level course taught in Spanish? Might we want to know whether students can form personal relationships with locals, with Spanish the medium of communication?

It can be challenging to narrow the list of goals. In the case of Boston College, when drafting its assessment plan, the OIP assessment working group began with 10 goals, each worthy of consideration. After much discussion, the list was winnowed to five. The working group determined that not everything could be measured, at least at the given moment, so preference was given to goals that aligned with institutional and office priorities. Other institutions such as Beloit College (see chapter 7) concentrate on one or two goals in a given year. Whatever the strategy, keeping the list manageable allows for a greater chance of success in carrying out the assessment plan, as well as in guaranteeing that students are able to achieve the stated goals.

A similar process applies to selecting learning outcomes, as there are inevitably very interesting and worthwhile questions that will go unanswered. If an outcome is not included in the current plan, this does not mean that it cannot be examined later; plans do and should change to stay relevant. Furthermore, within one goal, it may be necessary to split out learning outcomes to accommodate different types of students. In the earlier example of language development, certain outcomes may be relevant to advanced-level language speakers (e.g., the ability to succeed in a course taught in Spanish), whereas others may be reserved for beginners (e.g., the ability to carry out daily actions such as errands or use public transportation). The same assessment methods may sometimes be used for different sets of students to capture varying results, whereas in other cases different methods may be required.

Rather than entirely reinventing the wheel, it can be helpful to view examples of goals and learning outcomes created by other institutions, such as those accessed on the American Council on Education's (n.d.) website within the "Campus Internationalization Toolkit," the Forum on Education Abroad's (2014) Outcomes Assessment Toolbox, and the assessment plans obtained by asking colleagues at other institutions. There is considerable overlap in how institutions articulate outcomes for education abroad. Among common themes are global citizenship, intercultural awareness and skills, disciplinary knowledge, and language acquisition. Although looking at others' examples can be a good place to start, learning goals and outcomes ultimately need to be calibrated with the specific office's mission and aims.

A spreadsheet or table (see table 3.1) can be employed to organize the goals and learning outcomes with other components. Doing so will reveal any gaps. Keeping the information in cells avoids overly lengthy descriptions and encourages a focus on the most relevant points. This, of course, is not the only way to display a plan; each office needs to determine what works best for it.

TABLE 3.1
Assessment planning worksheet.

Goals	Learning Outcomes	Tools/Instruments	Recipients of Data
1.	a.		
	b.		
2.	a.		
	b.		
3.	a.		
	b.		
4.	a.		
	b.		

Instruments and Methods

Once learning goals and outcomes have been set, the next task is to identify assessment instruments and methods to evaluate the outcomes. The number of options can be overwhelming. It would certainly be ideal if there was a single list of recommended tools that could be implemented in any situation. The reality is that needs, capacities, and resources vary from one office to another. It is thus necessary to align instruments carefully with desired outcomes.

In selecting an instrument or method, one question to ask is whether to rely on self-reported data. These data derive from instruments that ask participants to respond to questions without researcher interference. A common example is that of program evaluations; these can prompt students to evaluate their own progress over time. Evaluations and other similar tools tend to be low cost and relatively easy to implement; however, they also present limitations in terms of accuracy. Respondents tend to report what they believe the researcher or evaluator expects to see (Cook & Campbell, 1979) or report what reflects positively on their own abilities, beliefs, or opinions (Yu, Ohlund, DiGangi, & Jannasch-Pennell, 2000). Some students, conversely, may underreport what they learned or how they grew; this may suggest that study abroad had a negative impact on their development. In truth, students may self-evaluate lower because they have gained a better understanding of how much they do not actually know. This in turn may be a sign of intellectual and personal maturity and a success in its own right. Self-reported data are equally problematic in that they rely on human memory, which has been shown to be fallible. Given that memories are not fixed, it can be difficult for students to evaluate objectively where they were developmentally months before.

If self-reported data are not ideal, this does not mean that they should be disregarded altogether; rather, they should be compared with results from other forms of measurement, including those that do not rely on participants to evaluate themselves. In this latter category, there are again many options. Instruments may be developed in house or purchased from outside vendors; there are pros and cons to each. A growing number of products have come on the market that can be implemented fairly quickly and easily. In the realm of intercultural and/or global competency, for example, widely used instruments include the Intercultural Development Inventory (IDI, n.d.), Global Perspective Inventory (GPI) (Global Perspective Institute, n.d.), and Beliefs, Events, and Values Inventory (BEVI, n.d.). These instruments offer the advantage of having been created and tested by experts, and because they are standardized, it is easier to compare results across campuses and between institutions. The IDI, for instance, was used in the large-scale, multiyear Georgetown Consortium Project (Vande Berg et al., 2009). One drawback can be the costs, which may include training for administrators, licensing, and fees for processing surveys. In addition, buyers should also be careful to select instruments that fit stated outcomes; just because "intercultural" or "global" is in the title does not mean that the tool measures what one hopes to assess. Another constraint is the time involved in administering the instrument and making sense of the data.

Some institutions have created their own instruments. Wesleyan University, for example, found that the IDI did not quite meet its needs in terms of costs and implementation. The Office of International Studies implemented a tool created by a faculty member on campus, the Wesleyan Intercultural Competence Scale (WICS; as discussed in chapter 13). In other cases, where there are not sufficient resources to develop a new instrument, offices have been able to tweak or add questions to larger surveys distributed regularly across campus, such as the CIRP first-year and senior surveys, as noted earlier.

Beyond standardized instruments, a variety of other methods exist for assessing students. Whenever possible, it is best to piggyback on existing practices, so as to maximize resources and reduce possible "survey fatigue" among students. Duke University, for example, has relied on student blogs as a creative way of tracking students' progress in areas such as global awareness and cross-cultural understanding. Students can be given prompts that align with desired learning outcomes, or they can be given liberty to write freely about their experiences. Duke's Office of Assessment has created rubrics to categorize and rate student development in key areas; results from the blogs are then compared with data from other sources, including the GPI. The same strategy of rubrics can be applied to student papers and examinations, as well as to qualitative questions added to pre- and postprogram evaluations.

Entering the selected instruments or methods into a spreadsheet or table (see table 3.1) allows one to see what gaps may exist in terms of data collection, as well as to determine whether existing instruments need to be recalibrated to align more closely with desired learning outcomes. With program evaluations, for example, questions may need to be added or rephrased to yield better results, and those that no longer serve an explicit purpose should be deleted. Eliminating can be easier said than done, given that there is a natural tendency to want to hold on to questions that "might" be used at some point. It is nonetheless necessary to streamline questions so as to maximize the chance of students completing the entire evaluation rather than stopping midway out of frustration.

Recipients

To close the assessment loop, assessment results need to be shared with key stakeholders. All too often considerable work goes into collecting data, which then remain locked away, neither fully analyzed nor disseminated. This tendency is understandable in that most of us juggle many duties; some, like assessment, can take a backseat. If we do not share and act on our findings, however, the hard truth is that there is no reason to assess; the time and energy used to collect data could be better spent elsewhere.

Potential recipients of assessment results include senior-level administrators, on-site staff, the education abroad office, students, parents, other departments and offices, accrediting agencies, and alumni. Not everyone will need to see all results. Foreign language faculty will likely be interested in findings related to language proficiency, for example, whereas colleagues in other disciplines might be less so.

Thought also needs to be given to how results are shared. Higher level administrators may want more concise résumés with brief explanation (from a couple of paragraphs to a page). These sorts of reports need to zero in on the most pertinent information; if more details are needed, they can be provided later. One tactic that can work well is to develop an executive summary of results, which can be absorbed quickly, along with appendices that provide greater detail. Knowing the audience can also help to determine whether more emphasis should be placed on quantitative or qualitative data, as well as the extent to which graphs and other illustrations should be incorporated. Preferences may be based on disciplinary training; for example, a faculty member or leader who has been trained in the sciences might be more easily persuaded by quantitative results than will a colleague who employs qualitative methodology in his or her own work.

Reading program evaluations and reviews can help students (and parents) select a program or prepare for the study abroad experience. Before making evaluations available, the education abroad office should ensure that inappropriate comments and any student identifiers have been removed, unless students have intentionally given permission for their name and/or other contact details to be revealed. Concern may be raised over whether evaluations color students' perceptions before they have had a chance to really learn about a program. This can be indeed problematic when one or two students pan a program, perhaps unfairly, while the silent majority does not complete an evaluation or offers minimal comment. On the flipside, systematically sharing results sends a positive signal to students that their feedback is valued. By providing regular updates and reports on assessment activities, furthermore, an office can assist in fostering a "culture of assessment" on campus (Weiner, 2009), by which assessment comes to be viewed as less of a chore and more as a valuable part of one's work.

Beyond internal reports, findings can be used for marketing and outreach. A number of institutions integrate quotes from evaluations, papers, blogs, and videos, with permission from students, into their online and print materials. At Boston College, special attention has been paid to excerpts that demonstrate the ways in which students have met desired learning outcomes; for example, students who have expressed progress in terms of the language gains, increased knowledge of the world, and growth in intercultural competency. When students articulate such outcomes in their own words, the conversation around study abroad can shift away from the fun of traveling and living abroad to focus on academic and student development. Getting away from the typical group shots, quotes can be paired with photos of students engaged in activities (e.g., research, community building, or conducting service), which similarly reinforce student learning and development.

Regardless of how and to whom data are distributed, it is always important to bear in mind that the assessment of learning outcomes should, in due course, benefit students. Results can help improve how students are advised prior to going abroad, while in country, and upon their return to campus. Clear and data-driven knowledge allows professionals in the field to ensure that experiences abroad are value added and effective in preparing students for future endeavors.

Reflecting on the Results and Restarting the Cycle

Once the final stage has been reached and the assessment plan has been implemented, it is time to examine the results and review the process. Before taking any drastic moves, one should verify that the assessment instruments and methods in use are accurately measuring outcomes. A homegrown tool may need to be fine-tuned, or a borrowed one reevaluated to ensure that it is capturing what it purports to measure. When an office may not have the necessary expertise or resources to adequately evaluate an instrument or method, others on campus may have relevant expertise.

Once verified for accuracy, the data can help strengthen programs and processes to ensure that students have the best chance of realizing stated outcomes. If assessment results demonstrate that students' language levels are not improving sufficiently on an immersion program, for example, it may be time to consider whether certain aspects of the program (e.g., course work, housing, activities) need to be revamped. An honest conversation with the program staff and faculty can yield new and innovative strategies not previously considered. These conversations need to be approached delicately, though openly, to assure staff that they themselves are not being criticized and allow them to brainstorm solutions. Staff may be able to offer a useful context, as well as corrections to some of the conclusions determined by the assessment results. It may be that there are circumstances outside the control of the program that need to be understood and mitigated.

For programs run by an external provider, there may be more of a hesitation in sharing results, for fear of offending colleagues or because of a sense that it is not one's responsibility to "fix" another's program. Much comes down to the relationship with the provider, though most organizations very much welcome feedback, particularly if it is grounded in data and presented in a respectful and collegial manner. In an ideal situation, the home institution and provider see each other as partners, with the latter wanting to do everything it can to help students realize anticipated gains. If a provider is unwilling to take feedback seriously, this can be seen as a red flag, leading the home institution to consider removing the program from its approved list.

Last, reviewing a plan on a regular basis entails relaunching the assessment cycle. After distributing results to key stakeholders and gaining feedback, one needs to return to the original mission and goals and verify that they continue to reflect the office's priorities. The time lag alone might have allowed for considerable change to take place on a campus, with new leadership and initiatives that require an alternative approach to assessing learning outcomes. When a plan is reviewed on a regular basis, it can be easier to make smaller changes over time rather than rethink the entire plan, which is a much more time-consuming venture.

Tips From the Trenches

We close by hearing from colleagues in the field who can pass on practical tips that have served them well. Although not an exhaustive list, these suggestions offer a starting point for launching into the assessment process.

Take Time to Plan

With a busy schedule, sitting down to develop a plan may seem like an unnecessary luxury. Adriane van Gils-Pierce at Clark University reminds us that it is, nonetheless, imperative to invest time in "considering what you are trying to assess and in what context." Like many in the field, she explained that her office has needed to think about how the office evaluates language learning on Spanish-immersion programs. There was an initial proposal to measure only the gains of study abroad students without a control group on the home campus, which would have yielded an incomplete data set. Van Gils-Pierce is now collaborating with colleagues in the department of languages, literature, and culture to devise a study that will compare both sets of students. All involved recognize that it was critical to plan carefully to obtain results useful for both the education abroad office and the department. Knowing that planning is an indispensable part of the process can alleviate some of the stress that might ensue from any sorts of delays.

Consider What You Want Your Students to Know

Others caution that it is easy to get lost in assessing for assessment's sake while forgetting to focus on what is really important: student learning. Heather Barclay Hamir at Boston University emphasized, "You have to start with the outcomes you would like students to achieve." She added, "It is energizing to think about what we really want for our students, how we help them achieve it, what learning activities or artifacts will allow us to assess their progress, and how we will then adapt to better align the courses and learning activities to support the desired outcomes." Hamir's office has extended this analysis to its overseas sites to confirm that student learning outcomes at each location are aligned with those of the home office. Figuring out what students should be learning requires engaging in discussions with key stakeholders, including students.

Use a Variety of Methods

Joe Hoff at the University of Richmond stressed that once your office is ready to select tools and methods that align to stated outcomes, you need "to use mixed methods in order to validate your findings. It is important to use both quantitative and qualitative methods to show the soundness of the results." One example of this is his office's use of random, qualitative interviews with students, which have been used to complement data derived from the IDI. Even though the IDI has been tested at a variety of institutions, the interviews have helped to ensure that the results are not only accurate but also aligned with the outcomes that Richmond hopes to measure. The particular combination of measures used at Richmond may not meet all office's needs;

however, the process of combining multiple methods, or "triangulating" results, is critical in the development of any well-thought-out plan.

Keep It Manageable

Many practitioners caution that an assessment plan needs to be realistic and grounded in daily practices. At Beloit College, Betsy Brewer explained that her office intentionally limits its assessment efforts to responding to one or two key questions in a given year; responding to more can be overwhelming and lead to nothing being accomplished. Others have noted that they have implemented their plan in stages, starting with the easiest tasks or "low-hanging fruit." Doing so allows an office to build confidence and demonstrate success before tackling more complicated and time-consuming projects. Regardless of the strategy, it is almost always better to try something rather than nothing at all and realize that no plan will be perfect. Even weak results can serve as a pilot for a more in-depth and better informed project down the line.

Similarly, Martha Johnson at the University of Minnesota noted that it is equally necessary to be clear and reasonable in anticipated student outcomes. She explained, "Historically, education abroad programs have often been assessed on a long and unrealistic list of gains that are not part of the program's intention." For example, asking students to immerse fully in a location when the program itself is not set up to allow for true integration only sets participants and on-site faculty and administrators up to fail. It is important to be specific in outlining learning outcomes for a given set of students, with an understanding that success may take time.

Reach Out to Others

Rather than relying solely on one's own resources and expertise, many point out that it is important to collaborate with others on campus. Christine Wintersteen at Bowdoin College recounted that she and her colleague, in a two-person office, established and implemented an assessment plan within a year of attending a Forum on Education Abroad workshop. One of the ways that they were able to accomplish this feat was by gaining buy-in from senior institutional research team members, who were thrilled to know "other offices were interested in and considering ways of looking at data." She added that it has also been "valuable to know what [the research team's] mandates are from the institutional perspective."

In addition to an assessment team or office, it can be worthwhile to reach out to other faculty and staff on campus with knowledge in assessment. At some institutions, representatives from various offices meet on a regular basis to share best practices and ideas, as well as provide a support network.

At Michigan State University, Brett Berquist reported that his office teams up with the Office of Faculty and Organizational Development to run a workshop each year during which faculty share ways of engaging in research on study abroad from various disciplinary vantage points. His institution also has a research advisory council that convenes twice a year to consider a longer term agenda, which permits collaboration around large-scale projects, at times in coordination with external universities and organizations.

Connect Assessment to Advising

If students are fundamental to a successful assessment plan, there is a benefit to linking assessment to advising. Michelle Gere at Yale University noted, "It is often through the advising process that students begin to set goals and expectations for their experience that will continue into the program and influence their overall attitude and approach about learning and living abroad." She added, "By looking at advising through the lens of assessment, we see how it can be both a vehicle to reach stated learning objectives and a tool to assess them." More generally, this point reminds us that assessment results need to inform processes and programs. By closing the assessment loop and distributing data to staff and faculty, one ensures that the resources required to implement an assessment plan ultimately yield better services and support for students.

Revisit the Plan

There was consensus that the assessment process is never complete. Time must be set aside on a regular and ongoing basis to revisit plans and consider ways to fine-tune them. One associate director reported that she and her colleague meet at least twice per year, at prearranged times, and go to an off-campus coffee shop or other venue. By carving out time in advance and leaving the office, they are able to quickly and efficiently review their assessment efforts, and, by meeting fairly regularly, they are not faced with a Herculean task of attempting to revise the entire plan. Instead, adjustments are more nuanced. In what has become a repeated theme throughout this chapter, investing time wisely can lead to assessment efforts that are better organized and easier to implement—a great help to all of us in the "trenches."

Author's Note

This chapter developed out of a workshop titled "From A to Z: Developing an Assessment Plan to Promote Student Learning and Development," which was offered at the 2012 Forum on Education Abroad's annual conference in

Chicago, Illinois. I would like to thank my copresenters at the workshop, Elizabeth Brewer, Dennis M. Doyle, and Kelly McLaughlin, for their contributions to the workshop and the development of this chapter.

References

American Council on Education. (n.d.). *CIGE model for comprehensive internationalization.* Retrieved from www.acenet.edu/news-room/Pages/CIGE-Model-for-Comprehensive-Internationalization.aspx

Beliefs, Events, and Values Inventory. (n.d.). *About the BEVI.* Retrieved from http://thebevi.com/aboutbevi.php

Boston College Board of Trustees. (n.d.). *The mission of Boston College.* Retrieved from www.bc.edu/offices/bylaws/mission.html

Cook, T., & Campbell, D. (1979). *Quasi-experimentation: Design and analysis for field settings.* Boston, MA: Houghton Mifflin.

Deardorff, D. (2009). Understanding the challenges of assessing global citizenship. In R. Lewin (Ed.), *The handbook of practice and research in study abroad: Higher education and the quest for global citizenship* (pp. 346–364). New York, NY: Routledge.

DiBiasio, D., & Mello, N. (2004). Multi-level assessment of program outcomes: Assessing a nontraditional study abroad program in the engineering disciplines. *Frontiers: The Interdisciplinary Journal of Study Abroad, 10,* 237–252.

Dwyer, M., & Peters, C. (2004). The benefits of study abroad: New study confirms gains. *Study Abroad Advisor.* Retrieved from www.transitionsabroad.com/publications/magazine/0403/benefits_study_abroad.shtml

Forum on Education Abroad. (2011). *Standards of good practice for education abroad* (4th ed.). Carlisle, PA: Forum on Education Abroad.

Forum on Education Abroad. (2014). Outcomes Assessment Toolbox. Retrieved from www.forumea.org/research-outcomes.cfm

Global Perspective Institute. (n.d.). Global Perspective Inventory. Retrieved from https://gpi.central.edu/supportDocs/GPI-Brochure.pdf

Gozik, N. (2014). The fundamentals of outcomes assessment in education abroad. In M. Wiedenhoeft, M. Hernandez, & D. Wick (Eds.), *NAFSA guide to education abroad for advisers and administrators* (4th ed., pp. 407–421). Washington, DC: NAFSA.

Hammer, M., Bennett, M., & Wiseman, R. (2003). The Intercultural Development Inventory: A measure of intercultural sensitivity. *International Journal of Intercultural Relations, 27,* 421–443.

Higher Education Research Group. (n.d.). *About CIRP.* Retrieved from www.heri.ucla.edu/

Hornfeck, W., & Jouny, I. (2010). The successful integration of study abroad and an engineering curriculum. In *Transforming engineering education: Creating interdisciplinary skills for complex global environments* (pp. 1–11). Dublin, Ireland: IEEE.

Institute for International Education. (2013). *Open doors 2013: International students in the United States and study abroad by American students are at all-time high.* Retrieved from www.iie.org/en/Who-We-Are/News-and-Events/Press-Center/Press-Releases/2013/2013–11–11-Open-Doors-Data

Intercultural Development Inventory. (n.d.). *The roadmap to intercultural competence using the IDI.* Retrieved from http://idiinventory.com/products/the-intercultural-development-inventory-idi

National Survey of Student Engagement. (n.d.). *About NSSE.* Retrieved from http://nsse.iub.edu

New York University. (n.d.). *About NYU.* Retrieved from www.nyu.edu/about.html

Ogden, A. (2014). Effective utilization of institutional data for strategic education abroad planning and campus advocacy. In M. Wiedenhoeft, M. Hernandez, & D. Wick (Eds.), *NAFSA guide to education abroad for advisers and administrators* (4th ed., pp. 331–355). Washington, DC: NAFSA.

Olson, C., Green, M., & Hill, B. (2005). *Building a strategic framework for comprehensive internationalization.* Washington, DC: American Council on Higher Education.

Sutton, R., & Rubin, D. (2004). The GLOSSARI Project: Initial findings from a system-wide research initiative on study abroad learning outcomes. *Frontiers: The Interdisciplinary Journal of Study Abroad, 10,* 65–82.

Twombly, S., Salisbury, M., Tumanut, S., & Klute, P. (2012). Study abroad in a new global century: Renewing the promise, refining the purpose. In K. Ward & L. E. Wolf-Wendel (Eds.), *ASHE Higher Education Report* (pp. i–154). Hoboken, NJ: Wiley.

Vande Berg, M., Connor-Linton, J., & Paige, R. (2009, Fall). The Georgetown Consortium project: Interventions for student learning abroad. *Frontiers: The Interdisciplinary Journal of Study Abroad, 18,* 1–75.

Weiner, W. (2009). Establishing a culture of assessment. *Academe, 95,* 28–32.

Yu, C., Ohlund, B., DiGangi, S., & Jannasch-Pennell, A. (2000). *Estimating the reliability of self-reported data for web-based instruction.* Retrieved from www.creative-wisdom.com/pub/aect2000.pdf

PART TWO

TOOLS AND STRATEGIES FOR ASSESSING STUDY ABROAD

4

CONTEXTUALIZING THE ASSESSMENT JOURNEY AND TOOLS FOR THE TREK

Kevin P. Saunders, Jen Hogan, and Christa Lee Olson

We have been thrust into situations where we have been unfamiliar/uncomfortable, and that has helped me as a student to learn about the culture as well as about myself. (Drake student, Egypt seminar, 2013)

My point is that excellent teaching . . . is not simply a matter of knowing the latest techniques and technologies. Excellence also entails an ethical and moral commitment . . . [to] inquire into the consequences of [our] work with students. This is an obligation that devolves on individual faculty members, on programs, on institutions, and even on disciplinary communities. A professional actively takes responsibility; she does not wait to be held accountable. (Shulman, 2003)

With growing interest and increasing participation rates across U.S. college campuses, education abroad or study abroad has become a priority for many institutions. Study abroad by American students has more than tripled over the past two decades, from approximately 71,000 students in 1991–1992 to 283,332 in 2011–2012 (Institute of International Education [IIE], 2013). Today's students recognize the importance of meaningful, international experiences and view these opportunities as an essential component to their undergraduate experience. Similarly, employers place a high value on students' abilities to develop critical intercultural skills. In a recent survey of employers, more than 9 in 10 of those surveyed said it is important that those they hire are comfortable working with colleagues, customers, and/or clients from diverse cultural backgrounds (Hart Research Associates, 2013).

Assessing education abroad in a systematic way is a relatively new phenomenon for our field, but it is a pressing one to tackle. The higher education sector in the United States and other countries around the world is facing calls for greater accountability from the public.

Enhanced attention to assessment is driven by these external trends, but it is matched by our long-standing commitment as education abroad practitioners to improve the field of international education (Deardorff, 2009). Over the past decade, we have seen an acceleration of surveys, projects, and other research. International studies by the International Association of Universities and the European Union Studies Association and national studies conducted by the American Council on Education (ACE), Association of American Colleges and Universities (AAC&U), Association of International Education Administrators, IIE, and Association of International Educators—to name a few—raise questions about the extent to which institutions have articulated global learning outcomes and are assessing for them. The ACE, AAC&U, and Forum on Education Abroad have engaged institutions in projects to pilot assessment of international education practices and document lessons learned. Multimethodological research conducted by scholars and practitioners at our PhD programs in international education are yielding results and deepening our discussions about reflection and impactful learning (Connor-Linton, Paige, & Vande Berg, 2009; Deardorff, 2009; Rubin & Sutton, 2004). Through this work, the field is establishing a theoretical foundation for assessment of education abroad. Furthermore, educational organizations are working to convey this theoretical foundation. As a field, we are embracing the value and importance of assessing education abroad.

Pondering the Landscape

Despite this progress, many institutions are still struggling to gain a foothold in assessment. Contributing factors include the capacity and expertise of the education abroad office, access to and cooperation with institutional research and assessment experts on campus, and sustained interest and motivation in going the "long haul" with the data. In addition, there are typically high expectations for the data to yield certain outcomes. It also takes time to test a variety of approaches to see which one or ones work the best for the institution. Moreover, most institutions are also likely to be employing more than one method of assessment at a time, which can take massive amounts of time and energy (Steinberg, 2007).

Study abroad professionals ponder questions such as the following: How does an institution get started in developing an education abroad assessment plan? What kinds of data are needed: direct data or indirect data? Is information already being collected? If so, by whom, and who has access to the data? What is working or not working? Who are the internal and external partners, and who is available to provide support? And last, what gaps need to be filled?

As we engage with these questions, we may struggle with how to translate the research and lessons learned to our own context. When we return from the conference or sign off from the webinar, as individual practitioners, we may find ourselves lonely in our renewed commitment and perplexed in how we move from theory to practice.

We may also find ourselves stressed because we have been tasked by campus leaders to assess the impact of education abroad. If this is the case for you, what was your response? How did you react to this undertaking? What kinds of questions were you asking yourself as the anxiety mounted and you found yourself under the hot lights, staring blankly into the audience? Perhaps you might have felt—as two of us coauthors felt before connecting with our calm coauthor and director of assessment—that the questions were at times spiraling out of control (see figure 4.1).

You are not alone and destined to remain perplexed. Others at your institution have experience with assessment, and others in education abroad have embarked effectively on this journey. We can draw on their expertise and apply lessons learned from their experiences.

To test our assumptions about the questions that others are asking and the challenges we are all facing as we move from theory to practice, we queried our colleagues through the Association of International Education Administrators LISTSERV. We asked the following questions:

- What specific assessment questions is your institution asking, and who is asking them?
- Have those questions evolved to another set of questions?
- If so, what are the current questions institutions are tackling in the areas of outcomes and assessment?

The response to the specific query about the assessment questions was too limited to generalize; however, we received valuable information. Several people responded by describing the people they were working with or sharing the approach they were using to advance their efforts, including

- working with current university strategic planning efforts,
- collaborating with assessment directors to get started on pilot projects,

Figure 4.1 Spiral of assessment questions

- modifying rubrics such as the AAC&U value and global learning rubrics to be used to evaluate student projects and participation in study abroad,
- administering intercultural surveys such as the IES (Intercultural Effectiveness Survey) to incoming freshmen and then again to outgoing seniors to gauge intercultural growth,
- assembling an assessment task force to assess student course work with rubrics via an e-portfolio or other matrices,
- experimenting with homegrown and/or established instruments to measure what an institution is doing internationally, and
- acknowledging the importance of student characteristics and program environment when looking at approaches to assessment.

Babson College offered the following noteworthy observation on how its guiding question and assessment approach has evolved over time:

As we have learned more through others' research and our own assessment of programs, we are able to ask more sophisticated research questions—so it's not just about whether or not students are gaining competencies, but what features of our programs are likely influencing their intercultural competence (both positive and negative). This can be researched from the perspective of the faculty that teach the programs, from the student participants, and through direct/indirect measures such as journals, interviews, and pre-post tests such as the Intercultural Development Inventory (IDI).

At the other end of the spectrum, respondents noted that as they were just getting started, they looked forward to receiving our summary of practices used at other institutions. Fundamentally, the pressing issue at hand now seems to be how to apply the theory advanced through the studies and the lessons learned by those institutions piloting innovations in education abroad assessment to the questions we are trying to address at our respective institutions.

Following this brief description of the landscape we as practitioners are attempting to navigate when pondering assessment of education abroad, this chapter will now offer practical principles or techniques for moving from theorizing about assessment to effectively implementing assessment and making use of the results.

Moving Forward

We now turn our attention to specific recommendations for how individuals can enhance their readiness for implementing an assessment plan. In this section, we outline practical techniques for clarifying the destination (purpose for assessment), mapping out the pathways (evidence needed), reviewing the resources readily available (data already in hand), and selectively identifying additional collection tools (instruments).

Clarifying the Destination

The assessment effort will be more successful if there is a clear understanding of the destination and how you plan to use the assessment information. Suskie (2009) offered a series of questions that can help identify the various perspectives or frames of reference for deciding the end goal of assessment (see table 4.1).

Each of these questions will help to focus on the type of question you hope to answer and therefore guide the best assessment design to provide useful information. Here we offer a few case examples to help illustrate how institutions might use the different perspectives. Imagine that an institution

TABLE 4.1
Assessment Framing Perspectives

Perspective	Question	Example
Standards based	Are students meeting our standards?	Percentage of students rated as "proficient" on global and multicultural rubric
Benchmarking	How do our students compare to peers?	Scores on Global Perspective Inventory compared to national average
Best practice	How do our students or programs compare to examples of best practice?	Percentage of students engaging in international service-learning experiences compared with select institutions
Value added	Are our students improving?	Longitudinal tracking of changes in students' self-rating of skills
Longitudinal	Is our program improving?	Comparison with scores on Global Perspective Inventory over time

is interested in learning more about the progress that students make in their development of global understanding. In this case, the institution decides to use the Global Perspective Inventory (Global Perspective Institute, n.d.) as one data source.

- A standards-based perspective should collect information at a suitable point in time (e.g., after study abroad–specific learning experiences) and would examine the students' progress against a shared understanding of a set institutional standard. Here the institution could review student scores to determine if students achieved the standard and to identify patterns among students who underperform.
- The benchmarking perspective would compare the institution scores against peer scores, which requires both the identification of appropriate peers and access to comparable information from peers. Here the institution could review the average student score in comparison to peer institutions to add an external viewpoint and to inform discussions about setting appropriate standards.
- The best practice perspective narrows the benchmarking effort to a comparison against best practices. Professionals in the international office might use a review of the literature or engage colleagues at professional conferences to learn about practices that result in demonstrated performance on the Global Perspective Inventory. This

requires a strong commitment to improvement regardless of current quality levels.

- The value-added perspective looks to see change over time, which can provide compelling information on change. There are several limitations to consider (e.g., student motivation, error margin in tools, difficulty in identifying source of change, time required for longitudinal data collection). Nonetheless, an institution may administer the instrument to the same students at different points in time to see value in exploring the change in student responses over time, coupled with additional information on the types of experiences students engage. This robust information could help to identify programmatic and curricular interventions that promote growth.
- The longitudinal perspective looks at differences in cohorts of students or changes in successive groups of students. This approach requires the application of an assessment tool to successive groups of students. Institutions then review this information to learn about changes across cohorts. The design of this effort should consider that changes over time may be related to extraneous factors. In addition, if there is little change in the programmatic or curricular interventions, longitudinal data may not offer useful information to guide program improvement.
- The capability perspective sees limited use in higher education because of the difficulty in accurately determining capability. The utility of this perspective may be in the ability to pursue important second-level questions (e.g., could our students be doing better?).

Each perspective offers advantages and disadvantages, along with an incomplete picture. As you design an assessment plan, it is useful to consider multiple perspectives to gain a more balanced understanding of your assessment questions. Practitioners may want to begin with the center column of table 4.1 to simply explore the types of assessment questions that are meaningful at the current moment.

Identifying Partners

To help guide the planning efforts, we also suggest appointing an assessment committee. The coordinator of this committee should have thorough knowledge of the institution, respect of colleagues, strong communication skills, and excellent organizational skills. Walvoord (2004) explained that these characteristics are more important than specific research skills, statistical knowledge, or previous experience in assessment efforts. We recommend providing the committee with a specific charge to understand the purpose of the assessment effort, conduct an audit of assessment activities, develop or review an assessment plan, recommend actions to enhance assessment, and write a report to audiences. Walvoord (2004) suggested that the membership of this committee should include

- someone who is good at "big picture" thinking and understands campus dynamics,
- a social science researcher,
- representation from the office of student affairs,
- a faculty member who knows the campus well,
- student representation, and
- someone from institutional research or the assessment office.

This last representative can assist in the development of an assessment plan, provide examples of how to conduct assessment, support the development of measures, and provide data. We also affirm the benefit of strategic recruiting to seek individuals who bring a spirit of cooperation and collaboration to the table (Gruenewald & Brooke, 2007).

Sternberger, LaBrack, and Whalen (2007) explained that there is a set of natural collaborators who will have an interest in the assessment of international learning. Natural collaborators include

- faculty and staff involved in study abroad;
- international programs offices;
- international student and scholar services;
- academic departments with international emphases;
- student affairs, multicultural affairs or diversity offices, and career services; and
- alumni offices and admissions offices.

The authors cautioned that it is crucial to consider how to motivate busy individuals to take on additional tasks related to assessment or research.

Mapping Out the Pathways

Once there is a clear purpose for the assessment effort, it is important to specify the connections among the purposes for the project, the specific assessment questions being asked, and the evidence used to answer those questions. Without strong links among these pieces, individuals are likely to encounter pitfalls as they implement assessment plans (Cooper, 2009; Deardorff, 2009). For example, imagine that a university is interested in exploring how students develop intercultural competence. The purpose of this assessment is to use the assessment information to guide the development of new curricular programs. The evidence used to support this assessment effort might include a critical review of cultural competence demonstrated in student work from course assignments. However, if the purpose of the project is instead to identify specific courses and experiences that address intercultural competence, the appropriate data collection methods might include an audit across the curriculum through a web-based survey of faculty or interviews with directors of cocurricular programs.

An effective strategy for mapping links is a three-stage backward design process. In the simplest terms, the stages include (a) identify desired results, (b) determine acceptable evidence, and (c) plan learning experiences and instruction (Wiggins & McTighe, 2005) (see figure 4.2). Wiggins and McTighe described this intentionality as building a wise itinerary through a map: Given a destination, what is the most effective and efficient route? Although it makes good sense to consider our assessment destination (purpose and questions), the specific route (type of evidence needed to answer the questions), and the modes of transportation (programmatic and curricular interventions), this is often backward from the habits of program or curricular design. Rather than create assessments after an intervention, backward design calls for us to make the assessment questions explicit, consider the best evidence to address those questions, and examine the alignment of interventions with both assessment questions and evidence.

Figure 4.2 aligns with a common outcome for study abroad experiences: the desire to engage students in critical awareness of how their cultural

Figure 4.2 Backward design example

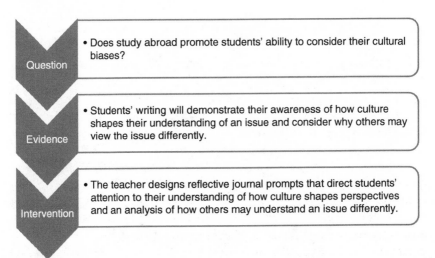

experiences shape their understanding. A backward design approach begins with this end goal and then considers what evidence might be useful in trying to examine students' understanding of cultural bias. Once a type of evidence is chosen, the design of the program should consider ways of structuring the experience to support the desired end point and integrate the chosen measure for evidence.

Thinking Like an Assessor

The backward design process encourages program developers to consider the connection between assessment questions and possible evidence. The task of refining lists of possible evidence into a clear set of data that you will collect is often daunting. Here we encourage teams to think like an assessor by asking the following questions:

Reflection

- What evidence can show that we've achieved the desired results?
- What criteria will we use to assess levels of quality?
- What do we need to look for to determine the extent of our impact (Wiggins & McTighe, 2005)?

Rather than thinking about program design or implementation, an assessor begins with the end goal and asks the question, "How would we know that we've arrived at our intended destination?" As educators, we have a natural inclination to start focusing on the design of interventions to accomplish an end goal. Here we suggest that it is very productive for teams to shift their thinking from the locus of the intervention (e.g., study abroad experiences, curricular structure, cocurricular experiences) to a specific focus on the type of evidence that is needed to shape our work.

Before we select measures, it is important to consider the type of information needed to address the assessment question. Instead of asking, "What activities help students gain a broader understanding of international perspectives?" ask, "What evidence would be sufficient and revealing of changes in students' understanding of international perspectives?" The distinction here is a clear focus on the intended impact rather than the design of an intervention. Using the assessment planning information from the previous efforts (clarifying the destination, mapping out the pathways), teams should have a clear understanding of specific assessment goals. Teams should then reflect on several broad-based questions that can help identify the type of evidence needed to address the goals. For example, an institution undertaking an effort to assess the effectiveness of predeparture orientation for study abroad experiences could begin by asking questions like the following:

- What would we notice in students who have successful predeparture orientation?
- What are the markers of effective transition to study abroad experiences?
- If our orientation programs were highly effective, what would we expect to hear from students and faculty?

Reviewing Existing Resources

An important part of the process that is often overlooked is gaining a clear understanding of existing information, including what information is routinely collected and how that information is being used. One of the best places to begin when considering types of data available at an institution is to spend time visiting with the "keepers" of information at the institution. This might initially include the institutional researcher, assessment office, registrar's office, or provost's office.

Initially you will want to find out what institution-wide data are being collected, distributed, and used. Common sites for collection include institutional research, assessment (office or committee), international programs, student life, student government, service-learning, first-year experience, and the like. It is useful to conduct interviews with these and other offices to gain a deeper understanding of what is currently being done (and what is not being done). This effort should extend to smaller areas (e.g., academic departments, administrative units) to understand assessment that is happening at multiple levels. Rather than asking a group to share its activities related to international assessment, you might consider asking if the unit has any specific goals that relate to international learning and experiences. The unit can then describe any efforts to support this goal and offer some ideas about its progress.

In addition to these informal conversations, teams should also consider conducting an audit of institutional data. Institutions may routinely collect data from the Multi-Institutional Study of Leadership, the National Survey of Student Engagement, the Beginning College Survey of Student Engagement, the Faculty Survey of Student Engagement, and the University Engaged Citizen Assessment, to name a few. The list is not exhaustive of the types of instruments, but it can offer some ideas of the types of tools that can be used on your campus. We share this broad set to encourage assessment teams to expand the scope of their audit work to include an exploration into a variety of existing measurement tools. Assessment teams can then establish partnerships to use this information in ways that intersect with study abroad experiences. Although most of these instruments are not designed to focus on students' study abroad learning, it can be very insightful to examine how these measures can offer insight into the impact of study abroad experiences (e.g., Do students who study abroad look different compared to those who do not?).

Assessment teams should consider ways to leverage available instruments to examine their established assessment questions. At our institution, we have looked for ways to embed measures in several tools that capture students' perceptions before they start at the institution and throughout their experiences. Here, we hope to gain powerful insights into the ways that different experiences interact to influence students' perceptions of their skills and knowledge, including areas relevant to study abroad (e.g., global and multicultural understanding).

One useful resource for this effort is an audit tool established for the Wabash Study (Wabash Study of Institutional Change, 2014). Although this tool focuses on general assessment information, the template offers a useful format for considering various types of information (e.g., standardized surveys, use of student work, student information system). The format of the tool asks institutions to name sources of student input data, student experience data, and student outcome data. We recommend that assessment teams consider using this template as a tool for opening conversations with other groups across campus. The variety of tools that ultimately are revealed by the audit can help to uncover sources of data that are not widely known across campus or that may not routinely be shared with groups exploring the impact of international experiences. This audit process will likely yield information you were not otherwise aware of and can assist in homing in on the gaps in information. The process of consulting with others on what information is already available may also open up opportunities for partnerships or address questions you are seeking to answer.

Identifying Additional Information Needs

The next issue is how to address the gaps in evidence or information that you uncover through your audit. After considering your purpose of assessing, articulating your assessment questions, and identifying the information already in hand, you may need to identify new instruments. Hopefully, you were able to resist the temptation of picking an instrument and jumping in before taking these preliminary steps. Continuing with our journey metaphor, to simply identify an instrument is like venturing off into the wilderness without having a specific destination in mind or a map to help you from wandering needlessly off the path. You may likely see and learn interesting things, but the data you gather may not address your fundamental purpose for conducting your assessment and assist you in answering the questions that external and internal voices are raising.

When you are clear about what additional information is needed, you might apply the following series of questions that Paige and Stallman (2007) offered up to make decisions about assessment instruments. First, does the instrument measure human development and learning in a manner relevant to education abroad? There are several useful sources that can help address this question, including the relevant literature, campus colleagues acting as consultants, and the experience of international educators on your campus or in your network. As mentioned earlier, an important next step is to probe beyond the alignment with education abroad to ensure that the measures are relevant to the research questions. Many times groups select measures because they might offer interesting information. It is important to remain focused on information that not only is simply interesting but also has promise in providing insight into your specific questions of interest.

Second, is there a theoretical foundation for the instrument? A review of the conceptual structure of the instrument will help you determine if the model aligns with your research questions and the institutional philosophy that guides the design of programs and learning experiences. For example, consider an institution that is looking to understand students' experiences with global and multicultural perspectives. Initial interest in a specific measure faded when the review team realized that the foundation and design of the instrument focused on perceptions of campus climate rather than individual student growth and understanding. The tool represented a widely used and valuable instrument, but it simply did not align with the question of interest for this project.

Third, is the instrument a valid and reliable measure? The utility of the data requires attention to the validity (measures what it is designed to measure) and reliability (consistency in responses) of the instrument. Qualitative researchers would refer to this effort as ensuring the quality or integrity of the data, along with a clear understanding of the process used to make meaning of the data. Again, the existing literature, colleague consultants, and international educators are useful resources in determining the likely utility of a given measure.

Fourth, are the administrative and logistical issues manageable? Here the assessment team will consider the logistics mentioned earlier, including cost, administration procedures, access to data, distribution of analysis responsibilities, resources available to support analysis, and any conditions and limitations to the instrument.

Engaging With Others to Maximize Use of the Results

This chapter's first section opened by framing the compelling need for assessment and noting the dizzying array of questions facing those who wish to venture into assessing education abroad but are not sure how or where to begin this journey. The second section offered practical techniques for clarifying the destination (purpose for assessment), mapping out the pathways (evidence needed), reviewing the resources readily available (data already in hand), and selectively identifying additional collection tools (instruments). Now, we turn our attention to productively engaging others on this journey to maximize the use of the assessment results.

Coordinating With Partners

How can you promote an assessment mind-set at your institution? This question is intended to signal attention to the ways that our understanding of assessment shapes our work. In a critical review of the Wabash National Study, the directors of the study noted that their initial hypothesis was that the assessment challenge facing institutions was the need for more and better data. Following their study, the directors concluded that institutions did not lack actionable assessment data but instead struggled to use the information effectively because they had limited experience in reviewing and making sense of data, they ignored the structural constraints that prompt inertia, they failed to embed assessment data in ongoing conversations about student learning, or they failed to connect the evidence to key questions that constituents want to understand (Blaich & Wise, 2011). We contend that an effective assessment effort will think through the ways to coordinate with partners to promote an assessment mind-set at the institution.

One lesson from the Wabash National Study was the importance of engaging partners at the institution to create sustained conversations about data and engage in collective sense-making activities. Participating institutions listed the individuals, constituencies, and governance structures that needed to be engaged in discussions of evidence and then developed plans for how to engage those constituencies. Participants developed a plan for structuring activities and conversations before sharing any data to make the conversations more effective. A related lesson was the importance of involving students as an integral partner in this effort (Blaich & Wise, 2011).

Campus leaders can also help to identify the importance of assessment and make explicit connections to the importance of this effort for continual improvement. Engaged campus leaders can help to demonstrate an institutional commitment to assessment, promote communication about assessment and its value, encourage risk-taking, set clear expectations for assessment, provide resources and support, and use assessment results to make decisions and set priorities (Suskie, 2009).

It's helpful to find a champion among the campus leaders. A senior international officer (SIO) who reports to the president, provost, or another VP and who regularly engages with other leaders can serve that champion role. At institutions without an SIO, you can offer your provost or a prominent dean a plan for engaging the campus leaders, demonstrating how the assessment of education abroad aligns with other efforts underway on campus and describing how you envision using results for improvement.

Reflection

Have you explicitly connected the work to institutional priorities?

- Have you conveyed how the work can count toward performance reviews and institutional service?
- Have you reviewed how the work connects to research activities?
- Have you publicly recognized the service with unit leaders?

Using Assessment as Generative Fodder

When you reach a vista on a mountain trek, you are able to see where you have been and where you might venture from a very different perspective. Likewise, once you have come to a significant milestone in collecting data along the journey of assessing education abroad, there are opportunities to review what those data say about your efforts to date and consider what the data are telling you about how you can improve your education abroad efforts going forward. All too many education abroad assessment efforts cave in on themselves without yielding their full potential. The appropriate partners, as noted previously, may not have been drawn in to assist with the effort and join along for the journey. Or the assessment efforts may have fallen into the pitfall of collecting massive amounts of data and stopping without further implementation.

By way of illustration, we will share how we just barely avoided falling into such a pitfall at Drake. It would have been all too easy to once again collect data about our diverse education abroad offerings and stop there. In 2013, as we headed into the final year of implementing our internationalization strategic plan, we decided to take some time at this important milestone to look at how we were achieving our goals. A handful of Drake faculty and staff serving on an existing cross-cutting body, the Global/International Implementation Team (GIIT), accepted the task of retroactively articulating indicators and metrics of success for the original 2010 plan. We were retrofitting our indicators because we had not understood and applied the technique of backward design, noted previously. The task force then reviewed the relevant data collected to date that might offer evidence of success. Among these data sets were quantitative and qualitative data about the impact of education abroad. At times, the group struggled in the effort to identify and collect information that would provide the greatest utility in trying to assess the strategic plan. Along the way we experienced the challenges noted in the swirl of questions at the start of the chapter.

If our director of assessment had not been on the GIIT and amenable to coleading the group, the group might not have considered the merits of backward design or had easy access to other relevant data. We would have missed an opportunity to understand how the data on education abroad connect with other efforts across campus and how we can improve student global learning. Instead, the GIIT has been able to bring these data to the professional staff and faculty champions from across the institution. The data have sparked meaningful conversations with these stakeholders on how we can promote even more global learning on these experiences. The data have informed the features of Drake's Global Vision 2020, and the strategies generated through the conversations about the data have fed directly into the development of our Drake's 2015–2020 Internationalization and Global Engagement plan.

The GIIT has also brought the data on education abroad (as an integral part of the conversation about indicators of success) to Drake's International Advisory Council. This is an external body that includes Drake's most important corporate and individual donors to the internationalization effort, as well as Drake alumni who are very invested in championing Drake's efforts. In sharing the data with this set of stakeholders, we are not shy in asking for their help in how we best present the data to others in order to promote visibility of our successes and solicit support for areas where we could use additional support. Because of our readiness to share our data, we have been equipped to have meaningful conversations with other external stakeholders who have assisted us in attracting education abroad scholarship endowments to Drake. This is to say that education abroad assessment data, used wisely, can stimulate important conversations among your external stakeholders that can further support your journey going forward.

Likewise, the director of institutional research and assessment, who coleads the GIIT on indicators of success, is able to infuse into relevant high-level conversations with Drake's academic leadership relevant questions about education abroad and service-learning. When sharing the results of the National Survey of Student Engagement (NSSE) data and first-year/senior seminars last spring with the Dean's Council, for example, the director highlighted results pertaining to high-impact learning. Study abroad and service-learning were among the prominent examples of high-impact learning in this data set. We then examined the impact of these experiences on students' engagement, noting that seniors who participated in more high-impact practices reported significantly higher engagement.

While highlighting areas of impact, this study also raised important questions about why education abroad, as a quintessential example of high-impact learning, did not seem to be correlated with stronger evidence of integrated learning among the student respondents. These questions were not lost in the mix; rather they were brought back to the Drake international team for deeper reflection.

We will continue to ask ourselves how well Drake's education abroad options (short-term faculty-led programs, semester and yearlong programs offered by affiliate providers, exchange options with partner institutions, and service-learning with organizational partners) are intentionally addressing our mission promise of graduating globally responsible students and attaining the relevant outcomes. But now as we ponder how we might structure our future assessment, we also want to know more. We want to know how well these programs are both deepening student global learning and fostering enhanced integrated thinking.

In charting the next leg of our journey, we are hypothesizing that enhanced attention to contextualizing our education abroad offerings with other learning experiences at Drake will foster more integrative learning. As such, we are actively making some changes in our approach. The director of Drake-administered programs abroad and the director of community engagement and service-learning, who both engaged directly with faculty in creating a January term and global service-learning programs, were inspired by these assessment results to redouble their efforts to encourage professors to include additional reflection techniques for the student participants. In addition to the one-on-one discussions with professors as they design the curriculum, they are also including workshops that focus on deepening reflection and integrative learning. Likewise, the director of education abroad is stepping up her collaboration with Drake's affiliate education providers to develop programs that are closely integrated with specific academic programs at Drake. She is also planning to work more intentionally with faculty in units across campus to identify and endorse courses from selected education abroad programs that are especially appropriate for their advisees.

Although few of these tactics are new to the field, they are novel for many of the faculty and staff who are engaged in conversations with us about these data. We now have a broader group of faculty and staff who are motivated to partner with us on these tactics.

In summary, an intentional interpretive process joined by carefully staged communication of the results with diverse stakeholders can be quite generative. Questions that are raised by the diverse stakeholders, if captured and digested productively, can generate new facilitative strategies that the education abroad professional staff can put in place. Sharing and discussing the data with faculty and staff can inspire them to make improvements in the education abroad programs they are instrumental in building. Likewise, deliberate conversations with selected groups of faculty and staff might galvanize additional energy among them for promoting education abroad. Furthermore, sharing these data with your academic leadership might foster thinking about how the learning from education abroad might be connected to other important learning targets for your students. Finally, sharing this data artfully with external stakeholders might inspire their engagement in acquiring additional scholarship and other funding to support your education abroad initiatives. In short, although the assessment process at times may feel like a side step from advancing our journey with internationalization, with due attention to interpreting and communicating about the results, the assessment process can be quite generative.

Conclusion

Much as one would begin a journey with a general understanding of the terrain of the region, we began this piece by describing the context within which education abroad practitioners now find themselves compelled to engage in assessment of education abroad. Well over a decade of intensive work by practitioner scholars, policy organizations, and researchers has provided the foundation on which we can draw to move forward with this work. Yet, many still find themselves at the beginning of their journey pondering a multitude of questions, wondering which way to go, caught between theory about assessment and the implementation of assessment at their home campuses.

After identifying some of the factors contributing to this bind, we offered suggestions for getting going with this journey. We presented perspectives that can be used to clarify the destination, a backward design process for determining a pathway forward, the technique of thinking like an assessor to unearth information already available, and guidance in selecting additional tools if needed. Then we discussed strategies for how to develop a mind-set of assessment and engage others effectively so that in the end you can maximize the usage of the resulting data.

Finally, we have humbly offered a practical illustration of how we have been striving to apply, albeit imperfectly, many of the principles that have been offered up. The intentional conversations we have had about assessment data have been generative. These conversations have yielded strategies for education abroad, enhanced partnerships between faculty and staff, inspired donor contributions to education abroad scholarships, and informed features for Drake's Global Vision 2020. We have experienced how assessment of education abroad can be an important catalyst for our comprehensive internationalization process and global engagement adventure. As we present our 2015–2020 Internationalization and Global Engagement plan, we are recommitting ourselves to another adventure with assessment. We are setting our sites on a pristine peak a bit further beyond where we ventured this round, but that is another tale for another time.

The chapter opened with a quote from a student that offers a glimpse into the impact of education abroad experiences. We then shared another quote that challenges us, as educators, to reflect on and critically examine the impact of our work. This chapter focuses on fulfilling the powerful promise we offer students by getting moving with assessment of student global learning. This work can help to highlight areas of success and illuminate needs for new approaches. We hope this piece will help others in the field take courage and renew their determination to venture into the foothills of assessing education abroad with their destination in mind, a map in hand, and good company for the journey. After all, it is the conversation with companions along the way—remarking on the sites you see and the things you learn together—that makes the journey so rich.

References

Blaich, C. F., & Wise, K. S. (2011). *From gathering to using assessment results: Lessons from the Wabash National Study* (NILOA Occasional Paper No. 8). Urbana, IL: National Institute for Learning Outcomes Assessment.

Connor-Linton, J., Paige, M., & Vande Berg, M. (2009). The Georgetown Consortium Project: Interventions for student learning abroad. *Frontiers: The Interdisciplinary Journal of Study Abroad, XVIII*, 1–75.

Cooper, R. M. (2009). Planning for and implementing data collection. In J. H. Schuh (Ed.), *Assessment methods for student affairs* (pp. 51–76). San Francisco, CA: Jossey-Bass.

Deardorff, D. K. (2009). Understanding the challenges of assessing global citizenship. In R. Lewin (Ed.), *Handbook of practice and research in study abroad* (pp. 346–348). New York, NY: Routledge.

Global Perspective Institute. (n.d.). Global Perspective Inventory. Retrieved from https://gpi.central.edu/

Gruenewald, D., & Brooke, C. (2007). Building collaborative student affairs-academic affairs connections through the development of learning communities at Iowa State University. In B. L. Smith & L. B. Williams (Eds.), *Learning communities and student affairs: Partnering for powerful learning* (pp. 35–46). Olympia, WA: National Association of Student Personnel Administrators and the Washington Center for Improving the Quality of Undergraduate Education.

Hart Research Associates. (2013). It takes more than a major: Employer priorities for college learning and student success. *Liberal Education, 99*(2), 22.

Institute of International Education. (2013). *Open doors report.* Retrieved from www .iie.org/Research-and-Publications/Open-Doors

Paige, R. M., & Stallman, E. M. (2007). Using instruments in education abroad outcomes assessment. In M. Bolen (Ed.), *A guide to outcomes assessment in education abroad* (pp. 137–162). Carlisle, PA: Forum on Education Abroad.

Rubin, D., & Sutton, R. (2004). The GLOSSARI Project: Initial findings from a system-wide research initiative on study abroad learning outcomes. *Frontiers: The Interdisciplinary Journal of Study Abroad, X,* 101–116.

Shulman, L. S. (2003). No drive-by teachers. *Carnegie Perspectives.* Retrieved from www.carnegiefoundation.org/perspectives/no-drive-teachers

Steinberg, M. (2007). The place of outcomes assessment in higher education today and the implications for education abroad. In M. Bolen (Ed.), *A guide to outcomes assessment in education abroad* (pp. 7–22). Carlisle, PA: Forum on Education Abroad.

Sternberger, L., LaBrack, B., & Whalen, B. (2007). How to begin: Key decision points in the assessment process. In M. Bolen (Ed.), *A guide to outcomes assessment in education abroad* (pp. 71–88). Carlisle, PA: Forum on Education Abroad.

Suskie, L. (2009). *Assessing student learning: A common sense guide.* San Francisco, CA: Jossey-Bass.

Wabash Study of Institutional Change. (2014). *Guide to outcome measures.* Retrieved from www.liberalarts.wabash.edu/storage/assessment-instruments/Guide_to_outcomes.pdf

Walvoord, B. E. (2004). *Assessment clear and simple: A practical guide for institutions, departments, and general education.* San Francisco, CA: Jossey-Bass.

Wiggins, G., & McTighe, J. (2005). *Understanding by design* (2nd ed.). Upper Saddle River, NJ: Pearson.

5

USING QUALITATIVE RESEARCH METHODS TO ASSESS EDUCATION ABROAD

The Value of Qualitative Methods in Education Abroad

Tasha Bleistein and Mary Shepard Wong

University funding and support for education abroad are often contingent on evidence of its effectiveness; thus, assessment is essential. Most likely you are keenly aware of the value of study abroad and know the impact it can have on students and their host communities or you would not be reading this volume. But what if your program is not accomplishing all it could? What is the point of offering study abroad if students are not increasing in intercultural competence (Bennett, 2009), making gains toward global citizenship (Morais & Ogden, 2011), enlarging their vision of the world, and contributing to the common good (Slimbach, 2014)? We posit that the methods used in qualitative research are well suited to assess these outcomes and the effectiveness of education abroad, whether it is a holistic evaluation of the study abroad program, its contribution to the campus community, or education abroad's various components of prefield orientation, language learning, homestay experiences, internships, excursions, student research projects, and academic study.

This chapter provides a distinction between qualitative and quantitative approaches, an overview of the research process, a brief background of the rise of the qualitative approach, an overview of a "mixed methods" approach, and a discussion of six qualitative methods useful in assessing international education. Other topics addressed are the importance of asking good questions, controlling for bias, and using triangulation. Case studies and examples of how qualitative methods have been used to assess study abroad are provided throughout.

Qualitative and Quantitative Distinction and Overview

Qualitative and quantitative research approaches are often contrasted, but they might be better understood on a continuum. Quantitative research is generally driven by a hypothesis and seeks to account for and control variables, frequently using large sample sizes that allow for generalizations. The results are typically in the form of numerical data that require statistical analysis. Qualitative research, on the other hand, seeks an in-depth understanding of a limited number of participants in a specific context. A qualitative approach allows for greater flexibility, is iterative and dynamic (less linear), and seeks more nuanced understandings. Analysis in qualitative research generally focuses on categorizing data and identifying themes. Put another way, qualitative research is an inductive process that seeks to provide information on "how people interpret their experiences, how they construct their worlds, and what meaning they attribute to their experiences" (Merriam, 2009, p. 5). Qualitative research is more complex than interviewing students to gain general impressions or seek a few quotes to support existing beliefs. It is a systematic process that is dependent on understanding how to ask quality questions, gather appropriate artifacts, and carefully interpret gathered data. When done properly, it is easy to see why qualitative research methods can be useful tools to gain rich and nuanced understandings of the complex issues in education abroad.

Qualitative approaches arose out of the desire of anthropologists and sociologists to understand the meanings that people attributed to the social contexts in which they lived. In 1967, Glaser and Strauss, in their book *The Discovery of Grounded Theory*, shifted the focus from testing theory to building theory through the process of inductive analysis. Since the 1970s, scores of disciplines have adopted qualitative approaches, and hundreds of books and journal articles that focus on qualitative research have been published. Four characteristics of qualitative inquiry include the following: (a) a focus on meanings and understandings that seeks an emic (insiders) perspectives and not just the etic (outsiders) perspective; (b) the researchers (and for our purposes, this would include students) are the primary instrument for data collection and analysis whose biases are identified and monitored; (c) it is an inductive process in which themes, categories, and concepts emerge from data analysis; and (d) results are provided in rich descriptions of words, quotes, and pictures rather than numbers.

Another distinction between quantitative and qualitative research is in their different philosophical approaches to how we know what we know (epistemology) and how we understand who we are (ontology). Although quantitative researchers maintain a positivistic understanding of the world, or the notion that reality is "out there" waiting to be discovered, qualitative researchers maintain a postpositivistic philosophical position that knowledge is socially constructed and more relative than absolute. In the study abroad context, quantitative research has its strengths in showing "the product" or determining "what is" or what was learned or not learned through a set of pre- and post-study abroad surveys, for example, with large sample sizes and statistical analysis, whereas qualitative research might provide more details about why and under what conditions such learning did or did not take place.

Mixed Methods Research

Although quantitative and qualitative approaches are often presented as coming from and supporting contrasting paradigms (positivistic versus post-positivistic), today a growing number of researchers use mixed methods, downplaying the philosophical divide and drawing from the strengths of both approaches. That said, mixed methods researchers generally emphasize one approach (i.e., qualitative *or* quantitative) and use the other to deepen or widen their understanding or to inform the next phase of the study. For example, surveys (considered a primarily quantitative method but used in both approaches) could be used to collect data on study abroad students' opinions of their prefield orientation, but the survey data may result in puzzling results or not clarify the reasons for inconsistent responses. Interviews and case studies (which are qualitative methods) could be used to explore the specific reasons and variation of students' responses to gain a more in-depth assessment of the orientation. Also, the survey could be used to identify interview participants, such as two students with vastly different reasons to study abroad. Mixed methods' "central premise is that the use of quantitative and qualitative approaches in combination provides a better understanding of research problems than either approach alone" (Creswell & Plano Clark, 2007, p. 5).

The strength of adding a qualitative component to assessment in education abroad is that it helps inform the process of learning and gets at the meaning students have constructed through their experiences living and studying abroad. Although what can be learned in purely quantitative studies is valuable, such studies may lack in-depth, nuanced understandings of the local setting and context that on-site observations might provide. For example, Rao and Woolcock (2003) encouraged the use of mixed methods when researching abroad, specifically working with poverty-stricken groups, so that data could be collected through observations in the context where the participants live.

Asking Good Questions and Finding the Right Scope

The research approach and methods selected for any study or assessment project should be determined primarily by the question it seeks to address. If the question focuses on how many students report deeper appreciation for other cultures or increased language fluency, then quantitative methods, such as a survey, would be a good way to gather these numerical data. In contrast, if a study abroad office wants to understand the impact study abroad experiences have on students' lifestyle changes or on the communities in which they work and live, then qualitative methods might be best. After one determines the question, the next step is to determine what data (e.g., student opinions, student actions, and homestay parent opinions) are needed to address the questions and then the best data collection methods (e.g., observations, interviews, and documents) and data analysis procedures one should use to find answers to the question. What is important is that there is a clear alignment among the question, the data being sought, and the methods of data collection and analysis. Once the analysis shows that enough data has been collected to respond to the question, the findings are written up and shared with stakeholders.

Our third-grade teachers were wrong, as there *are* such things as "dumb questions," as well as poorly worded, biased, leading, double-barreled, meaningless, ambiguous, and inappropriate questions, all of which need to be avoided in good research. Merriam (2009) asserted that the "key to getting good data . . . is to ask good questions" (p. 95), and articulating clear, meaningful questions that result in participants conveying rich, on-target responses is no easy task. Good research questions need to probe and explore what you consider to be essential in education abroad. For example, a dumb question might be "Study abroad produces many exciting experiences; how many such experiences did you have?" This one is a biased question that presupposes what the student may or may not have experienced. It could be rephrased as "Describe a study abroad experience that you have had and rate it on the level of excitement you did or did not feel about it."

Scope is another factor to consider. An exploratory study with a wide focus on the entire study abroad program may be helpful initially to determine what follow-up, more focused, in-depth studies and assessments are needed later. It is also important to know the limitations of one's resources

TABLE 5.1
Potential Components, Questions, Data, Collection Methods, and Details

Component	Sample Question or Prompt	Data	Collection Method	Collection By, From, and When
Prefield orientation	What specific task or advice best prepared you for living in X?	Student opinions of prefield orientation	Interview, focus group, and journals	Collected by the study abroad office from students at the end of the program
Homestay	How did the homestay experience enhance your understanding of local culture?	Student opinions of homestay's impact	Student documents (e.g., essays and posts)	Collected by students (peer to peer) at the beginning, middle, and end of a sojourn
Classroom study	What are the major crises facing X, and what is your responsibility?	Student knowledge and social vision	Student papers, journals, and interviews	Collected by instructors during or after the course from students

and not to attempt too much. Less done well is better than a lot done poorly. It is better to collect only the data that will address the specific questions you are asking rather than collect a lot of data that will not help to answer your questions or will never get analyzed.

Consider the questions, the research approach(es), the data that would respond to the questions, and the data collection methods as you read through table 5.1.

Additional rows with other program components (e.g., student research, language learning, excursions, internships) and columns with added details (e.g., time estimates for data collection and notes on analysis) could be included as needed. The suggestion that students ask each other about their homestay experiences brings up an important value in the use of qualitative methods in study abroad, and that is the potential it offers to be collaborative. Inviting students into the process of data collection and analysis provides them the opportunity to learn useful research skills and helps in assessment. At the very least, students could be asked, "What questions should our office be asking study abroad students?" Other stakeholders who can be brought into the collaborative research and assessment process to form questions, collect data, and analyze the data are faculty and staff from other campus units, study abroad providers, researchers, homestay providers, and local internship supervisors, among others. Bringing in voices of locals ("Data" and "Collection By, From, and When" columns in table 5.1) is an important consideration and adds credibility to the study, as discussed more in the following section.

Bias, Data, and Triangulation

The assumption when creating questions and analyzing data is that the researcher is able to clearly articulate any bias and account for that bias so that the data have a clear voice. Kinginger (2009) reminded researchers and anyone using qualitative methods that the questions we explore and how data are analyzed originate from one's "own sociocultural locus" (p. 215). She reminded those involved in study abroad of the tendency to analyze data solely using the sending institution's cultural lens, which condemns "practices of host communities . . . without a trial. At the very least, the qualitative literature needs to expand its scope beyond attempts to achieve an insider's perspective on student perceptions. It should include the perceptions of the host community as well" (Kinginger, 2009, p. 216).

Data, in the context of qualitative research, can include interview transcripts, photographs, videos, tests, journals, student papers, student posts, and field notes. But the raw data are not the answers. The answers to the questions are found only through data analysis. Understanding the types of data and analysis can help the researcher or evaluator plan for data collection and analysis. Sometimes more data are needed when findings are not "robust" or credible (i.e., students telling you what you want to hear).

Triangulation is used in research to increase the confidence in one's findings by seeking out and comparing the results of multiple data collection and/or analysis procedures. There are at least five types of triangulation used in research, including four identified by Denzin in 1978 (as cited in Janesick, 2000, p. 391): (a) *data triangulation*: using multiple data sources such as various stakeholders' opinions; (b) *investigator triangulation*: using more than one rater or researcher in analysis; (c) *theoretical triangulation*: using more than one theory to interpret the data set; and (d) *methodological triangulation*: using multiple methods such as journals and interviews to get at the same data. In addition, there is *temporal triangulation*: using data from multiple times. Qualitative research seeks a multifaceted approach, using a variety of ways to collect and analyze data to locate and verify one's findings. As you read the following methods for data collection and analysis, consider how you might increase the confidence in your findings by applying different types of triangulation.

Qualitative Methods and Student Learning Outcomes

External and internal pressures to justify the expense of a college degree have led institutions of higher education to embrace outcomes-based education. When a study abroad program is unsure of what constitutes success, it cannot determine whether it has been successful or demonstrate achievement to students and other institutional offices. Therefore, effective assessment is linked to clearly stated outcomes or goals. According to Selby (2008), study abroad should include "a stated set of objectives that include academic learning, intercultural analysis, and personal development" (p. 8). As stated earlier, impact on host communities and common good could be added to this list. The stated outcomes or objectives should be set yet still remain flexible as data are continually collected and analyzed. Even good outcomes often need to be revised as data reveal new areas and programs become more successful.

Rubrics are a helpful tool to assess outcomes, as they provide specific measures and scales that help increase reliability. An example of a rubric is the Intercultural Knowledge and Competence VALUE Rubric available from the Association of American Colleges and Universities (AAC&U, 2010).

Wu and Wong (2013) adopted the American Council of Education's (2008) International Learning Assessment Project rubric in their study of a dozen undergraduate and graduate student-teachers who participated in a three-week faculty-led study abroad trip in Myanmar in which students collaborated with local teachers to teach English in a school in Yangon. The researchers read the journals of the 13 students numerous times, looking for emerging themes and specific evidence demonstrating learning in cultural self-awareness, cultural knowledge, intercultural skills, and a positive disposition toward host nationals. Although some evidence was found to support cultural learning, the researchers agreed that asking students to provide the evidence would have helped. The researchers in this study found that combing student journals for evidence, in spite of strategic prompts, was extremely time-consuming and did not provide a complete representation of student learning. (The students may have experienced learning that was not noted in their journals.) Had the researchers prepared students to collaborate with them to investigate their own cultural learning, the data analysis phase would have been more feasible, and the students' ability to reflect on and take ownership of their learning would have been fostered in the process. In addition, because the researchers did not have confidence that the journals comprised every aspect of the students' learning, methodological triangulation could have been used, getting at the students' learning with more than one method of data collection. Pre- and post-study abroad interviews with the students would have provided this extra level of data that would have improved the study.

For example, in follow-up interviews, students could have been asked to provide evidence for the following learning outcome from Azusa Pacific University: "Students will demonstrate awareness of their own motivations, values, attitudes and biases, and how these influence interaction/relationships with others." Consider other ways that this outcome could be measured using qualitative methods. We will return to the outcome at the end of this chapter to see which of the methods might be used. Attitude and awareness outcomes such as this one are inherently more complex to reliably measure than cognitive or skills outcomes but are just as important to assess.

Qualitative Data Collection Methods

In this section, six data collection methods will be discussed: interviews, focus groups, observations, student artifacts and documents, open-ended questionnaires, and case studies (which use several methods). Researchers will frequently use multiple data collection methods.

Interviews

Interviews are the most common method for data collection in qualitative research, so it is not surprising that the interview was identified as the most often used method to assess intercultural competence in study abroad contexts (see Deardorff & Deardorff, 2007). Interviews should be used when they are the best way to gather the most data at the least expense, or when they are the only way to get data. Interviews are typically one-on-one, face-to-face, and classified in three ways: highly structured, which have a set list of questions to ask in a prescribed order; semistructured, which have topics to address, with the freedom for follow-up questions; and unstructured with hardly any preconceived or preformulated questions. Semistructured interviews are the most common, as highly structured interviews are often too rigid to allow for helpful follow-up questions, and unstructured interviews are more useful in inquiries that explore issues that are as yet unstudied.

Interviews, when done well, can provide what Geertz (1973) called "thick description" or detailed, rich, firsthand accounts of the actual lived experience of participants gained through a series of main questions, probes, and follow-up questions. Good questions and a well-prepared interview guide are essential to a successful qualitative interview. Patton (2002) suggested six types of questions to stimulate responses from interviewees: (a) *experience and behavior questions:* "Tell me about a typical day for you with your host family"; (b) *opinion and values questions:* "What is your opinion on your host country's policy of women in the workforce?"; (c) *feeling questions:* "How do you feel in your readjustment process?"; (d) *knowledge questions:* "Can you describe the type of government and current leadership in your host country in as much detail as possible?"; (e) *sensory questions:* "Can you describe in vivid detail what you smell, hear, touch, and experience at local markets?"; and (f) *demographics questions:* "What other countries have you lived in for more than three months?"

In additional to these six types of questions, hypothetical or "what-if" questions might be considered, such as "Suppose you wanted to apologize for an inappropriate comment; what phrases in the local language would you use?" Devil's advocate questions could be used to get at information that might be embarrassing to provide about oneself, such as "What might some of your peers say about their experience of working with host nationals?" Ideal position questions can get at both information and opinion, such as "What specific changes would improve the cultural learning for the excursion to X?" A list of questions and prompts might include the following:

- Tell me about a time when you had keen insight into a cultural bias you held.
- Give me an example of a cultural difference you noticed in classroom interaction.
- What was it like for you when your attempts to speak the local language did not succeed?

A list of probes to get more details and clarification might include the following:

- Tell me more about what you felt when you first arrived.
- What do you mean by difference in what "on time" means?
- Walk me through how you felt when you first entered the temple.

Questions to avoid are those with assumptions or that are leading, such as "What emotional problems have you had living with your host family?" or multiple questions within a single question such as "What attitudes and behaviors changed, and which stayed the same before and after the trip?" and yes-no questions like "Did you enjoy the experience?"

An interview guide is a list of questions to ask during an interview. If informed consent and permission to record the session are needed, you should begin by discussing your motives and intentions for collecting data; how you will protect participants' identity through the use of pseudonyms and other means; compensation, if any; and logistics of time and place of further interviews or member checks (where interviewees are provided the transcript to verify). This should be followed with a question that asks if they have any concerns and consent to proceed. A semi-structured interview would begin with "neutral" questions (if there are such things) that might ask about demographics (unless they are sensitive). Follow this with some general questions asked of all participants, lead to more open-ended questions with appropriate probes that may be more sensitive or challenging, and then ask some easier questions to end the interview. This sequence can help the person being interviewed ease into and out of the conversation. Usually no more than a dozen main questions are asked during an hour-long interview to allow time for follow-up questions and probes.

Because the interviewer is the main instrument for data collection, the experience and skills of the interviewer are crucial. Trained interviewers listen for not only what is said but also what is not said to hear the meanings of what the interviewees are telling them. They know how to set the interviewee at ease and how to get clarity and precision in responses. They can adjust the interview process and questions and understand its dynamic and iterative nature. They are aware of their personality and biases and can monitor them. They articulate their roles clearly and respect boundaries, act professionally and ethically, and thus engender trust, which provides more open and in-depth responses.

However, good interviews are not just the result of good questions and sensitive interviewers. Selecting appropriate interviewees and establishing an appropriate setting to conduct and record the interview are also needed. Appropriate interviewees are those who can provide useful information and who are experienced, knowledgeable, and communicative. Selection of interviewees is also affected by access and the need to understand multiple viewpoints. For example, responses from both men and women might be needed, as well as both student and host national perspectives. Because participant selection may affect the credibility of your findings, it is important to think through the criteria for selection (and nonselection) and to keep records of this so you can be explicit and transparent about your rationale and process. The goal is not to find those who support an agenda but to represent the myriad perspectives held by those involved in education abroad.

Focus Groups

Focus groups are interviews with a group of people who can provide insight into the questions being explored. One can select preexisting groups, such as all the participants in a study abroad program, or select groups of stakeholders, such as teachers, students, host family parents, and employers, to participate in a focus group. Focus groups often help participants interact with concepts at a deeper level as their ideas are challenged or supported by others in the group. Focus groups can be used to provide a general understanding of an issue (potentially to pick up terms used to develop survey or interview questions), inspire new ideas, gather participants' impressions, and discuss previously collected data.

Merriam (2009) suggested that focus groups consist of 6 to 12 participants. A moderator who has a clear understanding of the purpose should lead the group. Pre-focus group questionnaires or individual interviews can help the moderator guide the discussion. The moderator begins a session by introducing what will happen, establishing guidelines, and leading an opening activity (e.g., short participant introductions) before starting the discussion. Moderators should speak approximately 10% of the time, with the remaining 90% dedicated to participant discussion (Berg, 2009). Ideally, focus groups are video recorded to allow for more accurate transcription and analysis later. Some researchers use online focus groups, synchronously or asynchronously. The role of the moderator is often reduced in these settings, but collecting data in this way is economical, convenient, and realistic given geographic constraints encountered in study abroad.

There are several advantages to focus groups. One is that they are flexible, so various numbers of participants and session lengths can be used depending on what is being explored. Another is that they can provide significant insights as members interact and new or unanticipated questions are explored. Participants may feel free to participate more in a group of peers, but they may also feel inhibited for the same reason. Focus group success, like that with interviews, is dependent on the skill of the moderator to some extent. A potential shortcoming is the logistics of gathering groups of people together, which may be achievable in study abroad settings but complex upon people's return to home institutions. A final limitation is that fewer questions are addressed, and not all individuals will respond.

Brux and Fry (2010) provide an example of how focus groups were used to understand multicultural student participation in study abroad. Focus groups were held with members of three campus organizations. The Asian American Student Association focus group included 20 students, most of whom had participated in study abroad experiences. Subsidized and short-term study abroad opportunities were appreciated, but some reported that study abroad options did not fit with their majors. All seven students from the Latino Student Organization focus group indicated interest in study abroad, yet none knew of another student who had participated. The authors reported that "approximately" 15 Black Student Union members participated in the third focus group (p. 519). None of the students had participated in study abroad, but some had considered the opportunity. Finances, family responsibilities, and fears kept members from participating. In addition to the focus groups, a survey was distributed with a response rate of only 8%. Although these authors were not forthcoming about their procedures, the choice of topic may be of interest to study abroad personnel.

Observations

Observations are often used in qualitative research, as they add an important firsthand, on-site component that can triangulate findings that emerge from interview and document analysis. Much like good interviews, good observations require a keen focus in which researchers pay close attention to see what casual observers would miss. Just as a spy, thief, or detective is trained in observation techniques, researchers are trained in selective attentiveness, descriptive writing, and rigorous methods to validate observations. Researchers can use an unstructured approach, with just a blank notebook to record as much specific, detailed information as possible, or a more structured approach that uses code sheets with a complex matrix of actions in which the observer records what did and did not take place at specific intervals. Regardless of the level of structure used to record field notes, all of the following elements should be noted: (a) the physical settings, (b) the participants, (c) the activities and interactions, (d) conversations, (e) subtle factors such as nonverbal communication, and (f) the actions of the observer that may have affected the event.

The relationship between the observer and what is observed ranges along a continuum, from the observer acting as a full participant on one end, to an observer who does not participate on the other, and *participant*-observer and *observer*-participant in between, with dual roles, the priority given to the first (italicized) term. Collaborative partnership is also an option, in which the observer and actors involved in the event being observed are equal partners in the observation and research. If a participant role is chosen, note taking during the event will be limited, and observers will need to create a full account as soon after the observation as possible. Providing detailed, descriptive information and quotes separate from observer comments can be accomplished by using two columns for these types of information or by using brackets and the initials "OC" for observer's comments.

In some settings, such as classrooms, observers will need to first get permission and should be able to communicate what they will be doing, how disruptive they will be, what will be done with their findings, why that particular setting was selected, and what those observed might gain from the observation. The observer should be courteous, friendly, respectful, and be as unobtrusive as possible. Resources often limit the number of observations conducted, but, hopefully, enough will take place so that a "saturation" of information is obtained.

As the study by Williams (2009) noted, students in a study abroad context can be taught observation techniques. This serves a dual purpose of increasing their ability to learn about and from other cultures and of collecting data on their own cultural learning. Selby (2008) stated, "Some study abroad programs make this self-reflection an explicit part of the curriculum by requiring students to analyze both observed local patterns of behavior and their own reaction to those patterns" (p. 2). However, to increase confidence in the findings, in addition to student observations of their own cultural learning, teacher, researcher, and host national accounts could also be sought, applying investigator triangulation.

Student Artifacts and Documents

Document analysis is another commonly used method in qualitative research. The advantages of document analysis are that it does not intrude on participants, as observations can, and avoids the difficulties of scheduling that interviews create. *Document* is an umbrella term that encompasses both personal and public written, digital, visual, and physical data. Documents may include official records, letters, journals, test results, photos, blogs, websites, e-mails, memos, homework, lesson plans, posts to course websites, and artifacts or "things." Primary sources are those that the originator of the document is recounting firsthand experiences, and secondary sources are reports of accounts not witnessed, usually at a later date. Primary sources are usually more valuable than secondary sources, with the most value given to those closest in time and place to the event being investigated. Brewer's case study on Beloit College uses student essays, a type of document, to evaluate study abroad (see chapter 7 of this book).

Questionnaires or Surveys

Although questionnaires (also referred to as surveys) are primarily a method used in quantitative studies, qualitative data can be gathered in questionnaires with the use of open-ended questions. Writing clear questions is important for successful questionnaires, and, to determine their clarity, pilot testing is required. To pilot a questionnaire, a sample group of participants, who are not part of the study, completes the instrument to see if the questions are understood and whether they elicit the types of responses sought. After the pilot testing is completed, the questionnaires are distributed and collected, so the data analysis process can begin. Williams (2009) provided an example of how open-ended questions on an end-of-program evaluation form were used. Students were asked to provide demographic information and then were asked a number of questions (see the following two examples) that correlated to outcomes established by the study abroad office:

- What aspects of the country or culture where you studied abroad do you understand better? For example, did your experience increase your understanding of the country's people, values, culture, economy, politics, society, and/or environment? If yes, how? If no, why not?
- Describe any situation(s) where you were required to develop tolerance, flexibility, and a positive attitude in order to adapt to the situation. What did you learn from the experience? Examples of situations may include changes in housing, diet, conversational style with others, customary practices, transportation, and so on (p. 292).

According to Williams (2009), reading and analyzing surveys was "invigorating" (p. 304) and provided needed insights for a study abroad administrator who is often unable to observe learning in-country.

An obvious strength of questionnaires is that they can collect a significant amount of data with limited economic and time investment. In addition, a large number of participants can provide input. Conversely, open-ended items lack the flexibility of an interview setting where follow-up or expansion questions can lead to clarity. Response rates can be low with questionnaires and might not represent all students. One way to increase response rates is to offer a small incentive such as a drawing for a gift card. The reward should in no way influence participants' responses, and data should be collected separately from identifying information. SurveyMonkey is one of many providers who allow for open-ended question responses to be collected and for participants' identifying information to be collected separately.

Case Studies

Case studies have a specific focus but generally utilize a variety of data collection methods. For evaluation purposes, case studies provide explanation, description, illustration, and enlightenment (Yin, 2009). Yin (2009) defined a *case study* as "an empirical inquiry that investigates a contemporary phenomenon in depth and within its real-life contexts, especially when the boundaries between phenomenon and contexts are not clearly evident" (p. 18). The context-rich study abroad experience is a natural fit for case studies. Data need to be collected in a variety of ways. Therefore, a single interview or even a series of interviews is not enough to constitute a case study. In addition, it is important to be familiar with the existing research related to the area being explored and to address competing explanations (that do not match initial assumptions).

Some researchers criticize case studies because the findings are not generalizable. A case study of one or two study abroad participants does not allow for generalizations about all study abroad participants, but it can direct further research and help to provide a deeper understanding of individual experiences. Another disadvantage of case studies is that they are time-consuming. Although this is true, tracking study abroad experiences, especially over a long period of time, provides invaluable data to invested parties. Learning gains and long-term impact can be difficult to measure and understand, but the data gathered are compelling. Stories are powerful communication tools, and a case study can be a persuasive, well-researched story. Case studies are excellent companions to survey data or other research, because they can provide a rich picture to illustrate what the data are showing. When data are confusing, a case study can reveal potential reasons for unexpected or inexplicable results.

Two case studies of study abroad programs or their components are provided next for you to glean ideas for your assessment projects.

Case Study 1: Goode (2008) examined faculty study abroad directors. The research focused on the intercultural development of eight faculty leaders of study abroad experiences. The mixed methods study began with qualitative interviews followed by the administration of the Intercultural Development Inventory (IDI). The interviews were transcribed using a separate table for each interview question, so the interviewer could see all eight participants' answers to one question in the same table. A column was added to the table for the researcher to write memos or thoughts as he read through the answers. Patterns and themes were identified from the transcribed responses and matched to the four research questions: How do study abroad faculty directors conceptualize their role? How well do faculty's formal and informal experiences prepare them to serve as study abroad faculty directors? What degree of intercultural development do the study abroad faculty directors at North American College have? How do study abroad faculty directors conceptualize their role in the intercultural development of their study abroad students (Goode, 2008, p. 150)? A key finding resulted in the suggestion to raise the faculty directors' awareness of their intercultural sensitivity by administering the IDI before a mandatory faculty workshop.

Case Study 2: Allen (2010) provided a comparative case study that explored two North American female students involved in short-term (lasting fewer than eight weeks) study abroad experiences. The two participants were selected based on their similarities to the "average" study abroad student. A case study format allowed the researcher to explore the motives for participating in a study abroad experience as well as the students' initial and evolving goals and their language-learning motivation throughout the process. Data were collected from students' blogs, three semistructured interviews with each participant (predeparture, on field, and upon return), and questionnaires. Themes were identified, and the data were coded by the researcher, who was also the program director. The researcher looked for examples that did not match her conclusions and also invited the two female students to offer feedback on her analysis throughout the process. The results focus on how differing motivations impact the study abroad and language-learning experience, but other aspects of study abroad can be examined in a similar format.

Data Analysis

People naturally make meaning out of what they are reading, and the data analysis process helps to systematize that meaning-making. Before data can be coded, they need to be in a text-based format, so audio and video recordings need to be transcribed. Transcription is a time-consuming process, taking several hours to transcribe a one-hour interview. Transcription services can provide professional-quality transcripts, but this can be costly. Qualitative analysis is not about counting, but it generally focuses on coding. Although it may seem intimidating, "coding is nothing more than assigning some sort of shorthand designation to various aspects of your data so that you can easily retrieve specific pieces of the data" (Merriam, 2009, p. 173). Coding provides a way for messy and large amounts of data to be organized and for data to be taken apart and put back together again to gain understandings. How coding occurs depends on the types of data and the research questions.

Data need to be read and reviewed multiple times. Memos or notes can be recorded during the initial readings of the data to guide the next steps. The first round of coding is often referred to as "open coding." Open coding allows for the data to speak about the ideas included without the researcher trying to combine or analyze categories. Some codes use the participants' actual words as the title of the code or category, and others assign a term to help organize the information. Until the 1980s, qualitative researchers primarily utilized colored cards or pens to code their data (Weitzman, 2000). Although many researchers still enjoy the tactile process of highlighting and manipulating cards, sticky notes, or typed pages, a number of software programs are available to assist in the coding and analysis process, such as NVivo. University research offices or faculty who are qualitative research experts are excellent resources for training on how to use programs, if needed. Word processing and spreadsheet software are easy-to-use alternatives.

After initial or open coding, focused coding synthesizes data and helps to explain larger portions of data (Charmaz, 2006). During the focused coding stage, open codes are analyzed and larger categories identified. At this stage, those analyzing the data can start to look for patterns and ways to organize and reorganize the data. These larger categories of coding can lead to the identification of themes from reading, rereading, writing, drawing, and organizing the focused codes. It is important to keep asking the next question when analyzing the data. Do not stop at the first or simple answer, but look for multiple connections and interpretations. More data may need to be collected about themes that emerge but are not fully explored. The process of gathering, coding, and analyzing data occurs until theoretical saturation, "the point at which gathering more data about a theoretical category reveals no new properties nor yields any further theoretical insights," is reached (Charmaz, 2006, p. 169).

Wu and Wong (2013) provided an example of the process from planning to data collection to data analysis. To support learning, carefully selected assigned readings on Myanmar were required, and pretrip meetings focused on discussions of these readings and with an invited host national to discuss the current situation in Myanmar. Students were provided 16 journal prompts to respond to before, during, and after the trip that focused specifically on their cultural learning. The researchers applied a predesigned rubric to the analysis of student journal entries, searching for evidence of appreciation of the local people's culture, acceptance of cultural difference, and tolerance for cultural ambiguity.

Conclusion

Qualitative research methods are valuable tools to assess learning in education abroad. They are especially useful when assessing difficult-to-measure learning outcomes; for example, "Students will demonstrate awareness of their own motivations, values, attitudes, and biases and how these influence interaction and relationships with others." All of the data collection methods discussed in this chapter could be used to assess this outcome. One-on-one interviews could provide more in-depth responses regarding how the experience changed students' values, whereas focus groups could provide insights gained from a larger number of students at one time and could benefit from the interaction of group discussion. Open-ended survey questions that ask for examples of biases exposed and confronted would provide data from the largest number of people, although possibly less in-depth data because of researchers' inability to ask follow-up questions. Student narratives from journal entries responding to guided prompts about their motivations, values, attitudes, and biases collected before, during, and after the sojourn would provide rich data, as could student assignments and projects. Field notes from faculty and researchers would add a much needed on-site perspective of how students interact with host nationals, as would reports from homestay families and internship supervisors that ask about the students' relationships with host nationals and impact on the community. Analysis of the data would involve coding and could also be scored using an existing rubric or one adapted or developed for the assessment process. Finally, a case study of a few selected students could be conducted using a combination of these methods. Which and how many of these methods are used in assessing this or any outcome depends on the purpose of the assessment and the resources and support of your institution, as the options available in qualitative research methods to assess international education are plentiful.

References

Allen, H. W. (2010). What shapes short-term study abroad experiences? A comparative case study of students' motives and goals. *Journal of Studies in International Education, 14*(5), 452–470.

American Council of Education. (2008). *ACE/FIPSE project on assessing international learning.* Retrieved from www.acenet.edu/news-room/Pages/ACEFIPSE-Project-on-Assessing-International-Learning.aspx

Association of American Colleges and Universities. (2010). *VALUE rubrics.* Retrieved from www.aacu.org/value/rubrics/index_p.cfm?CFID=6634177&CFTOKEN=40351583

Bennett, J. M. (2009). Transformative training: Designing programs for culture learning. In M. A. Moodian (Ed.), *Contemporary leadership and intercultural competence: Understanding and utilizing cultural diversity to build successful organizations* (pp. 95–110). Thousand Oaks, CA: Sage.

Berg, B. L. (2009). *Qualitative research methods for the social sciences* (7th ed.). Boston, MA: Allyn & Bacon.

Brux, J. M., & Fry, B. (2010). Multicultural students in study abroad: Their interests, their issues, and their constraints. *Journal of Studies in International Education, 14*(5), 508–527.

Charmaz, K. (2006). *Constructing grounded theory: A practical guide through qualitative analysis.* Thousand Oaks, CA: Sage.

Creswell, J. W., & Plano Clark, V. L. (2007). *Designing and conducting mixed methods research.* Thousand Oaks, CA: Sage.

Deardorff, D. K., & Deardorff, D. L. (2007). An overview of the basic methods of outcomes assessment. In M. C. Bolen (Ed.), *A guide to outcomes assessment in education abroad* (pp. 89–96). Carlisle, PA: Forum on Education Abroad.

Geertz, C. (1973). *The interpretation of cultures: Selected essays.* New York, NY: Basic Books.

Glaser, B., & Strauss, A. (1967). *The discovery of grounded theory.* Chicago, IL: Aldine.

Goode, M. L. (2008). The role of faculty study abroad directors: A case study. *Frontiers: Interdisciplinary Journal of Study Abroad, 15*, 149–172.

Janesick, V. (2000). The choreography of qualitative research design: Minuets, improvisations, and crystallization. In N. K. Denzin & Y. S. Lincoln (Eds.), *Handbook of qualitative research* (pp. 379–399). Thousand Oaks, CA: Sage.

Kinginger, C. (2009). *Language learning and study abroad: A critical reading of research.* New York, NY: Palgrave Macmillan.

Merriam, S. B. (2009). *Qualitative research: A guide to design and implementation.* San Francisco, CA: Jossey-Bass.

Morais, D. B., & Ogden, A. C. (2011). Initial development and validation of the global citizenship scale. *Journal of Studies in International Education, 15*(5), 445–466.

Patton, M. Q. (2002). *Qualitative research and evaluation methods.* Thousand Oaks, CA: Sage.

Rao, V., & Woolcock, M. (2003). Integrating qualitative and quantitative approaches in program evaluation. In S. Bourguignon & L. Pereira da Silva (Eds.), *The impact of economic policies on poverty and income distribution* (pp. 165–190). Washington, DC: World Bank.

Selby, R. (2008). Designing transformation in international education. In V. Savicki (Ed.), *Developing intercultural competence and transformation: Theory, research, and application in international education* (pp. 1–12). Sterling, VA: Stylus.

Slimbach, R. (2014, September–October). Reinventing international education: On what pattern? *International Educator,* pp. 58–63.

Weitzman, E. A. (2000). Software and qualitative research. In N. K. Denzin & Y. S. Lincoln (Eds.), *Handbook of qualitative research* (2nd ed., pp. 803–820). Thousand Oaks, CA: Sage.

Williams, T. R. (2009). The reflective model of intercultural competency: A multidimensional, qualitative approach to study abroad assessment. *Frontiers: Interdisciplinary Journal of Study Abroad, 18*, 289–306.

Wu, S. F., & Wong, M. S. (2013). "Forever changed": Emerging TESOL educators' global learning and spiritual formation on a study abroad trip in Myanmar. In M. S. Wong, C. Kristjánsson, & Z. Dörnyei (Eds.), *Christian faith and English language teaching and learning: Research on the interrelationship of religion and ELT* (pp. 47–65). New York, NY: Routledge.

Yin, R. K. (2009). *Case study research: Design and methods* (4th ed.). Thousand Oaks, CA: Sage.

6

QUANTITATIVE APPROACHES TO STUDY ABROAD ASSESSMENT

Mark E. Engberg and Lisa M. Davidson

I n an era of increased accountability and transparency, study abroad practitioners must account for the overall impact of their programs and, in many cases, demonstrate the value added to student learning and development. In response, practitioners have utilized a number of commercially and locally developed surveys to assess their programs; yet, all too often the utility of these efforts is never fully realized, and the data and corresponding reports simply "collect dust" over time (Engberg, Manderino, & Dollard, 2014). Approaching assessment from the perspective of maximizing utility requires a proactive stance in which important questions surrounding use are negotiated among relevant stakeholders at the onset of the process. The formation and prioritization of assessment questions will concomitantly influence the research design, drive the selection of appropriate instrumentation, and dictate the types of analytic approaches necessary to make programmatic improvements. The analytic choices in relation to quantitative data—particularly data collected from surveys—present a number of opportunities to explore and better understand the impact of study abroad programs, although this task can often feel daunting for those new to statistical applications and data conditioning.

In this chapter, we examine the process by which study abroad practitioners can approach the analysis of quantitative data collected through surveys of their respective programs. We begin with a brief overview of the assessment process, paying particular attention to the various approaches to research design that are most commonly used among study abroad practitioners, while highlighting the applied nature of such endeavors. Next, we discuss the important preliminary steps in relation to data conditioning and data cleaning, including data accuracy, response rates, missing data, outliers, and correlations. We then provide more specific examples of quantitative techniques used in both cross-sectional and longitudinal designs, with attention to how such techniques can be used to answer important questions about group differences and change over time, respectively. In doing so, we focus on those approaches most commonly used in study abroad programs, while emphasizing the applied nature of these techniques in addressing program improvement and impact. Throughout the chapter, we refer to and utilize the Statistical Package for the Social Sciences (SPSS) software (Version 22.0) to illustrate different statistical procedures. Although there are several popular statistical software packages from which to choose, the accessibility and intuitive pull-down menus within SPSS make its navigation fairly straightforward and a good choice for those unfamiliar with using statistical software. In addition, it is usually available at institutions of higher education.

Overview of the Assessment Process

Before delving into the specific processes involved in quantitative analysis, we will briefly review a few of the important questions and procedures that ultimately drive the choice of different analytic procedures. We view the assessment process as a highly collaborative endeavor that works best when a variety of stakeholders (both direct and indirect) are involved in the initial discussions regarding the prioritization of assessment questions, design decisions, instrumentation selection, and subsequent conversations regarding data interpretation and implications for practice (see Braskamp & Engberg, 2014, for guidelines in assessing student learning). For those new to the assessment process, we recommend reviewing an appropriate textbook (see Fitzpatrick, Sanders, & Worthen, 2011; Wholey, Hatry, & Newcomer, 2010) to learn the major tenets of program evaluation. Of critical importance is recognizing the inherent trade-offs in any assessment plan in relation to its utility, feasibility, accuracy, and propriety (Fitzpatrick et al., 2011). For instance, although it may be important to design a study that demonstrates causality in relation to a particular study abroad program, such a design may not be feasible given the naturalistic setting of study abroad programs and the difficulty in randomly assigning students to both treatment and control groups.

Once an assessment team has been delegated, it is essential to create and prioritize a list of questions that will eventually drive the assessment process. In our experience, the question development process should include both a divergent stage, in which multiple stakeholder voices are included to generate a laundry list of important questions, and a convergent stage, in which questions are prioritized by their frequency, utility, and relative importance, the latter of which is often influenced by the context of the political landscape that situates the program (Fitzpatrick et al., 2011). Questions can often be categorized as well by their relative focus on either outcomes or processes, understanding student change over time versus understanding differences among students, and the relative weight placed on understanding the overall impact of the program.

When discerning whether questions focus on process or outcomes (or both), evaluators and researchers have a number of opportunities to choose between locally and commercially developed surveys that attend to these differing priorities. Locally developed surveys are beneficial in that questions can be specifically tailored to institutional priorities and concerns, often increasing their overall utility, but there are additional trade-offs in relation to the accuracy and validity of such surveys. Commercially developed instruments typically address the validity concerns inherent in more locally developed surveys, provide opportunities for national benchmarking of student outcomes, and are often accompanied by interpretative guides that help in discerning the meaning of the data, though they may not focus as intently on local questions and issues. A number of different commercial instruments are available that relate specifically to the study abroad experience—including the Global Perspective Inventory (GPI) (Global Perspective Institute, n.d.), the Intercultural Development Inventory (IDI, n.d.), and the Beliefs, Events, and Values Inventory (BEVI, n.d.)—each with different foci on student outcomes and the emphasis placed on specific process elements related to the study abroad experience.

In addition to the careful attention placed on the selection of instrumentation, it is equally important to take into consideration the type of assessment design that aligns most closely with the questions driving the assessment process. For instance, programs that are largely concerned with making between-group comparisons (e.g., across student demographic characteristics, study abroad locations, or peer institutions) will often employ a cross-sectional design in which a survey is typically administered at one time at the end of the study abroad experience. Alternatively, programs that are most interested in understanding how students change over the course of the study abroad experience will employ a longitudinal design in which they will administer a survey twice—once at the time of predeparture and again at the conclusion of the experience. In addition to including the same student outcome questions on the pre- and posttest surveys, pretest questions often include information about predeparture experiences that may have influenced the decision to study abroad or the initial assessment of outcomes, whereas posttest items often include specific process-related questions that delve more deeply into the nature of the study abroad experience. Finally, for those programs interested in addressing questions about the overall impact of the study abroad program, more advanced designs, such as those that include a comparison group, can be employed along with appropriate statistical procedures that minimize selection biases. We recommend reviewing the work by Creswell (2014) and Shadish, Cook, and Campbell (2002) for a more in-depth discussion of research design.

Preliminary Steps in Quantitative Data Analysis

After collecting and before analyzing survey data, we recommend closely examining the data set to ensure the accuracy and representativeness of the information and the integrity of subsequent analyses. Data conditioning involves attending to detailed components of both an actual data set and the particular analytic techniques chosen to examine the data. This often requires more time and attention to detail than either the data collection or the subsequent analytic procedures. Though data conditioning can be a time-intensive step, carefully executing these practices allows one to responsibly proceed with accurately analyzing, interpreting, and reporting quantitative data. In addition, it offers a more fine-grained picture of the study abroad student sample, which can be quite informative even before more focused statistical analyses are begun.

This section outlines several important issues in data conditioning and highlights the specific steps to consider prior to engaging in data analysis. We begin the section with an examination of issues surrounding data accuracy and understanding participant response rates. We then discuss handling missing data, unusual or extreme responses, and patterns of relationships among the variables under study.

Data Accuracy

The initial step in data conditioning attends to the issue of accurate data entry. This step requires an examination of how data have been entered (or uploaded) into a data file and a consideration of issues that could yield inaccurate analyses. Comparing the actual obtained data to the final data file is an essential step; however, the size of the sample under study affects the methods by which this is typically executed. Tabachnick and Fidell (2013) outlined several components to consider in ensuring data accuracy; for example, with small data sets, careful proofreading of all variable values is recommended, but for larger data sets, analyzing particular descriptive statistics and graphic representations of variables is typically more efficient in ensuring appropriate variable value ranges (e.g., possible minimum and maximum values). Analyzing descriptive statistics of variables differs depending on the types of variables examined (i.e., categorical or continuous variables). Categorical variables consist of data that are grouped into discrete categories: either nominal classifications devoid of any particular order or ordinal classifications that have a meaningful ranked order. For example, the location of a study abroad program (e.g., Asia, Europe, or South America) is a nominal variable, whereas asking participants to rate their responses to questions along a Likert-type rating scale (e.g., 1 = *strongly disagree* to 5 = *strongly agree*, or 1 = *poor* to 7 = *excellent*) is an example of an ordinal variable. Though Likert-type scale responses are technically categorical variables, these responses are often treated as continuous variables in data conditioning and later analyses. Continuous variables take on numeric values within a defined range and have equal intervals between data points (e.g., a student's age or number of months immersed in a host country).

To check data accuracy for categorical variables, evaluators and researchers must examine the frequencies of responses in each possible category. For example, utilizing the frequency function in SPSS will display tables that include the number and percentage of responses in each of a variable's categories, as well as the number of valid and missing values (after opening SPSS and loading your data file, follow these SPSS menu choices: Analyze > Descriptive Statistics > Frequencies). In addition, various types of charts can also be generated through the same SPSS navigation menu to graphically display frequencies, including bar charts, pie charts, and histograms. In looking at the frequency tables, we can find several questions that are helpful to ask. Are any values out of the range of the numbered categories (e.g., there are three categories of study abroad program types—arbitrarily numbered 1 through 3—but the frequency table or chart indicates other number categories beyond these three values)? Finding nonexistent categories easily brings to light these types of data-entry errors. What do the frequencies suggest? How many responses are in each category? Which category contains the lowest and highest number of responses? What are the implications of low or high frequencies in particular categories?

To examine data accuracy for continuous variables (including Likert-type scales), we must analyze other descriptive statistics beyond frequencies. For instance, we often analyze the mean values (the averages) and dispersion (i.e., ranges and minimum-maximum values) of the continuous variables in SPSS (follow these SPSS menu choices: Analyze > Descriptive Statistics > Descriptives > Options) to answer important questions about the accuracy of the data. Do all of the values fall within the range of possible scores? If not, this points to data-entry errors. Do the mean values for the variables make sense based on what is already known about the population under study? The dispersion of a variable is also important to examine, particularly if there are any out-of-range values (i.e., below the minimum or beyond the maximum possible values). In addition, the standard deviation (the amount of variation from the mean) is also important to consider, as this indicates how closely values are dispersed around the sample's mean. A low standard deviation value suggests that overall scores are generally clustered around the mean with little variation, making the likelihood of finding differences across the sample relatively small. Conversely, a high standard deviation value indicates that the sample's scores are more widely dispersed across a wider range of scores, indicating a greater likelihood of differences in scores within a sample.

Finally, it is important to ensure that missing data are properly entered and coded in the data file. Data are missing from data files for several reasons, and these must be identified for accurate analyses and reporting. Participants, for instance, may choose not to answer particular questions on a survey, whereas others may have inadvertently skipped several questions or run out of time to complete the survey, leaving some answers blank. Finally, the nature of some survey questions may require participants to legitimately skip particular questions or blocks of questions. In SPSS, missing values are indicated by either an asterisk or the absence of any values. A more thorough discussion of missing data is found later.

Participant Response Rates

Once the data are checked for accuracy, response rates must be carefully examined to understand the representativeness of the sample. For several reasons, it is often not possible to survey, interview, or otherwise investigate every individual from a population of interest. Comparing the sample participants to the larger overall population of interest—examining how representative the sample is—and discussing any significant distinctions between the two is critical before findings can be understood and applied more broadly. Furthermore, external validity—which considers the generalizability of one's findings or the extent to which one's findings generalize beyond the current sample to the overall population under study—is an important aim of quantitative inquiry.

It is essential to know and report a participant response rate by determining the total number of individuals invited to participate in a study and those who actually participated. This is a simple proportion to calculate by dividing those who participated by the total invited, although it is important to take into account those who never received the initial invitation because of invalid e-mail addresses or returned mail. Beyond understanding response rates, it is necessary to consider how representative a sample is relative to the overall population of interest. How many and what types of individuals compose the overall population under study, and how does this compare to your final sample? Is the sample representative of important demographics of the total population, including race, ethnicity, gender, age, and other salient characteristics? Are there over- or underrepresented groups in your sample? What are the implications of these disparities? If these data are not readily accessible, campus institutional research or enrollment management areas can typically provide assistance in obtaining population data. Although beyond the scope of this chapter, weighting techniques can also be applied to correct for nonresponse biases (see NSSE, 2014).

Missing Data

The issue of missing data is one of the most prevalent quandaries in quantitative research and assessment efforts. In an extended discussion on the implications of and strategies for handling missing data, Tabachnick and Fidell (2013) stated that it is essential to first determine the severity of any missing data, particularly the patterns of missing data, the amount of data missing, and the reasons why the data may be missing. In quantitative research, missing data are often categorized as MCAR (missing completely at random), MAR (missing at random, which constitutes ignorable nonresponses), and MNAR (missing not at random, which constitutes nonignorable nonresponses) (Little, Jorgensen, Lang, & Moore, 2014). Randomly scattered missing values are less serious than nonrandom missing values, as the latter can affect the generalizability of results.

We can determine random from nonrandom missing data by testing for patterns in the missing data. Tabachnick and Fidell (2013) recommended two ways to test for this: First, one can construct a new variable that represents cases with missing and nonmissing values for an independent variable (e.g., a new variable could be created and coded as 0 = missing and 1 = not missing) and then test for mean differences on a continuous outcome measure between the groups using an independent-samples *t*-test (follow these SPSS menu choices: Analyze > Compare Means > Independent Samples *t*-Test). We can then examine the SPSS output and determine whether the two means differ significantly. The second strategy Tabachnick and Fidell (2013) outlined is SPSS's missing value analysis (follow these SPSS menu choices: Analyze > Missing Value Analysis), which highlights the numbers and patterns of missing values by providing statistics including frequencies of missing values, *t*-tests, and missing patterns.

Once the missing data patterns have been identified, there are a few different approaches—and resulting implications—in handling missing data that emphasize either excluding or substituting missing values. Excluding cases (participants) with missing data from analyses is a reasonable option if there is a random pattern of missing values, very few participants have missing data, and the participants are missing data on different variables and it appears that the missing cases represent a random subsample of the aggregate sample (Tabachnick & Fidell, 2013). By default, cases with missing values are usually excluded from most analyses in SPSS based on a listwise deletion technique. Although an acceptable approach—provided that the previous points are considered—excluding cases with extensive missing values (over 10% in most cases) can compromise the external validity of the results.

Tabachnick and Fidell (2013) recommended a number of different imputation or substitution approaches to use if a variable is missing extensive data yet is important to the analysis: First, one can use prior knowledge to replace missing values with an informed estimate if the sample is large and the number of missing values is small. For instance, if—given experience or expertise in a field—one is sure that the missing values would equate to the median, mean, or most frequent response, it is acceptable to substitute those values and note the reasons for doing so. Second, one can transform an ordinal or continuous variable into a dichotomous variable (e.g., participated or did not participate in study abroad; low or high engagement) and predict into which category to place the missing case. For longitudinal data, one can use the last observed value to fill in missing data, but this implies that there was no change over time. Third, one can substitute missing values by inserting an overall sample mean or a subsample mean defined by a particular grouping variable. Finally, one can utilize a regression-based technique on those cases with complete data to generate an equation that substitutes estimated missing values for incomplete cases. In the long run, effective methods of reducing missing data may focus on well-constructed surveys in which students are less likely to leave data blank and exhortations for students to leave no answers blank as they work through the questions.

For those interested in a much more in-depth discussion of missing data analysis, see Enders (2010) for quite thorough overviews and methods of different techniques to handle various types of missing data.

Detecting Outliers (Extreme Values)

Occasionally, outliers—or extreme, unexpected values—surface in the data and must be addressed, especially with small sample sizes. Participants can randomly respond to questions or represent genuinely rare cases, so it is often helpful to examine the other items attached to a particular participant to see a fuller picture and possibly explain any extreme values. Univariate outliers (an extreme value on *one* variable) and multivariate outliers (an unusual combination of scores on *two or more* variables) distort sample statistics (i.e., can lead to either stating there is a relationship or effect when there is not one or failing to detect a relationship or effect when there is one) and interfere with generalizability.

Tabachnick and Fidell (2013) discussed several reasons for outliers: First, incorrect data entry can produce incorrect values, some of which may be outliers (e.g., accidentally typing a value of 22 instead of 2). Second, failure to specify missing-value codes for data that should be read as real data can also produce outliers. Third, an outlier could be from outside of the population from which we wish to sample; we should delete these cases once they are detected, as they are not relevant to our analyses. Finally, an outlier could be from the population of interest, but the distribution of the variable has more extreme values than expected in a normal distribution. In this final case, we can retain these outliers but change the value on the variable so that the outlier's impact on the analyses is attenuated. Given the more advanced nature of identifying and handling multivariate outliers, we recommend referring to Tabachnick and Fidell (2013) for a more extended discussion.

Looking for Correlations Among Variables

Data conditioning also involves examining the degree to which continuous variables (including Likert-type scales) are correlated—or related—to one another. Note that correlations are not viable using categorical data, as the numerical values of these variables are not meaningful (the numerical values solely serve to categorize data into discrete groups). When examining correlations between continuous variables, correlation coefficients in SPSS will indicate the direction and strength of the correlation between the variables. Correlation coefficients are reported as values between −1.0 and +1.0. (*Note:* A positive relationship indicates that as one variable either increases or decreases, the other variable increases or decreases in the same manner; a negative relationship indicates that as one variable either increases or decreases, the other variable moves in the opposite direction.) To examine the correlations among all of the continuous variables in a data set, we can produce a correlation matrix in SPSS (follow these SPSS menu choices: Analyze > Correlate > Bivariate), which is simply a table that allows one to see the correlation coefficients for the specified variables to determine the direction (positive or negative) and degree to which they are related with each other. The closer correlation coefficients are to a value of −1.0 or +1.0, the stronger the negative or positive relationships, whereas the closer these values are to zero, the weaker the relationships.

For example, using responses from two survey items found on the GPI, we are interested in understanding the relationship between the number of multicultural courses taken at college and the degree to which students felt informed of current issues that impact international relations. Intuitively, it might seem that there could be a relationship between these two items, but whether this is statistically significant—and if so, the strength of this relationship—will be useful to understand. Using the SPSS navigation described earlier, we ran a bivariate (two-variable) correlation on these two items and found a correlation coefficient of .058 that was statistically significant. This value indicates that there is a statistically significant and positive (the correlation coefficient was greater than zero) relationship between these variables; in other words, as students complete more multicultural courses, their understanding of current global issues also increases. This correlation coefficient also illustrates, though, that although statistically significant, it is a weak relationship, as the value is very close to zero at .058. In this case, our intuition was correct in that these GPI items are, indeed, related, but the weak relationship between them is not that meaningful.

Of particular concern in the data conditioning stage for multivariate analyses is when two or more variables are strongly correlated with each other. For instance, problems can occur when independent variables are highly correlated with each other in the same multivariate model, which may lead to unstable findings, larger standard errors, and a reduced likelihood of statistical significance (see Grimm & Yarnold, 1995, for an expanded discussion of multicollinearity issues). As such, it is important to examine a correlation matrix prior to engaging in multivariate analyses.

Quantitative Approaches to Data Analysis

Once the data have been sufficiently cleaned and conditioned, a number of different statistical procedures can be utilized depending on the underlying questions driving the assessment. In the following examples we utilize survey data collected from the GPI (Global Perspective Institute, n.d.) to demonstrate some of the common techniques employed in cross-sectional and longitudinal designs. We present each example using as straightforward language as possible and focus on the applied nature of the results rather than the mathematical equations used to derive the various test statistics. We do, however, recommend the following resources for those interested in a more thorough understanding of the underlying assumptions and mathematical equations used in each of the examples: Grimm and Yarnold (1995), Huck (2012), and Tabachnick and Fidell (2013).

Example 1: Cross-Sectional Research Design: Study Abroad Class Differences

As mentioned earlier, descriptive analyses are often conducted during the data conditioning process in which frequencies and means are analyzed for all categorical and continuous variables, respectively. In the examples that follow, we analyze data collected from a cross-sectional study of 510 students at the completion of their study abroad experience, which included students in their second, third, and fourth years of study. Given the variations in class standing, one of the first questions we posed was whether there were statistical differences in how students representing different class years responded to the various Likert-type questions on the GPI Study Abroad Survey.

To answer this question, we utilized the crosstab function in SPSS (follow these SPSS menu choices: Analyze > Descriptives > Crosstab), placing the class-standing grouping variable (1 = second year, 2 = third year, and 3 = fourth year) in the column box and selecting the GPI survey question "How often did you feel immersed in the culture of the host country?" in the row box. In addition, under the "Statistics" tab, we checked the chi-square box and under the "Cells" tab, we checked the row percentages, which will aid in interpreting the table output. The chi-square (χ^2) test is used when comparing two categorical variables (either nominal or ordinal), and in this example, it will help us to determine whether students of different class standing responded significantly differently from one another in relation to the question.

As shown in table 6.1, the chi-square statistic is associated with a probability, or p value, of less than .05, which indicates that students' responses to the survey question were significantly different from one another based on their class standing. In statistics, the p value represents the probability of observing a more extreme test statistic, and when the p value falls below 5% (or .05), we would consider the finding to have reached statistical significance given the low probability of finding such an extreme value if additional samples were drawn from the population and tested. Although the p value indicates statistical differences, we must closely examine the distributions to determine where the differences lie. For instance, in referencing table 6.1, we note that the majority (51%) of fourth-year students felt immersed *very often* versus only 37% and 29% of third- and second-year students, respectively.

As in most assessments of surveys, these findings suggest a number of additional questions to further our understanding of the results. To what extent did fourth-year students differ on other survey questions compared to their second- and third-year counterparts? If other differences were found,

TABLE 6.1
Crosstab Analysis Example

Class Standing		How Often Did You Feel Immersed in the Culture of the Host Country?					
		Never	Rarely	Sometimes	Often	Very Often	Total
Second year	Count	0	1	11	30	17	59
	Row %	0.0	1.7	18.6	50.8	28.8	100.0
Third year	Count	0	3	34	120	92	249
	Row %	0.0	1.2	13.7	48.2	36.9	100.0
Fourth year	Count	1	3	29	67	102	202
	Row %	0.5	1.5	14.4	33.2	50.5	100.0

Note. χ^2 = 16.95, *p* value = .031.

what is the relationship between these other questions and students' level of immersion? Finally, to the extent that these differences are important to the program, additional qualitative research—including interviews or focus groups—may be necessary to better understand the differences uncovered in this question in relation to class standing.

In the next example, we consider a similar question related to group differences; however, in this example, we consider a continuous outcome based on the Knowing scale included in the GPI using the same cross-sectional sample and class-standing grouping variable. Thus, we ask a similar question, "Do students' average scores on the Knowing scale differ by class standing?" and utilize a different statistical test—the analysis of variance or ANOVA test—to determine whether there are statistically significant mean differences on the Knowing scale across class standing (follow these SPSS menu choices: Analyze > Compare Means > One Way ANOVA). When using SPSS in this example, note the "factor" box refers simply to the class-standing grouping variable, and the "dependent list" refers to the Knowing scale.

In interpreting the ANOVA results in table 6.2, note the *p* value in the final column is less than 5% (or .05), the typical statistical cutoff to determine significance, and thus we can conclude that the mean scores on the Knowing scale are significantly different from one another based on class standing. However, once determining that significant group differences exist, it is often important to perform an after-the-fact (or post hoc) test to determine where the differences lie (e.g., between second- and third-year students or third- and fourth-year students). There are a number of options for post hoc tests when clicking on the post hoc tab in the one-way ANOVA box in

TABLE 6.2
ANOVA Example

		Sum of Squares	df	Mean Square	F	p Value
Knowing	Between groups	1.847	2	.924	4.592	.011
	Within groups	101.958	507	.201		
	Total	103.805	509			

TABLE 6.3
Tukey Post Hoc Test Example

Dependent Variable	(I) Class Standing	(J) Class Standing	Mean Difference (I-J)	Standard Error	Significance
Knowing	Second year	Third year	−.02664	.06493	.911
		Fourth year	−.14346	.06636	.079
	Third year	Second year	.02664	.06493	.911
		Fourth year	−.11681	.04246	.017
	Fourth year	Second year	.14346	.06636	.079
		Third year	.11681	.04246	.017

SPSS; the two most common tests are the Tukey and Bonferonni tests, with other tests used to correct for sample size differences and other important statistical nuances.

As shown in table 6.3, the post hoc tests examine each of the possible pairings within the class-standing grouping variable and include a test of mean differences to determine whether the means of each pairing are significantly different from one another. The results indicate that there are statistical differences in the mean scores of the Knowing scale only between third- and fourth-year students ($p = .017$, which is less than the .05 threshold for significance) and no statistical differences between second-year students and the other groups.

It should be noted that the ANOVA is used only when examining a grouping variable with at least three levels. When comparing a grouping variable with only two levels—such as whether English was the primary language spoken in the country where one studied abroad (yes or no are the two levels)—the appropriate test to use is the independent-samples *t*-test (follow these SPSS menu choices: Analyze > Compare Means > Independent Samples *t*-Test). Finally, more sophisticated approaches, such as the analysis of covariance (ANCOVA), allow one to test for group differences across a continuous outcome variable while controlling for different covariates. We recommend reviewing this procedure in the noted references if such controls are important to one's assessment work.

Example 2: Longitudinal Research Design: Student Growth

In the next example, we examine a similar group of students who initially completed the GPI survey at the time of predeparture and then completed a follow-up survey shortly after they completed their one semester studying abroad. Just as we noted in the previous example, it is important to examine the frequencies and means of the categorical and continuous variables, respectively; although, there are now two sets of data to consider. Similarly, prior to examining student change over time, both the pre- and posttest survey must be merged together using a unique identifier for each survey respondent. There are two important caveats to keep in mind. First, both data sets must be sorted in ascending order based on the unique identifier; second, there cannot be any duplicate cases (e.g., a student who for some reason took the survey twice at either the pre- or the posttest administration). It is important to recognize that often some sample attrition will occur unless all students in the target population completed both the pre- and the posttest, which has rarely been the case in our experience.

One of the common questions we try to answer first when analyzing a longitudinal sample is whether students demonstrated significant growth across the different learning outcomes over the course of their semester abroad. In the following example, we look at three different outcomes from the GPI pre- and posttest survey (i.e., the Knowing, Identity, and Social Interaction scales). To calculate whether students increased their learning over the course of the semester, we utilized the paired-samples *t*-test function in SPSS (follow these SPSS menu choices: Analyze > Compare Means > Paired Samples *t*-Test), dragging each pair of outcomes into the variable 1 and variable 2 slots.

As shown in table 6.4, across each of the three GPI learning outcomes, students demonstrated positive growth over the course of the semester, and the associated *p* values (less than .05) for each of the paired outcomes suggest that the differences are statistically significant. It is also possible to calculate the effect size for each of the paired differences, which allows one to better understand the magnitude of the change over time. Using a simple formula to calculate Cohen's *d* (mean difference/pooled standard deviation),

TABLE 6.4
Paired Samples *t*-Test Example

	Time 1 Mean	*Time 2 Mean*	*Mean Difference*	p *Value*	*Pooled SD*	*Cohen's d*
Knowing	3.7793	3.8815	0.10224	.000	.44576	.229
Identity	3.9742	4.1376	0.16340	.000	.42061	.388
Social Interaction	2.7980	2.9402	0.14216	.000	.61728	.230

we found a small to moderate effect size across the three learning outcomes (.2 = small, .5 = medium, and .8 = high).

In addition to understanding whether students change over time, practitioners are often interested in examining how different facets of a study abroad experience contribute to student growth and development. In the next example, we utilize a regression method to investigate how a number of different process-oriented elements of a study abroad experience contributed to student learning over the course of a semester.

Using the SPSS regression command (follow these SPSS menu choices: Analyze > Regression > Linear Regression), we regress the posttest Social Interaction scale (i.e., a continuous and normally distributed dependent variable) on three groups of independent variables: student background characteristics, the pretest Social Interaction measure, and a number of process-related variables. (*Note:* The independent variables can be entered either simultaneously or in blocks using the "Next" tab to enter each subsequent block.) Entering variables in blocks allows one to understand how each block of variables adds to the overall amount of variance explained, while also understanding how subsequent blocks may influence the significance of earlier blocks of variables. This design aligns with Astin's (1993) input-environment-output (I-E-O) assessment model, which has been used extensively in higher education research to control for student inputs (e.g., what students bring to an experience) and to better understand how different environmental aspects (in this case, process-related elements) contribute to student change over the course of an educational experience.

As shown in table 6.5, the model summary provides a number of diagnostic indicators to better understand the overall viability of the regression model. In this case, the *R*-squared indicates that approximately 46% of the variance in student scores (i.e., distribution of scores around the mean) is explained by the regression model. If the *R*-squared were 100%, the model would explain all of the variability in student scores, so in this example, we are able to explain just under half of the variability in students' posttest

TABLE 6.5
Model Summary for Longitudinal Regression

	R	R-*Squared*	*Adjusted* R-*Squared*	*Standard Error of the Estimate*
Social interaction model	.675	.456	.441	.51062

scores, and by most educational standards, this would be considered a moderately robust explanatory model.

Table 6.6 provides the results of the full regression model after all blocks have been entered into the equation. This analysis yields many useful findings, so we provide an extended discussion of the results in this section. There are a few important things to consider before we discuss the model results. First, SPSS calculates both standardized and unstandardized beta coefficients: Unstandardized beta coefficients (*B*) demonstrate the *actual* amount of change expected in the dependent variable and are quite useful when comparing the effects of independent variables across different outcomes. Standardized beta coefficients (β) are most useful when interpreting the comparative effects of different independent variables within the same model, as the unit of analysis is standardized among the different independent variables. By taking into account the comparative magnitude of different effects, we found it easier to prioritize those variables that are malleable and most important in relation to program improvement. Second, the *p* value estimates are interpreted in a manner that is similar to that in earlier examples, and they are quite useful in discerning which effects are statistically significant and most likely to influence student learning and development. Finally, several of the student background characteristics were transformed from nominal variables into numerical dummy variables (0 = no and 1 = yes) in the model, and the parentheses indicate the appropriate referent group to use when interpreting the results. It is important to note that all nominal variables must be transformed into numerical values prior to performing any regression analyses.

Four of the independent variables in table 6.6 were statistically significant (*p* values of less than .05). First, White students scored significantly lower, on average, than students of color on the posttest Social Interaction measure (β = −.160), which suggests that students of color have higher average preferences toward interacting across difference than White students. The significance of this finding suggests that students respond differently by race in relation to their preferences toward social interaction, and this is an area that may warrant further investigation by examining other salient groups' differences in relation to different outcomes, by running separate group models or through

TABLE 6.6
Longitudinal Regression Example

	Unstandardized Coefficients		Standardized Coefficients	
	B	Standard Error	β	p Value
Student background characteristics				
Female (male)	.038	.052	.026	.461
White (students of color)	−.277	.061	−.160	.000
Second year (fourth year)	−.058	.077	−.027	.448
Third year (fourth year)	−.034	.049	−.025	.491
College grade point average	.104	.058	.060	.074
Pretest variable				
Social Interaction pretest	.507	.036	.503	.000
Process-related variables				
Usefulness of predeparture orientation	.008	.024	.013	.727
Developmental influence of faculty and staff	−.007	.029	−.009	.809
Spoke host language inside and outside of classroom	.010	.019	.018	.608
Class assignments involved community	.056	.025	.085	.025
Classroom-based reflective activities	.016	.019	.030	.407
Shared or discussed experience with others	−.032	.034	−.033	.357
Intercultural wonderment	.274	.043	.237	.000

qualitative methods to better understand the origins and meaning behind these differences. Second, students' pretest Social Interaction scores are highly predictive of their posttest scores (β = .503), controlling for other influences. Third, students who were exposed to class assignments that involved the community were associated with higher average scores on the Social Interaction measure (β = .085), which suggests that this is an important practice to retain and to consider expanding in future programs if social interaction is an important programmatic outcome. Fourth, students with higher levels of intercultural wonderment (i.e., their curiosity to explore new habits, make new friendships, and feel immersed in the host country) were also associated with higher posttest Social Interaction scores, and the magnitude of this effect was considerably larger than the finding related to class assignments in the community (β = .237 versus .085), suggesting that this may be the most useful opportunity to focus on in terms of increasing students' preferences toward interacting across difference. Finally, it should be noted that a lack of significance does not necessarily imply that a particular process variable is unimportant; rather, one should look at the comparative patterns to better understand how different experiences and practices influence a full range of student learning and developmental outcomes. In summary, the regression analysis shown in table 6.6 answers several meaningful questions and points the way to further potential improvements in study abroad practices. Quantitative methods provide a rich set of alternatives for education abroad assessment, an array of tools to discover answers to issues important for understanding student progress and for improving program effectiveness.

It is important to also recognize that, although this is beyond the scope of this chapter, longitudinal designs that include a comparison group can be useful if it becomes necessary to demonstrate the causal impact of a particular program. However, given the naturalistic setting of study abroad programs, voluntary nature of survey research, and difficulty of randomly assigning students to treatment or control groups, it can be quite challenging to create a comparison group that is not susceptible to selection biases. Much of study abroad assessment follows an "action research" model in which new programmatic approaches are evaluated on the fly rather than in a more pristine, experimentally controlled manner. More advanced statistical techniques can be used to minimize selection biases (i.e., propensity score matching; see Grunwald & Mayhew, 2008), and similar techniques (e.g., repeated ANOVA and regression-based methods) can be used to analyze the treatment effects.

Conclusion

This chapter presented an overview of the processes, issues, and steps involved in analyzing quantitative survey data. As the demands for accountability continue to increase and extend into all regions of colleges and universities, we are hopeful that this chapter is useful to practitioners who are both new to and experienced in quantitative analysis. We have provided a number of additional references to guide in this process and to further one's knowledge of the varied approaches to data analysis. If you are somewhat bewildered by parts of this chapter, we recommend finding a local consultant, coach, or mentor to further explain and elaborate these approaches. In our experience, it is only through regular practice and a willingness to learn, experiment, and ask questions that further mastery of these skills is possible. Such mastery is useful in not only meeting both the external and the internal demands for accountability but also empowering oneself with the necessary tools to make continuous programmatic improvements and better understand how students learn and develop during their study abroad experiences.

References

Astin, A. (1993). *Assessment for excellence: The philosophy and practice of assessment and evaluation in higher education.* Washington, DC: Oryx Press.

Beliefs, Events, and Values Inventory. (n.d.). Retrieved from www.thebevi.com/aboutbevi.php

Braskamp, L. A., & Engberg, M. E. (2014). *Guidelines for judging the effectiveness of assessing student learning.* Chicago, IL: Loyola University Chicago. Retrieved from https://gpi.central.edu/index.cfm?myAction=JudgingEffectiveness

Creswell, J. W. (2014). *Research design: Qualitative, quantitative, and mixed method approaches* (4th ed.). Thousand Oaks, CA: Sage.

Enders, C. K. (2010). *Applied missing data analysis.* New York, NY: Guilford.

Engberg, M. E., Manderino, M., & Dollard, K. (2014). Collecting dust or creating change: A multi-campus utility study of student survey results. *Journal of Assessment and Institutional Effectiveness, 4*(1), 27–51.

Fitzpatrick, J., Sanders, J., & Worthen, B. (2011). *Program evaluation: Alternative approaches and practical guidelines* (4th ed.). New York, NY: Longman.

Global Perspective Institute. (n.d.). Global Perspective Inventory. Retrieved from https://gpi.central.edu/

Grimm, L. G., & Yarnold, P. R. (1995). *Reading and understanding multivariate statistics.* Washington, DC: American Psychological Association.

Grunwald, H. E., & Mayhew, M. J. (2008). Using propensity scores for estimating causal effects: A study in the development of moral reasoning. *Research in Higher Education, 49*(8), 758–775.

Huck, S. W. (2012). *Reading statistics and research* (6th ed.). Boston, MA: Pearson.

Intercultural Development Inventory. (n.d.). Retrieved from http://idiinventory.com/

Little, T. D., Jorgensen, T. D., Lang, K. M., & Moore, E. W. G. (2014). On the joys of missing data. *Journal of Pediatric Psychology, 39*(2), 151–162.

NSSE. (2014). *An explanation of weighting in the NSSE institutional report.* Retrieved from http://nsse.iub.edu/html/weighting.cfm

Shadish, W. R., Cook, T. D., & Campbell, D. (2002). *Experimental and quasi-experimental designs for generalized causal inference.* Belmont, CA: Wadsworth, Cengage Learning.

Tabachnick, B. G., & Fidell, L. S. (2013). *Using multivariate statistics* (6th ed.). Upper Saddle River, NJ: Pearson.

Wholey, J. S., Hatry, H. P., & Newcomer, K. E. (Eds.). (2010). *Handbook of practical program evaluation* (3rd ed.). San Francisco, CA: Jossey-Bass.

PART THREE

CASE STUDIES OF PRACTICE
IN ASSESSING STUDY ABROAD

7

WHERE AND HOW DO STUDENTS LEARN ABROAD?

Using Reflective Writing for Meaning-Making and Assessment

Elizabeth Brewer and Joshua Moore

Just as students learn and develop over time, so do institutions and their faculty and staff. Though often perceived as an onerous and burdensome add-on, assessment, by providing data about what students are learning and where and how, can help faculty and staff members, as well as institutions, reflect on their practices and make changes to deepen student learning. Furthermore, assessment practices that also help students reflect on their learning can shift the assessment paradigm from assessment *of* learning to assessment *as* learning (Earl, 2003). Indeed, assessment is one of several new forms of teaching that institutions can and should employ to ensure student success, as in itself, can provide significant learning experiences (Fink, 2003).

Through years of trial and error, Beloit College has become an example of an institution slowly learning and evolving from assessing (or evaluating) individual student learning to embracing assessment as a learning experience for both students and the college. Evidence of this shift can be found in the assessment of study abroad learning outcomes, where "reflection products" (Ash, Clayton, & Atkinson, 2005) captured in study abroad applications and post-study abroad evaluations are used both to help individual students drive, monitor, and plan for future learning and to assess study abroad learning outcomes across students.

Context: Building Momentum for Broad Ownership of Study Abroad

Beloit College, a small, liberal arts, undergraduate college enrolling 1,250 students, has allowed financial aid to support study abroad since 1931. However, real growth in study abroad participation rates did not take place until 1960, when a new Educational Blueprint called for greater internationalization of the curriculum and increased opportunities to study abroad. That same year, the World Affairs Center and the World Outlook (study abroad) Program were established to support the call. Student performance in faculty-led seminars abroad was graded; it is to be assumed that experiences from one seminar informed planning for the next. However, the assessment of student learning was not yet attempted. Methods to distinguish between individual student learning and performance based on a variety of factors, including factors not directly related to learning (attendance, participation, effort) *and* learning across courses and programs, as measured by both graded assignments and other means (Carnegie Mellon Eberly Center for Teaching Excellence, n.d.), were not yet developed.

Later, when the model for study abroad shifted from faculty-led "seminars" to other kinds of opportunities, what students were getting out of study abroad was mostly reported in student satisfaction evaluations. The potential usefulness of this information is unknown; the evaluations, collected and stored in filing cabinets, were largely left unread and, therefore, also unanalyzed. Today, approximately 75% of students who study abroad at Beloit do so by enrolling in universities abroad on a visiting or exchange basis without using a provider for admissions purposes or other supports. This activity is referred to as *direct enrollment*. Twenty-five percent of students participate in provider programs.

In 2000, Beloit began to reexamine its international engagement to ask, for example, whether students who did not study abroad were receiving an international education and what study abroad was yielding at and beyond the individual student level. In response, an annual international symposium was established to allow returned study abroad students to report on their experiences abroad. A mission statement for international education and learning goals for study abroad were also adopted, and the study abroad application and post-study abroad evaluation aligned with these. The study abroad application was also modified to invite students to articulate their own learning goals and to anticipate how they might achieve them.

Eventually, rubrics with which to evaluate study abroad application essays were created, and post-study abroad evaluations were shared with faculty advisors. They were also made available to prospective study abroad students to help them anticipate their own experiences. At the same time, faculty volunteers worked with the Office of International Education to create pre- and post-study abroad courses to help strengthen the learning outcomes of study abroad. Eventually, grants from the Andrew W. Mellon Foundation, the Freeman Foundation, and the American Council on Education's Internationalization Collaborative enabled faculty members to experiment with ways to integrate study abroad into their teaching and advising. A collaborative project with Kalamazoo College eventually led to publication of a book on study abroad integration (Brewer & Cunningham, 2009), helping cement the idea that study abroad at Beloit College is integral to students' educational trajectories. The experiment also demonstrated that faculty could and should play a role in making study abroad a meaningful activity for students' academic and personal growth.

Combined, these actions helped raise expectations for the study abroad experience, for preparation for it, and for post-study abroad integration. Subsequent surveys of graduating seniors, faculty, and staff have indicated that study abroad is perceived to be the most significant and successful feature of the college's international education program. This perception is shared by non-study abroad students, although they are less likely than their study abroad counterparts to recognize the international dimensions of the curriculum, even when majoring in the same subject. As noted by Murphy and Hall (2008), our identities (in this case, as study abroad and non-study abroad students) influence how we experience a curriculum.

Despite progress made to strengthen study abroad and secure its place in students' ongoing educations and development, outcomes *across* the study abroad population remained unclear. Many could point to benefits to individual students, but the broader institutional benefits of study abroad were not clear in terms of helping students achieve the Beloit College mission and learning goals. The next step, therefore, would be to embark on a study abroad assessment project that would align with other assessment efforts at Beloit.

Toward Embedded Assessment

For much of Beloit College's history, student learning was not assessed. This was not atypical. After all, grades were thought to be sufficient evidence of student learning and the effectiveness of a college's curriculum. This promised to change at Beloit when a college examiner was appointed in 1965 and charged with "conducting research and analysis about the college and its populations." The appointment coincided with the introduction of the Beloit Plan: year-round instruction and required experiential learning terms away from the campus (Beloit College, n.d.). Economic woes eventually led to termination of the plan and also positions, including the examiner's, in 1971. Nonetheless, that year Beloit began participating in Cooperative Institutional Research Program (CIRP) first-year and senior surveys, using the first-year data to inform the work of its admissions office. Senior data would not be matched with first-year data until a more robust infrastructure could be put in place. Comparisons of this data can help illuminate students' development from admission to graduation.

Going forward, accreditation was to drive assessment, until assessment was sufficiently well established to be incorporated into academic programming and administration as a general practice. The first step in this direction was the reestablishment of the examiner's office as the Office of Institutional Research in 1987; this followed a 1986–1987 accreditation visit by the Higher Education Commission of the North Central Association of Colleges and Schools. Despite this step, the 1996–1997 accreditation review found the college's assessment practices wanting; improvements would need to be made. Thanks to a recommendation from the accreditation team, Beloit began participating in the National Survey of Student Engagement (NSSE) in 2001 but was unable to do more. Preparations for the 2006–2007 review made glaringly obvious that a single institutional researcher, acting alone, could not both conduct institutional research and develop an assessment program. Urgent discussions—among the senior staff, in the academic senate, and in other deliberative bodies—led to the appointment of a Committee for the Assessment of Student Learning, placing responsibility for the assessment of student learning in the hands of the faculty. This would prove key to building momentum for assessment.

In 2005, the Teagle Foundation awarded a joint grant titled Missions and Majors to Beloit College and three other members of the Associated Colleges of the Midwest (Knox, Monmouth, and Ripon). During Missions and Majors, over two years, four departments at each institution devised assessment methods to better understand the contributions of their academic programs to institutional learning goals. Focusing on critical thinking, civic engagement, and quantitative reasoning (Fass, 2008), the colleges sought to integrate findings from assessment activities with NSSE and Collegiate Learning Assessment data. Workshops, conferences, and regular conference calls helped move the project forward. Although the approaches to assessment varied (from senior surveys plus analysis of course evaluations to student writing, oral presentations, and course content), the method that resonated most at Beloit College was embedding assessment in existing course assignments. In other words, student work could be analyzed both to measure the degree to which *individual* students were satisfying course requirements and to assess the degree to which learning goals set by the broader institution were being met *across* students. This, in turn, taught the faculty participants how their teaching and assignments correlated with learning outcomes and where changes might improve learning. This could be "unnerving," but it enabled one participant to better "tailor goals to specific learning environments and level of student knowledge" and pay "close attention to the ways in which student writing 'speaks'" (Fass, 2008, p. 9).

The scope of the project was small. Nonetheless, it demonstrated that departments' teaching and curricula were critical to students' abilities to achieve Beloit's learning goals, and the visibility of the project raised interest in assessment beyond the project participants. Beloit College then pursued two more collaborative assessment projects (through the Associated Colleges of the Midwest, or the ACM, a consortium of liberal arts colleges, and the Center of Inquiry in the Liberal Arts at Wabash College) to experiment with methods; earlier, it had begun experimenting with rubrics in a project sponsored by the Association of American Colleges and Universities (AAC&U, 2010).

Today, Beloit College tries to ensure that all academic committees, departments, and programs use assessment to ensure they are contributing to college-wide learning goals and to embed assessment practices from the start when initiating new programs. Many of these efforts analyze student work (writing, poster sessions, presentations) to determine if desired learning outcomes are being met. Assessment is also being embedded in study abroad processes.

The rationales for assigning responsibility for assessment broadly and using embedded assessment are threefold: (a) assessment should focus on things the campus cares about (e.g., graduation requirements and study abroad), (b) it should benefit students (through meaningful assignments and reflective activities), and (c) it should provide information that can suggest which assignments, activities, and tasks are working and where improvements can be made. However, beyond these, embedded assessment avoids asking students (and programs and departments) to undertake "extra" tasks and allows outcomes and rubrics to be applied to programs or sets of courses with common but not identical characteristics (Garretson & Golson, 2005), such as first-year courses and study abroad experiences.

Using teams to develop assessment questions and methods and do the analysis also creates shared ownership of assessment and increases understanding of where learning is or is not taking place. Such collaborative assessment of student learning, used in elementary and high schools as a tool for teachers to monitor their teaching methods and work together to address common problems (Langer & Colton, 2005), has been shown to generate increased faculty engagement in learning and to "develop a sense of collective efficacy . . . [to ensure] student success" (p. 26). Beloit College's work with assessment teams has shown similar results. Indeed, student members of teams have reported that the assessment work has taught them more about learning goals, the learning process, and "grading" than any other activity.

As Beloit begins new initiatives, stakeholders from across the campus are being enlisted to design assessment questions and processes, and work is underway to allow learning that takes place outside course work to be incorporated into an advising record made accessible to advisors and students. This information will complement academic transcripts to provide a more complete picture of students' educational experiences.

Learning to Assess Study Abroad

When Beloit College students apply to study abroad, they are asked to respond to four prompts asking about (a) their learning goals in relation to the university or program where they will study and its location, (b) the relationship of the planned study abroad to their prior and future studies, (c) their knowledge of the host country and how they will structure their unstructured time (i.e., learn independently and experientially), and (d) the role social identities may play in their experience. (Social identity is an idea introduced to students in Beloit College's first-year seminar program to help them recognize, navigate, and appreciate the cultural and social diversity of the campus and larger world and understand how identities shape their experiences.) Applicants are given rubrics to use as a guide as they prepare their essays. The rubrics are also used by faculty to evaluate students' study abroad plans. In essence, the study abroad application process serves to cultivate students' metacognition, essential skills for which are planning, monitoring, and evaluating (Schraw, 1998).

To arrive at an assessment plan and method, Beloit looked at a variety of models and instruments. In reviewing these, Beloit determined that it wanted to find a way to make the assessment of study abroad learning outcomes meaningful for the students themselves. That is, an assessment method was needed that would allow students to (a) better understand what and how they learned while abroad and (b) allow that learning to help guide their ongoing educational and personal development (Kaplan, Silver, LaVaque-Manty, & Meizlish, 2013). The assessment process would therefore need to facilitate reflection and meaning-making and encourage students to continue to take ownership of their learning. At the same time, the assessment method also had to yield information that would enable the college to improve institutional practice around study abroad. Finally, the assessment had to be doable, on the part of both the students and those analyzing the data, and involve minimal, if any, additional expenditure.

As this process began, Beloit was invited to participate in a collaborative, multi-institutional project to understand how study abroad might contribute to liberal learning outcomes. As the project developed, it focused on the development and administration of a pre- and post-study abroad instrument. However, using such an instrument was incompatible with Beloit's move toward embedded assessment. Beloit was already asking students to develop specific plans for study abroad, and assessment would need to take these into consideration. The Beloit project team was thus reluctant to ask students to complete an assessment instrument that did not. Beloit therefore withdrew from the project.

The search for methods and instruments had been productive, however, and the team proposed that, as was done to evaluate study abroad applications, rubrics be used to examine post-study abroad evaluations. Ideally, applications and evaluations would also serve for pre- and post-study abroad comparisons. The first step would be to modify the post-study abroad evaluation to prompt greater reflection, and the second step would be to develop or adapt a rubric.

Round 1: Testing Methods and Processes

To modify the post-study abroad evaluation questions, staff members in the Office of International Education (OIE) reviewed responses to the current short answer prompts. Although the alignment of these with application prompts lent comparison, the prompts were too closed, tending to produce yes-no and good-bad responses. A prompt about the liberal arts, for example, elicited comparisons (host university not so good–Beloit College better) instead of encouraged students to think more deeply about educational differences and their own roles in the learning process. Furthermore, the actual experiences of students and their responses to them were largely hidden. The prompts also were not elastic enough to allow students to discuss the difference between what they had envisioned for themselves pre-study abroad and what they actually experienced. (See Engle [2012] for a helpful discussion of evaluation prompts.)

Simultaneously, Beloit's first- and second-year Initiatives Program was experimenting with ways to encourage students to take greater ownership of their learning. Influenced by Flavell's work on metacognition (Kaplan et al., 2013) and experience with the study abroad application, students in the Initiatives Program would write reflective essays midway through each of their first four semesters, discussing what they had learned and setting goals for their next semesters. Beloit's director of Institutional Research, Assessment, and Planning (IRAP) and the Initiatives Program director then helped OIE modify post-study abroad reflection prompts as follows:

> From: What were your learning goals for study abroad? Did you achieve them? If yes, how? If no, why?
> To: What were your original goals for study abroad? How did they change? What conditions and actions by you and others influenced your ability to achieve the goals?
> From: What were the biggest benefits of studying abroad? The biggest challenges?
> To: Discuss experiences abroad, small or large, that were especially meaningful and memorable. Explain why and how these will have a lasting effect on you (500 words).
> From: How did studying abroad enrich your liberal arts education?
> To: How did your learning abroad intersect with your studies at Beloit College, past and future?

Two prompts did not change:

> How did your experiences abroad, including others' perceptions of you, impact how you think about yourself and your relationship to society?
> In three sentences or fewer, how would you describe your study abroad experience to a future employer or graduate school admissions office?

Two prompts suggest text lengths; the others do not. Text boxes, however, are sized to welcome longer responses. Longer essays tend to yield higher scores; students who write more appear to be more invested in reflection. However, there are exceptions. Succinct essays can provide strong evidence of growth, whereas longer essays may not correlate with the outcomes under examination.

Administration of the Instrument and Essay Analysis

Near or following the conclusion of their study abroad experience, students are invited to complete a series of short reflective essays and to use Likert scales to indicate agreement with a set of statements. They also are asked to provide information on such things as housing and spending. The request is sent via SurveyMonkey, with periodic reminders sent to students who have not yet completed them. (Because students' study abroad dates differ, the window for completing the survey is wide.)

To analyze the essays, in round 1, a team of 15 faculty, students, and staff members took part in a five-hour workshop on a Saturday. Joining members of the Committee on International Education were a representative of the Curriculum Oversight and Administration Committee, an IRAP student intern and the IRAP director, two OIE staff members, a staff member in the college's Liberal Arts in Practice Center, and two returned study abroad students. A two-and-a-half-hour norming session was used to come to consensus on how to apply the rubric and to clarify terminology. Norming is critical; without it, scores may differ radically from reviewer to reviewer.

Working in teams of two, the participants then read and analyzed 36 essays submitted the previous semester. As compensation, students received an hourly wage and faculty members were each paid $100. (Staff members cannot receive additional compensation for such activities but in principle may be able to take time off during the workweek as compensation.) Breakfast, lunch, and a mid-morning snack were served.

The rubrics used for the analysis were adapted from the AAC&U's VALUE rubrics on the development of "Integrative Learning," "Critical Thinking," and "Intercultural Knowledge and Competence" (AAC&U, 2010). The study abroad learning outcomes to be assessed were the ability to transfer (skills, abilities, theories, or methodologies gained in one situation to new situations), reflect (on multiple interrelated factors in past and future), and take ownership (recognize the role of self and others in learning and strategize to achieve goals). Additional outcomes were cultural self-knowledge and knowledge of others' cultural frameworks.

The rubrics were applied across sets of essays, both because information pertinent to the rubrics emerged in different essays depending on the respondents and because some individual essays would not have yielded enough information for analysis on their own.

Round 1 Assessment Findings

Each set of essays was evaluated using scores from 0 (low) to 3 (high) for each rubric subcategory. If a response seemed to fall between scores, the lower score was assigned. No partial scores were allowed. Very few scores of 3 were assigned, and, when students were not interested in reflecting, some essay sets received all 0s or 0s and an occasional 1. Thanks to the norming session, scores given by team members either were identical or differed by only one point. If scores had differed by more than one point, scoring by a third person would have been required to achieve consistency.

Scores were highest for ownership, closely followed by reflection and then transfer. Some research on intercultural learning suggests that less intercultural learning takes place during study abroad than generally understood (Twombly, Salisbury, Tumanut, & Klute, 2012). Findings underscored this. Scores for intercultural knowledge and competence were lowest, with evidence of cultural self-knowledge higher than knowledge of cultural world frameworks.

As Beloit College offers a variety of study abroad opportunities, an analysis was undertaken by program type, using Forum on Education Abroad classifications. Differences by program type were found, with scores distinctly higher for direct enrollment than for other kinds of study abroad across all five measures (see table 7.1). The scores related to intercultural development contradict some research on the relationship between facilitated learning and intercultural learning (Vande Berg, Paige, & Connor-Linton, 2009). These differences moderated in the next round of assessment, however, when 115 essay sets were scored. Nonetheless, round 1 findings suggested that increasing the proportion of study abroad taking place through direct enrollment was not negatively affecting learning outcomes on the selected measures.

For those doing the scoring, most compelling were the *stories* the *students* were telling about their experiences abroad. In particular, the prompt about an "impactful experience" allowed students to be selective and specific in telling a story about how and where they had learned abroad. For example, a math student had not only asked questions about terms and concepts he had previously taken for granted, but also realized, at the end of the semester, that his favorite part of the day was navigating several forms of public

TABLE 7.1
Round 1 Rubric Average Scores

Program Types	Rubric Categories				
	Transfer	Reflection	Ownership	Cultural Self-Knowledge	Others' Cultural Frameworks
Across program types ($N = 35$)	1.00	1.29	1.30	0.85	0.70
Direct enrollment ($n = 6$)	1.50	2.0	1.58	1.69	1.22
Facilitated direct enrollment ($n = 9$)	0.87	1.30	1.13	0.59	0.61
Field research program ($n = 4$)	0.88	1.00	1.50	0.50	0.25
Hybrid program ($n = 6$)	0.97	1.08	1.08	0.58	0.50
Study center ($n = 10$)	0.88	1.10	1.32	0.87	0.55

transportation to get to and from the university, an initially unnerving task. He now felt like a local resident.

Round 2: Applying Round 1 Lessons: New Questions and Tools of Analysis

In the following year, a 21-member team of faculty, staff, and students was assembled to read and analyze post-study abroad reflective essays. Using a PowerPoint slide presentation to give an overview of the session and its goals and methods helped reduce the amount of time spent on norming, as did a review of a set of application essays annotated to indicate which parts of the essays correlated with the measures. Teams worked at different paces, but all were finished within the five-hour workshop framework. Eighteen of the team members were new to the analysis, expanding the circle of campus members becoming more familiar with study abroad learning outcomes and this kind of assessment. Compensation for the workshop consisted of meals and the learning experience; no stipends were offered, and students did not receive wages. One hundred and fifteen essays received over two semesters were read. The Pivot Tables function available within Microsoft Excel was used for cross-tabulations of data to look for correlations.

Round 2 Findings

As seen in table 7.2, in this round, scores across program types were higher than in round 1. Differences between scores associated with lifelong learning skills and intercultural development held, with the former higher than the latter. In general, scores associated with study center enrollment were lower than scores for other program types, as was the case in round 1. However, ownership of learning correlated most highly with hybrid programs, as did cultural self-knowledge.

The highest scores for transfer, reflection, and others' cultural frameworks were associated with field research programs. This may be associated with the higher bar for acceptance to such programs at Beloit. To qualify for field research programs, students must demonstrate strong rationales and preparation through course work and other activities. They must also discuss their plans for the independent studies they will conduct abroad and how they will build on these upon return to campus. Although this is expected of all applicants, the bar is higher for field research programs, and thus applicants have to demonstrate greater capacity for lifelong learning, greater self-awareness, and greater knowledge of the host country before they go abroad than do other students.

TABLE 7.2
Round 2 Rubric Average Scores

	Rubric Categories				
Program Types	*Transfer*	*Reflection*	*Ownership*	*Cultural Self-Knowledge*	*Others' Cultural Frameworks*
Across program types (*N* = 115)	1.10	1.46	1.45	1.18	0.93
Direct enrollment (*n* = 45)	1.08	1.48	1.40	1.12	0.76
Facilitated direct enrollment (*n* = 18)	1.01	1. 55	1.29	1.12	0.97
Field research program (*n* = 18)	1.42	1.70	1.54	1.33	1.30
Hybrid program (*n* = 16)	1.19	1.33	1.89	1.51	0.86
Study center (*n* = 18)	0.81	1.19	1.23	0.96	0.96

We also combined the scores from both rounds, yielding results similar to the second-round scores (see figure 7.1).

After round 1, scales (1 = *not at all*, 5 = *very much so*) were inserted after each essay prompt asking how helpful the prompt was in facilitating meaningful reflection on the study abroad experience. The greater the helpfulness of the prompt for the essay, the higher the score for reflection.

Limitations

- The findings by program type are only suggestive; although, as indicated in the discussion of round 1 assessment, for Beloit's purposes, they suggest that Beloit's prioritization of direct enrollment over other kinds of study abroad is not hindering learning.
- As the essays are not a course requirement, and students do not receive credit, students vary in the degree to which they invest in them and the reflection process. If similar essays were assigned in courses in faculty-led or provider programs, and/or if group reflective discussions took

Figure 7.1 Combined rubric average scores for rounds 1 and 2 across program types

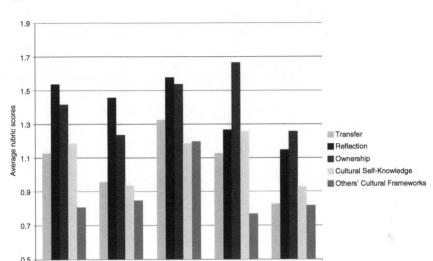

place before the essays were written, the reflection might be deeper across students, resulting in higher scores.

- Beloit's study abroad assessment captures data at a particular point in time. A student still working through an incident that occurred abroad or who is deeply engaged in another activity may not be fully open to reflecting on study abroad when the request to complete the instrument arrives.

- A rubric is not a reflection of a "permanent and absolute reality" (Griffin, 2009, p. 9) but rather the product of the people who have collaborated to produce it. Subject to change as knowledge and values develop, it also balances "generality and specificity" (p. 10). Rubrics are thus constructed and limiting. They will not capture all the learning evident in the essays.

- Lifelong learning skills and intercultural knowledge and competence are developed over time. It should not be surprising, therefore, that by the junior year when most students study abroad, these are still in development.

- There are limitations to the methodology. Other kinds of data are therefore needed to arrive at a fuller understanding of what and how students learn abroad and how this affects their subsequent studies and other activities.

To this end, NSSE data have been examined to determine if study abroad students differ from non-study abroad students; although the data do not indicate why the students differ, study abroad students are more likely than their non-study abroad counterparts to participate in high-impact learning practices and to both be more open to others' perspectives and draw on more diverse perspectives in classroom discussions and assignments. In addition, the Committee on International Education examined 387 abstracts from international symposia held from 2002–2014 to understand the relationship between Beloit College's goals for study abroad and abstract content. Changes in content appear to relate to strengthen study abroad learning outcomes through messaging about study abroad's purpose and advising; these underscore study abroad learning goals introduced in 2002 after the first international symposium was held. The changes are significant: In 2002, 32% of abstracts discussed connections to studies, whereas 96% did in 2014, and 4% of abstracts in 2002 included a focus on how the student's assumptions and values had been challenged, whereas 36% of the 2014 abstracts did so.

Finally, in a current assessment project, post-study abroad reflective essays are being read to discover patterns in outcomes, such as the development of resilience. Interviews will then be conducted to explore the factors contributing to the outcomes. And in a next step, a collaborative project with the college's curriculum committee will examine the development of intercultural literacy, including through study abroad.

Lessons for Study Abroad

Beloit's experience with assessing study abroad learning outcomes suggests a number of lessons for study abroad in general. First, the more students can be taught to approach study abroad as a learning experience for which they must take responsibility, the more they will learn. The same is true of connecting study abroad to their ongoing studies, interests, and postcollege planning. Second, opportunities to reflect must be created, and students must be taught to reflect. Third, colleges and universities need to provide curricular and cocurricular opportunities for students to prepare for study abroad and to integrate it post-study abroad.

Concretely at Beloit, based on the findings, questions on the study abroad application have been modified to use language more accessible to applicants and to bring them in-line with what is being learned about Beloit College students' study abroad experiences. For example, instead of asking students about their ability to learn experientially, the application asks students to discuss plans for structuring unstructured (out-of-classroom) time. This helps them develop the agency that will enable them to use out-of-classroom time wisely. In addition, greater emphasis is being placed in study abroad advising on helping students research study abroad opportunities, identify what they hope to gain from study abroad, and make connections with their studies, cocurricular and extracurricular activities, and future hopes.

The study abroad orientation has also been redesigned as a four-hour conference with plenary and concurrent sessions promoting active engagement and critical thinking. Returned study abroad students help plan and facilitate the orientation, furthering their own reflection and learning.

Finally, as discussed earlier in this case study, Beloit College has worked for over a dozen years to strengthen study abroad. As it continues this work, it would like to find additional ways to help students monitor their activities and learning while abroad and to translate this reflection into next steps. In other words, Beloit hopes to continue to help students "intervene" in their own learning, to borrow an oft-used term in the literature on study abroad (Vande Berg, 2007).

Lessons for Assessment Practice

Using student reflective writing to assess learning outcomes fosters reflection and meaning-making among returned study abroad students. The writing also lends itself to fruitful and rich discussions of the goals and outcomes of study abroad and the relationship of these to overall desired outcomes for undergraduate education. Specific lessons for assessment practice include the following:

- Open-ended questions yield richer reflection. Of round 2 respondents, 67.2% reported the prompt to discuss small and/or large experiences was either "helpful" or "very helpful." The prompt seems to give students permission to recognize that significant learning can emerge from small and/or routine experiences. In this sense, the prompt liberates them from the rhetoric around study abroad as involving big, life-transforming experiences.
- The analysis of post-study abroad essays may suggest few gains from study abroad for some students. The essay may not be the best vehicle for some students to demonstrate what they put into and got out of study abroad. That is, very rich learning experiences will not emerge in these kinds of essays, but they may emerge elsewhere. It is thus important to have multiple opportunities for returned students to reflect on and express what they have learned both formally and informally, along with ways to capture this information.

- As experience with assessment is gained, and new questions arise, literature on learning and student development can provide valuable theoretical perspectives that in turn can inform not only assessment but also study abroad practices, including advising, program design, and messaging.
- It is important to embark on assessment incrementally. Make modest starts that do not demand a large learning curve. As experience is gained, new tools are learned, and findings suggest new questions, assessment practice can evolve and become richer. At Beloit, a student intern in the assessment office will analyze CIRP and NSSE data in the coming semester. We also hope to use transcript analysis to see if this can help illuminate the essay data and to compare data by disciplinary focus (arts and humanities, social sciences, mathematics, and natural sciences).
- Make assessment a shared enterprise. Doing so will invite perspectives and expertise from colleagues, widen the circle of individuals and campus units invested in study abroad, and make the assessment both more achievable and enjoyable.
- Finally, subsets of student products (e.g., essays, posters, presentations) can be mined to discover what students are learning. It is not imperative to analyze a product from every student.

References

Ash, S. L., Clayton, P. H., & Atkinson, M. P. (2005). Integrating reflection and assessment to capture and improve student learning. *Michigan Journal of Community Service Learning, 11*(2), 49–60.

Association of American Colleges and Universities. (2010). *VALUE rubrics.* Retrieved from www.aacu.org/value/rubrics/index_p.cfm?CFID=6634177&CFTOKEN=40351583

Beloit College. (n.d.). *Guide to the Beloit College institutional research records 1956–2000* (AC 67). Beloit College Archives.

Brewer, E., & Cunningham, K. (Eds.). (2009). *Integrating study abroad into the curriculum: Theory and practice across the disciplines.* Sterling, VA: Stylus.

Carnegie Mellon Eberly Center for Teaching Excellence. (n.d.). *What is the difference between assessment and grading?* Retrieved from www.cmu.edu/teaching/assessment/basics/grading-assessment.html

Earl, L. M. (2003). *Assessment as learning: Using classroom assessment to maximize student learning.* Thousand Oaks, CA: Corwin.

Engle, L. (2012). The rewards of qualitative assessment appropriate to study abroad. *Frontiers: Interdisciplinary Journal of Study Abroad, XXII.* Retrieved from www.frontiersjournal.com/frontiersxxiiwinter2012spring2013.htm

Fass, M. (2008, July 31). *Missions and majors: An assessment project funded by the Teagle Foundation; Beloit, Knox, Monmouth and Ripon colleges* (2nd annual report). Retrieved June 11, 2014, from http://bioquest.org/teagle/Missions-and-Majors-08-01-08.pdf

Fink, L. D. (2003). *Creating significant learning experiences: An integrated approach to designing college courses.* San Francisco, CA: Jossey-Bass.

Garretson, H., & Golson, E. (2005). Synopsis of the use of course-embedded assessment in a medium sized public university's general education program. *Journal of General Education, 4*(2), 139–149.

Griffin, M. (2009). What is a rubric? *Assessment Update: Progress, Trends, and Practices in Higher Education, 21*(6). Reprinted in Rhodes, T. (2010). *Assessing outcomes and improving achievement: Tips and tools for using rubrics.* Washington, DC: Association of American Colleges and Universities. Retrieved from http://apir.wisc.edu/assessment/What_is_a_Rubric%28Griffin2010%29.pdf

Kaplan, M., Silver, N., LaVaque-Manty, D., & Meizlish, D. (2013). *Using reflection and metacognition to improve student learning: Across the disciplines, across the academy.* Sterling, VA: Stylus.

Langer, G. M., & Colton, A. B. (2005). Looking at student work. *Educational Leadership, 62*(5), 22–26.

Murphy, P., & Hall, K. (2008). *Learning and practice: Agency and identities.* Thousand Oaks, CA: Sage.

Schraw, G. (1998). Promoting general metacognitive awareness. *Instructional Science, 26*, 113–125.

Twombly, S., Salisbury, M., Tumanut, S., & Klute, P. (2012). *Study abroad in a new global century: Renewing the promise, refining the purpose* (ASHE Higher Education Report). Hoboken, NJ: Wiley.

Vande Berg, M. (2007). Intervening in the learning of U.S. students abroad. *Journal of Studies in International Education, 11*(3–4), 392–399.

Vande Berg, M., Paige, R. M., & Connor-Linton, J. (2009, Fall). The Georgetown Consortium project: Interventions for student learning abroad. *Frontiers: Interdisciplinary Journal of Study Abroad, 18*, 1–75.

8

ADAPTING THE OFFICE MISSION AND ASSESSMENT PRACTICES TO INSTITUTIONAL NEEDS

Nick Gozik

R egardless of where we work, many of us have the tendency to work diligently on perfecting a mission statement and goals, only to leave both to collect dust, either figuratively or quite literally in a framed picture on the wall. Why do we do this? In some cases, we are instructed by those at the top or an external accrediting body to engage in assessment efforts, so there is little choice but to comply. At other times, an organization may feel that a mission and goals are simply required, along with a potted ficus in the lobby and water cooler in the break room. However, in such scenarios little thought may be given to the ways in which a mission and goals, along with other aspects of a fully formed assessment plan, can play a vital and enduring role in an organization's activities.

By taking the example of the Global Education Office for Undergraduates (GEO-U) at Duke University, I argue that assessment efforts must evolve in tandem with an organization's needs. This is all the more essential within the field of international education, which has grown at an exponential rate over the past several decades, in terms of both the overall number of activities and the complexity and variety of program offerings. An assessment plan written 5 or 10 years ago may have little to do with the programs and services offered by an education abroad office today.

Here we trace the evolution of assessment efforts in Duke's GEO-U, which can be divided roughly into three stages: the development of an initial assessment plan, drafted as part of the university's reaccreditation process; the creation of a more fully formed plan, along with other assessment activities; and a critical review and rearticulation of the office's assessment efforts based on the expansion of international activities on campus. Although this chapter focuses primarily on one office's activities, the types of questions and concerns raised throughout are common for many institutions.

About the University

Duke University traces its roots to 1838 with the establishment of Trinity College, located in Randolph County, North Carolina. In 1892, the college moved to Durham through the financing of its primary benefactor, tobacco and electric power industrialist Benjamin Newton Duke. In 1924, James B. Duke, Benjamin's brother, created the Duke Endowment, a philanthropic foundation that allowed for the expansion of Trinity College into Duke University, named in honor of Washington Duke, the brothers' deceased father. For many years Duke remained largely a regional university, drawing students from North Carolina and nearby states. Within the past several decades, the university has gained greater prestige, ultimately becoming a national research institution. Within the university, undergraduate students are enrolled in the Trinity College of Arts and Sciences (from this point forward, "Trinity College" refers to the Trinity College of Arts and Sciences, not the former name of the university) and the Pratt School of Engineering.

International initiatives have played a key role in Duke's surge to the top. Today, between 45% and 50% of Duke's approximately 6,500 undergraduates study abroad at some point, with the greater percentage going abroad during the academic year. The GEO-U offers 13 semester and academic year abroad programs and around 20 summer abroad programs each year, and it also permits students to study in more than 150 approved non-Duke programs. In addition to study abroad, the university has developed international programs within areas such as global health, business, and public policy. The recent construction of Duke Kunshan University, located outside of Shanghai, as well as the establishment of centers around the world by the Fuqua School of Business, exemplifies this outward reach.

Although Duke has touted certain successes (e.g., a robust study abroad program, the existence of a senior international officer, and a healthy number of international students), such activities have not always been woven together within what Green and Shoenberg (2006) called a "comprehensive internationalization approach." In 2009, the reaccreditation of Duke through the Southern Association of Colleges and Schools (SACS) provided an opportunity for the university to review its internationalization strategy and determine ways of better integrating international programming into the curricula. As part of the reaccreditation process, Duke developed a quality enhancement plan (QEP), titled "Global Duke: Enhancing Students' Capacity for World Citizenship," which outlined three new projects designed to help students become more globally competent: the Winter Forum, the Global Semester Abroad, and the Global Advising Program.

Duke was also obligated to provide SACS reviewers with a blueprint for assessing academic programs and activities across the university, at both the undergraduate and the graduate levels. The provost's office oversaw an effort to collect assessment plans and activities and developed two committees to track the progress of individual schools, departments, and offices. As an academic unit within the Trinity College of Arts and Sciences, the study abroad office was required to develop an assessment plan, as we will see next.

Phase I: Responding to SACS

By the time of writing its first assessment plan, the GEO-U, then called the Office of Study Abroad (OSA), had long engaged in various forms of assessment. Most notable were the postprogram evaluations, which were regularly collected and housed in the office's resource room. Largely to gauge student satisfaction, staff members consulted the evaluations to make improvements to Duke-administered programs, monitor non-Duke programs, and advise students. Prospective study abroad students were likewise encouraged to read the evaluations for firsthand accounts about the programs that they were considering. The office had also engaged in program reviews to evaluate academics, health and safety, housing, activities, and staffing needs. Semester program reviews were carried out by external reviewers, composed of two faculty members and one administrator, who conducted two- to three-day site visits. Reviews were conducted on a 10-year cycle, with approximately two reviews per year. Summer reviews were held less formally, usually by one staff member from the OSA.

Although the office had been collecting data, there was no overall assessment strategy or assessment plan. It was in spring 2008 that the respective directors of the OSA and the Trinity College Office of Assessment created the first actual plan. Scheduled to commence in the fall of the same year, the plan outlined four general learning outcomes: "Study abroad [will increase] inter-cultural understanding; study abroad [will develop] language and/or inter-cultural communication skills and provide language development opportunities appropriate to the mission of the OSA; study abroad [will develop] students' tolerance for ambiguity, problem-solving skills and empathy; and study abroad [will complement] discipline specific learning outcomes appropriate to departmental/certificate programs curriculum" (Duke University Office of Study Abroad, 2008).

For each of these outcomes, the OSA and assessment office directors selected three to four assessment tools or general methods (see table 8.1). Wisely, each tool was listed as part of the first, second, or third wave of implementation so that OSA staff members could begin with simpler tasks, or "low-hanging fruit," and then move on to more complicated ones. Within the first outcome related to intercultural understanding, for example, the OSA would begin by mining already existing data from Cooperative Institutional Research Program and Consortium on Financing Higher Education surveys, as well as study abroad postprogram evaluations. Because these data were already accessible, the emphasis was on analysis, not on collection. In a second wave, it was expected that a new instrument would be used to gauge students' progress before, during, and after the study abroad experience. As can be seen, not all tools were selected at the time of the plan's creation, particularly those in stages II and III. Time was built into the proposed implementation, with the understanding that it was necessary to do due diligence before investing significant resources.

Phase II: Taking Ownership of Assessment

This initial assessment plan marked a significant achievement for the OSA. For the first time, the OSA had articulated clear learning outcomes that were linked to specific tools for tracking students' progress. The top-down approach resulting from SACS reaccreditation equally had drawn attention to the necessity of assessing programs and activities. However, it would take a further step for an office like the OSA to embrace the process fully and for the outcomes to be linked more directly to Duke's mission. Here it was up to individuals to move the ball forward. In fall 2008, all of the pieces came together within the OSA with the formation of a working group. This group was able to take stock of the initial assessment plan, solicit input from experts, and develop a more detailed plan that would best serve the needs of the office and broader university community, as will be explored next.

Assessment Working Group

Three OSA staff members were selected to form the first assessment working group (AWG). Rather than creating a "committee," which suggested that the team would meet in perpetuity, the working group was intended to be more flexible, with the primary objective of reevaluating and implementing the assessment plan. The working group has, in fact, not since disbanded, given that it continues to be challenged with new assessment needs. The group

TABLE 8.1

Goals, Measurements, and Phases

Goal	Measurements	Phase
Goal 1: Increase intercultural understanding	Cooperative Institutional Research Program and Consortium on Financing Higher Education first-year survey, senior survey, alumni survey	I
	Predeparture survey and program evaluation	I
	Intercultural assessment tool (e.g., Intercultural Development Inventory, Global Perspective Inventory)	II
Goal 2: Develop language and/or intercultural communication skills and provide language development opportunities appropriate to the mission of the Office of Study Abroad	Pre- and postlanguage test (where appropriate)	I
	Method for tracking individual success in content courses taught in foreign language abroad	II
Goal 3: Develop tolerance for ambiguity, problem-solving skills, and empathy	Cooperative Institutional Research Program and Consortium on Financing Higher Education first-year survey, senior survey, alumni survey	I
	Predeparture survey and program evaluation results	I
	Capstone essay required of all students before release of grades	III
Goal 4: Complement discipline-specific learning outcomes appropriate to departmental and certificate programs curriculum	Mechanism for demonstrating successful completion of courses abroad in major disciplines that are used to satisfy Duke graduation requirements	II
	Mechanism for tracking involvement of students who have studied abroad in these various programs and whether students' departmental-related research projects (i.e., honors thesis, graduation with distinction projects, independent study projects, etc.) relate to their study abroad experience	III

was initially composed of an associate director and an assistant director, both with research degrees and expertise in quantitative and qualitative methods, and a computer operations manager, who was able to provide statistical and technical assistance. With personnel changes, the composition of the AWG has since evolved over time and now includes four staff members with different skill sets and experiences.

The AWG continues to meet on average once per month, finding that it is necessary to assemble, even if much has not been completed during peak work periods, so as to maintain a momentum on projects. The AWG chair sets a simple agenda, and notes are taken at each meeting, which help to keep the group on track. In addition to the primary members, the AWG frequently invites on-campus experts to offer assistance on various activities. In the revision of the office's assessment plan, team members were fortunate to be able to consult with a nationally recognized intercultural trainer and researcher, as well as the director of Trinity College's Office of Assessment.

Reviewing the Assessment Plan

The first task of the newly created AWG was to review the assessment plan that had been developed as part of the QEP. After careful analysis, group members concluded that the plan had made significant headway in identifying several key learning outcomes and appreciated the fact that it was intended to be rolled out in phases, so that there would be realistic expectations as to when newer and more intensive projects would be implemented. At the same time, it was agreed that the plan would benefit from a more clearly established link between the GEO-U's learning outcomes and the university's overall mission and goals. Likewise, it would help to have greater detail in how the outcomes would be measured, and data resulting from the assessments would be relayed to key stakeholders.

Environmental Scan

The AWG began with an environmental scan of Duke's website and other sources to gain a sense of the university's mission and strategic plan, both stated and implied through the directives of senior-level administrators. Within a much longer statement found on the university website, which was first developed in 1994 and revised in 2001, the following was of particular relevance to the GEO-U's activities:

> The mission of Duke University is to provide a superior liberal education to undergraduate students, attending not only to their intellectual growth

but also to their development as adults committed to high ethical standards and full participation as leaders in their communities. (Duke University Board of Trustees, n.d.)

One word that stood out here and throughout the rest of the mission was *leaders*. As Duke is a highly selective institution, which aims to cultivate graduates who will go out into the world and assume top positions in a range of sectors, it was not surprising that leadership was featured so prominently. Furthermore, a search on the same website for *leader* yielded approximately 48,800 results. Although search engines are imprecise instruments for gauging an institution's commitment to any one goal, the sheer repetition of this term highlighted its salience on campus.

Despite such ubiquity, the AWG found it challenging to consider how *leadership* might be defined and assessed within the context of education abroad and in turn how such activities might promote better leaders (Earnest, 2003; Ricketts & Morgan, 2009). The idea of training leaders—at least in the traditional way of mentoring students to take on roles in student government, sports, clubs, and classroom activities—was perhaps even incongruous with the fundamental objective of encouraging students to immerse fully in host cultures. Yes, students were encouraged to get involved in organizations while abroad as a way of befriending locals and practicing foreign language skills as applicable. However, students who were most successful in immersion were often best at playing a less conspicuous role than they might at home (i.e., blending into their surroundings, engaging more thoughtfully with the host community). As a result, the AWG concluded that other characteristics of being a good leader were more applicable to students' experiences abroad, including developing *a sense of independence, adaptability,* and *an ability to think critically.*

The other key phrase of "high ethical standards" was easier to incorporate, for it related to a broader desire to encourage students to be more aware of their impact on others, including those in other cultures. The focus on ethics dovetailed with new initiatives at the time, including the creation of DukeEngage, cofunded by the Duke Endowment and Bill and Melinda Gates Foundation. With a focus on civic engagement, this high-profile program was established "to empower students to address critical human needs through immersive service . . . and provid[e] meaningful assistance to communities in the U.S. and abroad" (DukeEngage, n.d.). The GEO-U had been offering service-learning opportunities on study abroad programs for quite some time, including on the Duke in the Andes program in Ecuador, and so it was easy to consider ethical and social responsibility within this context. For other programs without service-learning, the connection to ethics and social responsibility was thinner;

instead, it was concluded that the GEO-U's program could more directly help students gain a general *awareness of and respect for cultural differences*, in preparation for students to appreciate their impact on others.

A final key concept that was not highlighted in the university's mission statement, yet implied by the very nature of the type of institution, was that of research. Classified by the Carnegie Foundation for the Advancement of Teaching as a research university with very high research activity, previously referred to as a "Research I" university (McCormick & Zhao, 2005), Duke's charge largely rests on producing new knowledge and training scholars, primarily at the graduate level though also increasingly among undergraduates. Here too it was possible to look to existing GEO-U programs like Duke/Organization for Tropical Studies, which provides opportunities for students to engage in hands-on fieldwork in Costa Rica and South Africa. For programs without a research component, students could seek funding through the Undergraduate Research Support Office to engage in research upon returning from study abroad. For the GEO-U assessment plan, it was determined that it was fruitful to gauge the extent to which students were gaining *disciplinary* and *analytical skills* abroad, which would eventually prepare them for research activities.

Resources in the Field

In addition to the environmental scan, the AWG investigated assessment plans at other institutions for inspiration and to ensure that any revisions to the GEO-U's plan were in line with best practices on other campuses. At the time, few education abroad offices had fully developed plans, much less stated learning outcomes on their website or in written materials. Even so, there were few examples from which to draw, particularly within the field of education abroad.

One of the most helpful resources was a page on the American Council on Education (ACE) website titled "Statements of International Learning Outcomes," which featured learning outcomes from the internationalization plans of a variety of colleges and universities. The ACE's resources have since been expanded into a much more comprehensive site called the "Internationalization Toolkit," which comprises examples from a wider variety of institutions—including Duke—and a more robust selection of projects (American Council on Education, n.d.). Then, as now, the AWG recognized that Duke was unique in many respects and that the GEO-U could not simply adopt another institution's learning outcomes without modification. Group members nonetheless discovered quite a few overlapping themes within the plans outlined on the ACE website, many of which were relevant to Duke's needs.

The AWG also consulted the GLOSSARI project, which was conducted within the University of Georgia system. The first phase of that project focused on a comparison of study abroad participants and nonparticipants, measured through a large-scale survey of students across the 16 University of Georgia campuses and summarized in a report by Sutton and Rubin (2004). Although the scale of this project was unlike anything that could have been attempted by one institution alone, the content domains outlined served as useful examples. It was likewise helpful to see how the outcomes were actually measured through a quantitative survey.

More general resources included *A Guide to Outcomes Assessment in Education Abroad* (Bolen, 2007) and *The SAGE Handbook of Intercultural Competence* (Deardorff, 2009). These works reminded the AWG that the assessment plan needed to be holistic, so that all of its parts—from mission to learning outcomes to tools to the distribution of results—were aligned as part of an assessment cycle. Group members likewise recognized that assessment is not always straightforward "in the trenches," making it necessary to adapt theory to practice. Most notably, the AWG needed to account for limitations of time, expertise, and funding. And, as previously mentioned, it was also necessary to allow for an ever-changing institutional context, requiring that the assessment plan be revised on a routine basis.

Office Mission

Having conducted an environmental scan and research on other plans, the AWG was ready to direct its attention toward GEO-U's mission statement, which had recently been revised. The committee felt that the mission itself did not need to be tweaked and that it was broad enough to capture the primary objectives of the office. One question did arise over the references to "international" and "internationalization." Some argued that "global" rather than "international" was more appropriate—a shift in terminology that was also reflected in the office's name change from the Office of Study Abroad to the Global Education Office for Undergraduates.

The name had been altered when the office took over the management of Duke's domestic programs in Los Angeles, New York City, and Washington, DC, and thus was no longer responsible solely for study abroad. In this discussion, it was determined that *global* was a better fit than *international* in the office title because the former seemed to more easily embrace activities at home and abroad. For the mission statement, the substitution from *internationalization* to *globalization* did not work as neatly, given that the latter had a very different connotation—one that was rooted in greater economic, political, and societal forces rather than the sorts of "international" or "global" initiatives that might take place on a university campus (Altbach & Knight, 2007). In the end, the mission statement was mostly left intact.

Goals and Learning Outcomes

The AWG found that some institutions merge learning goals and outcomes. Group members determined that it was preferable to maintain a distinction between the two to ensure sufficient nuance to the plan. Goals were intended to provide broad direction, whereas learning outcomes were designed to gauge a more specific set of anticipated student gains. Outcomes were also to be measureable; they could be linked to actual assessment tools and were consequently far more concrete than goals.

After much deliberation, the group settled on four goals: global perspectives, cross-cultural adjustment, language development (for participants in non-English-speaking countries), and student learning outcomes related to departmental and certificate programs and general graduation goals (see table 8.2). Many more goals were considered, but group members opted to keep the list succinct; taking a more ambitious route would have simply overwhelmed all involved, perhaps leading to nothing being accomplished.

Global perspectives. For the first goal, some consideration was given to the idea of employing the catchphrase "global citizenship." There were nonetheless concerns about the ambiguity of this phrase because of its overuse and frequent lack of definition. The AWG preferred the notion of global perspectives—often considered one aspect of global citizenship—with the objective of having students "connect the dots of [their] contemporary world, with attention to the global as well as the local" (Adams & Carfagna, 2006, p. 12). Admittedly, students can "connect the dots" on their home campus, given their access to media and the fact that connections can take place anywhere and at any time. It was posited that this process may be accelerated during study abroad.

The goal of understanding global perspectives was parsed out into three outcomes: the ability to identify varying cultural viewpoints, the ability to demonstrate the recognition of cultural differences, and the ability to communicate effectively and appropriately from the host culture's viewpoint, both verbally and nonverbally. The first two were accepted as more passive in that they expected students to learn how to recognize and articulate others' perspectives and cultural nuances, such as through a paper or journal entry written on the subject. With the third outcome, students needed to actively demonstrate their ability to communicate across cultural lines. This might entail, simply enough, respecting cultural cues like knowing how to greet someone (e.g., one kiss on each cheek or a handshake). On a deeper level, students would learn to navigate the intricacies of establishing meaningful relationships in the host culture.

Cross-cultural adjustment. The second goal was related to the first, yet it focused more specifically on students' ability to adapt to new environments. Referenced frequently in the literature on expatriates, *cross-cultural*

TABLE 8.2

Goals and Learning Outcomes

Goal	Learning Outcomes	Assessment Tools	Recipients of Data
Global perspectives	Students will be able to identify varying cultural viewpoints.	Self-reported on postprogram survey Writing sample Global Perspective Inventory (GPI) or other tool Senior survey, Part A, #5	Program directors and administrators Assessment office Publications and marketing as appropriate
	Students will be able to demonstrate recognition of cultural differences.	Self-reported on postprogram survey Writing sample GPI Senior survey, Part A, #5 Photos	Program directors and administrators Assessment office Publications and marketing as appropriate
	Students will learn to communicate effectively and appropriately from the host culture's viewpoint, both verbally and nonverbally.	Self-reported on postprogram survey GPI Senior survey, Part A, #5 Writing sample Observation by program director and staff	Program directors and administrators Assessment office Publications and marketing as appropriate
Cross-cultural adjustment	Students will show increased ability to empathize with people from different cultures and perspectives.	Self-reported on postprogram survey GPI Writing sample	Program directors and administrators Assessment office Publications and marketing as appropriate
	Students will show increased ability to tolerate ambiguity.	Self-reported on postprogram survey GPI or other tool Writing sample	Program directors and administrators Assessment office Publications and marketing as appropriate
	Students will develop critical thinking skills and be able to apply them when encountering unfamiliar environments.	Capstone essay GPI or other tool Self-reported on postprogram survey	Program directors and administrators Assessment office Publications and marketing as appropriate

Language development (for participants in non-English-speaking countries; varies by type of program)	Students will demonstrate an ability to carry out daily tasks in the host country language (all programs in non-English-speaking host countries).	Successful completion of at least one language course in host country language Pre- and postprogram language testing in certain programs Self-reported on postprogram survey Senior survey, Part A, #5	Appropriate academic departments Academic deans Program directors and administrators Assessment office Publications and marketing as appropriate
	Students will demonstrate advanced proficiency in the host language, such as the ability to complete content courses in the host language and to communicate complex ideas (immersion programs in non-English-speaking countries).	Successful completion of content courses in host country language Pre- and postprogram language testing in certain programs Self-reported on postprogram survey Senior survey, Part A, #5	Appropriate academic departments Academic deans Program directors and administrators Assessment office Publications and marketing as appropriate
Student learning outcomes related to departmental and certificate programs and general graduation goals	Students will gain knowledge that can be applied to major, minor, and certificate requirements.	Auditing of credits from off-campus programs Self-reported on postprogram survey	Appropriate academic departments Academic deans Program directors and administrators Assessment office Publications and marketing as appropriate
	Students will gain knowledge that will contribute to students' general education requirements as defined in Duke University's undergraduate curriculum.	Auditing of course codes, including areas of knowledge and modes of inquiry for Trinity students and modes of inquiry for engineering students Self-reported on postprogram survey	Appropriate academic departments Academic deans Program directors and administrators Assessment office Publications and marketing as appropriate

adjustment is often defined simply as "the degree of psychological comfort and familiarity that the individual has for the new environment" (Black, as cited in Takeuchi, Yun, & Tesluk, 2002, p. 655). For the AWG's purposes, this definition was expanded to include three primary components, which were also expressed as learning outcomes: the ability to empathize with people from different cultures and perspectives, the ability to tolerate ambiguity, and the development of critical thinking skills and ability to apply them when encountering unfamiliar environments. All of these outcomes might be difficult to observe externally; students often best expressed them through verbal and written communication.

Language development. Of all of the outcomes, the third goal, *language development,* was the easiest to define. This goal was not relevant to all students, particularly those studying in a country or program where English or another of the student's native language was the host language. Students also went into their abroad experience with different levels of language skills. It was expected that students studying in a language immersion program, who had the requisite speaking and writing skills, would begin at a higher level and develop their proficiency. They would need to demonstrate the ability to successfully complete content courses and express complex ideas in the host country language. For students in nonimmersion programs, and who were usually taking a beginning- or intermediate-level skills course, the expectations were more modest: They were expected to carry out daily tasks in the local language.

It would have been ideal to find one instrument that could be used across all programs and languages, allowing for comparative analysis; however, there was little consensus among language instructors, even within any given language section, as to which tool might serve such a purpose. Instead, the AWG allowed each Duke program director to determine his or her own method for measuring language gains. Students studying on non-Duke programs would be measured by the third-party provider when possible. In addition, all students, on both Duke and non-Duke programs, were asked to report on their own development through the pre- and postprogram evaluations. Here, biases needed to be considered, as students frequently under- or overevaluated their own skills. In analyzing evaluations, for instance, there was a bit of alarm when some students rated their skills lower following their time abroad. In fact, although some students' language skills may have declined, students typically became increasingly critical of their proficiency, having learned more about their needed areas of improvement.

Student learning outcomes. The fourth and final goal was for students to gain disciplinary knowledge that would contribute to major, minor, certificate, or general graduation objectives. This goal fit into a broader curriculum integration project, which sought to correct the common misperception of study abroad being viewed as "time off" or a "vacation" from academic work on campus. Students were to be reminded that study abroad is an integral component of their undergraduate academic career, which in the case of semester and academic year programs is equal to one eighth or one quarter of their time at Duke, respectively.

One of the easiest ways to evaluate students' progress was to track the types of courses that they took abroad. Calculating how many students took at least one course in their major, for example, would provide a sense of whether students were continuing to meet curricular requirements. Of course, this method alone could not indicate whether students were integrating what they learned abroad into their major studies, and so it was also necessary to enlist the assistance of faculty in the home department. It was anticipated that faculty could gauge the extent to which students had developed along disciplinary lines, as well as their ability to incorporate case studies and examples from abroad within class discussions and projects. This part of the plan has remained the least scripted without common methods or measurements across departments and thus presents an area for further development.

Finalizing and Implementing the Plan

The revised assessment plan took a year and a half to develop. This may seem quite long, yet members of the AWG considered the time worthwhile, as it was necessary to gain feedback from key stakeholders and experts. Group members presented various versions at an Atlantic Assessment Conference, as well as a conference sponsored by NAFSA: Association of International Educators. In addition, roundtable discussions were held on campus. Others in the new GEO-U offered additional input. The AWG recognized that although the plan was not flawless, it offered a comprehensive strategy for moving forward. In actually implementing the plan, the AWG would find out that it was necessary to continually update the plan based on logistics, resources, and changes in leadership, as will be explored next.

Phase III: Adapting the Plan and Reaching Out to Others

Beginning in spring 2013, new initiatives throughout Duke have required the GEO-U to further review and recalibrate its assessment plan to stay current with and relevant to other priorities on campus. Although discussions are ongoing, the movement toward a more collaborative approach among international units around assessment is exciting and worth noting. The dialogue has been driven largely by the directors of academic engagement for global and civic opportunities (DAEs), initially known as the global advisors, whose positions were created as part the university's QEP and thus linked to the reaccreditation process. These directors are housed within the Academic Advising Center and have no reporting line to the GEO-U or any other global unit, which permits them to talk objectively to students about opportunities on campus and abroad. Rather than seeing any one experience as a stand-alone event, the goal has been for "students to imagine and plot their global and civic engagement at Duke as a four-year journey in which curricular, cocurricular and away-from-Duke experiences complement each other in enhancing students' capacities to reflect and engage in global learning" (Duke University Undergraduate Global Advising, n.d.).

In setting up the program, the DAEs met with a large number of units across campus, which allowed them to catalog the vast array of international and domestic offerings available at Duke. Working with the Office of Institutional Research and the provost's office, they subsequently sought to chart the ways in which students were engaging in multiple activities (e.g., study abroad *and* DukeEngage), leading to a deeper and more complex understanding of students' decision-making processes. To present the results, the DAE's hosted an off-campus retreat in 2013.

In addition to discussing the assembled data, representatives from the various global units at Duke used the retreat to consider possible areas for collaboration. They agreed to establish working groups around five topics that cut across multiple units and were deemed most pressing: ways of engaging in multiprogram assessments, reentry programming from immersive experiences, an examination of the cohort of students who combined study abroad and DukeEngage, methods for encouraging local opportunities for global engagement, and an examination of the "nones" or students that were not engaged in any sort of global programming. It has since been recognized that the latter is challenging in that many of the "nones" are difficult to track and less willing to participate in assessment activities.

The recent discussions and working group efforts are notable for many reasons, not the least of which is that all has been done on a grassroots level. Senior-level administrators have been kept in the loop and have provided encouragement, yet they have not orchestrated the latest collaborations between international units around assessment. Instead individuals have opted to work together to better serve their students, many of whom engage with more than one of the offices. It can be argued that earlier efforts to encourage global programming and assessment are paying off, particularly through accreditation, so that campus leaders can now step back and allow those on the ground to move forward without direct oversight. As Matt Serra, director of the Office of Assessment in Duke's Trinity College of Arts and Sciences, noted, recent efforts at Duke are a great example of the need of external motivators to play a larger role initially and then take somewhat of a backseat to internal motivators as the process matures (personal communication, December 12, 2013).

Recent efforts also represent a shift for the GEO-U. Although study abroad still represents the most common international activity for undergraduates, the proliferation of international or global units in recent years means the learning outcomes from study abroad need to dovetail with those in other programs. The GEO-U is waiting to see where the dust falls, though it is clear that its assessment plan will need to be further adapted to align with the activities of other units on campus. Serra noted that all of this is a sign of a good assessment plan; it is necessary for formative assessment to loop back and allow for adaptation.

Lessons Learned and Concluding Thoughts

The case of Duke provides a view from the trenches of an education abroad office. Rather than a pristine, pretty process, we have seen how the creation of an assessment plan involves much trial and error. The Duke example demonstrates the need for all involved to remain open to change, with an understanding that an effective assessment strategy must be revised frequently to ensure that it reflects the office's current mission and needs. Here, I conclude with a few lessons learned, which may aid others beginning the assessment process. Although Duke is a large university with a great deal of resources, the following ideas and suggestions can scale well to organizations of many different sizes and types.

Develop a Team

Regardless of the size of the office, it is critical to form some sort of assessment team, which will ideally include both members from the office and outsiders, such as assessment experts and faculty with relevant skills and knowledge. At Duke, the director of the Office of Assessment was involved from the start and provided much needed support. In the second phase, participation was expanded to include other members of the office, who formed an assessment working group, as well as others on campus. The development of this group allowed the office to fine-tune and expedite the implementation of the assessment plan.

Consider Reasons for Assessing

It is necessary to determine why one is assessing and what will be gained from the effort. In the Duke case, the office began by responding to an outside demand: Staff members were following top-down measures designed to meet accreditation requirements. After the initial plan was developed, it was easier to determine what types of data would truly aid the office in measuring student outcomes. Team members ultimately had to ask, "What do we want to know, and what is the best way of finding out what we want to know?" By considering the end goals, the team found it possible to work backward to outline an effective strategy. Generally speaking, it is necessary to have a mix of external and internal motivation factors; the blend of each will shift as the team moves forward with the process.

Do Not Seek Perfection

Throughout all three stages, there was a potential pitfall in wanting to spend an indefinite amount of time perfecting the assessment plan. It does, in fact, take time to develop a well-thought-out plan, and the preparation is well worth the investment. At a certain point, however, the AWG recognized that the plan was good enough, if not ideal, and that the group was ready to begin assessing.

Adapt, Adapt, and Adapt Some More

The most important takeaway was the recognition that an assessment plan is a living document that needs to be revised on a regular basis. Even as the AWG sought to hone its plan, the office itself was changing around it. With the transition to a new office name and slightly adapted office mission—prompted by the addition of domestic programming, new leadership and reporting lines, and adjustments in office personnel and hierarchy—team members were required to remain nimble in their approach to assessment. It is impossible to ever imagine a moment when change will not be occurring. The goal, then, is to continually scrutinize and adapt the plan, realizing that it will never be totally optimal yet always optimized.

References

Adams, J. M., & Carfagna, A. (2006). *Coming of age in a globalized world*. West Hartford, CT: Kumarian Press.

Altbach, P. G., & Knight, J. (2007). The internationalization of higher education: Motivations and realities. *Journal of Studies in International Education, 11*, 290–305.

American Council on Education. (n.d.). *The internationalization toolkit*. Retrieved from www.acenet.edu/news-room/Pages/Internationalization-Toolkit .aspx#curriculum

Bolen, M. (Ed.). (2007). *A guide to outcomes assessment in education abroad.* Carlisle, PA: Forum on Education Abroad.

Deardorff, D. (Ed.). (2009). *The SAGE handbook of intercultural competence.* Thousand Oaks, CA: Sage.

Duke University Board of Trustees. (n.d.). *Mission statement.* Retrieved from http://trustees.duke.edu/governing/mission.php

Duke University Office of Study Abroad. (2008). *Assessment plan.* Unpublished internal document.

Duke University Undergraduate Global Advising. (n.d.). *Mission and values.* Retrieved from http://globaladvising.duke.edu/who/mission

DukeEngage. (n.d.). *About DukeEngage.* Retrieved from http://dukeengage.duke.edu/about-dukeengage

Earnest, G. (2003). Study abroad: A powerful new approach for developing leadership capacities. *Journal of Leadership Education, 2*(2), 46–56.

Green, M. F., & Shoenberg, R. (2006). *Where faculty live: Internationalizing the disciplines.* Washington, DC: American Council on Education.

McCormick, A. C., & Zhao, C. (2005). Rethinking and reframing the Carnegie Classification. *Change, 37*(5), 50–57.

Ricketts, K., & Morgan, C. (2009). Internationalizing leadership development: Important components within educational international leadership experiences. *Journal of International Agricultural and Extension Education, 16*(2), 21–34.

Sutton, R. C., & Rubin, D. (2004). The GLOSSARI project: Initial findings from a system-wide research initiative on study abroad learning outcomes. *Frontiers, X,* 65–82. Retrieved from www.frontiersjournal.com/issues/vol10/vol10-04_SuttonRubin.pdf

Takeuchi, R., Yun, S., & Tesluk, P. (2002). An examination of crossover and spillover effects of spousal and expatriate cross-cultural adjustment on expatriate outcomes. *Journal of Applied Psychology, 87*(4), 655–666.

9

INTEGRATED ASSESSMENT STRATEGIES

Linking Study Abroad Outcomes to the Liberal Arts Core Curriculum

Dennis M. Doyle

Colleges and universities in the United States increasingly view global learning as essential to undergraduate education; they are developing initiatives to integrate curricula featuring a global perspective. Global learning has long been the emphasis of study abroad programming, so study abroad practitioners are now assuming prominent advisory roles in institutional curriculum reviews. As Braskamp and Engberg (2011) explained, global learning involves a type of perspective-taking whereby one develops the "disposition and capacity to think with complexity" regarding multiple worldviews, while forming a unique sense of self that is value based and authentic and also relating to others—especially those unlike oneself—with openness and respect. Situating study abroad within a core curriculum requires close attention to exactly how study abroad aligns with the broader institutional goals and mission. Brewer and Cunningham (2009) argued that the goals of study abroad must be placed in dialogue with campus-wide learning goals for students. Furthermore, institutions should enable all students, faculty, and staff to be internationally engaged at one or more points by developing "a conceptually integrated systems approach to international education that encompasses the entire university" (NAFSA, 2008). Vande Berg, Paige, and Lou (2013) also emphasized that an integrated approach to global learning expands the role and significance of a study abroad experience within a student's journey through college. They argued, "The primary goal of learning abroad is not, then, simply to acquire knowledge but to develop in ways that allow students to learn to shift cultural perspective and to adapt their behavior to other cultural contexts—knowledge that will allow them to interact more effectively and appropriately with others throughout their lives" (p. 18).

Central College recently completed a self-study and core curriculum review that further exemplifies this trend in higher education. The goal was to learn how the mission of the college and general education goals for students might be more fully integrated within the core curriculum and its learning objectives. The self-study reaffirmed Central's educational priority to create "an international community of global learners . . . in which the demarcations between the campus, the community, and the world become more porous as learning extends across boundaries of culture, language, and nations" (Central College, 2012, pp. 4–5). Seven integrated goals for students were developed, with four specific learning outcomes for each goal identified as focal points for each year of student development. One of the integrated goals, for example, calls for students "to develop competencies for responsible global citizenship," with a specific outcome for second-year students to "seek opportunities to interact with persons with differing world views" (Central College, 2013–2014). The institutional self-study also brought to the foreground the importance of aligning assessment strategies across all parts of the general education curriculum to monitor student progress toward the integrated learning goals.

In this case study, I report why and how Central College developed an assessment plan to gauge the educational impact of a newly created global perspective requirement within the core curriculum. Creating such a plan required significant cooperation and collaboration from offices and stakeholders across campus, as the plan must serve the needs of study abroad programming and the institution's general education curriculum. Braskamp and Engberg (2011) observed that today's students live in "a pluralistic and global society, where multiple worldviews, and salient traditions have a lasting influence on how we think, feel, and relate to others" (p. 34). Study abroad educators fully understand that assessing student growth in global learning is an increasingly complex endeavor and that how this assessment is conducted and what the assessment finds may significantly affect students' overall education.

I present here the journey Central College has traveled thus far to accomplish a task put forward during the self-examination to "identify the learning outcomes sought for global experiential education, and take steps to assure that both study abroad and the core curriculum support these global learning outcomes" (Central College, 2012, p. 6). First, I provide some historical context to Central's current culture of integrated assessment. Second, I outline recent curricular decisions regarding the core requirement that link student learning goals specific to Central College's study abroad programs with the general education core curriculum. Third, I identify the steps the college has taken thus far to strategically integrate these assessment strategies. Fourth, I reflect on what we are learning and present next steps in the assessment process.

Assessment Context and Culture

Central is a residential liberal arts college dedicated to undergraduate education of approximately 1,500 students. Founded in 1853, in Pella, Iowa, it is accredited by the Higher Learning Commission of the North Central Association of Colleges and Schools. By featuring core requirements in global sustainability and global perspectives, Central demonstrates a commitment to nurture in students a desire to actively and ethically engage the world beyond the campus borders. Over 70% of students complete internships, and over 90% are involved in some form of service work. Nearly 50% of students study abroad at least once during their four years at Central, most participating in one of six semester-long programs administered by the college. Cocurricular programs involving internships and service-learning assist in guiding students toward habits and attitudes of global civic engagement.

Central College has nearly 50 years of involvement in international education and runs program sites in Western Europe; Merida, Mexico; and Ghana, Africa. The programs serve Central students and students from over 100 affiliated colleges and universities (Central College, 2013). On the home campus, Central College Abroad is staffed with a director and four full-time professionals who manage recruitment, advising, and program development tasks. An on-site director who is a full-time resident of the country and interacts regularly with the Central faculty leads each program. Directors report to the associate dean of global education and oversee the operation of the programs, teach courses, organize experiential learning opportunities, and serve as key resource persons to program participants. The associate dean of global education, a position was created in 2012, guides and coordinates efforts to integrate global perspective learning goals on the home campus with the six study abroad programs. Central College Abroad, Academic Internships, and the Center for Community-Based Learning all report to the associate dean; this ensures consistent leadership and provides a common structure for global learning programming.

The desire to integrate global learning into the core curriculum grew out of a rigorous curriculum review undertaken by the faculty from 2006–2009. Coinciding with the arrival of new senior administrative leadership (i.e., president and academic dean), the college also completed a three-year self-study examining its educational mission, goals, and priorities. Upon reflection, faculty realized that too much emphasis was placed on study abroad programming rather than college-wide global learning goals and that student global learning abroad was not well integrated with educational experiences available on the home campus. The self-study made it clear that all areas of the campus—from student life programming to core curriculum to academic majors and departments—needed greater investment in global learning outcomes. A key curricular development involved the creation of a global perspective core requirement (instituted in fall 2012) to systematically embed global learning goals and values into the general education curriculum. This action encouraged Central College Abroad to review its own program assessment strategy in light of the new core requirement. For example, study abroad staff examined the relationship between language studies occurring at the study abroad site and student learning goals for language fluency outlined in the college-wide curriculum. Similarly, staff explored whether internships and service-learning opportunities offered on-site were meeting global learning goals. Finally, the self-study and campus review processes renewed Central's commitment to recruit international students to the home campus, because, ironically, the approach to global education had been primarily focused on sending students abroad rather than nurturing a more culturally diverse home campus.

Central is currently engaged in a 10-year assessment plan initially developed by the Institutional Assessment Coordinating Council and is now managed jointly by the faculty Assessment Committee, the director of institutional research, and the Office of Academic Affairs. The plan provides structure and direction to Central's efforts to carry out an educational mission that develops in students "moral character that is evident in ethical behavior, intercultural effectiveness, environmental stewardship, and service to humanity" (Central College, 2013–2014). In short, a global perspective core requirement was created as an important link between the institution's mission, educational goals for students, and learning outcomes that could be regularly assessed. To assist the college in developing global learning goals, selected faculty and staff participated in the Association of American Colleges and Universities (AAC&U) national initiative titled Shared Futures: General Education for a Global Century (2009). The results of this participation helped guide faculty as they explored ways to align the general education curriculum with global learning goals for students.

This assessment activity has clarified and deepened the campus commitment to global learning. A culture of continuous self-examination emphasizes the value of developing attainable, measureable student learning outcomes for all core courses. In particular, the global perspective requirement is understood as a bridge between foundational student learning goals and the broader mission of the college.

The Global Perspective Core Requirement

Although there are many different terms and models that can guide one's understanding of global learning (Hovland, 2014), institutions must choose terms that resonate best with their needs and culture. In 2008, Central selected *global perspective* as the name for its new requirement as it evokes an active, engaged process whereby students seek a broader understanding of themselves and the world. *Global perspective* is also a unifying term for the campus, as it places emphasis on a holistic approach to global learning that includes developing international and intercultural perspectives. The core requirement is designed to work in tandem with Central College Abroad and foreign-language instruction on Central's campus to support its long-standing commitment to global learning; that is, to assist in "bringing the world not just to the doorstep but to the very heart of the academic community" (Central College, 2012, p. 5). The term *global perspective*, therefore, captures well Central's learning goals for students and communicates a shared understanding that "we live in a global world in which multiple perspectives about knowing, identity, and relationships with others serve as powerful influences in our society" (Braskamp, Braskamp, & Engberg, 2014).

The use of the term *global perspective* is also consistent with the primary tool, the Global Perspective Inventory (GPI) (Braskamp et al., 2014), used by the college to gather information about student development in global perspective taking. The GPI was created as a means "to study and promote global holistic human development, especially among college students" and is composed of 35 statements designed to reveal respondent reactions to three major questions: How do I know? Who am I? How do I relate to others? (Braskamp et al., 2014). These responses are clustered within three dimensions—cognitive, intrapersonal, and interpersonal—of student learning and development. The three dimensions represent desired learning and developmental goals for students and interact with campus experiences—community, curriculum, and cocurriculum—that represent the means by which the learning goals can be achieved. All students are invited to complete (electronically) the GPI survey at the beginning of each academic year. Data have been gathered over the past five years, with three classes (first year to graduation) represented in the pool of participants. The GPI data provide Central with the most complete information as to how students are progressing toward meeting global perspective learning goals.

To meet the global perspective requirement, students need to demonstrate

1. a minimum proficiency in a second language;
2. awareness, knowledge, and understanding of international and cultural groups other than their own;
3. an ability to see their own cultural group from a different perspective; and
4. an ability to interact ethically and responsibly with local, national, and international communities. (Central College, 2013–2014)

Students can demonstrate the first learning outcome by passing a proficiency exam, completing eight semester hours of foreign-language study, or studying the target language abroad for one academic semester. To meet the other three goals, students either participate in a Central College Abroad (or other approved) semester-long study abroad program or enroll in six semester hours of course work specifically committed to meeting global perspective learning goals. These courses are taught on the home campus and emphasize international or intercultural topics, themes, and issues. Courses with an international focus use conceptual or practical frameworks to focus primarily on a significant cultural dimension of one or more international groups, such as art, history, literature, music, politics, and religion. Courses with an intercultural focus use conceptual or practical frameworks to focus primarily on interactions between and among cultural groups. Some examples of cultural groups that are created and maintained as a result of social identifiers include race or ethnicity, immigrant or indigenous status, sex or gender identity and expression, and socioeconomic status or class (Central College, 2013–2014).

In developing the core requirement, the faculty recognized that learning outcomes demonstrating practical and ethical dimensions cannot be achieved without substantial experiential learning. Therefore, academic internships and service-learning modules serve as important companions to traditional classroom learning both at home and abroad. Many of these opportunities focus on fostering intercultural awareness and integration by partnering with local not-for-profit agencies and community organizers. For example, the study abroad program in Paris, which was historically known for the rigors of classroom language instruction, has integrated a service-learning component into the required core course to provide students an immersive language experience that extends the traditional classroom into local communities. Credit-bearing service-learning components are also built into courses on the home campus where students have the opportunity to work with a range of not-for-profit agencies and community partners in Central Iowa that serve refugees and immigrants from Sudan, Liberia, Iraq, Afghanistan, Mexico, Guatemala, El Salvador, and other nations. These experiential opportunities are primarily developed and assessed by the Center for Community-Based Learning in coordination with Central College Abroad and the associate dean for global education.

The development of the global perspective core requirement is illustrative of the commitment to global learning present across campus. Although the four learning outcomes described here can guide assessment planning, developing effective strategies is complex and challenging given the various means by which students can meet the requirement. The action steps described in the next section are the result of a great deal of cooperation and coordination among various individuals, each bringing unique perspectives, approaches, and talents to the task. In particular, arriving at an assessment plan involved the associate dean for global education, Central College Abroad (staff and on-site directors), the Center for Community-Based Learning, the director of institutional research, college faculty, and various faculty committees. Three action steps outline where we are in creating a foundation for assessment that brings questions of student development regarding global learning into focus. These steps are (a) increasing involvement of the faculty, (b) revising predeparture and reentry courses, and (c) coordinating teaching efforts with the culture course abroad.

Increasing Involvement of the Faculty

An important action step involves increasing faculty investment in the learning objectives of the global perspective requirement. Faculty discussions during the self-study revealed a need for clarity related to how the learning goals of the new requirement could be met, both on campus and through Central's study abroad programs. In other words, some faculty asked how a study abroad experience accomplishes Central's global learning goals for students. Faculty who viewed themselves as global citizens and/or embraced the educational values of experiential learning seemed more intuitively aware of how global learning outcomes can be achieved abroad, whereas others struggled to fully grasp what was being asked of our students with the requirement and how outcomes could be measured to evaluate progress.

The faculty and staff who attended the AAC&U Shared Futures: General Education for a Global Century summer workshop learned that faculty involvement or "buy-in" was essential to the effectiveness of new global learning initiatives. In a report to senior leadership, they proposed creating faculty development workshops to facilitate faculty members' personal connections with global learning. So far, the administration has supported faculty workshops at Central's program sites in Merida, Mexico, and Granada, Spain. During the 8- to 12-day workshops, faculty are immersed in the host culture through language study, homestays, local lectures on topics of interest, and excursions similar to those students experience while studying abroad. Workshops are designed to develop individual faculty members' global perspectives and also provide each participant greater insight into the study abroad experience from the student perspective. The workshop experience is also designed to encourage follow-up upon return, such as improving academic advising and student mentoring and developing assessment measures linking the global perspective core requirements to study abroad programming and the broader campus curriculum. Workshops held from January 2012 through January 2014 involved approximately half of Central's full-time faculty.

Brewer and Cunningham (2009) argued, "Faculty travel overseas is a powerful tool in the internationalization of a college or university and in the delivery of an internationalized curriculum to students" (p. 211). Central's faculty workshops abroad are an effective illustration of this argument. Anecdotal information suggests that participating faculty are more engaged in all aspects of global learning upon return to campus. They integrate their workshop experiences into class exercises, discussions, and assignments, as well as into academic advising and curriculum planning. The faculty Assessment Committee currently collaborates with individual departments to align their respective global learning goals for student majors and minors with college-wide learning outcomes. Because practically every academic department now has a faculty member who has participated in a workshop, discussions about the assessment of student development and global learning are more focused. Now that Central has collected data, through the GPI, for a complete student cohort, from first year through graduation, departments have rich data with which to examine how global learning is affected by students' educational pathways, including the decision to study abroad or remain on campus.

Revising Predeparture and Reentry Courses

The GPI has been administered to Central study abroad students prior to departure and upon reentry for the past five years. The Central College Abroad office uses the information to guide the program review and revision process. For example, one study (Doyle, 2009) collected student interviews before and after the study abroad experience and compared emergent themes to GPI data collected from the same students. The study reported that the GPI

> responses and the in-depth interviews [together] reinforce the manner in which the study abroad experience guides students to realize their personal strides toward maturity and social awareness. They come to recognize that at every turn there are important interpersonal episodes that can be used for building community across cultural and social boundaries. (Doyle, 2009, p. 151)

However, when both the interviews and the GPI data revealed general student dissatisfaction with the design of predeparture and reentry courses, study abroad staff reviewed their programming and initiated curricular changes.

In one important change, the GPI analytical framework was incorporated into the courses. Students had often found the predeparture course ineffective because they approached it from a viewpoint guided by immediate needs (e.g., packing lists, travel logistics, medical needs, banking, etc.) rather than considering the importance of the more abstract interpersonal and cross-cultural issues they would confront (e.g., culture shock, negotiating international roommates and student life, educational expectations, etc.). Study abroad staff restructured the course to feature assignments and activities highlighting the GPI's three dimensions of student learning and development—cognitive, intrapersonal, and interpersonal—as a way to sensitize students to a broader range of possible predeparture goals. Assignments and discussions now intentionally encourage students to examine their readiness in terms of each developmental dimension. They engage in self-reflection (intrapersonal) exercises exploring personal hopes and concerns about leaving the familiarity of friends and family. Students also complete fact sheets and conduct informational Internet searches that reveal their level of knowledge and understanding (cognitive) about the host culture's customs, traditions, and belief systems. And study abroad staff facilitate class discussions focused on the relational challenges and opportunities (interpersonal) presented by homestays, rooming with international students, and interacting with instructors. These curriculum changes are expected to help students develop a deeper awareness of their readiness when it comes to the degrees of difference and personal change that await them.

Central College Abroad has also reorganized its reentry course. When comparing predeparture and reentry, GPI data showed significant growth within all six learning development scales. Students demonstrated progress ranging from .21 to .72 differences in their development of a global perspective, with the largest gain on the Knowledge scale followed by the Social Interaction scale (Central College, 2014). Although it was encouraging to have evidence confirming significant development, study abroad staff also recognized a need to assist returning students in processing their personal gains in global perspective taking as they reintegrated into campus life. Twombly, Salisbury, Tumanut, and Klute (2012) asserted, "The experiences in which students engage before and after studying abroad cannot be ignored, minimized, or left to chance" (p. 113). In other words, carefully considered strategies need to be established to assist returning students in understanding the personal impact of their study abroad experience, how it is influencing their feelings about home, and how to meaningfully express these understandings to others. Guiding student experiences in the "three Cs" (curriculum, cocurriculum, community) of the GPI has become an important focal point for the reentry class. From a curricular standpoint, students use the reentry course to explore ways to integrate their learning abroad into current course assignments (e.g., research projects, personal essay writing, and class presentations). Students who are motivated to continue their language study explore scheduling options with language instructors. Students are also reminded about course offerings within the global perspective core that can extend their study of international topics.

In terms of the cocurriculum, Center for Community-Based Learning staff talk with students during a class session about experiential opportunities such as internships and service-learning within the central Iowa area that can assist them in furthering their global perspective development while also enhancing a professional résumé. The director of career services conducts a workshop to help students strategize about how to use their study abroad experience for career planning. Finally, students are encouraged to share their study abroad experiences with the larger campus community through class presentations, social event planning, or active participation in campus cultural events such as cultural holiday celebrations, fine arts performances, or historic commemorations. In fact, a requirement of the reentry course is for students to share their experience with the campus community through a structured activity. This requirement is specifically intended to connect reentering students to the life of the campus. Personal interviews and GPI data (Doyle, 2009) reveal that students often feel isolated when they return and when others seem not to care to hear about their experiences. The reentry course helps students reenter campus life and guides them in developing strategies to articulate to themselves and others in the community how their study abroad experiences have influenced their overall global perspective.

Coordinating Teaching Efforts With the Culture Course Abroad

Another action step involved a review of the culture course required in Central's study abroad programs, learning goals, and faculty teaching strategies for accomplishing the goals. The culture course is intended to build community among the student cohort and orient students to the host country and region. The course uses a seminar format to provide a forum for discussing historical and contemporary issues (e.g., cultural identity, family customs, economy, politics, religious practices, etc.) as they are revealed through the students' personal insights, observations, and research. In terms of the global perspective learning goals, the course presents a common experience for the student cohort but allows program directors to choose the instructional and assessment methods they deem will best foster student progress toward global learning on-site. Recent data reported through the GPI, class reflection papers, and personal interviews have been encouraging in that they show students are building meaningful relationships with on-site faculty, developing effective coping strategies for encountering differences, and appreciating the way staff personally invest in their development.

Central College Abroad's curricular review process made clear that different teaching philosophies, strategies, and evaluation methods have shaped course development and implementation in its different program locations. Study abroad staff are now working with program directors to collaborate on the teaching of the culture course. For example, during the 2013–2014 academic year, a dialogue was facilitated among directors to clarify institutional, core curricular, and Central College Abroad program student learning goals and to use these to guide the organizational structure of the class. Although directors are given freedom to employ a range of assessment methods (examinations, reflection papers, journaling, blogging, personal interviews, etc.), the methods should be designed to contribute to the overall assessment of students' global learning development. One illustration of this collaboration is the development of a rubric for evaluating the effectiveness of experiential learning elements (e.g., group excursions, internships, service-learning, and personal travel) to meet learning goals in both the global perspective and the study abroad program contexts. The example presented in table 9.1 illustrates how the rubric could be used to provide common points of emphasis for activities and assignments. By incorporating common terminology into the rubric, directors are reminded of institutional student learning goals. As this rubric is implemented, Central College Abroad plans to gather samples of student work from the culture course and use it as another means to assess student progress toward meeting the core global perspective learning goals.

Next Steps

This case study describes how a range of offices and committees, as well as study abroad personnel, are collaborating to assess global learning at Central

TABLE 9.1

Sample Rubric Linking Student Learning Outcome Goals to Program Strategies

Global Perspective Student Learning Outcomes	List Primary Program Elements or Strategies That Help Achieve This Outcome	Describe How Each Element Contributes to This Particular Outcome
Cognitive: Students will demonstrate awareness, knowledge, and understanding of international and cultural groups other than their own.	Social issue comparison paper (three to five pages; use sources beyond personal observations and opinions)	Students will identify one social issue of current significance in the host country and compare it to a similar issue in the United States in terms of social attitudes, policies, and impact.
Interpersonal: Students will demonstrate an ability to interact ethically and responsibly with local, national, and international communities.	Homestay reflection (required journal entry)	Students will describe a specific conversation with a host family member and reflect on the level of success in meeting communication goals.
Intrapersonal: Students will demonstrate an ability to see their own cultural group from a different perspective.	Internship reflection (required journal entry)	Students will describe the workplace environment (tasks, communication, professionalism, etc.) and compare it to their personal work experience in the United States.

College. Perhaps the greatest benefit of this process is that faculty, study abroad staff, and administrators have developed a common understanding of global learning's influential role within the general education experience of Central's students. When addressing the value of outcomes assessment, Madeleine Green (2013) argued, "The most important step in this continuous process is disseminating the findings and discussing their implications for improving student learning" (p. 7). An important "next step," therefore, involves expanding the study abroad assessment process beyond the action steps taken within Central College Abroad. A good place to start would be to conduct an analysis combining the five years of GPI data with data from several other instruments also being used in the college-wide 10-year assessment plan. These include the National Survey of Student Engagement (NSSE), administered annually to first-year and senior students, and the paired surveys (Cooperative Institutional Research Program freshman survey and Your First College Year) conducted every three years. Placing the data in a comparative relationship would create a holistic view of student global learning. For example, recent GPI data (2013–2014) indicate that when compared nationally, Central students rate more favorably in several areas—especially the cognitive and intrapersonal domains—of global perspective development (Central College, 2014). What do other data tell us about how our students compare in their development? How do factors such as gender, grade level, amount of study abroad participation, and academic major influence student development in global learning?

Another "next step" involves broadening the assessment process to include other pathways (i.e., on-campus courses and experiential learning) available to students to meet the global perspective learning goals. The Assessment Committee could initiate a dialogue among faculty to examine how the on-campus courses designated as focusing on global learning are specifically addressing the core learning goals. This dialogue could lead to a stronger alignment between the core requirement, specific course offerings, and cocurricular programming.

A final "next step" builds on the growing collaborative spirit among the study abroad program directors generated through their work on the culture course. The study abroad office plans to gather and analyze samples of student work from this course as an additional means of assessment. Standardized journal assignments and reflection papers, for example, will be used to compare student growth and development across programs with respect to global perspective learning goals. As needed, directors could then discuss together specific intervention strategies to assist students to stay on track for meeting their goals.

The assessment strategy outlined here is part of Central's long-term evaluative process. It is also a representative report, because other discussions are taking place involving other means of assessment (e.g., creating a study abroad alumni survey, developing rubrics for language proficiency comparisons) that are early in planning stages. Still, the assessment strategy plays a critical role in unifying the college community in its commitment to integrate overall student development and global learning goals.

Conclusion

The arrival of new senior administrative leaders, coupled with the 10-year assessment plan, the completion of the college-wide self-study, and the conclusion of a third academic year of the new core requirements collectively, has created a strong motivation for refining assessment strategies related to global experiential learning in the general education curriculum. A range of quantitative and qualitative methods is being used to assess student learning outcomes within the global perspective core requirement. A challenge we face involves developing effective and efficient ways to coordinate the collection of data and then to evaluate the data meaningfully. Central College Abroad staff are making significant progress in integrating programmatic learning goals with learning goals associated with the core curriculum. Milton Bennett (2012) stated, "If a study abroad program is claiming that its outcome is intercultural learning, then the program needs to be providing coherent intercultural learning schemata to enable that kind of experience" (p. 109). Central's assessment story thus far seems to adhere to this claim, as a structure links the various levels of global learning (core curriculum, goals for study abroad students, on-site programming) together in what promises to be a holistic assessment plan. As it refines the assessment process, Central College will be challenged to effectively coordinate the diverse perspectives, strategies, and methods influencing academic experiences both on the home campus and at Central's study abroad sites. Although a challenging project to be sure, this kind of coordination should not only improve our understanding of how best to accomplish the student development and learning goals outlined in the global perspective core requirement but also assist the college in preparing students for a diverse and ever-changing world. Although a holistic outcomes assessment process may be a challenging undertaking, it is well worth the effort.

Author's Note

Many thanks to Lyn Isaccson, Larry Braskamp, and the editors of this book for their helpful comments on previous drafts of this case study. Thanks also to Central College for its ongoing support of my research and scholarship.

References

Association of American Colleges and Universities. (2009). *Shared futures: General education for a global century*. Retrieved from http://aacu.org/SharedFutures/global_century/index.cfm

Bennett, M. J. (2012). Paradigmatic assumptions and a developmental approach to intercultural learning. In M. Vande Berg, R. M. Paige, & K. H. Lou (Eds.), *Student learning abroad: What our students are learning, what they're not, and what we can do about it* (pp. 90–114). Sterling, VA: Stylus.

Braskamp, L. A., Braskamp, D. C., & Engberg, M. E. (2014). *Global Perspective Inventory*. Chicago, IL: Global Perspective Institute. Retrieved from https://gpi.central.edu

Braskamp, L. A., & Engberg, M. E. (2011). How colleges can influence the development of a global perspective. *Liberal Education, 97*, 34–39.

Brewer, E., & Cunningham, K. (2009). *Integrating study abroad into the curriculum: Theory and practice across the disciplines*. Sterling, VA: Stylus.

Central College. (2012). A strategic framework for academic planning at Central College. Retrieved from https://my.central.edu/facultystaff/Documents/A%20Strategic%20Framework%20for%20Academic%20Planning%20at%20Central%20College.pdf

Central College. (2013). *Central College Abroad: About us*. Retrieved from www.central.edu/abroad/aboutUs

Central College. (2013–2014). Central College mission statement. In Central College catalog (p. 7). Retrieved from http://departments.central.edu/registrar/files/2011/08/Central-Briefly-MissionHistory2.pdf

Central College. (2014). *Summary of GPI results for Central College*. Pella, IA: Office of Institutional Research, Central College.

Doyle, D. (2009, Fall). Holistic assessment and study abroad. *Frontiers: The Interdisciplinary Journal of Study Abroad, XVIII*, 143–155.

Green, M. F. (2013). *Improving and assessing global learning*. NAFSA: Association of International Educators. Retrieved from http://nafsa.org/Find_Resources/Publications/Periodicals/Epublications/Improving and Assessing Global Learning

Hovland, K. (2014). What can global learners do? *Diversity and Democracy, 17*(2), 8–11.

NAFSA: Association of International Educators. (2008). *Internationalization at home*. Retrieved from www.nafsa.org/knowledge_community_network.sec/teaching_learning_and/internationalizing_the_3/practice_resources_24/iah_best_practices

Twombly, S. B., Salisbury, M. H., Tumanut, S. D., & Klute, P. (2012). *Study abroad in a new global century: Renewing the promise, refining the purpose*. Hoboken, NJ: Wiley Periodicals.

Vande Berg, M., Paige, R. M., & Lou, K. H. (2013). *Student learning abroad: What our students are learning, what they're not, and what we can do about it*. Sterling, VA: Stylus.

IO

ENGAGEMENT

Assessment's Ability to Connect People, Ideas, and Practice

Kelly McLaughlin

Yale College's Center for International and Professional Experience (CIPE) is utilizing the assessment process to help students define and take greater *ownership* over their own development. To this end, CIPE is focusing on how experiences abroad, particularly when guided by *reflection*, *intentionality*, and *assessment*, can help students gain greater facility in taking the next steps in their academic and professional lives.

Context

Founded in 1701 to promote and preserve a liberal arts education, Yale College enrolled 5,430 students in 2013–2014. Yale University's enrollment, including graduate and professional schools, was 12,109.

Institutional support for undergraduate international experiences (study, work, research, and independent projects) has grown significantly in Yale College over the past decade. The number of students thus engaged grew from 500 in 2003 to approximately 1,300 in 2014.

To manage and encourage international experience, Yale established the Center for International Experience (CIE) in 2007, uniting the offices for fellowships, study abroad, and summer study (faculty-led international and domestic summer programs abroad). With the addition of the career services office, the CIE became the Center for International and Professional Experience in 2010. Outcomes assessment, approached collectively, has provided a framework for bringing the units together to improve both student and staff development.

As is the case elsewhere, sustained assessment of student learning outcomes beyond course grades has not been an institutional priority beyond accreditation needs. Nevertheless, CIPE's director, who also serves as Yale College's senior associate dean for international and professional experience, prioritized assessment when CIPE was established. One third of CIPE's deputy director's time was reserved for assessment.

Neither the dean nor the deputy director had formal backgrounds in assessment, but through iterative development, Yale College has recognized the benefits of CIPE's assessment processes for the college. This case study addresses questions faced by international educators contemplating outcomes assessment: How do I get started? How do I pick an assessment method? How do I link assessment to the larger goals of my organization or institution? How do I communicate findings?

Inputs Alignment (How Do I Get Started?)

A number of key questions should be asked before gathering data (Sternberger, LaBrack, & Whalen, 2007). Thankfully, examples of assessment frameworks in international education have grown, making getting started less daunting than it was just five years ago (Deardorff, 2009). The primary challenge—and opportunity—remains, however, of developing an approach that addresses specific office and institutional aims.

CIPE began its assessment work with an environmental scan to ask what goals CIPE's constituent areas already had and how, if at all, these aligned with institutional aims as expressed in mission statements, reports on Yale College education, fund-raising campaigns, and speeches given by the university president or Yale College dean. The scan laid the groundwork for the assessments to come and proved, in and of itself, a helpful exercise in clarifying and documenting goals.

The environmental scan additionally helped CIPE identify opportunities for contributing to the institutional mission in ways that had not been obvious and ensured that CIPE assessments would be informed by Yale's stated goals. The environmental scan ultimately drove the following questions:

1. What are CIPE's and Yale College's goals for international experience?
2. Where and how are those goals articulated?

3. Are these goals aligned with each other?

4. How, if at all, are these goals being operationalized and assessed?

Answers to the questions revealed that CIPE's goals were largely hidden from view, often vaguely defined, only loosely connected with institutional aims (which were also rather hidden and vaguely defined), and not recognizable in CIPE's approach to assessment, namely, student satisfaction surveys. This led CIPE to create a schema of Yale College's most apparent goals for international experience that borrows heavily from Bloom's (1984) *Taxonomy of Educational Objectives*. Bloom's taxonomy provides a framework for classifying learning objectives within an educational system.

Overview of an Environmental Scan of Yale College's Mission

Foster students' knowledge of the

1. World
2. Curriculum
3. Self

Foster students' skills in

1. Leadership
2. Service
3. Networking

Foster students' attitudes of

1. Humility (less focus on self)
2. Open-mindedness (more focus on others)
3. Flexibility and adaptability

In fact, Yale's aims primarily concerned knowledge, with skills a distant second and virtually no focus on attitude. The CIPE director, however, felt that these attitudes might make the difference in not only students' own learning but also in how Yale students are perceived and remembered off campus. Reliance on students' knowledge and skills while ignoring attitudes could undermine CIPE's efforts to maintain good relationships with partners around the world and project a positive image of Yale students as thoughtful and considerate guests.

Even before collecting assessment data, CIPE was now better situated to determine, instill, and report on student learning outcomes that contribute directly to the larger institutional mission and to possibly also address elements of that mission that had not been given adequate attention (e.g., student attitude). The assessment journey could now continue.

Adapting and Adopting (How Do I Pick an Assessment Method?)

Commercially Available Assessment Tools

There is no lack of commercially available assessment tools from which to choose, and new tools are continually under development. The Intercultural Communication Institute (ICI, n.d.), for example, lists 14 assessment tools that are geared specifically to intercultural training and assessment. Creating, testing, and validating assessment measures takes more expertise and resources than most education abroad professionals can bring to bear on their own. However, there is no guarantee that any particular existing tool is the right fit for specific assessment aims, and the costs and complexities of administering externally developed instruments should not be overlooked.

Nonetheless, CIPE decided to experiment with the Global Perspective Inventory (GPI) (Global Perspective Institute, n.d.) in fall 2010, both to develop familiarity with commercially available resources and to determine if results from the GPI would validate its own findings. Ideally CIPE would also have administered the GPI to a control group of students who had not undertaken experiences abroad, but such an effort was more aspirational than feasible for CIPE at this early moment in its assessment work.

The GPI was administered pre- and postexperience and showed positive gains in four of the five GPI scales; only Social Responsibility indicated no statistical difference between pre- and postexperience, apparently a common finding among study abroad participants. However, although GPI administrators' data interpretation was of great service in enabling CIPE staff to make use of the aggregated data, it was difficult to translate findings into specific actions to improve student or staff development. Furthermore, CIPE lacked the skill set to look at individual items to see which items show the largest difference between post- and pretest administration, as suggested. In addition, without qualitative findings expressed in students' own voices, the aggregated data would not make a compelling case to the Yale College leadership.

Moreover, CIPE was not able to break down the aggregated findings by program. For example, how did GPI results for structured study abroad compare with results for independent projects? Because CIPE administered the same pre- and postexperience GPI surveys to both sets of students at once, the results captured the entire group's change from pre- to postexperience, without differentiating by type of experience. Ultimately, a partnership between CIPE and a professor of psychology at another institution helped CIPE utilize the GPI data more effectively. This partnership is explained in more detail later in this chapter.

The GPI itself is not flawed. It does what it was designed to do, which is "to study and promote global holistic human development, especially among college students" (https://gpi.central.edu/index.cfm?myAction=About). Such development is a key consideration for CIPE as well, and validation through the GPI of some of CIPE's more general questions was highly useful. CIPE simply was not yet ready to disaggregate large data sets to answer its programmatic and individual student-level questions about learning outcomes. The lesson? High-quality, third-party assessment tools can provide a starting point and/or supplement other assessment efforts and are useful to large-scale research projects. Furthermore, although CIPE could benefit by gaining more experience working with data, no single measure or tool would suffice for its assessment purposes. The question for CIPE, therefore, was how to proceed to find additional assessment methods.

Tensions in Assessment

Many of the challenges CIPE faced reflect tensions that are inherent with assessment efforts generally. Although such tensions can be addressed, and possibly even resolved, they cannot be avoided entirely (Ewell, 2009). Fortunately, deciding how to address or resolve the tensions makes follow-up decisions easier. CIPE's list of such tensions, for example, includes the following:

- Accountability ⇔ Improvement
- Summative ⇔ Formative
- Adopting ⇔ Adapting
- Direct Measure ⇔ Indirect Measure
- Quantitative ⇔ Qualitative
- Aspirational ⇔ Feasible
- Interdependent ⇔ Independent
- Satisfaction ⇔ Learning

This list led CIPE to initially focus on items on the right side and to design an assessment process that would

- place primary importance on improving its work (rather than on demonstrating accountability to an external group);
- help students reflect critically on their own development (rather than summarize that development);

- adapt methodologies to suit CIPE's needs (rather than adopt tools);
- utilize indirect measures and qualitative data (student self-reporting rather than testing);
- be feasible and iterative given CIPE's limited experience and resources;
- evolve independently from, but aware of, assessment efforts elsewhere (rather than join a larger effort beyond CIPE); and
- keep student learning and development at the forefront (rather than count student satisfaction as a learning or developmental outcome).

Several years later, the focus on items on the right-hand side of the tensions list has positioned CIPE staff to begin addressing items on the left side of the list more confidently and ably. Furthermore, the Yale College leadership is seeing CIPE hold itself accountable for the resources its work requires, CIPE is becoming more adept at turning a formative process into one that also reliably summarizes student experiences, and CIPE better understands its options for using commercially available tools in the future to measure specific aspects of its assessment portfolio.

CIPE, however, excludes student satisfaction from assessment. Survey questions focused on consumerism ("How would you rank your host family?"), qualitative terms ("I received *timely* feedback on my academic progress."), and negative judgments ("What were the weakest points of the program?") do not correspond with learning outcomes and can yield data that are ambiguous if not misleading (Engle & Martin, 2010).

For example, if a student ranks a host family very low, is that because the family often engaged the student in conversation or because the family left that student alone completely? Or is it because the student did not want to live with a host family? CIPE does not ignore comfort, convenience, and safety for its students. Rather, it has rethought every satisfaction measure it had been watching to focus instead on learning and developmental outcomes important to Yale College and on outcomes reliably measurable through student surveys.

Designing Your Own Assessment Tools

CIPE, it should be emphasized, did not have outside pressure to adhere to a particular protocol or a mandate to produce certain kinds of data validated in particular ways. Instead, it had considerable freedom in approaching its assessment work. This freedom, however, could be overwhelming; a seemingly infinite number of items could potentially be assessed. Interesting questions never seemed to end; how much was CIPE ready and able to undertake? By determining CIPE's office- and institutional-level goals for student learning outcomes and development (i.e., the things CIPE was addressing), CIPE could much more easily focus its assessment efforts on how well it was contributing to Yale College's mission (i.e., the things CIPE should be assessing). So, too, could CIPE see more clearly what tools, purchased or self-designed, would best fit a particular assessment effort.

Following its experimentation with the GPI, CIPE designed a postexperience survey instrument aimed at capturing mission-driven data *and* prompting students to reflect critically on their experiences. The survey strives to be formative for students and provide targeted data gleaned from their self-reports. The approach has limits; ideally outcomes would be assessed holistically, through a mix of self-reported and additional measures, in-depth interviews, direct testing of student knowledge pre- and postexperience, and so on (Doyle, 2009). Holistic data provide a fuller view of outcomes.

That said, the tension between feasible and aspirational assessment is real. Furthermore, student self-reporting may not be less reliable than other types of assessment (Ewell, McClenney, & McCormick, 2011). Thus, any particular approach is not necessarily inferior to another, and too much reliance should not be given to any single instrument. Of course, the value of self-reported data in particular is closely tied to the quality of the questions asked (Engle, 2013). Questions should also neither confuse nor bias the students answering them (Fowler, 2009).

CIPE's most recent survey prompts included the following:

- The primary goal(s) that I set for this experience was (were) . . . .
- The most helpful step(s) I took to help me achieve my goals was (were) . . . .
- The best result(s) of my experience was (were) . . . .
- As I reflect upon this experience, something that surprised me is . . . .
- The next step(s) I plan to take toward building upon this experience is (are) . . . .

These prompts largely focus on students' role in setting and achieving goals and building on experience. The number of questions is deliberately limited to facilitate completion of the survey and still afford CIPE actionable (and manageable) data and students an opportunity to reflect and make connections to future endeavors. Responses to prompts range from one or two sentences to entire paragraphs.

The data yield insights into students' goals, the agency they exercise to achieve the goals, the best and most surprising aspects of their experience, and their plans for build on the experience upon return. Answers are coded into categories, which allows for quantitative analysis of the responses. As coding the data lends insight into student experiences, it plays an important role in CIPE staff development.

Knowledge of student behavior and student learning has empowered CIPE to encourage students to take ownership over their own development. CIPE is better able to help students think more explicitly about how international experiences can form an integral part of their Yale education.

For example, how might courses taken abroad enrich the student's participation in related courses back at Yale? How might skills gained through independent research abroad help prepare the student for a capstone project or senior thesis? And how might international experiences be discussed with faculty and advisors before, during, and after to maximize the benefits, as opposed to ticking a check box of things that "successful" students seem to do?

Operationalizing Assessment (How Do I Link Assessment to the Larger Goals of My Organization or Institution?)

Having come this far, CIPE discovered that gathering useful data was, in some respects, the easy part. Now the findings had to be operationalized, and tangible resources and changes to practice had to be put in place to improve CIPE's work. That, after all, is the purpose for undertaking assessment to begin with.

Model of Student Engagement (Resource Example 1)

One difficulty was finding a way for heretofore independently run offices to contribute discrete (if periodically overlapping) pieces to the student and staff development puzzle. The model of student engagement was CIPE's answer (see figure 10.1).

CIPE units administer experiences with either highly structured support or little or no support. Some experiences take place mostly or entirely in a classroom (*academic*). Similarly, some experiences take place mostly or entirely outside of the classroom (*experiential*). In addition to activity type, CIPE focused on "agency," that is, whether the program (*programmatic*) largely controls the experience or the student (*independent*).

As figure 10.1 illustrates, for each quadrant (academic, experiential, programmatic, and independent), CIPE defined some key characteristics and aligned these with the student competencies needed for a successful experience.

CIPE's use of this advising model is relatively new. Nonetheless, anecdotal feedback from students suggests the model works; the distinctions between the types of opportunities are clear and help students choose an experience appropriate to their goals and background.

Figure 10.1 Model of student engagement

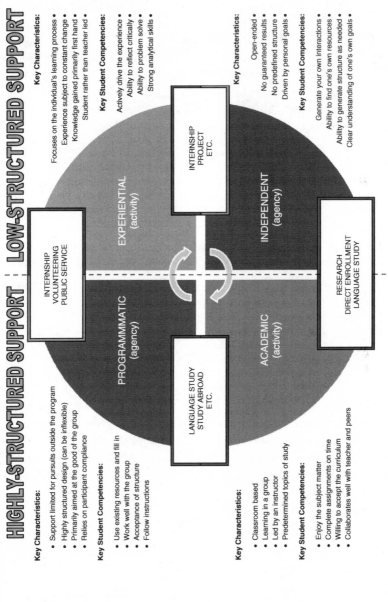

HIGHLY-STRUCTURED SUPPORT : LOW-STRUCTURED SUPPORT

Key Characteristics:

Focuses on the individual's learning process •
Experience subject to constant change •
Knowledge gained primarily first hand •
Student rather than teacher led •

Key Student Competencies:

Actively drive the experience •
Ability to reflect critically •
Ability to problem solve •
Strong analytical skills •

INTERNSHIP
PROJECT
ETC.

EXPERIENTIAL
(activity)

INTERNSHIP
VOLUNTEERING
PUBLIC SERVICE

PROGRAMMATIC
(agency)

INDEPENDENT
(agency)

ACADEMIC
(activity)

LANGUAGE STUDY
STUDY ABROAD
ETC.

RESEARCH
DIRECT ENROLLMENT
LANGUAGE STUDY

Key Characteristics:

Open-ended •
No guaranteed results •
No predefined structure •
Driven by personal goals •

Key Student Competencies:

Generate your own interactions •
Ability to find one's own resources •
Ability to generate structure as needed •
Clear understanding of one's own goals •

Key Characteristics:

• Support limited for pursuits outside the program
• Highly structured design (can be inflexible)
• Primarily aimed at the good of the group
• Relies on participant compliance

Key Student Competencies:

• Use existing resources and fill in
• Work well with the group
• Acceptance of structure
• Follow instructions

Key Characteristics:

• Classroom based
• Learning in a group
• Led by an instructor
• Predetermined topics of study

Key Student Competencies:

• Enjoy the subject matter
• Complete assignments on time
• Willing to accept the curriculum
• Collaborates well with teacher and peers

Note. © 2011, Yale University Center for International and Professional Experience. Created by Kelly C. McLaughlin.

CIPE then mapped the experiences it offers against the model to determine the types of activities and agency most clearly present in particular offerings. Offerings correspond to one or more quadrants (e.g., academic + programmatic = structured study abroad experience).

A sample of CIPE offerings mapped against the model of student engagement finds the following:

- *Academic-programmatic:* Study Abroad: Center-Based/Hybrid // Language Study: Yale Summer Session // Yale-in-London // Richard U. Light Fellowship (language study in East Asia) // Waseda Global Sustainability Seminar
- *Programmatic-experiential:* Bulldogs (Yale College) Internships // Monterey Tech Sustainable Development Internship // Fulbright English Teaching Assistantships
- *Experiential-independent:* Project or Public Service Fellowship // Self-Designed Internship // Fulbright Fellowships
- *Independent-academic:* Direct Enrollment // Research Fellowship, including Fulbright, and so on // Yale Fields Language Study Program
- *Academic-programmatic-experiential:* Study Abroad Field-Based Program // Project-Based Course
- *Academic:* U.K. Fellowships // Graduate/Professional School // Postgraduate Fellowships
- *Experiential:* Work // Public Service
- *Independent:* [Create your own internship/project] // [International science opportunities]

CIPE staff conversations leading to the model of student engagement were critical to clarify the possible learning and developmental implications for structured versus unstructured opportunities and academic versus experiential opportunities. Understanding how CIPE's constituent offices can work in holistic and synergistic fashion to promote desired learning outcomes has helped staff appreciate that experiences across CIPE's spectrum of opportunities can help students design a clearer road map for defining and achieving their goals in highly personalized ways.

Terms of Engagement (Resource Example 2)

CIPE's *terms of engagement* makes more explicit the roles that CIPE and students should play to ensure desired learning outcomes. Some students expect a fee-for-services model. The following terms therefore attempt to clarify that the student must take ownership over learning.

CIPE Terms of Engagement
To what end? To help students

- develop and actively pursue a plan of action over time and across multiple experiences if possible,
- build positive relationships with others through mutual respect,
- understand the ways in which their experiences have contributed to meeting (or revising) their long-term goals and to their personal growth, and
- articulate and communicate this knowledge effectively.

CIPE offers

- the opportunity to discuss the student's plan of action with an advisor who will guide critical reflection, goal-oriented activity, and thoughtful program selection;
- opportunities for experiences away from campus that offer quality, safety, and strong potential for meeting goals (the student's and Yale's);
- support throughout the application process, after selection, during the experience, and upon return;
- one courtesy reminder to complete requirements; and
- a culture of mutual respect for student and staff time.

Students are expected to

- be active participants in their own development by utilizing CIPE's resources (online tools, advising, peers, funding, etc.);
- rely directly on CIPE for CIPE-related information;
- be able to conceptualize and express how their plans connect to their own short- and long-term development;
- engage with faculty, the dean, and family members in a timely manner about plans for activity away from Yale;
- act as positive ambassadors for Yale College in the United States and abroad; and
- respect peer and staff time by meeting deadlines, keeping appointments, and completing requirements associated with the experience.

The terms of engagement both serve as a touch point for CIPE's interactions with students and provide further material for context-specific assessment. Any of these bulleted items could form part of a productive assessment effort; some, in fact, are evident in the CIPE survey questions.

Fellowship Preadvising Questionnaire (Resource Example 3)

CIPE's Fellowship Programs unit employs a preadvising questionnaire to operationalize assessment aims. Students must complete and submit the questionnaire to secure an advising appointment.

Fellowship Programs seeks to empower students to take greater ownership of their fellowship application efforts and their learning. However, despite offering general information sessions, staff found themselves repeating basic information in individual advising sessions. This was not only inefficient but also undercut the goal of fostering student agency over their own development.

Staff and students were concerned that requiring the submission of a completed questionnaire to secure an advising appointment would negatively and perhaps unfairly impact students' access to resources. This touches on the fee-for-service dynamic mentioned previously. Fellowship Programs, however, believed that a preadvising questionnaire was commensurate with its emphasis on learning outcomes. In essence, pondering basic questions before meeting with an advisor would help students "intervene" in their own learning (Lou, Vande Berg, & Paige, 2012).

The preadvising questionnaire also signals to students that failure to take this initial step means they are not taking enough ownership over the process. Students who neither complete the questionnaire nor meet with an advisor can still apply for fellowships. However, staff time is now better used, and completing the questionnaire lessens the need for advising for many students.

Fellowship Programs does not expect students to have detailed answers for each item on the questionnaire. Rather, as evident in the terms of engagement already discussed, students must partner with CIPE, especially if seeking one-on-one advising. The following preadvising questionnaire is aimed primarily at freshmen and sophomores contemplating applications for fellowships:

Yale College CIPE Fellowship Programs Preadvising Questionnaire

To make the most of your individual appointment, we ask that you fill out this questionnaire to the best of your ability. In this way, not only will our advisors be better prepared to answer your questions, but also you will be better prepared to reflect on and engage in a conversation about your proposed idea, your application strategy, and your long-term goals.

1. Please provide general information about what you will be proposing to do and where you are proposing to do it (in two or three sentences).

2. With whom have you discussed your application and/or proposed idea? Please include any contacts you have made at your activity site (e.g., Professor Eli O'Yalieberg, Yale history department; Dr. Maria Sanchez, Healthy Health, an NGO in Bolivia).
3. Briefly (two or three sentences), what is one of your longer term goals, and how might your proposed experience relate to this?
4. Please list the fellowships to which you plan on applying.
5. Click here to verify that you and your proposed activity (if applicable) are eligible for the fellowships you've listed.
6. Name(s) of possible recommender(s).
7. Name of possible language evaluator (if applicable).
8. If you have any particularly challenging circumstances or questions that you would like to discuss with an advisor, please describe these here.

Questionnaires are received at least 24 hours prior to advising sessions, so that advisors and students are on the same page when they meet. This also gives advisors time to prepare for particularly difficult or unusual questions. This kind of partnership is what CIPE aims for in its terms of engagement.

Interestingly, Fellowship Programs now sees fewer students for individual advising appointments, particularly freshmen and sophomores. Also, although the total number of fellowship applications initially dipped following the changes, the quality of fellowship applications increased, as evidenced by feedback from faculty reviewing applications, scores awarded to applications, and the yield of fellowship winners. Furthermore, advisors and students are able to focus on outcomes in a single meeting, something that used to require much more time.

Advisors were concerned that a reduction in individual advising sessions would result in a drop in the quality or number of fellowship applications. They therefore devoted the time freed up from reducing individual advising sessions to providing additional (and more interactive and effective) general information sessions. A two-item survey administered at the end of the information sessions provides feedback on the usefulness of the sessions to student learning; the feedback is then used to improve the sessions:

1. As a result of attending this meeting, I feel better prepared to take the next steps in my application.
    Strongly Agree ☐   *Agree* ☐   *Disagree* ☐   *Strongly Disagree* ☐
2. Is there anything you expected to learn in today's session that was not covered?

Some students, by virtue of more clearly understanding the work required for a strong fellowship application, delay application until they are better prepared; others realize applying for a fellowship does not make sense. Although such decisions result in fewer fellowship applications, students better understand the fellowship application process and their own developmental stage and future direction. This outcome makes good use of everybody's time and resources.

Recording and Reporting (How Do I Communicate Findings?)

CIPE communicates its findings formally within Yale College through yearly presentations to the college's administrative leaders and through online assessment reports (see www.yale.edu/yalecollege/international/welcome).

One result of CIPE's emphasis on students' greater ownership of their academic and personal development has been the creation of a college committee to "change the narrative" so that students arrive on campus not as passive consumers but as active participants in a community that hosts remarkable but still limited resources. To an extent, the committee hopes to counteract student entitlement or consumerism. More important, it aspires to help students take productive and ethical advantage of their time at Yale. CIPE's director chairs the committee and also shares CIPE's assessment reports and methodology for inclusion in Yale College's reports to the New England Association of Schools and Colleges.

In disseminating CIPE's assessment methods and findings, the CIPE director has consistently sought to ensure that these remain an active topic of conversation among Yale College's senior administrators. Assessment reports are also shared with current or prospective Yale College donors; CIPE's careful stewardship of student learning is a positive argument for increased funding for international learning experiences. Communicating the aims and practical implications of CIPE's assessment work remains an ongoing challenge both inside and outside CIPE. Such communication, however, which continues to evolve and expand, is important for the long-term relevance of the work for CIPE and Yale College.

Lessons Learned (Counting What Counts)

In 1963, sociologist William Bruce Cameron wrote,

> It would be nice if all of the data which sociologists require could be enumerated because then we could run them through IBM machines and draw charts as the economists do. However, not everything that can be counted counts, and not everything that counts can be counted. (p. 13)

CIPE has also learned that specifying first what "counts" has proven fundamental to measuring (counting) its contributions and progress. Otherwise the universe of things to assess is simply too large and, at any given time, not helpful or feasible to study.

Data Limitations

CIPE initially struggled to find data to explain nuanced phenomena. Eventually, it realized that although data inform, they do not explain. No perfect data sets exist to explain fully the complexities of student learning. With these limitations understood, the pressure to find "perfect" lifted, and CIPE was able to focus on its local context. The data that would be gathered would have the best chance of improving CIPE's work in ways that resonated with institutional aims.

A recurring question is, "How could we use the results on this item to improve our work?" Questions that might yield interesting but nonactionable data are quickly set aside, at least for assessment purposes. Collecting data that have the potential for practical applications also aids greatly in limiting the volume of data that needs to be analyzed, reported, and acted upon.

Intentionality + Iteration = Improvement

Productive assessment requires intentionality about what is being assessed and why; collecting data without first asking "what" and "why" is unlikely to prove helpful. At the same time, what is being assessed and why will likely evolve with experience and time. What appeared to be actionable data may prove not to be. Institutional priorities may change. Intentionality and iteration are, therefore, key if assessment efforts are to have high potential for continually improving (and documenting) practice.

Partnerships

Critical to CIPE's ability to develop its approach to assessment were several breakthrough partnerships. Consultant Patti Clayton, who has expertise in student learning through critical reflection, led workshops to help CIPE staff define its "North Star"—the guiding principles that would help define CIPE's assessment efforts and its engagement with students (Ash, Atkinson, & Clayton, 2005).

Now, on many occasions, CIPE staff ask, "What would North Star say?" when confronted with an issue around assessment or a desired student learning outcome. For example, what happens when students miss a scheduled appointment? What would North Star say? The North Star framework also guided the creation of the model of student engagement and the terms of engagement. If CIPE asked students to reflect critically and to define better goals, shouldn't CIPE staff be held to the same standard?

As discussed earlier, another partnership helped CIPE interpret GPI data. CIPE was fortunate to have connections with a professor of psychology who hoped to give "live" data to her students so they could practice data analysis and reporting to clients. In the end, she was unable to create this assignment and instead did the GPI data analysis and reported to CIPE herself. The report allowed CIPE to see that GPI scores correlated in interesting ways with students' backgrounds.

International students, for example, tended to have higher scores on the GPI preexperience survey, but demonstrated less gain on the postexperience survey. Perhaps they had already gained much of what the GPI attempts to measure by studying abroad in the United States. This reminded CIPE that many students come to Yale with international experience that has allowed them to acquire GPI-relevant knowledge, skills, and attitudes. Students come to CIPE at different starting points in terms of international experience and goals.

CIPE also has long partnered with Yale College's Office of Institutional Research (OIR), which "provides information to support university decision-making through a variety of analytic activities, data-gathering tasks, and research projects" (Yale College, 2015). OIR staff tend to large projects throughout the year but have nonetheless always supported CIPE's data collection and documentation. A newer partnership is with Yale's Center for Science and Social Science Information (CSSSI), which "provides Yale faculty, students, and staff with state-of-the-art information services in a technology-rich environment" (CSSSI, n.d.).

Most recently, CSSSI advised CIPE to create a "perfect assessment report" of assessment questions that CIPE, in an ideal world, would be able to answer. The aim is not to be overly aspirational but to underscore which data would be needed to answer particular questions. As a result, CIPE will inventory data currently collected in CIPE and elsewhere at Yale that might provide a richer picture of students' development.

Such partnerships are proving pivotal in CIPE's efforts to move its assessment work forward. However, CIPE would likely have benefited much less from them had it not first spent more than a year to determine its assessment focus and gain experience gathering and reporting on data. This made CIPE's subsequent partnerships far more productive. Nonetheless, it might have been helpful to partner earlier and more often with experts in and around Yale's campus, even if just in an exploratory manner.

Additional Resources

CIPE has been particularly influenced by the author's participation in the Forum on Education Abroad's Outcomes Assessment and Research

Committee. Indeed, the author chaired the committee when it created and launched an online toolbox as "a platform for sharing assessment tools and strategies among professionals in the education abroad community" (Forum on Education Abroad, n.d.). The National Institute for Learning Outcomes Assessment (NILOA) also was a wealth of useful assessment resources, including its occasional papers, the first of which is titled "Assessment, Accountability, and Improvement: Revisiting the Tension" (Ewell, 2009). Several of NILOA's papers helped CIPE resolve the tensions it faced in developing its assessment approach. Other resources beyond the Yale campus could also be mentioned.

Conclusion

Well-designed and intentionally resourced assessment efforts can help determine, instill, and report on the most important learning outcomes for local and institutional aims. Findings can help to address valid concerns about the reasons and the resources behind the large and growing emphasis on international experience. Indeed, there are many compelling reasons, at both the institutional and student levels, for U.S. colleges and universities to devote resources to study abroad (Sterns, 2009).

However, intellectual rigor and honesty are essential to these endeavors. For all of its positive potential, study abroad can also foster imperialism, exclusivity, wasted resources, health risks, and other undesirable outcomes (Twombly, Salisbury, Tumanut, & Klute, 2012). Indeed, beyond determining study abroad's benefits, understanding its potentially negative outcomes—and working to avoid them—is the work of outcomes assessment.

The number of U.S. students studying abroad tripled from fewer than 100,000 students in 1994 to nearly 300,000 by 2012 (Institute of International Education, 2013). International educators must balance the logistical pressures of sending greater numbers of students abroad against a professional and moral obligation to work for desired outcomes. The "Lincoln Commission Report" raised the pressure to increase the number of study abroad participants by setting a goal of one million U.S. students abroad each year by 2016–2017 (Commission on the Abraham Lincoln Study Abroad Fellowship Program, 2005). That target will almost certainly not be met, and the United States may not even have the capacity to triple once again participation rates. This is just as well.

Greater focus should first be given to better defining, deepening, and documenting the desired outcomes of study abroad before pinning success on blunt, if well-intentioned, measures such as participation rates. Although the path toward practical, meaningful, and impactful assessment is neither straight nor short, as a community of professionals, we need to continue to pursue the path collaboratively. Understanding students' development and their impacts on people and places abroad is an imperative and exciting mission.

References

Ash, S. L., Atkinson, M. P., & Clayton, P. H. (2005). Integrating reflection and assessment to capture and improve student learning. *Michigan Journal of Community Service Learning, 11*(2), 49–60.

Bloom, B. S. (Ed.). (1984). *Taxonomy of educational objectives: The classification of education goals.* White Plains, NY: Longman.

Cameron, W. B. (1963). *Informal sociology: A casual introduction to sociological thinking.* New York, NY: Random House.

Commission on the Abraham Lincoln Study Abroad Fellowship Program. (2005). *Global competence and national needs: One million Americans studying abroad.* Retrieved from www.culturalinsurance.com/pdf/lincoln_final_report.pdf

CSSSI. (n.d.). Retrieved from http://web.library.yale.edu/building/center-science-and-social-science-information

Deardorff, D. K. (2009). Understanding the challenges of assessing global citizenship. In R. Lewin (Ed.), *The handbook of practice and research in study abroad: Higher education and the quest for global citizenship* (pp. 346–364). New York, NY: Routledge.

Doyle, D. (2009). Holistic assessment and the study abroad experience. *Frontiers: The Interdisciplinary Journal of Study Abroad, 18*, 143–154.

Engle, L. (2013). The rewards of qualitative assessment appropriate to study abroad. *Frontiers: The Interdisciplinary Journal of Study Abroad, 22*, 111–126.

Engle, L., & Martin, P. C. (2010). *Alignment and accountability in education abroad: A handbook for the effective design and implementation of qualitative assessment based on student evaluations.* Carlisle, PA: Forum on Education Abroad. Retrieved from www.forumea.org/documents/AlignmentandAccountabilityEdAbroad.pdf

Ewell, P. T. (2009). *Assessment, accountability, and improvement: Revisiting the tension* (NILOA Occasional Paper No. 1). Urbana, IL: University of Illinois and Indiana University, National Institute for Learning Outcomes Assessment.

Ewell, P. T., McClenney, K., & McCormick, C. (2011). Measuring engagement. *Inside Higher Education.* Retrieved from www.insidehighered.com/views/2011/09/20/measuring-engagement#sthash.xbqKf4J9.dpbs

Forum on Education Abroad. (n.d.). Retrieved from http://www.forumea.org/resources/member-resources/outcomes-toolbox

Fowler, J. F., Jr. (2009). Survey research methods. In L. Bickman & D. J. Rog (Eds.), *Applied social research methods series* (4th ed., pp. 87–111). Thousand Oaks, CA: Sage.

Global Perspective Institute. (n.d.). Global Perspective Inventory. Retrieved from https://gpi.central.edu/

Institute of International Education. (2013). *Fast facts open doors 2013.* Retrieved from www.iie.org/Research-and-Publications/Open-Doors

Intercultural Communication Institute. (n.d.). *Intercultural training and assessment tools.* Retrieved from www.intercultural.org/tools.php

Lou, K. H., Vande Berg, M., & Paige, R. M. (2012). Intervening in student learning abroad. In M. Vande Berg, R. M. Paige, & K. H. Lou (Eds.), *Student learning abroad: What our students are learning, what they're not, and what we can do about it* (pp. 411–420). Sterling, VA: Stylus.

Sternberger, L., LaBrack, B., & Whalen, B. (2007). How to begin: Key decision points in the assessment process. In M. Bolen (Ed.), *A guide to outcomes assessment in education abroad* (pp. 71–88). Carlisle, PA: Forum on Education Abroad.

Sterns, P. N. (2009). *Educating global citizens in colleges and universities: Challenges and opportunities.* New York, NY: Routledge.

Twombly, S., Salisbury, M., Tumanut, S., & Klute, P. (2012). *Study abroad in a new global century: Renewing the promise, refining the purpose* (ASHE Higher Education Report). Hoboken, NJ: Wiley.

Yale College. (2015). Retrieved from http://oir.yale.edu/

11

USING DATA FOR IMPROVEMENT AND ADVOCACY

A 10-Year Retrospective on Outcomes Assessment Through Multimethod Longitudinal Studies and Institutional Data

Elaine Meyer-Lee and Karen Chambers

Assessment Context: Mission and Goals

Over 10 years ago, Saint Mary's College, a Catholic women's liberal arts college with about 1,500 students in Notre Dame, Indiana, set out to rigorously assess student growth within the context of its robust education abroad. Before that, typical satisfaction surveys had been administered and participation tracked, but no real attempt had been made to gauge the impact on student growth and learning. The college itself is an example of international learning since its founding in 1844 by four Sisters of the Holy Cross, and it has run significant study abroad programs of its own since the 1960s. Its mission "prepares [women] to make a difference in the world" and "promotes . . . social responsibility [and] responds to the complex needs and challenges of the contemporary world." In 2001, the college accelerated these priorities by establishing a Center for Women's Intercultural Leadership (CWIL), which houses all of the education abroad programs, among other things, with a mission statement that includes "empowering women to realize their

call to leadership and to develop the intercultural knowledge and competence critical in today's increasingly interdependent world" (see https://cwil
.saintmarys.edu/cwil-mission). As far as the inputs and outputs of study
abroad, 51% of Saint Mary's graduates study abroad, mostly on one of the
11 semester or year programs Saint Mary's operates, and the rest participate
in the college's 14 short-term programs. This case study will focus, however,
on assessment of the *outcomes* or results of these programs. Incidentally, Saint
Mary's as a whole recently adopted undergraduate learning outcomes for
general education, which include separate requirements in global learning,
intercultural competence, and social responsibility.

When we at CWIL first established our assessment program, we had several goals, which have remained relevant. Of course, as a general rule, it is
crucial to have a clear question to answer prior to collecting data of any type.
First and foremost, then, in broad terms we are focused on assessing the extent
to which students achieve both their own goals and those of Saint Mary's, so
that we can better assist future students in doing so. Flowing from the mission of the college, we try to understand how the study abroad experience
supports students' developing self-knowledge, intercultural communication
skills, and understanding of human cultures. We use these findings to evaluate CWIL's effectiveness and inform our curricular, pedagogical, and advising
continuous quality improvement. Second, we assess meaningful outcomes so
as to better advocate for the value of international education, both internally to
our administration, trustees, and other stakeholders and externally, such as for
accreditation. Finally, as psychologists by discipline, we, the principal investigators in CWIL's assessment activities and the authors of this chapter, endeavor to
add to the field's basic understanding of student growth in this domain. At the
time we began, there was little encouragement to assess from outside our office,
but it should be noted that there has been a sea change more recently at Saint
Mary's where all units have been asked to construct assessment plans in preparation for reaccreditation. Eventually, CWIL will also integrate its assessment
efforts with those of the broader general education program at Saint Mary's.

With these broad goals and the college and center missions in mind, we
set about to define the specific outcomes that we wanted to measure. When
we began over 10 years ago, we brainstormed broadly with the faculty, our
institutional research office, and other stakeholders and then narrowed down
to what seemed to be of highest priority to our audience and realistic to our
resources. Through this process we decided to focus on assessing intercultural
competence and personal growth rather than, for example, language learning
or disciplinary knowledge. Of course, intercultural competence is a complex
combination of knowledge, attitudes, and skills, so we needed to refine further what evidence of success we most wanted to study.

We therefore decided we wanted to look at student changes in three ways. First, we wanted to know how students thought they had grown in terms of the goals they and we would articulate. Second, we had heard many of our returnees say that their time abroad was the first time they had reflected on what it means to be American and that it shifted their identities, so we wanted to explore that. Third, we wanted to try to capture broader changes related to intercultural competence in some way that could be objectively measured and compared to other populations.

To meet our goals, our questions about outcomes, however, could not be as simple as, for example, "Did change occur during study abroad, and if so, of what type?" The real usefulness of assessment data comes in looking at what factors correlate with the degree of change, such as country, program model, duration, student demographic characteristics, and student engagement choices while abroad. These comparative or differential impact analyses yield the information that is actually helpful to us as educators, program developers, and advisors. We were also interested in changes in impact over time—does immediate change disappear over time, stay stable, or even increase as seeds planted continue to blossom?

Having clearly established our intended outcomes and research questions, we only then set about to identify appropriate assessment methods for the Saint Mary's context. We knew we would need to use multiple methods to capture the rich complexity of the growth processes in question. We wanted some indirect measures where we asked students to self-report their own growth and also some direct pre-post standardized measures to document change longitudinally. Ideally, we wanted both quantitative measures of change and qualitative descriptions. Initially, we did collect written reflections and focus group comments from students in a reentry course, and we have experimented more recently with beta testing the Association of American Colleges and Universities (2010) value rubrics on global learning and intercultural competence. These have proven too labor intensive for us to implement consistently to date, but we hope to add some analysis of student writing from a new online study abroad reflection course we are launching. We wanted our data collection to be ongoing and integrated into all of our processes. Although we have also collected data on the impact of on-campus aspects of our international learning, the rest of this case study will lay out our approach related to education abroad only.

Methodology: Study Data Collection, Sample Analyses, Findings, and Uses

To assess our questions, we collected and analyzed data on three broad classes of variables: student outcomes, program predictor variables, and student predictor variables. Student outcomes refer to the changes in the student that are associated with the study abroad experience. Program variables are both features of the programs that we can influence and change and the extent to which the students' own choices abroad support intercultural interaction and engagement. Finally, student variables are those qualities that students bring with them prior to studying abroad and over which we have no influence.

Student outcomes. In an effort to capture broad changes related to inter-cultural competence in a way that could be objectively measured and com-pared to other populations, we have, over the past decade, sequentially utilized three of the most commonly used standardized measurement tools of intercultural development available. We used the Intercultural Develop-ment Inventory (IDI) (Hammer, 1999) for the first three years, then after evaluating those results, we changed to the Beliefs, Events, and Values Inven-tory (BEVI) (Shealy, 2004) for the next three years as part of its beta testing, leading to another period of considering what we had learned about the pros and cons of each. Now we are using the Global Perspective Inventory (GPI), a nationally normed measure that is designed to assess holistic development of intercultural maturity on the dimensions of cognitive, intrapersonal, and interpersonal domains (Braskamp, Braskamp, & Merrill, 2007). To summa-rize a rather involved decision-making process, we settled on the GPI because it is grounded in solid research-based yet accessible developmental theory, is transparent in its analytic methods, best captures—with concise simplicity—the kinds of changes we hope and believe are occurring, is user friendly to students, is continually updated by the author who is open to user feedback and committed to contributing to basic knowledge in the field, and is afford-able with no required certification to administer it. In addition, the GPI is particularly aligned with Saint Mary's mission statement in that it assesses self-knowledge, complexity of one's thinking about intercultural issues, and the degree of understanding and awareness of various cultures.

The the American Identity Measure (AIM) (Meyer-Lee & Evans, 2008) was adapted from the Multigroup Ethnic Identity Measure (Phinney, 1992) to try to confirm anecdotal stories that students shared with us upon return about new insights into what it means to be an American. (See appendix A for the full measure.) One dimension of intercultural competence is better understanding one's own cultural perspectives, and so we wanted to try to capture in an objective way whether students think more complexly about what their national identity is and what it means to them. The AIM assesses two processes of national identity development (exploration and commit-ment) based on the identity development theory of Erik Erikson and James Marcia. Erikson (1968) proposed that a central task for adolescents and young adults is to explore their identity—who they are and what their ide-als are. Marcia (1980) operationalized the level of exploration/search and commitment/belonging/affirmation to yield four types of identity outcomes. Thus, students can be in moratorium (high exploration/low commitment), foreclosure (low exploration/high commitment), diffusion (low exploration/ low commitment), or achievement (high exploration/high commitment). Phinney and Rosenthal (1992) adapted this work to create a measure of how ethnic minorities come to understand their ethnic identity, and Phinney approved the adaptation of her psychometrically validated measure to apply to national identity instead.

The AIM has 10 Likert-style items (5 each for exploration and commitment). As with any homegrown scale, it took some years of testing, analysis, and refining, but now it has been established to have good reliability and validity. For an example of some findings from analyses of the AIM data, we have generally found that many of our students are in a state of foreclosure prior to the semester-long study abroad experience and have moved to a state of moratorium or achievement at the end of the study abroad experience. In addition, we have found that our predeparture goals assessment correlates positively with AIM scores, such that students with more intercultural goals are likely to show more increase in exploration of their own national identity (Meyer-Lee, Chambers, & Savicki, 2013).

We administer the GPI and the AIM both before and after study abroad to objectively document changes in students' intercultural awareness and identity in association with study abroad. The final aspect of outcomes on which we collect data postreturn (as well as five years after graduating to look at the longer term impacts) is a self-report scale on students' own growth. To do this, we use another homegrown series of Likert-style items articulating both our main goals for study abroad and many of the goals we have heard our students express. In fact, we use the goals (although not phrased as growth) in our predeparture data collection as an important predictor, as will be discussed next. Factor analysis has shown that these goals can be divided into some that are more intercultural and others that are more about personal development such as increases in independence and maturity.

Program predictor variables. Given that our main goal for our assessment is program improvement, it is essential that we correlate the outcomes we find with aspects of our programs. Our focus on program variables helps us to identify for our use in further program development aspects of our programs that are more supportive of growth. To get beyond basic program characteristics such as content and duration to the more fine-grained program design elements, we use our own adaption of Engle and Engle's (2003) typology. Engle and Engle argued for a categorization scale that outlines the degree of cultural immersion of individual program types along several dimensions, with the assumption that the degree of immersion in program types might facilitate cross-cultural competence of participants to different degrees. Rather than focus on discrete program types, we adapted the categories proposed by Engle and Engle to describe each of our individual programs on their five dimensions of "immersiveness." These five dimensions include entry target language, language required for course work, academic work context, housing, and level of experiential learning. Each dimension has a scale that reflects the level of immersion; for example, experiential learning is rated on a scale of no opportunity, limited opportunity, optional opportunity, and required and regular opportunity.

We have found that some of these dimensions are positively correlated with student outcomes. For example, both the amount of experiential learning built in and more international contact in the classroom correlate with larger increases in American identity development. Thus, we are able to be more systematic in our student advising and help students to be realistic in what they can expect of each program they are considering and what the program will require of them. In addition, as we have developed new programs, we have been able to focus on these dimensions in thinking about individual program specifics and about desired variability in our overall program offerings.

In contrast, the second type of program variable we assess uses another homegrown measure we created to try to quantify—after students return—the part over which the CWIL has little to no control: the degree of intercultural engagement students personally pursued while abroad. We created this Measure of Intercultural Engagement (MIE) in an attempt to capture the variance in student choice; again, in recognition that although we might have programs that provide students numerous opportunities, they still need to choose to take advantage of them (as the old saying goes, "You can lead a horse to water, but you can't make him drink!"). (See appendix B for the full measure.) The MIE has two factors: *multicultural interaction* and *multicultural engagement*. Multicultural interaction assesses the students' frequency of interacting with local people such as visiting local families, attending cocurricular campus events, watching local news, volunteering, and so on, whereas multicultural reflection assesses frequency of explicit reflection on this interaction through activities such as journaling, photography, conversations with locals, and so on. Interestingly, we have found that students' pre-AIM scores are negatively correlated with students' MIE scores; thus, low scores on exploration and commitment prior to departure are associated with more multicultural engagement than are high scores. It is not a surprise that engagement in general is correlated with growth (Meyer-Lee et al., 2013).

Student predictor variables. Another factor over which the CWIL has little control but that can be quite significantly related to outcomes is student demographics (e.g., GPA, age, major, ethnic identity, year, etc.). Using these as predictors to correlate with outcomes allows us to understand how student preparation and other personal characteristics influence later outcomes and improve our policies and advising. Thus, we have found that certain programs require a higher GPA than others for students to be both academically and personally successful. Understanding who our students are and what their needs are allows us to shape program development and adjust existing programs. We have also seen that age is correlated with certain types of growth, which has helped us to advise first-year students somewhat differently than sophomores. The fact that older students show more intercultural growth suggests an optimal readiness factor that has led us to reduce barriers to students going as juniors, as the majority of Saint Mary's students currently study abroad as sophomores. Student demographic data also indicate that Latina students have different personal experiences of intercultural identity while attending Spanish immersion programs, and this is an issue we try to address individually in predeparture meetings.

In addition to collecting demographic information, we ask students to articulate their own goals predeparture, as mentioned previously. We classify student goals into two broad classes: *personal development* and *intercultural development*. Personal development goals include, for example, questions about the desire for greater autonomy, the opportunity to travel, and growth in interpersonal skills. Intercultural goals include, for example, the desire to understand different cultures, to learn a different language, and to develop a new perspective on American culture. Surveying goals at predeparture serves pedagogical interests because it has been demonstrated in broader research on learning that when students are primed by reflecting on their own goals, they are more mindful about their encounters, choices, and learning (Paige, Cohen, Kappler-Mikk, Chi, & Lassegard, 2006). We can also link predeparture goals to student outcomes, allowing us to recognize that student goals might differ from institutional goals, and that student intention has an independent impact on outcomes. In other words, as one might expect, students who are hoping to learn more about world affairs and their place in the world are more likely to show growth on the GPI and AIM than those whose motivations are more about independence and adventure or even shopping (which students do sometimes honestly admit!). See table 11.1 for a summary of variable types and timing of data collection.

Challenges in Study Design

The gold standard in psychological research on development is a study with a stable control group. So with a "condition" such as study abroad, if one wants to make truly causal claims that changes measured between the pre- and the

TABLE 11.1
Schematic of Variable Types and Collection Points

Student Variables Predeparture	Program Variables During	Outcome Variables Postreturn
Demographics	MEI (collected post)	Post-AIM (and change)
Student goals	Engle and Engle (2003): "immersiveness"	Post-GPI (and change)
Pre-AIM		Self-rated growth
Pre-GPI		

Note. See "Study Abroad Levels: Towards a Classification of Program Types," by L. Engle and J. Engle, 2003, *Frontiers, IX,* pp. 1–20. AIM = American Identity Measure; GPI = Global Perspective Inventory.

postmeasures are caused by study abroad rather than just by maturation, one also needs to measure a "control" group of students who do not study abroad. In our first three-year study, we did obtain such a control group of students who did not intend to participate in study abroad, but it proved quite difficult to use as a true control for a number of reasons. First, some of the students changed their minds and studied abroad. Second, some of those who didn't study abroad participated in the many on-campus opportunities we have for global learning, which may have also had an impact on them. Third, those who had not done either of these were of course much less intrinsically interested in the topic, and it was therefore difficult to get a decent response rate for the "post." Therefore, although we did find evidence of greater growth in those who studied abroad, the main use to us of including a control group was helping us establish a baseline difference in "pre-" data between the two groups. In other words, were there were big differences in those who chose to study abroad and those who did not that might explain away differences noted afterward? There were not as many as we expected. This is probably due to the fact that more than half of our students study abroad in a wide variety of programs rather than just a small minority of self-selecting students. Thus, we no longer go to the trouble of recruiting a control group, but we are also careful, in principle, because of this study limitation to avoid using language of causation (e.g., claiming that study abroad causes x or y) and instead talk about correlates of change (those who studied abroad are also more likely to x or y).

Through trial and error, our approach to assessment has evolved over a number of years. One of the major limitations that we repeatedly encountered is the amount of time that some assessment procedures take. One example of this was the inability to follow through on assessment plans that involve qualitative data, as mentioned previously. Although we are often interested in gathering student responses in a more unfiltered way, from either application essays or classroom assignments, we have found the amount of time needed to analyze this data stream unfeasible because of the many other more immediate tasks that are required of our office. As a result, we have relied primarily on quantitative assessment procedures but continue to try to find ways to work in at least some qualitative methods.

Time constraints are also one of the reasons that we have found the GPI so useful, given the GPI's automatically generated reports about our student outcomes and changes. This enables us to keep a pulse on the students' learning each year, without investing significant time, until we are ready to engage in a more in-depth analysis. The other major time-saving process that we have implemented over the years is the automated collection of assessment data through our study abroad database. Thus, rather than collecting data from students in person, we are able to have students respond to all survey questions on their own time, via computer, directly into the database. Although there have been a few challenges in integrating the online assessment tools into this database, they seem to be surmountable, and this automation has decreased the overall time required of the office staff and also increased our overall response rates, which are generally quite good, around 70%. Earlier, we used grant money to incentivize participation, but we have found that to be unnecessary.

A final strategy, which has been very successful in our office to sustain a level of rigorous assessment when staff members are already quite overextended, is to bring qualified faculty, students, and, occasionally, external volunteer assistants onto the research team. Psychology students have recieved credit for independent studies or internships to assist in the assessment work, whereas faculty who have a professional interest in the research have joined us. We also draw on our own institutional research office as appropriate. At the beginning, we had grant funding to hire an evaluator to help the first author and the director of Saint Mary's Office of Institutional Research create the assessment plan, and the assistant director for study abroad assisted with data collection. Now the second author has come from the faculty to work part-time to coordinate study abroad programs and lead CWIL's ongoing assessment initiative.

Using the Study Evidence for Improvement

By weaving together in this case study the phases of data collection and analysis, reflection on results to discern needed changes, and then implementation of the changes, we want to emphasize how these phases form

USING DATA FOR IMPROVEMENT AND ADVOCACY   *223*

a continuous cycle that must not stop after data collection, despite the time constraints that can make assessment difficult to see through. We have shown how our own collected assessment data have helped us choose, advocate for, and implement pedagogical and curricular program design elements, policy changes (e.g., GPA requirements), advising approaches (taking into account program features and students' goals, age, and even ethnicity), and our predeparture preparation (talking more about goals and engagement choices).

The data have also led us to think in a more sophisticated way about program-specific outcomes. For example, the data suggested that one of our programs was not yielding optimum intercultural learning, although it met many other of our and students' objectives. In this specific case, it was possible for the director to make minor design changes. Beyond this, however, we also modified advising and preparation to (a) clarify the program-specific outcomes that could be expected, (b) draw on student goals and class standing in advising, (c) adjust the eligibility requirements, and (d) stress personal choice predeparture. As a result, students have shown somewhat improved outcomes in this program. We would like to think more in the future about assessing program-specific outcomes more directly and also adding some language proficiency assessment for our language-based programs.

Drawing on Institutional-Level Data on Outcomes for Advocacy Purposes

Beyond program improvement, our secondary reason for assessment was to advocate for the value of international education to various audiences. In addition to the multiple types of growth, which we have documented from our own multimethod longitudinal study data, we also take every opportunity to draw on broader academic or institutional-level data that might be relevant.

The very first type of datum Saint Mary's collects from a student is the admitted student survey administered by our Office of Institutional Research. This is a much larger survey that the college administers, but we have been able to work with the Office of Institutional Research to embed a couple of questions about incoming students' interest in study abroad. Specifically, the new questions ask students to rate features of the college as compared to those of other schools to which they applied, and we also ask explicit questions about whether they are planning to study abroad and, if so, where. Students consistently give our study abroad opportunities the second-highest rating among the 17 different features of Saint Mary's queried. As one might imagine, this statistic alone has been very helpful in advocating for study abroad with the administration and trustees. In addition, figures about how many students want to study abroad and in which country have been useful for not only showing the value of international education in attracting students but also predicting, to some extent, fluctuating student interests so CWIL can predict and plan for shifting resources. For example, when we saw there may be an increase in future demand for a particular program, we inquired study abroad sites about whether we can increase the total number of students that can attend. Similarly, when we saw an increase in the interest in our intended nursing majors in studying in Spanish-speaking countries, we worked with our partner provider to modify the programming to fit the level of language the nursing majors generally have during the semester they must study abroad. Finally, the fact that approximately 80% of our incoming student body indicates that they want to study abroad prior to the start of college but only about 51% of our students actually do keeps us focused on trying to identify the remaining barriers to study abroad.

On the other end of the student experience, we also disaggregate quite a few of our outgoing student institutional data sets to get at the impact of study abroad. For example, our students who study abroad have higher retention rates, GPAs, and institutional loyalty as measured by their saying they would choose the same institution again and higher rates of alumnae giving to the college. They also report more growth on many of the National Survey of Student Engagement or Higher Education Data Sharing items on critical thinking, leadership, transformative learning, and preparation for life. These data take very little effort to generate and can be of great assistance in demonstrating the importance and effectiveness of international education to advocate for its critical role in these difficult financial times.

Although we have had plenty of challenges in our assessment journey, we hope this case study will serve not so much as a road map but rather as an affirmation of the opportunity for even small schools to develop a productive culture of assessment within their international education units that is authentic to their own missions, contexts, questions, and goals. There is no need to reach for the nearest shrink-wrapped solution; as the saying goes, "If your only tool is a hammer, everything looks like a nail." By intentionally creating a realistic multimethod longitudinal plan that addresses our real questions, we have been able to improve and advocate for study abroad. We hope to continue to disseminate the results of Saint Mary's study abroad assessment efforts to contribute to the general body of empirical knowledge about growth in the context of international education for the benefit of the larger field.

References

Association of American Colleges and Universities. (2010). *VALUE rubrics.* Retrieved from www.aacu.org/value/rubrics/index_p.cfm?CFID=6634177&CF TOKEN=40351583

Braskamp, L. A., Braskamp, D. C., & Merrill, K. C. (2007). *Global Perspective Inventory.* Chicago, IL: Global Perspective Institute. Retrieved from http://gpi .central.edu

Engle, L., & Engle, J. (2003). Study abroad levels: Towards a classification of program types. *Frontiers, IX,* 1–20.

Erikson, E. H. (1968). *Identity: Youth and crisis.* Oxford, UK: Norton.

Hammer, M. R. (1999). A measure of intercultural sensitivity: The Intercultural Development Inventory. In S. M. Fowler & M. G. Fowler (Eds.), *The intercultural sourcebook* (Vol. 2, pp. 61–72). Yarmouth, ME: Intercultural Press.

Marcia, J. E. (1980). Identity in adolescence. In J. Adelson (Ed.), *Handbook of adolescent psychology* (pp. 159–187). New York, NY: Wiley.

Meyer-Lee, E., Chambers, K. L., & Savicki, V. (2013, May). *Making meaning of assessment: Recognizing the impact of national identity.* Presented at the 65th annual conference of NAFSA: Association of International Educators, St. Louis, MO.

Meyer-Lee, E., & Evans, J. (2008, May). New tools for intercultural outcomes learning assessment. In D. Deardorff (Chair), *Assessment toolbox for international educators.* Symposium presented at the annual conference of NAFSA: Association of International Educators, Washington, DC.

Paige, M. R., Cohen, A. D., Kappler-Mikk, B., Chi, J. C., & Lassegard, J. P. (2006). *Maximizing study abroad: A students' guide to strategies for language and culture learning and use.* Minneapolis, MN: Center for Advanced Research on Language Acquisition, University of Minnesota.

Phinney, J. (1992). The Multigroup Ethnic Identity Measure: A new scale for use with diverse groups. *Journal of Adolescent Research, 7,* 156–176.

Phinney, J., & Rosenthal, D. A. (1992). Ethnic identity in adolescence: Process, context, and outcome. In G. Adams, T. Gullotta, & R. Montemayor (Eds.), *Adolescent identity formation* (Vol. 4, pp. 145–172). Thousand Oaks, CA: Sage.

Shealy, C. N. (2004). A model and method for "making" a C-I psychologist: Equilintegration (EI) theory and the Beliefs, Events, and Values Inventory (BEVI) [Special series]. *Journal of Clinical Psychology, 60,* 1065–1090.

Appendix 11.A

⊞

Saint Mary's College
NOTRE DAME · INDIANA

AMERICAN IDENTITY
MEASURE

The Multigroup Ethnic Identity Measure was originally from J. Phinney ([1992]. The Multigroup Ethnic Identity Measure: A new scale for use with adolescents and young adults from diverse groups. *Journal of Adolescent Research, 7,* 156–176). It has since been revised. The American Identity Questionnaire is from J. Phinney and M. Devich-Navarro ([1997]. Variations in bicultural identification among African American and Mexican American adolescents. *Journal of Research on Adolescence, 7,* 3–32).

The adaptation of some items from these two scales for use with U.S. students studying abroad to examine American identity was done by Elaine Meyer-Lee and Joy Evans, Saint Mary's College, and presented at NAFSA in Minneapolis on June 1, 2007. The scale is available for research purposes. If you use the measure in a study, please use the previous citations and send a copy of your results to Dr. Elaine Meyer-Lee, Associate Vice President for Global Learning and Leadership Development, Agnes Scott College.

Use the the following numbers to indicate how much you agree or disagree with each statement:

4: Strongly Agree	*3: Somewhat Agree*	*2: Somewhat Disagree*	*1: Strongly Disagree*

1. I think of myself as being American. (Phinney AIQ 1)
2. Being American plays an important part in my life. (Phinney AIQ 3)

3. I have a strong sense of being American. (Phinney AIQ 6 and MEIM-R 2)
4. I have spent time trying to find out more about what being American means by exploring its history, traditions, and customs. (MEIM-R 1)
5. I have thought a lot about how my life will be affected by my American identity. (10-item MEIM 2)
6. I have often talked to other people about being American. (MEIM-R 5)
7. I understand pretty well what being American means to me. (MEIM-R 3)
8. I have often done things that will help me understand my American nationality better. (MEIM-R 4)
9. I have sometimes wondered about the meaning or implications of being American. (10-item MEIM 6)
10. I feel a strong attachment toward my American nationality. (MEIM-R 6)

Subscales according to Phinney and validated by SMC factor analysis:

Commitment/Affirmation, items 1, 2, 3, 7, 10
Exploration/Search, items 4, 5, 6, 8, 9

The preferred scoring is to use the mean of the item scores; that is, the mean of the 10 items for an overall score and the mean of the 5 items for search and the 5 items for affirmation. Thus, the range of scores is from 1 to 4.

Appendix 11.B

✠
Saint Mary's College
NOTRE DAME · INDIANA

MEASURE OF
INTERCULTURAL
ENGAGEMENT

This scale was created by Elaine Meyer-Lee and Joy Evans, Saint Mary's College, for use with U.S. students studying abroad to quantify how much students choose to interact with local people and reflect on those interactions. The scale is available for research purposes. If you use the measure in a study, please cite this chapter and send a copy of your results to Dr. Elaine Meyer-Lee, Director, Associate Vice President for Global Learning and Leadership Development Agnes, Scott College.

We would like to know how you were able to immerse yourself in the host country's local culture. We are not suggesting that more often is necessarily better, and some options may be "Not Available" to your program, but your honest reply will help us advise future students about what to expect. Please indicate only one number.

*How often did you **interact** with local people in the following contexts?*

Frequently   Occasionally   Infrequently   Never/Not Available
(3–5/week)   (1–2/week)   (<1/ week)   (0 times)

1. Local media (TV, newspaper, magazine, radio)
2. Shopping/visiting local markets
3. Movies/entertainment catering to locals
4. Restaurants/pubs/cafés catering to locals

  5. Visiting local families/friends in their homes
  6. Participating in worship services
  7. On-campus informal conversations
  8. Events sponsored by the study abroad program
  9. Extracurricular activities (student clubs, intramurals, etc.)
  10. Volunteering/service-learning/internships/shadowing

*Individuals **reflect** on abroad experiences in many different ways. Please indicate **how often you reflected on your interactions with the culture** in the following ways while you were studying abroad:*

  11. Journaling/blogging
  12. Photography
  13. Other artistic expression (painting, drawing, collages, etc.)
  14. Class discussions
  15. Informal conversations with locals
  16. Informal conversations with students studying abroad
  17. Calling/e-mailing family/friends/faculty in America

Items 1–10 are grouped into an interaction subscale, and items 11–17 are grouped into a reflection subscale. All items are reverse coded, so there is a range of scores from 0–5. The mean of the subscales is used as our metric of engagement.

12

CONTINUOUS IMPROVEMENT IN A SMALL STUDY ABROAD OFFICE USING OUTCOMES ASSESSMENT

Victor Savicki and Michele V. Price

Τhis extended case study of study abroad outcomes assessment illustrates a long-term investment in assessment and a continuous improvement framework for using assessment results to guide changes in program design. The concept of "continuous improvement" is based on management practices successful in business and industry (van Aartsengel & Kurtoglu, 2013). The goal is simple: Assess your efforts, make adjustments based on data to improve your goal attainment, and do it over and over again. The process has not been easy or always smooth, yet this case documents how adherence to the idea of continuous improvement can be implemented in the face of constraints and impediments facing study abroad and international education offices.

Phase 1: Making Lemonade

Context

In an attempt to increase the head count of students during a time of budgetary crisis, the administration at Western Oregon University required study abroad students to enroll in a one-credit course parallel to their study abroad. Approximately 100–120 students studied abroad each year, slightly less than 2% of the total student population. Western Europe was the primary destination, followed by Spanish-language sites mostly in Latin America. Short programs, four to eight weeks, were the most popular, though some students did study abroad for a full term or year. This course did not have an academic home but rather was taught by personnel in the campus study abroad office—without additional funding. The course originally was offered as pass–no credit, and the requirements to earn a pass were minimal. In 2001, the newly installed director (second author of this chapter) inherited the course in this format. Determined to make the best of this unfunded mandate and to create an academically sound course, the director, in collaboration with Western Oregon University's writing center, redesigned the course and requested a grading method change from pass–no credit to A–F. Thus began the continuous redesigning and improvement of this course, the study abroad capstone project.

Several years later, when university accreditation loomed, additional requirements for assessment were assigned to meet the needs for self-study as a part of preparation for the accrediting agency visit and evaluation. Again, no specific funds were allocated to support this process; the office was staffed with one study abroad professional, a half-time secretary, and occasional work-study students. At that time, the study abroad office director invited an emeritus faculty (first author of this chapter) to design an assessment methodology that would both meet the needs of the university and actually deliver meaningful results for the study abroad office. Thus this assessment project was launched.

Goals

After some discussion (between the director and the faculty assessor), we determined typical, global, subjective, student-satisfaction-oriented evaluations were too ambiguous for developing findings that would guide future improvement of the capstone course, yet both our interests remained on psychological gains that might illustrate intercultural competence. The goal of the assessment design was focused on determining what changes, if any, study abroad students underwent as a result of their experience. The focus of these changes was on areas of personal growth and development. The results would be used both to satisfy institutional assessment requirements and to offer data-driven feedback concerning the effectiveness of study abroad office programming.

Methodology

Because of budgetary constraints, we decided to search journal articles, the *Mental Measurements Yearbook* (Buros Institute of Mental Measurements,

2014), and other sources in the public domain for examples of measures that would quantify key features that we believed would reflect changes that might be expected in successful study abroad student experiences. The following is a list of the measures we used:

- *Goals for studying abroad* (Kitsantas, 2004) are defined as intentions to attain a specific standard of proficiency, usually within a specified time limit. Subgoals include cross-cultural competence, subject interest and competence, and social gathering (including heritage search).
- *General self-efficacy* (Chen, Gully, & Eden, 2001) is one's belief in one's overall competence to effect requisite performances across a wide variety of achievement situations and to view oneself as capable of meeting task demands in a broad array of contexts.
- *Social self-efficacy* (Smith & Betz, 2000) is an individual's confidence in his or her ability to engage in the social interactional tasks necessary to initiate and maintain interpersonal relationships.
- *Global perspective-ethnocentrism* (Wielkiewicz, 2000) has two subscales:

  - *Systemic thinking* reflects one's ability to relate a variety of ideas and concepts to organizational success and to relate organizational success to the complex interaction of a number of factors.
  - *Hierarchical thinking* suggests that organizations should be organized in a stable hierarchical manner, with power and control focused in the upper levels of the hierarchy and with the belief that control and authority extend downward, and members should seek guidance from the level above them.

- *Intercultural adjustment potential* (Matsumoto et al., 2001) is one's ability to adapt successfully to life in a cultural environment different from that to which one is accustomed. Subscales include *emotion regulation*, the ability to modulate one's emotional reactions to avoid employing psychological defenses; *openness*, the ability to engage in learning about the new culture; *flexibility*, the ability to avoid over-attachment to previous ways of thinking and willingness to tolerate ambiguity; and *critical thinking*, the ability to generate creative, new hypotheses about incidents in the new culture that go beyond one's home cultural framework.
- *Satisfaction with life (general well-being)* (Diener, Emmons, Larsen, & Griffin, 1985) is an overall indicator of satisfaction with life and relates with other measures of psychological well-being.

- *Perspective taking and empathy (Interpersonal Reactivity Index)* (Davis, 1996). *Perspective taking* is one's tendency to naturally examine another's point of view; *empathic concern* is having feelings of sympathy and concern for others.

Separate pre- and post-study abroad versions were constructed with the only difference between the two versions in the *goals for studying abroad*; the pre-departure version asked for anticipated goals, and the postreturn version asked for goal completion. The survey was posted online via web-based survey software. Prior to departure, students completed the preversion questions and provided relevant demographic information (age, gender, class standing) in 20 to 30 minutes. After students returned and completed the final requirements of the study abroad capstone course, they completed the postversion. Not all students completed both pre- and postversions. On average, 60 students per year completed the surveys.

Assessment Findings

Results for the first year indicated that students mostly changed in the desired direction on the scales. However, those changes did not often reach statistical significance. It seemed that students with high general self-esteem prior to departure, for example, had high general self-esteem upon return. They were generally above the norm for these measures, but study abroad, and specifically the capstone course of the study abroad office, seemed not to have boosted these measures significantly.

Lessons Learned

We were disappointed that the pre- and postmeasures were not sensitive to the impact of study abroad. However, we decided that students' experiences while they were abroad were very different from each other in terms of host culture, duration of stay, level of immersion, language expectations, and many other factors, so it is unreasonable for our set of measures to be able to capture the differences over such a broad range of study abroad site configurations. Instead, we decided to focus on the aspect of the student experience for which we were directly responsible: the study abroad capstone course.

Phase 2: 90 Degree Pivot

Context

In light of our previous efforts, we decided to keep the online survey in place because the measures in the survey might help us provide background for whatever results we might find in our next iteration. In addition, adding students to our database over several years might give us a more stable and reliable source of information. At this point, the requirement for assessment by the university quieted, but we were required to produce a yearly report.

Goals

As a part of the capstone course, students were required to write a final paper. For this paper, students were to capture and describe the key events and insights that they gained as a result of their study abroad experiences. The study abroad director and her staff, work-study students (three in all), and the writing center director committed significant efforts into crafting a rubric for this paper that would guide student reflection and writing. Our goal was to determine how well students engaged in this activity.

Methodology

A two-pronged approach to assessment was taken. First, students' final papers were subjected to content analysis using the Linguistic Inquiry and Word Count (LIWC) software (Pennebaker, Chung, Ireland, Gonzales, & Booth, 2007). This software has several "dictionaries" that identify key types of psychological phenomena. We scored the final paper content for cognitive processes (insight, causality, inclusiveness, etc.), affective processes (positive affect, negative affect, anxiety, etc.), and personal concerns (leisure, work, eating and drinking, etc.). We compared study abroad student responses in these categories to those of a normative sample supplied by the LIWC manual.

The second prong of this assessment was to compare student reports of goal attainment while abroad with both content categories from the analysis of their papers and predeparture measures on the online survey. Goal attainment was determined by using the Kitsantas (2004) Goals Survey with rephrasing to ask for how much they thought that they had actually attained the goals specified. These goals focused on the subscales of cross-cultural competence, subject interest competence, and social gathering (the degree of social contacts with American peers and host culture natives, and heritage concerns). The idea was to determine what characteristics defined *readiness to succeed* in study abroad.

Assessment Findings

Comparison of study abroad student final papers in the capstone course with the norm group developed by the LIWC software developers indicated that the study abroad student papers showed important differences in the desired directions on many categories identified by the LIWC content analysis software. Three general areas of content analysis are discussed: cognitive processes, affective processes, and personal concerns.

Cognitive processes. Study abroad students showed elevated levels of *inclusiveness* and *insight.* These content codes indicated that students discussed their study abroad experiences in a way that incorporated both home and host culture aspects in a thoughtful and reflective way. Unfortunately, the *certainty* category is also a bit elevated, possibly indicating a less tentative approach to discussing these issues.

Affective processes. Study abroad students show lower negative affect overall and in several of the negative affect categories: sadness, anger, and anxiety. Overall positive affect is elevated, indicating that the students evaluated their study abroad experience positively despite difficulties they may have encountered.

Personal concerns. Adolescent study abroad students in the midst of solidifying their identities are likely to consider study abroad situations, events, and encounters in the light of important personal concerns related to identity. Clearly, personal values and expectations related to how space is used and how one relates to time are likely to be challenged by exposure to values in a different culture. The data support that these issues were quite salient for the study abroad students. Other issues relating to food and drink, leisure activity and expectations, activity level, and religion were all mentioned by the students in their papers. Overall, students showed that they were processing this type of identity-relevant information during their study abroad.

In summary, the content analysis of student reentry essays indicated that students were addressing important issues in regard to their study abroad experience and processing that information at both a cognitive level and an affective level. The study abroad student deviations from the LIWC norm group, for the most part, indicated that study abroad students found their experience positive and intellectually challenging.

Postdiction correlations to goal attainment. Correlations between predeparture measures of individual student characteristics and their reports of attainment of study abroad goals indicate that self-efficacy and systemic thinking at predeparture were positively related to reports of goal attainment. The measure of flexibility was probably more related to independence of action. Its inverse relation to goal attainment may indicate a lack of engagement with the host culture. Likewise, language-usage aspects of student capstone essays related to goal attainment (e.g., affect, causality, inhibition, motion). These correlations give clues as to important processes active during the study abroad sojourn.

In summary, the postdiction correlations between predeparture individual characteristics and reentry goal attainment give some indication of what aspects of personal orientation to study abroad to emphasize in preparation for study abroad. Likewise, the content analysis correlations with reentry goal attainment yield suggestions as to the process the students underwent while studying abroad.

Lessons Learned

Although the content analysis and postdiction study in relation to goal achievement gave us some interesting confirmation of the capstone paper efficacy and some ideas about redesigning our orientation session, some of the results were a bit obscure. It was difficult to know exactly what to do as a result of the findings. Also, on a more intuitive level, many of the students' final papers were not descriptive or reflective enough regarding their intercultural learning to capture the insights that we had hoped to see.

Phase 3: More Relevant Content Analysis

Context

Although we found that returning students wrote richer final essays than students in the comparison norm group, the essays did not consistently reveal student thinking about cultural differences or explain the emotional and cognitive connections that would indicate deep reflection about self and culture. We still could not afford to purchase any of the commercial measurement instruments that might uncover these connections more directly. Therefore, we decided to, again, focus on students' final essays but to use a content analysis process that employed the developmental model of intercultural sensitivity (DMIS) (Bennett, 1993).

Goals

Our goal was to be able to describe the level of intercultural sensitivity displayed by students in writing their reflections on study abroad as expressed in their final essays. We wanted to use the language of the DMIS (Bennett, 1993) as a guideline in this process. The hope was to have a more easily understood description of our students' reflection process.

Methodology

Students' final essays were coded by independent raters in a two-step process. The coders were four graduate students, all of whom had extensive experience with living abroad. They were all compensated at the work-study student rate. In step one, sentences in students' essays were identified as discussing overt or implied differences between cultures. In step two, these sentences were assessed as belonging to one of the DMIS stages. Interrater reliability for assignment of DMIS stage codes was 82.9%. Coder training placed special emphasis on verbal expressions that fit into the six DMIS categories: denial, defense, minimization, acceptance, adaptation, and integration. We used training materials from the Intercultural Development Inventory (Hammer, Bennett, & Wiseman, 2003) as part of the coder-training manual. Comprehensive understanding of the DMIS was part of the training. The training and coding were very labor intensive. All coders had extensive experience in living abroad and in dealing with study abroad students, thus they had a perspective on intercultural sensitivity that would not be available to someone without such background.

An intercultural sensitivity summary score was developed by summing the weighted number of stage examples in each essay using the following scheme: ([Denial × –3] + [Defense × –2] + [Minimization × –1] + [Acceptance × +1] + [Adaptation × +2] + [Integration × +3]). This score was then correlated to predeparture measures of personality and study abroad readiness.

Assessment Findings

The average length of the essays was 1,925 words or roughly 6.5 pages. Proportions of codable content in essays averaged 20.6%, with a range of 1.9% to 51.2%. Women wrote significantly more codable content in their essays than men. Essay lengths between men and women were not significantly different.

Anecdotally, students' strategies for avoiding discussing reactions to cultural difference include

1. external-only focus (e.g., travelogues: "It's Tuesday; it must be Venice."),
2. internal-only focus (e.g., "I changed so much but not in relation to any outside events. It's all about me."), and
3. intellectualization (e.g., "My experience was pristine, unrelated to feelings.").

Proportions of intercultural sensitivity statements were not evenly distributed, with fewer denial, minimization, and integration statements and more defense, acceptance, and adaptation ones.

Figure 12.1 shows average intercultural sensitivity summary scores were distributed 57% in ethnocentrism and 43% in ethnorelativism. Neither gender, age, class standing, nor duration of study abroad was significantly related to the intercultural sensitivity summary score.

Postsojourn student essay intercultural sensitivity summary scores were significantly positively correlated with predeparture scores of the openness

Figure 12.1 Distribution of intercultural sensitivity summary scores

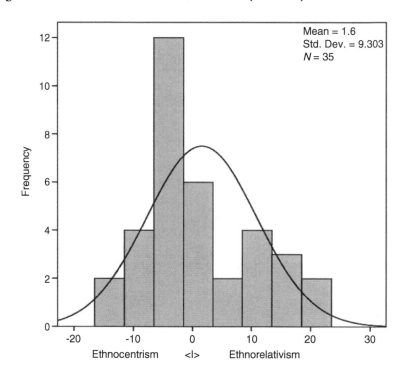

($r = .409$) and critical thinking ($r = .364$) subscales from the Intercultural Adjustment Potential Scale and significantly negatively correlated with empathic concern ($r = -.370$).

Prior abilities to be open to new experience, to process information in a critical and creative fashion, and to focus on one's own internal processes were related to higher levels of intercultural sensitivity.

Lessons Learned

It is unclear whether students who focused only on their internal reaction or focused only on external events were unaware of the other information source. Experiential learning theory suggests that the combination of experience and cognitive understanding leads to richer learning (Kolb, 1984). Student inclinations to deny or ignore one or the other aspect led to unscorable statements. Training or prompts to combine both internal and environmental (cultural) events might lead to a greater awareness of cultural issues and a higher level of intercultural sensitivity.

Although the findings were interesting and understandable, the methodology of this type of content analysis was slow and burdensome. We decided that finding appropriate coders, training them in the theoretical context, and training them in the specific coding methodology was beyond the scope of the regular ongoing assessment activities of the study abroad office. We could not devote this amount of time and effort on a continual basis. A different approach was called for.

Phase 4: Priming the Pump: Reflection and Cognitive Complexity

Context

Over the duration of this project, it has become more and more evident that students need both focus important intercultural issues over the span of their sojourn and guidance to unpack their experience not only while they are abroad but also after they return home. To that end, in 2008–2009, the director implemented a journal assignment modeled on the "Strategies for Keeping a Journal" chapter of the University of Minnesota's text *Maximizing Study Abroad* (Paige, Cohen, Kappler, Chi, & Lassegard, 2002) and also added a reentry session. Following this model of journal writing, students divided their journal into four sections: impressions, description, narrative, and expressive. They could write their entries in any section, but they were encouraged to try them all. Unfortunately, students didn't embrace the concept of a handwritten reflective journal, and most produced sporadic entries of the "this is what I did today" nature rather than entries that demonstrated that they were observing and engaging in the culture around them.

Nevertheless, we felt we were on the right track, and in 2010, we revised the journal assignment. The new assignment focused on asking what we hoped were the "right questions" or at least better questions, predeparture, while abroad, and on return, and was designed to encourage students to view their study abroad experience as an integrated whole and to help them articulate why the experience was important. Chisholm's book *Charting a Hero's Journey* (2000) provided inspiration for the questions. The predeparture questions planted seeds, which students had to cultivate by reflecting back while abroad and then again after returning.

The before and during time points were added to encourage thinking about key issues from the beginning and as a point of reference when students looked back on their experiences. The previous, more general, journal assignment and the final essay assignment had failed to elicit the kind of reflection that we hoped that students would describe. Therefore, we crafted more specific and more time-relevant questions that prompted for the integration of cultural concerns and the cognitive and emotional responses of students (see Savicki & Price, in press, for more details on this approach).

Goals

The goal of this phase of assessment was to track student reflection on specific topics over the span of their study abroad: before, during, and after. We were particularly interested in the processes that students employed in reflection. What cognitive patterns and emotional aspects were involved in their reflection? Were the components of critical thinking evident? The goal was to be more specific about the language and thought patterns students used so that we could prompt effective patterns in future questions asking for reflection about the study abroad experience.

Methodology

Table 12.1 shows the reflective questions for this part of the assessment series. These questions were adapted from *Charting a Hero's Journey* (Chisholm, 2000), which is often used as a guide to journal writing for college students engaged in study abroad, off-campus study, and service-learning. Again, the LIWC content analysis software (Pennebaker, Booth, & Francis, 2007) analyzed the questions for language relevant to categories of cognitive processes (insight, causality, discrepancies, tentativeness, certainty, inhibition, inclusivity, exclusivity, and negations), categories of affect (positive emotions, negative emotions, anxiety, anger, and sadness), and characteristics of the writing task itself (word count, words per sentence, and long words [six letters or more]). Students submitted answers to assigned questions via e-mail at the designated times (prior to leaving on their study abroad, prior to the end of their sojourn abroad, and after reentry to their university life in the United States). Three specific content areas were selected for analysis: academic expectations (four), cultural expectations (five), and psychological issues (two). Answers to these three areas were scored over the three time periods.

Assessment Findings

Overall, students' written expression, cognitive process, and affective language indicate thoughtful written responses. Changes over time and differences between content areas indicate a nuanced and psychologically healthy manner of processing study abroad experiences.

Written expression. Figure 12.2 shows that word count for both academic expectations and psychological issues peaked during the study abroad sojourn. However, the amount written for cultural expectations rose across all time periods, suggesting continued challenges to students in deciphering their study abroad and home cultures. Words per sentence and long words are consistently higher for academic expectations, possibly reflecting academic jargon and attempts at a more scholarly approach to content. For psychological

TABLE 12.1

Specific Reflection Questions for Before, During, and After Study Abroad

Prior	During	After
1. How and why did you choose the particular location of your study abroad? Who or what influenced your choice?	Describe the scene that greeted you upon arrival in the airport, and recount the behavior you observed. What bewildered, delighted, interested, amused, or frightened you? Why?	What hard skills did you learn or build on while abroad? How can these be reflected on your résumé? How will these skills support your desired employment? How will you articulate these skills during an interview with a prospective employer?
2. How do you feel about leaving home and campus? What are you glad to be leaving behind? What do you think you'll miss?	What has the separation from friends, family, school, and a familiar way of life revealed to you about yourself?	How do you feel about being home and back on campus? Are you glad to be home? What do you miss the most about your host country?
3. What ideologies are you taking with you? Identifying these beliefs and their source may help you when you are challenged abroad by those with a different point of view.	Have your relationships with individuals or your understanding of the culture become more complicated as your stay lengthens? How long do you think it takes to begin to understand and be part of the complexities of your host culture?	What soft skills did you learn or build on while abroad? How can these be reflected on your résumé? How will these skills support your desired employment? How will you articulate these strengths during an interview with a prospective employer?
4. What are your expectations and what are your preconceived notions about your academic program? What do you hope to learn, and how do you envision the instructors and learning environments?	Systems of education and forms of teaching vary from country to country. What have you discovered about the system of education in your host nation compared to the system of education you experience in the United States? Are your preconceived notions hindering your progress or aiding you in navigating new academic rules?	Were the expectations you had of your academic program abroad met? Why or why not? What about your preconceived notions? Which have you changed, and which beliefs or attitudes have you retained?
5. What expectations and what preconceived notions do you have of your host culture? How do you see yourself interacting with the host culture in light of your expectations and preconceived notions?	Describe how your expectations and preconceived notions of the host culture are being met or not. How have your first impressions of the country and its people changed since your arrival?	Were the expectations you had of your host culture met? Why or why not? Was the vision of yourself in interaction with the host culture realized? Why or why not? What about your preconceived notions? Which have you changed, and which beliefs or attitudes have you retained?

Figure 12.2 Mean word count on students' reflections before, during, and after study abroad

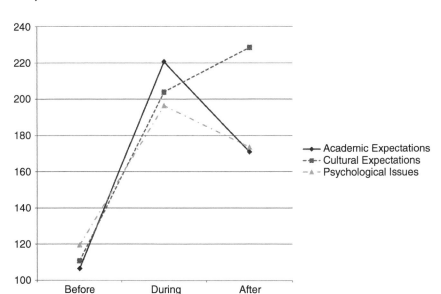

issues, all written expression indicators peaked during the sojourn but are lower before and after, indicating struggles with psychological adjustment. These struggles may be neither anticipated nor lingering but demand higher attention during the immediacy of demands of acculturative stress.

Academic expectations. For academic expectations, students showed a somewhat similar pattern of cognitive processes before and after their sojourn, with fewer indications of reflective thinking during it. Students in the midst of struggling with academic requirements of their study abroad were less able to write about these struggles in an insightful and cognitively complex way. For example,

> I really struggled with some of the academics here. . . . I would receive written requirements for classes, and then, in class, the professors would add on additional requirements. They also would tell one student and expect every student to know the new requirements! There have been a few crazy games of 'telephone' with no one really knowing what is going on.

Cultural expectations. For cultural expectations, the pattern of cognitive processing indicated both reflective and reactive thinking. Again, despite study abroad students showing cognitive complexity above the norm in most cases, cognitive processes employed during the sojourn often dipped in comparison with levels used before and after. For example, "I definitely see the world differently; I just think that there are so many wonderful places out there to explore and see. I am open to try new experiences, and I appreciate everything that I have in my life."

Psychological issues. Psychological issues also showed mixed reflective and nonreflective approaches to cognitive processing. Uses of causality and insight peaked, and inclusiveness dropped during the sojourn, illustrating students used a reflective approach while abroad. Cognitive complexity and reflection were mixed with indicators of more reactive and simplistic thinking. For example, "Everything else was just different; it felt weird to come back home, but I was glad to be home at the same time."

Affective language. Affective language might be used intensely in dealing with psychological issues such as separation and feelings regarding reentry. Affective language may better be understood in tandem with cognitive processing in the sense that more thorough and complex thinking about psychological issues might best analyze both positive and negative emotions in order to view them from a different perspective. For example, "Even though I felt out of sorts listening to a new form of language, I enjoyed everyone's cheerful and bright nature. The energy was amazing! It seemed that every person I met was so willing to help. I found this both interesting and delightful because many Americans I've met seem to be just the opposite; they tend to keep to themselves, and they aren't that helpful."

Lessons Learned

Reflective questions used in the current assessment iteration, probing responses to specific content areas across three time periods, allowed students to demonstrate reflection and cognitive complexity in their responses. At most times, students used insight, discrepancy, conjunctions, and prepositions well above the level of the norm group. Clearly, they were attempting to process their reactions to the questions in detail and in depth. The strategy of asking questions about content areas in this manner seems to have yielded meaningful student responses. The psychological issues content area showed the most distinctive responses, with its intense processing while students were experiencing the stressors of their encounters during the sojourn in the host culture. Similarly, cultural expectations showed continued intense thought upon reentry, thus signaling the need for further processing of those issues. Affective responding seems to be a critical component of the processing that students did at all time periods. Focusing only on cognitive processes would have missed this dynamic interplay between cognition and affect.

The concept of reflection can be vague and elusive. How students thought in this study showed a variety of cognitive processes that gives some body to the workings of reflection. Insights do not necessarily spring full blown into the students' minds but rather may emerge as a product of pondering multiple ideas and connections in relation both to their current situation and to their past meaning frameworks. Couching reflective questions in language that promotes both integration of experience and students' cognitive and affective responses improves the probability that students will reflect on that content. Also, asking questions that prompt language of causality, insight, exclusiveness, comparison, and connection among concepts may set the stage for more cognitively complex thinking.

Overall, using the LIWC to track the student writing and reflection process across time added interesting insights into student reflection, and the computer-based content analysis was, by far, more reliable and easier to use than was training human coders. Transitions from single final essays to shorter writings over time (both highly focused and more open-ended) have helped us coach students in near real-time. This timely guidance has reaped positive results.

Phase 5 and Beyond: The Next Iterations

Assessment continues, as does continuous improvement of program design based on lessons learned from the ongoing assessment projects. On the basis of our previous steps, we have moved to following students' writing via computer blogs on an almost weekly basis. This will expand our knowledge of student development over time, beginning at predeparture and ending at reentry. Our journey has been marked by small assessment projects focused, for the most part, on specific program components (e.g., students' final essays). Assessment results have directed our attention to ways of enhancing our goals and ideas of broadening our impact. The continuous improvement process does not end, but it does morph based on previous findings. Hopefully, our study abroad assessment experience in a small, underfunded, understaffed study abroad office can give readers ideas and optimism concerning the assessment process.

References

Bennett, M. J. (1993). Toward ethnorelativism: A developmental model of intercultural sensitivity. In R. M. Paige (Ed.), *Education for the intercultural experience* (2nd ed., pp. 21–71). Yarmouth, ME: Intercultural Press.

Buros Institute of Mental Measurements. (2014). *Mental measurements yearbook*. New York, NY: Ovid Technologies. Retrieved from http://buros.org/mental-measurements-yearbook

Chen, G., Gully, S. M., & Eden, D. (2001). Validation of a new general self-efficacy scale: New General Self-Efficacy Scale. *Organizational Research Methods, 4,* 62–83.

Chisholm, L. A. (2000). *Charting a hero's journey.* New York, NY: International Partnership for Service-Learning and Leadership.

Davis, M. H. (1996). *Empathy: A social psychological approach.* Boulder, CO: Westview.

Diener, E., Emmons, R. A., Larsen, R. J., & Griffin, S. (1985). The Satisfaction With Life Scale. *Journal of Personality Assessment, 49,* 71–75.

Hammer, M. R., Bennett, M. J., & Wiseman, R. (2003). Measuring intercultural sensitivity: The intercultural development inventory. *International Journal of Intercultural Relations, 27,* 421–443.

Kitsantas, A. (2004). Studying abroad: The role of college students' goals on the development of cross-cultural skills and global understanding. *College Student Journal, 38,* 441–452.

Kolb, D. (1984). *Experiential learning as the science of learning and development.* Englewood Cliffs, NJ: Prentice Hall.

Matsumoto, D., Leroux, J. A., Ratzlaff, C., Tatani, H., Uchida, H., Kim, C., & Araki, S. (2001). Development and validation of a measure of intercultural adjustment potential in Japanese sojourners: The Intercultural Adjustment Potential Scale (ICAPS). *International Journal of Intercultural Relations, 25*(5), 483–510.

Paige, R. M., Cohen, A. D., Kappler, B., Chi, J. C., & Lassegard, J. P. (2002). *Maximizing study abroad: A student's guide to strategies in language and culture learning and use.* Minneapolis, MN: Center for Advanced Research on Language Acquisition, University of Minnesota.

Pennebaker, J. W., Booth, R. J., & Francis, M. E. (2007). Linguistic Inquiry and Word Count: LIWC [Computer software]. Austin, TX: LIWC.net.

Pennebaker, J. W., Chung, C. K., Ireland, M., Gonzales, A., & Booth, R. J. (2007). *The development and psychometric properties of the LIWC2007.* Austin, TX: LIWC .net.

Savicki, V., & Price, M. V. (in press). Student reflective writing: Cognition and affect before, during, and after study abroad. *Journal of College Student Development.*

Smith, H. M., & Betz, N. E. (2000). Development and validation of a scale of perceived social self-efficacy. *Journal of Career Assessment, 8,* 283–301.

Van Aartsengel, A., & Kurtoglu, S. (2013). *A guide to continuous improvement transformation: Concepts, processes, implementation.* New York, NY: Springer.

Wielkiewicz, R. M. (2000). The Leadership Attitudes and Beliefs Scale: An instrument for evaluating college students' thinking about leadership and organizations. *Journal of College Student Development, 41,* 335–347.

13

A CLOSER LOOK AT THE WESLEYAN INTERCULTURAL COMPETENCE SCALE

A New Tool for Measuring Study Abroad Outcomes

Steven E. Stemler and Carolyn K. Sorkin

In this case study, we describe the development and use of the Wesleyan Intercultural Competence Scale (WICS), a new instrument for assessing the effectiveness of study abroad programs. We begin by discussing the institutional and political context in which this instrument was developed. We then discuss different approaches to assessing intercultural competence found in the literature. Finally, we summarize the methodology used in our work, as well as some results from early studies with the WICS. Along the way, we discuss false starts and challenges we encountered. We end by reflecting on lessons learned and providing recommendations for future research.

Context

Wesleyan University is a small, private, highly selective liberal arts university located in the state of Connecticut in a small town equidistant from Boston and New York. Wesleyan enrolls 2,900 undergraduate and 200 graduate students, plus 200 students in a Graduate Liberal Studies program. The student body is 52% women and hails from 49 states, the District of Columbia, the Virgin Islands, Puerto Rico, and 52 countries outside the United States.

Thirty-one percent of the classes of 2014–2017 are students of color (7% Black/African American, 8% Asian/Asian American, 10% Latino/Hispanic, 0.07% Native American, 0.1% Native Hawaiian or other Pacific Islander, 6% multiracial); another 8% hold foreign passports. All 385 faculty members (48% women, 17% persons of color) teach undergraduates and undertake scholarly research.

Wesleyan has long enjoyed high participation rates in study abroad. Some 45% of students study abroad for a semester or year. Although Wesleyan does not track summer study abroad, anecdotal evidence suggests the percentage would rise markedly were it to do so. Students fan out across the globe, with less emphasis on Western Europe than at many U.S. institutions. Three academic departments require study abroad for their majors.

As is true at other institutions, five or six years ago Wesleyan's Office of International Studies (OIS) began to recognize a need to assess study abroad outcomes. What were students gaining from their experiences abroad? Although Wesleyan requires students to earn grades for courses taken abroad, OIS research showed that these were largely the same as grades earned on campus. Furthermore, grades reflect only a small part of the study abroad experience, namely, mastery of content inside the classroom. We began to wonder how and how well students were immersing themselves in their host cultures and what they were taking away from the experience.

Background

Stemler (2012) used Wesleyan's 10 "Essential Capabilities," to be developed through academic work at Wesleyan and sometimes referred to as "essential outcomes" (www.wesleyan.edu/capabilities), as a framework for systematically reviewing similar statements from the top 125 U.S. national universities and the top 125 liberal arts colleges identified by the 2010 *U.S. News & World Report* college rankings. The development of intercultural competence was the most highly rated priority among highly selective national universities (85% mentioned it), beating out all other skills, including writing, quantitative reasoning skills, civic engagement, and information literacy. Furthermore, intercultural competence was second to only writing at highly selective liberal arts universities (68%).

One of the key challenges in the study abroad field is that, despite relative consensus regarding the importance of developing intercultural competence, scholars vary greatly in how they define or even name the construct (Spitzberg & Changnon, 2009). Indeed, the construct of "culture" itself is defined in a wide variety of ways that do not necessarily equate simply to "nationality." A review of the literature reveals that the variety of existing approaches to assess intercultural competence can be broadly categorized into measures of knowledge, attitudes, and behaviors.

Assessing Intercultural Competence as a Knowledge-Based Construct

Some researchers, such as Hirsch (1987), have conceptualized intercultural competence as the mastery of a particular body of knowledge. To operationalize this type of approach, Corbitt (1998) developed the Global Awareness Profile (GAP) test, which consists of 120 multiple-choice items designed to test cultural knowledge in 13 areas. These include one general section, six sections related to geographic knowledge of different regions (e.g., Asia, Africa, North America), and six separate sections dealing with knowledge related to the broad contexts of (a) environment, (b) politics, (c) geography, (d) religion, (e) socioeconomics, and (f) culture.

The knowledge-based approach to assessing intercultural competence has several limitations within the context of study abroad assessment. Chief among these is that knowledge-based assessments are necessarily domain specific. In other words, the knowledge one acquires by visiting Japan relates primarily to Japan. What we were seeking instead was an assessment of domain-general skills, those we would expect anyone studying abroad in any culture to acquire and that tend to focus on basic cognitive process elements (e.g., recognition of patterns, recognizing when one has made a faux pas or said something offensive, understanding how to adapt one's habits to thrive in another context).

In addition, within the context of higher education, perhaps the least important elements acquired from being exposed to culturally diverse friends are the benign details of etiquette (e.g., which cheek to kiss when greeting someone, how close to stand to someone, etc.). To be certain, there is a place for this knowledge, but such knowledge does not constitute what universities mean when they speak of a desire to develop students' "intercultural competence." Therefore, the GAP may act as a useful supplement to study abroad assessment but cannot be used alone.

Assessing Intercultural Competence via Attitudes and Behaviors

Two other approaches to measuring intercultural competence involve the assessment of attitudes and specific behaviors. An instrument that successfully integrates both dimensions is the Attitudinal and Behavioral Openness Scale (ABOS) (Caligiuri, Jacobs, & Farr, 2000). The ABOS is based on the theory that personality characteristics, which are stable, enduring traits, will be the best predictors of successful adaptation in a cross-cultural environment. The ABOS consists of 24 items divided across four subscales designed to measure (a) attitudes (e.g., "other cultures fascinate me"), (b) past experience (e.g.,

"I am fluent in another language"), (c) comfort with differences (e.g., "my friends' ethnic backgrounds are different than mine"), and (d) participation in cultural activities (e.g., "I eat at a variety of ethnic restaurants").

However, this trait conceptualization leaves little room for the development of cognitive skills or personality characteristics that lead to enhanced intercultural competence. With personality traits assumed to be relatively stable, little change over time would be expected.

The Development of the WICS and the Nature of Our Target Audience

Within the study abroad community, we found a tremendous appetite for a practical, economical way to assess study abroad outcomes. Increasingly, study abroad offices were being asked by their institutions to show proof that study abroad provided the outcomes that, for many years, had been claimed without much concrete evidence. What we needed was something domain-general in terms of skills, without a focus on a particular culture. It needed to capture learning by registering changes in perspective rather than simply in attitudes.

One of the most widely used attitudinal tests of intercultural competence, based on Bennett's (1986) developmental model of intercultural sensitivity (DMIS), is the Intercultural Development Inventory (IDI) (Hammer, 1999; Hammer, Bennett, & Wiseman, 2003). The IDI consists of 60 general statements to which participants rate their agreement or disagreement on a 7-point scale. Examples of items include "People should avoid individuals from other cultures who behave differently" and "Cultural differences are less important than the fact that people have the same needs, interests, and goals in life." The main advantage of the IDI is that it has a strong theoretical basis that assumes intercultural competence can be developed over time and experience. It has been used to measure the development of intercultural competence within the context of study abroad (Engle & Engle, 2004), and it has been shown to have reasonably good psychometric properties (Paige, Jacobs-Cassuto, Yershova, & DeJaeghere, 2003). The IDI suffers from certain limitations, however. Specifically, it is a self-report measure, which increases its susceptibility to faking (van de Mortel, 2008). It asks abstract attitudinal questions rather than relate each question to a specific context—an approach to questioning that has been shown to relate poorly to actual behavior (DeVellis, 1991). Finally, the IDI is a commercial test and is costly for institutions of higher education to administer and score.

Stemler had been working with a different approach to assessment, known as *situational judgment tests*, for quite some time (Stemler, Elliott, Grigorenko, & Sternberg, 2006; Stemler & Sternberg, 2006) and saw this method as a way to preserve the theoretical advantages of Bennett's model while overcoming some of the technical limitations of the IDI. Situational judgment tests are an approach to assessment in which individuals are presented with a specific scenario and asked to rate the extent to which they endorse several specific alternatives for responding to the scenario.

Goals

When one is developing a new instrument, the first step is to establish its reliability and validity. After that, one can proceed to use it to answer substantive research questions. Therefore, we had two initial goals for our study. First, we wanted to examine the psychometric characteristics of the WICS (reliability and validity) for use in the assessment of study abroad. Second, while we were interested in a number of substantive research questions, we primarily wanted to know if WICS could measure change in the development of intercultural competence over time.

From there we had all sorts of questions. Are there gender differences from the get-go and in terms of gains? Do people who start lower on the intercultural development scale end up gaining more than those who start higher? Do they gain at the same rate? Do those who start higher gain more? Are there differences among the types of study abroad programs (island, hybrid, direct enrollment)? If a student speaks the host country's language, and this is a different language than his or her native tongue, does this relate to the development of intercultural competence? Next, we briefly summarize the findings from our initial efforts at instrument validation and our study designed to measure change over time.

Methods

The WICS was developed to build on Bennett's theoretical work but overcome the limitations associated with the IDI.

The WICS presents 16 situations that study abroad students are likely to encounter (e.g., making a trip to the grocery store, navigating local transportation; see Stemler, Imada, & Sorkin, 2014, for the list of situations and the frequency with which they were encountered). Associated with each situation are six different response options designed to reflect the six levels of intercultural competence proposed by Bennett (1986). Participants were asked to rate each response on a scale of 1 (*very inaccurate*) to 5 (*very accurate*) to indicate the degree to which each response statement described their actual responses during their most recent experience abroad. Participants who had not encountered the situations chose "did not encounter such a situation" and did not rate the responses. Table 13.1 provides an example of how the items were mapped onto the DMIS (see Stemler et al., 2014, for the complete instrument and scoring key).

The WICS score is computed by weighing the developmental stage scores differently using the following formula: WICS Score = $(-2.5 \times \text{Denial})$ + $(-1.5 \times \text{Defense})$ + $(-0.5 \times \text{Minimization})$ + $(0.5 \times \text{Acceptance})$ + $(1.5 \times \text{Adaptation})$ + $(2.5 \times \text{Integration})$ + 18. The weights are useful for detecting the relative importance an individual places on the responses associated with each stage. In other words, the weights capture the relative positioning of a given individual and account for the fact that different individuals may use the scale values differently. What really matters is whether an individual states that a particular item in a situation is more or less characteristic of his or her own behavior (e.g., with this approach to scoring, a rating of 4 on an item, reflecting the *adaptation* stage, a rating of 2 on another item, reflecting the *denial* stage, and ratings of 3s on all subsequent items would suggest that the individual is actually closer to the adaptation stage than the acceptance stage). Ultimately, an individual score can be computed for each situation based on this formula. The scores across each of the 16 situations are then added together and averaged. Theoretically, the possible scores for the scale range from -18 to 18, with higher scores indicating greater intercultural competence. A constant value of 18 is added to all scores to eliminate the possibility of negative WICS scores and to make scale interpretation more user-friendly. Thus, the potential scores range from 0 to 36. Scores indicate DMIS categories as follows: denial (0–6), defense (7–12), minimization (13–18), acceptance (19–24), adaptation (25–30), and integration (31–36). See Stemler et al. (2014) for a worked scoring example.

Assessment Findings

Content-Related Validity Evidence

To evaluate the content validity of the test, five undergraduate research assistants not directly involved with the project were recruited as coders. They were provided with a brief description of the six stages of intercultural competence development proposed by Bennett (1986) and asked to independently categorize each response for each situation into one of the six theoretical stages (denial, defense, etc.). The research assistants were deliberately chosen as coders because, unlike experts, they had no prior knowledge of Bennett's DMIS or similar constructs. Thus, their judgment would be based solely on the information they received. This process, which would make the testing of

TABLE 13.1

Example WICS Items Mapped Onto Bennett's Developmental Model of Intercultural Sensitivity

Bennett's Stage	Description of the Stage	Response Example
Denial	Individuals deny the existence of other cultures or the difference between them.	I tried to go shopping with other Americans or find a store that catered to Americans.
Defense	Individuals react against the threat of other cultures by denigrating the other cultures and promoting the superiority of one's own culture.	I just got the things that were usually sold in the United States because I was afraid of wasting money for something terrible.
Minimization	Individuals acknowledge cultural differences on the surface but consider all cultures as fundamentally similar.	I found that the stores were pretty much like the ones in the United States, and I did not find any big differences. Grocery stores are just grocery stores anywhere.
Acceptance	Individuals accept and respect cultural differences with regard to behavior and values.	I enjoyed finding things that I never saw in the United States, and I was curious about what they were.
Adaptation	Individuals develop the ability to shift their frame of reference to other culturally diverse worldviews through empathy and pluralism.	I often bought local products that were a little different from the products I get in the United States, and I used them a lot in my everyday living.
Integration	Individuals expand and incorporate other worldviews into their own worldview.	I bought and tried local products and discovered really good ones. So I became more open-minded and less restricted by familiarity and brand names when choosing right products for myself.

Note. Adapted from "A Developmental Approach to Training for Intercultural Sensitivity," by M. J. Bennett, 1986, *International Journal of Intercultural Relations, 10*(2), 179–195.

intercoder agreement more conservative, is recommended by authors in the field of content analysis (Holsti, 1969; Krippendorff, 2003; Stemler, 2001) to prevent the buildup of shared meaning that can occur among experts with specialized knowledge. The average consensus estimate of intercoder reliability (Stemler, 2004) across all raters and items was 77% agreement (Cohen's Kappa = .86), providing strong evidence for the instrument's content validity.

Criterion-Related Validity Evidence

The WICS score for the sample was normally distributed (M = 25.42, SD = 2.74). The correlation between the WICS score and the scores from eight validity measures are shown in table 13.2. Because the validity measure items often referred to the United States as the home country, six participants who were not U.S. nationals were excluded from the analyses.

As expected, the WICS score was positively correlated with perspective-taking (r = .25, p < .05), empathy (r = .27, p < .01), and internationalism (r = .39, p < .001) and negatively correlated with nationalism (r = –.36, p < .01) and smugness (r = –.32, p < .01). Correlations between the WICS score and openness, patriotism, and ambiguity tolerance were not significant. As indicated by the high mean score of openness (M = 4.27), it is possible that study abroad participants are already high in openness, such that the magnitude of the correlation between these two variables was likely restricted and therefore prevented from reaching statistical significance. If a correction for restricted range (Cohen, Cohen, West, & Aiken, 2003) is applied, the correlation value becomes statistically significant (r = .27, p < .01).

Construct-Related Validity Evidence

To examine the construct validity of the scale, we analyzed the correlations among the six stage scores. Overall, the stages closer to one another (e.g., denial and defense) showed larger positive correlations, whereas the stages more distant from one another (e.g., denial and integration) showed larger negative correlations, indicating that the response items represented well the order of the six developmental stages proposed by Bennett's DMIS.

Factors Associated With Intercultural Competence

In addition to the responses on the WICS and validity measures, we also collected participants' demographic data, their language use during their time abroad, program types, and students' prior experience abroad to learn what factors might be associated with individuals' level of intercultural competence.

Of the 16 situations presented in the instrument, the mean number of situations participants experienced was 11.96 (SD = 2.45), suggesting that

TABLE 13.2
Means of Eight Validity Measures and Correlation With WICS Score (U.S. National Participants Only)

	Openness	Perspective-Taking	Empathy	Patriotism	Internationalism	Nationalism	Smugness	Ambiguity Tolerance
Mean	4.27	3.80	3.89	3.29	3.92	1.86	1.97	10.89
(SD)	(0.54)	(0.60)	(0.65)	(0.63)	(0.69)	(0.73)	(0.78)	(3.43)
Correlation with WICS score	.06	.25*	.27**	−.09	.39***	−.36**	−.32**	.13

*p < .05, **p < .01, ***p < .001.

the situations were commonly encountered by study abroad participants. It was not surprising that those who had completed one-semester study abroad programs (n = 73) reported that they encountered significantly more situations (M = 12.45, SD = 2.24) than those who had just begun their study abroad programs (n = 24, M = 10.46, SD = 2.50, $t[95]$ = 3.67, $p < .001$, d = .84). The number of different situations participants experienced (of the 16 on the test) was significantly positively associated with the WICS score (M = 11.96, SD = 2.45, r = .37, $p < .001$), suggesting that the greater the number of situations students experienced when studying abroad (e.g., taking local transportation, attending local sporting events), the higher the intercultural competence score.

In addition, the percentage of time spent speaking the local language (English-speaking countries were excluded) was also significantly positively correlated with the WICS score (M = 45.9%, SD = 30.5%, r = .37, $p < .001$). Finally, female participants (M = 7.88, SD = 2.82) showed significantly higher intercultural competence than their male counterparts (M = 6.57, SD = 2.12, $t[93]$ = 2.21, $p < .03$, d = 1.86). Differences in ethnicity, program type, and participants' prior study abroad experience were not significantly related to differences in intercultural competence.

Assessment of Changes in Intercultural Competence

Thirty participants responded to the survey twice (at the beginning and the end of their semester abroad). Their WICS scores were therefore examined to see if they captured changes in participants' intercultural competence. The length between the two responses ranged between 45 and 185 days (M = 101.87, SD = 36.16).

As shown in table 13.3, the WICS score of participants at the end of the study abroad program was significantly higher than at the beginning of the program, indicating that the participants increased their intercultural competence within a short period of time. The effect size was large (d = .71). In contrast, most of the eight validity measure scores showed no significant differences. The only measure besides the WICS that showed significant difference was ambiguity tolerance, with a moderate effect size (d = .47, see table 13.3).

We also tested whether any available variables (e.g., gender, program type, prior experience abroad) significantly predicted the size of the change in the WICS score. None of the variables were found to be significant, perhaps because of the small sample size. However, although only marginally so, the length between Time 1 and Time 2 and the change in the number of situations experienced between Time 1 and Time 2 were positively correlated with the size of change in the WICS score (r = .31 and .35, respectively;

TABLE 13.3

Score Changes in WICS Score and Eight Validity Measures (*N* = 30)

	Time 1	*Time 2*	*Score Change*	
	Mean (SD)	*Mean* (SD)	*Mean* (SD)	*Effect Size* (d)
WICS score	25.02 (2.92)	26.85 (2.18)	1.82 (2.11)***	.71
Openness	4.41 (0.28)	4.45 (0.34)	0.05 (0.23)	.15
Perspective-taking	3.78 (0.58)	3.78 (0.56)	0.00 (0.38)	.00
Empathy	3.92 (0.68)	3.99 (0.76)	0.07 (0.47)	.10
Internationalism	3.92 (0.53)	4.11 (0.69)	0.20 (0.60)	.32
Nationalism	1.86 (0.46)	1.89 (0.70)	0.03 (0.58)	.05
Smugness	2.05 (0.54)	2.06 (0.61)	0.01 (0.68)	.02
Patriotism	3.29 (0.46)	3.51 (0.61)	0.23 (0.48)	.42
Ambiguity tolerance	10.45 (3.02)	11.90 (3.21)	1.45 (2.39)*	.47

*$p < .05$, ***$p < .001$.

$p < .10$). That is, intercultural competence increased more for those who stayed longer and experienced more variability of situations abroad than for those whose participation was of shorter duration and/or who experienced lower variability of situations.

Discussion

The data from our initial studies provide strong support for the reliability and the content, criterion, and construct validity of the WICS. The first key substantive finding is that participants who experience a wider variety of situations (i.e., not only using transportation but also interacting more widely and/or deeply with the host community) tend to score higher on the WICS. This is consistent with findings from previous research suggesting that the more exposure students have to a new culture, the more likely they are to learn and develop (Lou & Bosley, 2008; Savicki & Selby, 2008). However, our data suggest that it may not be the amount of time that matters so much to the development of intercultural competence as the variety of experiences a student encounters.

A second substantive finding from this study is that students who reported spending a great amount of time speaking a foreign language while abroad tended to score more highly on the WICS than those who reported spending less time using the language. This suggests that students who embrace the language and immerse themselves in speaking it will be more fully engaged and will develop their intercultural competence at a more rapid rate than those who spend less time speaking the local language. This finding is consistent with much prior research in the area of study abroad (Hoffa, 2007). However, the finding is all the more interesting because the WICS items do not ask about time spent speaking the language. Rather, WICS asks how individuals dealt with relatively more or less common cultural experiences in their chosen country.

In a third substantive finding, women outperformed men on the WICS. This is consistent with other findings in study abroad research (Vande Berg, Connor-Linton, & Paige, 2009) and suggests that there may be gender differences in the development of intercultural competence that warrant further investigation. Specifically, do women also gain at a greater rate than men? Or do they start with more intercultural competence and finish higher, whereas men make greater gains?

Overall, the data from the study suggest that the WICS holds promise as a new tool for measuring the development of intercultural competence during study abroad. The WICS has several advantages, both psychometric and pragmatic, over current measures. First, it is freely available for use by any institution, provided that it is properly cited and acknowledged. Second, it can easily be expanded and adapted, with new situations being added to the scale, provided they are validated. Third, it is easy to administer and score. Fourth, it is sensitive to developmental changes in intercultural competence even over a relatively brief period of time. Fifth, it avoids many of the problems of self-enhancement that plague self-report measures and lead to ceiling effects. Sixth, the WICS can be used to not only evaluate individuals' intercultural competence but also investigate what elements of study abroad programs might play a more important role in fostering participants' intercultural competence. It can also investigate the interaction between participants' personal factors and program characteristics (e.g., a hybrid program is better for advanced language speakers, but an island program is better for beginners). Such information could be used to help existing study abroad programs redesign their content and help students select programs that fit them well. Finally, the WICS may be useful in a professional development context. For example, the instrument may be used to help students reflect on their responses prior to their study abroad departure and debrief upon their return to the home country. The instrument thus can be used to not only select and evaluate programs but also enhance intercultural competence development.

Lessons Learned

The results from our early studies with the WICS are promising; however, they need to be replicated across a wider variety of students. Furthermore, a large-scale study that increases the total number of study abroad participants would allow for the investigation of a broader range of research questions (see section titled "Goals"). Some progress toward this goal has been made by soliciting participation from institutions via electronic mailing lists and professional conferences. Indeed, over the past 1.5 years, we have collected pre- and posttest data from study abroad participants at eight higher education institutions and two major study abroad program providers. We are currently in the process of writing up the results.

The first major lesson learned in our effort to scale up the project was that many study abroad offices are not yet accustomed to using assessment instruments for research purposes. Although most institutions require students to submit a postexperience evaluation as part of their standard educational practices, the perceived logistics of participating in a large-scale research project proved an impediment to many already overworked study abroad offices. In reality, however, because most institutions already assess students as part of their normal educational practices, the project qualifies for "exempt status" and, therefore, for expedited review at most institutions' institutional review boards.

Second, although our preliminary studies provide excellent evidence for the internal validity of the WICS, we remain quite interested in comparing the scores on the WICS to the scores received by the same students on other measures that are currently being used in the study abroad community (e.g., IDI, GAP, ABOS). During the course of our research, we have, at times, encountered resistance from individuals with a financial or professional stake in their own instrument or perspective on assessment. Comparative data would be tremendously useful for further evaluating the validity and utility of the WICS relative to other instruments used for study abroad assessment. We are actively seeking partners interested in participating in such a research project.

A third lesson from our efforts to coordinate such a study is that many study abroad offices do not see the value in participating if they are already paying for and using one of the standard commercial measures. Why ask students to complete a second instrument? We sympathize with this sentiment; however, we would argue that the long-term benefit to their institution and the greater study abroad research community could be substantial. Because both the instrument and the scoring algorithm for the WICS are freely available (see Stemler et al., 2014), evidence that demonstrates that the WICS is providing as much information as commercial tests would suggest that there is a tremendous cost saving to be found while using an instrument with demonstrated scientific validity.

Finally, perhaps one of the key limitations of the WICS is that the pretest cannot be taken before participants leave for their study abroad sites. The pretest only makes sense once participants have spent one to two weeks in situ.

Conclusion

The thirst for a free instrument that does not contain a proprietary scoring algorithm and that yields specific, useful information usable in the context of training and assessment is tremendous. The WICS meets these criteria, and we encourage its broad use for all those in the study abroad community who feel they, their students, and their institutions might benefit from it. Although Wesleyan was our first point of departure, we are continuing to expand our research across institutions and encourage others to use the WICS and contribute their data to a research repository. We seek additional input and commentary from the study abroad community regarding key questions to address during the next phases of research. It is our hope that a professional organization in study abroad might develop a repository or other mechanism for sharing findings from institutions that use the WICS. Ideally, this would take place via peer-reviewed publications, but even submissions of anonymized data sets to a website would be of great benefit to researchers, including ourselves, wishing to do secondary analyses of these data.

References

Bennett, M. J. (1986). A developmental approach to training for intercultural sensitivity. *International Journal of Intercultural Relations, 10*(2), 179–195.

Caligiuri, P. M., Jacobs, R. R., & Farr, J. L. (2000). The Attitudinal and Behavioral Openness Scale: Scale development and construct validation. *International Journal of Intercultural Relations, 24*, 27–46.

Cohen, J., Cohen, P., West, S. G., & Aiken, L. S. (2003). *Applied multiple regression/ correlation analysis for the behavioral sciences* (3rd ed.). Mahwah, NJ: Lawrence Erlbaum.

Corbitt, J. N. (1998). *Global Awareness Profile: GAP facilitator's manual*. Yarmouth, ME: Intercultural Press.

DeVellis, R. F. (1991). *Scale development: Theory and applications* (Vol. 26). Newbury Park, CA: Sage.

Engle, L., & Engle, J. (2004). Assessing language acquisition and intercultural sensitivity development in relation to study abroad program design. *Frontiers: The Interdisciplinary Journal of Study Abroad, 10,* 253–276.

Hammer, M. R. (1999). A measure of intercultural sensitivity: The Intercultural Development Inventory. In S. Fowler & M. Fowler (Eds.), *The intercultural sourcebook* (Vol. 2, pp. 61–72). Yarmouth, ME: Intercultural Press.

Hammer, M. R., Bennett, M. J., & Wiseman, R. (2003). Measuring intercultural sensitivity: The Intercultural Development Inventory. *International Journal of Intercultural Relations: Special Training Issue, 27*(4), 421–443.

Hirsch, E. D. (1987). *Cultural literacy: What every American needs to know.* Boston, MA: Houghton Mifflin.

Hoffa, W. W. (2007). *A history of U.S. study abroad: Beginnings to 1965.* Carlisle, PA: Forum on Education Abroad.

Holsti, O. R. (1969). *Content analysis for the social sciences and humanities.* Reading, MA: Addison-Wesley.

Krippendorff, K. (2003). *Content analysis: An introduction to its methodology* (2nd ed.). Newbury Park, CA: Sage.

Lou, K., & Bosley, G. (2008). Dynamics of cultural contexts: Meta-level interventions in the study abroad experience. In V. Savicki (Ed.), *Developing intercultural competence and transformation: Theory, research, and applications in international education* (pp. 276–296). Sterling, VA: Stylus.

Paige, R. M., Jacobs-Cassuto, M., Yershova, Y. A., & DeJaeghere, J. (2003). Assessing intercultural sensitivity: An empirical analysis of the Hammer and Bennett Intercultural Development Inventory. *International Journal of Intercultural Relations, 27,* 467–486.

Savicki, V., & Selby, R. (2008). Synthesis and conclusions. In V. Savicki (Ed.), *Developing intercultural competence and transformation: Theory, research, and applications in international education* (pp. 276–296). Sterling, VA: Stylus.

Spitzberg, B. H., & Changnon, G. (2009). Conceptualizing intercultural competence. In D. K. Deardorff (Ed.), *The SAGE handbook of intercultural competence* (pp. 2–52). Thousand Oaks, CA: Sage.

Stemler, S. E. (2001). An overview of content analysis. *Practical Assessment, Research, and Evaluation, 7*(17). Retrieved from http://PAREonline.net/getvn.asp?v=7&n=17

Stemler, S. E. (2004). A comparison of consensus, consistency, and measurement approaches to estimating interrater reliability. *Practical Assessment, Research, and Evaluation, 9*(4). Retrieved from http://PAREonline.net/getvn.asp?v=9&n=4

Stemler, S. E. (2012). What should university admissions tests predict? *Educational Psychologist, 41*(1), 5–17.

Stemler, S. E., Elliott, J. G., Grigorenko, E. G., & Sternberg, R. J. (2006). There's more to teaching than instruction: Seven strategies for dealing with the practical side of teaching. *Educational Studies, 32*(1), 85–102.

Stemler, S. E., Imada, T., & Sorkin, C. (2014). Development and validation of the Wesleyan Intercultural Competence Scale (WICS). *Frontiers: The Interdiscipli-*

nary Journal of Study Abroad, XXIV, 25–47. Retrieved from www.frontiersjournal.com/documents/StemlerImadaSorkinFrontiersXXIV-Fall2014-withappendix.pdf

Stemler, S. E., & Sternberg, R. J. (2006). Using situational judgment tests to measure practical intelligence. In J. Weekley & R. E. Ployhart (Eds.), *Situational judgment tests* (pp. 107–131). Mahwah, NJ: Lawrence Erlbaum.

Van de Mortel, T. F. (2008). Faking it: Social desirability response bias in self-report research. *Australian Journal of Advanced Nursing, 25*(4), 40–48.

Vande Berg, M., Connor-Linton, J., & Paige, M. R. (2009, Fall). The Georgetown Consortium project: Interventions for student learning abroad. *Frontiers: The Interdisciplinary Journal of International Education, 18*, 1–75.

14

ENGAGING STAKEHOLDERS IN ASSESSMENT OF STUDENT LEARNING IN OFF-CAMPUS PROGRAMS

Joan Gillespie, Elizabeth Ciner, and David Schodt

One of the guidelines for creating an effective process to assess student learning calls for the involvement of stakeholders from the early planning stages through the implementation of the assessment tool and interpretation of findings (Braskamp & Engberg, 2014). Fortuitously, involving stakeholders in effective assessment encourages their further involvement. The Associated Colleges of the Midwest (ACM), a consortium of 14 residential liberal arts colleges in Colorado, Illinois, Iowa, Minnesota, and Wisconsin, relies on and benefits from a high level of engagement among faculty members and administrators with the off-campus programs that are jointly owned and managed by the member colleges. This engagement served as the starting point to create a pilot for an embedded assessment to measure student learning at four of the consortium's off-campus programs. The process included the on-site program staff and faculty and, eventually, faculty advisors at the campuses. The pilot generated findings tied to student learning that support the continuing process of program development, and it also produced important results for stakeholder involvement. Among these results were a new appreciation for assessment itself and recognition of the value of a systematic process for examining student learning in an off-campus program.

This chapter describes the pilot project, Learning From Study Away, beginning with the major questions that the ACM sought to answer and concluding with the examination of student writing to determine if certain learning outcomes were being met. It follows the steps through the design of the assessment, the development of a rubric, scoring sessions of student writing, and samples of the findings. (The pilot was carried out from May 2013 to June 2014 with an extension of a grant from the Teagle Foundation, "Expanded Contexts for Liberal Arts Learning.") The involvement of stakeholders is described at each phase. Although the project took its shape within the particular structure of the ACM consortium and the administrative framework of its off-campus programs, some phases of the project may serve as a model for other institutions and programs that both see the potential for involving stakeholders in the assessment of student learning in off-campus programs and may want to employ embedded assessment techniques.

Project Development

Learning From Study Away followed an earlier joint project of the ACM, Great Lakes Colleges Association, and Center of Inquiry in the Liberal Arts at Wabash College that included the design and use of a pre- and postsurvey instrument that sought to establish correlation between off-campus study variables and liberal arts learning. Conducted over a three-year period, the final phase of the project called for two workshops to review and analyze the findings from the survey instrument. The quantitative results of the instrument showed no statistically significant correlations between off-campus programming and student learning, and workshop participants noted concerns about the process, such as the small number of pre- and postsurvey responses and variations in length of time spent completing the survey. Nonetheless, the workshops underscored the need for effective assessment of student learning, with program learning goals as the key reference point. The ACM drew on these findings to propose the next iteration of Learning From Study Abroad, which became the pilot under discussion here.

One of the recommendations from the first phase was to identify opportunities for embedded assessment, which refers to the use of student work generated by an actual assignment, for example, a learning activity or written work that students complete for a course or a program. Such an assignment may be evaluated and graded by the instructor as part of the course or program. However, as an assessment of the entire program, the assignment is evaluated with program outcomes in mind, for example, by measuring students' progress toward an overall learning goal of the program, such as recognizing cultural difference. The advantages of an embedded assessment are that it is based on a pedagogically valid activity in the context of a course or program, as opposed to a method that occurs after the fact, and students are more likely to take the assignment seriously as a course requirement. Students' work becomes a source of information about how clearly the program and the course or courses state their learning goals and how close the activities come to achieving them.

In following the recommendation to use embedded assessment, the ACM stated that the pilot's purpose is to devise a methodology that would guide program improvement, deepen student learning, and improve faculty advising. Two questions sharpened the focus on student learning:

- Does students' work demonstrate what students learned at the end of the term by seeing something new or in a new light, compared to observations when they first arrived on-site?
- Are students able to draw on their academic work to interpret the culture and society in which they are living, that is, transfer skills and knowledge from one context to another?

The pilot also served as a means to gauge the effectiveness of the assessment process, directed by the following questions:

- Does embedded assessment generate findings that are useful in determining how to adjust the content and delivery of ACM programming to support student learning?
- Is involvement of stakeholders in the assessment a vehicle for their greater engagement in the off-campus program?

ACM drew on a number of resources through all phases of the project. Beloit College had been experimenting with embedded assessment of study abroad, and Elizabeth Brewer (Beloit College, director of international education) agreed to serve as project advisor. She made the initial presentation to the on-site program directors tasked with planning and implementing the pilot. Karl Wirth (Macalester College, Department of Geology), with significant experience in the pedagogy of experiential learning and student learning assessment, also served as project advisor. On-site program directors, staff, and faculty commented on and implemented the pilot project. ACM campus faculty advisors participated in the actual assessment alongside ACM program staff in Chicago. They brought to the project organizational history, broad knowledge of the sites, and commitment to advising students regarding off-campus study. They also read student applications, serve on selection committees for visiting faculty to the programs, contribute to self-study documents for program reviews, and meet annually in Chicago with the on-site staff to discuss program development. Workshops held during the final stage of the initial Learning From Study Abroad project also generated many useful suggestions from participants. Among those suggestions implemented in the new project was to ask students to write in an open-ended fashion rather than respond to multiple-choice survey questions.

The assessment project comprised five stages:

1. Identify and develop two pairs of assignments that could be used to assess student learning gains from an off-campus study program relative to the program's student learning goals.
2. Administer the two assignments to four ACM off-campus study programs in collaboration with the on-site directors and program faculty.
3. Develop rubrics for scoring students' written work.
4. Score students' work according to the rubrics.
5. Assess the assessment: Was one of the two methods superior to the other for ACM purposes? Did either assessment yield useful results? Did stakeholders believe their efforts were useful?

Developing the Assignments: The Neighborhood Walk and Reflections on Goals

Although the student learning goals vary somewhat across the different off-campus study programs offered by the ACM, most have broadly similar elements. These goals are exemplified by the goals of the ACM Costa Rica, Community Engagement in Public Health, Education, and the Environment program: to (a) develop (Spanish) language proficiency to a specified level, (b) develop broad understanding of (Latin American) society and intercultural literacy through cultural immersion, and (c) deepen knowledge of (Latin American) development and environmental and cultural issues through course work, firsthand experience, and field inquiry.

One pair of assignments was developed from an orientation activity that is used by several of the ACM programs and familiar in off-campus study—the neighborhood walk—in which students are given an itinerary and markers for a neighborhood. The ACM program goal is immersion in the culture and community, and this activity is consistent with other program and course assignments in that students are expected to interact with their new environment and come to think of themselves as residents, albeit short-term residents. The assignment seeks to engage students with their milieu by asking them to interview someone they meet along the route, buy something to eat, and reflect on their impressions and experiences. To use this assignment to measure students' progress from the start of the term to the end of it, the ACM gave students detailed instructions, prompts to guide them, and a writing requirement. The prompts needed to be open-ended so students would feel free to write about what strikes them; in general, if prompts are too specific, students respond in kind, and their writing is more difficult to evaluate in terms of intellectual and personal growth and development (see figure 14.1).

To assess student learning from the off-campus study program, this activity, with slight variations, was repeated at the end of the program, when

Figure 14.1 First neighborhood walk: Florence

Exercise Learning Goals:

- Establish a marker for your understanding of the culture
- Develop or use navigation skills (the city, public transit, crossing streets, maps, etc.)
- Practice skills of observation and analysis
- Practice interviewing skills
- Explore writing as a strategy for recording your experience in an environment

Assignment: For this assignment, you will be (a) making observations of Florence: its piazzas (squares), monuments, churches, fountains, statues, markets, shops, and so forth; (b) reflecting on what you see; and (c) turning in 500 to 1,000 words about what you saw and your thoughts about it. You'll be assigned the locations to visit, and your first job will be to locate the sites and then visit them. Remember to bring along something to keep notes on!

While you are going to the sites with other students, this is your opportunity to learn something not only about the sites but also about yourself: What do *you* notice? What do *you* experience (see, hear, smell, feel)? What do you think about what you notice and experience? To that end, to the extent possible, you should explore the sites on your own, noting *your* observations, experiencing what *you* experience. There will be ample opportunity to share with others once you have completed this phase of the assignment.

Required: As you walk through the various sites, what are your first impressions? What seems familiar, strange, unusual, or otherwise notable? What are one or two things that puzzle you? That impress you? That surprise you? Why? How does knowing or not knowing the languages you hear or see help you understand the neighborhood? Are there ways in which the academic work you have done in the past or other experiences you have had previously help you understand and interpret what you are observing? What skills help you navigate your way?

Find at least one person to interview at the location. What does the location mean to that person? How does he or she see it? How often does he or she come here? What strikes him or her about it?

The walk ends with you trying out an Italian pizza.

Optional: Feel free to take a photo of something that strikes you as familiar or strange (do not photograph people without their permission, and do not photograph children).

Required: Once you have noted your observations and the answers to your interview(s), write 500 to 1,000 words describing what you have observed and your thoughts about it. This isn't a formal essay; instead, think of it as "talking on paper." But you should write this with some care, as you will be sharing what you write with your classmates and your instructor.

students completed a second neighborhood walk. In addition to its value for assessment purposes, the opportunity to revisit the neighborhood, follow the same prompts, and write about their observations and interactions was expected to provide students with direct evidence of their own learning and thus have metacognitive value.

A second approach to assessing student learning also was developed, again, following a recommendation from an earlier phase of the project that the ACM revise its student application to include an essay question asking students to reflect on "how the program learning goals relate to your own academic and personal goals" (ACM, 2013, p. 5). In that earlier phase, ACM undertook steps to focus students' attention on program learning goals; the application was revised with a question that required students to link the program goals to their own goals for their term at the site, and the end-of-term evaluation instrument used for all ACM programs was similarly revised, asking students to indicate on a scale of one to three how well they met program goals. Building on work done by Beloit College with reflective student essays, ACM staff developed a pair of structured assignments focused on learning goals for the students to complete during the initial orientation for their off-campus study programs and the program debriefing (see figure 14.2).

Administration of the Assignments

The international programs chosen for the pilot (Pune, India; San José, Costa Rica; and Florence, Italy) are administered and staffed by individuals who are long-time residents or host nationals with vested interests in the programs and commitment to program development. The director and faculty of the Chicago Program, also part of the pilot, had particular expertise with the pedagogy of experiential learning and community engagement. They had already structured a neighborhood walk as an early assignment to teach students to begin to read neighborhoods in terms of their assets. The four programs share several commonalities in their curricula: Language instruction is

Figure 14.2 Beginning of program reflection assignment: Costa Rica

Several months ago, in applying for this program, you were asked to describe how the program's learning goals related to your own academic and personal goals. To refresh your memory, Costa Rica program's stated program goals are

- to develop Spanish-language proficiency to the advanced level,
- to develop broad understanding of Latin American society and intercultural literacy through cultural immersion, and
- to deepen knowledge of Latin American development and environmental and cultural issues through course work, firsthand experience, and field inquiry.

This is a first opportunity to revisit the question of goals (you'll have another at the end of the program). Please describe the relation you see between your personal goals on the program and the program's learning goals. What are your plans to achieve the learning goals?

Please write your answer in 500 to 750 words (two to three typewritten pages).

required in Costa Rica, Florence, and Pune, and integrative programming is offered at all the sites, with required internships in Chicago and internships in Florence for students with advanced Italian, a four-week rural community practicum in Costa Rica, and independent study projects in Chicago and Pune. On all four programs, students choose electives in the humanities and social sciences to complete their course load. The international programs house students with host families; in Chicago, when the pilot was conducted, students lived in shared apartments in two urban neighborhoods.

In introducing the neighborhood walk to program directors, project coordinators only loosely defined it. This gave program staff opportunities to experiment. The only stipulation was that the walk cover an area that students would regularly frequent over the program, by virtue of either living in the vicinity or traversing it as they commuted from their home to another part of the city for program-related activities. In the weeks preceding the start of the term, the program directors corresponded with each other and with the project coordinators about potential itineraries to confirm they would be consistent with the goals of the assessment. Students' housing arrangements served as the starting point in Chicago and Costa Rica for program staff and faculty to plan the itineraries; in both cases, the communities where the students reside directly relate to course themes. Students were assigned to follow the itineraries in pairs. In Florence and Pune, the itineraries more broadly reflected program themes rather than course themes, and students took the walks in groups of four to five. In Pune, staff members accompanied each group, but students were expected to navigate on their own. Although language skills varied at the international sites, an interview or conversation with someone encountered during the walk was an expectation in each location. In all instances, the assignment specified that although students might travel with others, their observations were meant to be their own.

As soon as they arrived at their sites, students at these four programs were invited to participate in the pilot, and permission to use their work for purposes of research was secured. All but one student gave permission. To minimize the burden on on-site directors, the ACM office prepared and sent students the two assignments electronically; toward the end of the program, each student was sent a copy of his or her original submissions and asked to write a second reflection, retrace the neighborhood walk, and write a new essay. Students were instructed to submit their essays electronically both to the on-site program directors and to ACM staff.

The Rubric

Two rubrics—one for the neighborhood walk, the other for the reflective essay—were developed, piloted, and revised. The rubrics draw from work done by Elizabeth Brewer (Beloit College) and Nina Namaste (Elon University), from the Association of American Colleges and Universities' (n.d.) *VALUE Rubrics*, including the *Global Learning VALUE Rubric*, and from Hammer (2012), "The Intercultural Development Inventory: A New Frontier in Assessment and Development of Intercultural Competence." Because the rubrics would need to be applicable across a range of programs to identify patterns, criteria were kept general. The rubric for scoring student reflections identifies four criteria: goals, knowledge, reflections, and intercultural development, with four levels of mastery—benchmark, milestones 1 and 2, and capstone (see table 14.1). The rubric for the neighborhood walk translates the ACM off-campus program student learning goals into three criteria: knowledge, intercultural development, and skills with four levels of mastery—benchmark and milestones 1, 2, and 3. *Knowledge* is defined as what students have learned from their course work plus their own experiences, as conveyed in their observations on the walks. *Intercultural development* focuses on students' perception and recognition of cultural difference and their ability to move between cultures as demonstrated by behavior. *Skills* address students' ability to navigate daily activities and situations, including interactions with local residents, and to explore novel situations.

Scoring Student Writing

ACM campuses assign a faculty advisor to each of the off-campus study programs, and, early in the process, project coordinators decided to involve several faculty advisors in a scoring session because of their familiarity with the program sites. Site knowledge had emerged as an issue in earlier efforts: Was learning that it is considered inappropriate to walk barefoot inside a Costa Rican house, as one student reported, important or trivial? Was it peculiar to one family, or did it constitute cultural knowledge? Would faculty who had expertise in the site read students' writings differently than faculty without this expertise? Pilot scoring sessions were designed to include some faculty with knowledge of the site and others who had knowledge of an off-campus site but not necessarily the one being assessed, with two sites being scored at each of two sessions.

Scoring sessions began with a norming exercise to give scorers practice working with a rubric and to ensure the rubric was applied in the same way. Using a sample student essay to read and score, participants assigned a score of 1–4 for each item of the rubric. Scores were recorded on a chart on the blackboard, at which point participants were invited to explain why they had given a particular score for a particular criterion. Discussion and a second sample followed. Once a consensus emerged, participants scored the remaining set. This process was repeated with the reflective essays.

In addition to questions about who might be optimal scorers, a second set of questions involved scoring mechanics: How long would it take to read and score a set of essays? Would faculty feel that involvement in assessment of actual student work was worth their time and effort? Did it help them in their role *as* faculty advisors? That is, would this activity give advisors a clear sense of program strengths, as well as areas to work on? And would it help them talk with students about the program from the students' point of view?

The first scoring session involved student work from both the Chicago and the Florence off-campus study programs. Sixteen faculty and staff participated, including 8 ACM staff; Elizabeth Brewer, advisor to the project; 3 faculty and staff from the Chicago Program; 3 ACM faculty advisors to the Pune, India, program; and a faculty member who serves as chair of the Spanish department at an ACM member college.

Project coordinators invited participants to critique the rubrics, which they did enthusiastically. The discussion addressed questions such as the following: Given a program's learning goals, were the criteria right for the programs, or had something important been left out? Were the various levels of mastery clearly distinguishable? Were the descriptors easily understood? The criteria for intercultural development prompted the following questions: Can the rubric account for an international student who already has lived in a diverse community? Could the descriptors be modified to better reflect the way that Chicago Program faculty and staff present urban culture to students?

TABLE 14.1

Learning in Study Abroad Assessment Rubric/Reflection Essay

	1: Benchmark	2: Milestone 1	3: Milestone 2	4: Capstone
Goals	Makes little or no reference to student's and program's goals.	References student's goals. Provides at least one example to illustrate how the student's goals have or have not been met.	Uses more than one example to show how the student's or program's goals have been met, not met, or changed over the course of the semester.	Makes specific reference to both the student's original goals and the program goals. Uses specific examples to reflect on how these goals have been met, not met, or changed. Illustrates self-awareness of change (or lack of).
Knowledge	Response is entirely in personal terms.	Discusses or mentions one or two aspects of the site and/or society, but the discussion shows only limited reference to the academic program. Largely experiential.	Combines personal experience and academic learning to reflect on the site and society but somewhat superficially. Shows some ability to generalize from specific experiences. Little or no indication of what questions the student might have about the site or the culture.	Cites specific examples of how the student's out-of-class experiences and academic learning during the program inform his or her understanding of himself- or herself and the site. Shows an ability to generalize from these specifics to a deep understanding of the society. Poses or raises thoughtful questions.
Reflections	Does not respond to any of the essay prompts, or does so superficially. Does not demonstrate thinking about learning.	Makes an attempt to respond to one or more of the essay prompts but explores off-campus study only superficially, with few or no specific examples of ways they may think, understand, or see differently. Demonstrates limited ability to think about learning.	Provides at least one specific example of something that the student thinks, understands, or sees differently. Provides at least one example of a strength or a challenge, and suggests the value of this knowledge outside of the immediate study abroad context. Contains some discussion of the student's own learning processes.	Provides a rich discussion with multiple examples of ways in which the study abroad experience has changed or enhanced the student's understanding of self and site. Speaks directly about the student's own thinking and learning processes, as well as implications for future learning.
Intercultural development	Cultural difference is not referenced, is denigrated, or is romanticized.	Student's cultural worldview is perceived as universal; other cultures are essentially similar to one's own.	Student's culture is perceived as one of many valid world cultures; other cultures are viewed as equally complex but different constructions of reality.	Recognizes cultural difference, and demonstrates the ability to move between cultures by changing behavior (or writing about the need to) in culturally appropriate ways.

The rubrics also generated discussion about the assignments themselves. Should the prompts and the rubric of the "neighborhood walk" be more closely aligned, for example, by directly referencing culture in the prompts with a question such as "What cultural elements do you observe?" and asking students to describe their interactions with people? Scorers suggested that students be required to take photos on the first neighborhood walk rather than have this as an option; interpreting them could then be included in students' writing. Scorers also discussed the issue of "transfer"; that is, that students demonstrate that they can apply, or transfer, what they learned in the classroom to situations outside the classroom. How can a faculty member know if students have learned what's important to the course if they do not reference something in the course in their writing? Some faculty advocated for weekly writing that would require students to apply academic or classroom learning to make sense of the site. Such weekly assignments would identify the points at which students' reflections about their observations change and grow more nuanced. Feedback from the first scoring session proved invaluable in revising the rubrics for the second session.

That second session, to score the essays from the Costa Rica and Florence programs, involved 16 individuals, including 7 ACM staff, 4 faculty advisors from the Costa Rica program, 2 faculty advisors and a program coordinator from the Florence program, and 2 ACM faculty, including project advisor Karl Wirth.

Analysis of the Results

Each student essay was read and scored independently by program directors and faculty advisors, as described previously. In both sessions, scores from the different readers tended to cluster, demonstrating that the rubric was working well. Table 14.2 illustrates individual scores for two students in Costa Rica: student A1 received scores of 2 (knowledge), 3 (intercultural development), and 1 (skills) from one reader, which gave that student a combined score of 6 out of a possible 12 points. Student A2 received scores of 3 (knowledge), 4 (intercultural development), and 3 (skills) for a combined score of 10 out of 12. These combined scores were averaged across all of the scorers for each student in the program.

In one analysis, combined scores for each student in the program from the first and second neighborhood walk essays were compared to measure students' progress in each of the categories. Alternatively, the student scores from each scorer were averaged by rubric item. As shown in table 14.2, the average score for students A1 and A2 on the knowledge item is 2.5 out of a maximum of 4. These average scores were then averaged across the scorers.

TABLE 14.2
Individual Scores for Two Students in Costa Rica

Walk 2				
Student ID	*Knowledge (1–4)*	*Intercultural Development (1–4)*	*Skills (1–4)*	*Sum*
A1	2	3	1	6
A2	3	4	3	10
Average	2.5	3.5	2	0

Figure 14.3 Average rubric scores for first and second neighborhood walks in Costa Rica

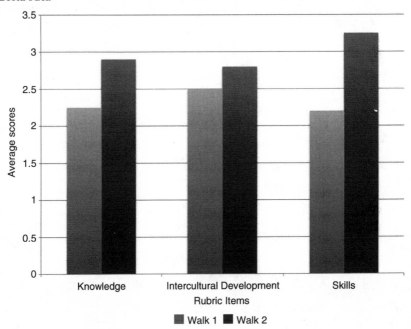

Scores by rubric item for the first and second neighborhood walks in Costa Rica appear in figure 14.3.

Although an important objective for this pilot was to develop quantitative assessment data by applying the rubric criteria to them, an unforeseen benefit was the degree to which the essays provided rich qualitative information about the students' experiences for the program directors. Faculty members were equally interested in the stories that the essays told. Although a particular comment may not be an indicator in the rubric, nonetheless, it might reveal, for example, the student's level of comfort in using a language other than English or his or her level of confidence in being able to interpret what he or she sees.

Lessons Learned

The project underscored the importance of treating assessment as an iterative process. Although the assessment results provide important and useful information for program improvement, the assessment process itself offers an opportunity to review the program's learning goals, the course content, the assignments used to generate the assessment data, the rubric used for scoring, and the scoring procedures, all of which affect the results.

Although project coordinators intended to create assignments and rubrics that were consistent across sites, the pilot demonstrated that cultural context must be taken into consideration. This applied in particular to the neighborhood walk assignments. In India, for example, safety concerns related to students' unfamiliarity with the area, and particularly concerns for female students, meant that the initial walk needed to be done in small groups with a staff member rather than independently. The scoring session generated questions such as the following: Is the neighborhood walk the best assignment in Pune, given that students walk less in this location than in other program locations? Where are the "neighborhoods" where host nationals walk? Should the homestay neighborhood be the focus for the assignment? Would the assignment be more meaningful to students if it were part of the required core course in the program? In Costa Rica, local residents give directions using compass points and landmarks rather than street addresses. How can this model be adapted to the assignment to reflect students' progress in the categories of knowledge, intercultural development, and skills? Furthermore, it was important to ask faculty or staff who understand the local culture and society to score the students' work. The discussion following the scoring sessions strongly suggests that using faculty who know a site is optimal.

Even before the scoring sessions, it was clear that the prompt for students' essays in which they reflect on the goals would need to be improved to be useful for assessing learning gains; in particular, students' initial reflections tended to slide over program goals and focus on students' personal goals instead. These reflections on goals were clearly an important metacognitive exercise for students, but the prompts used in the pilot were too complex for the essays to work well as embedded assessment. In extending the pilot to another year, the project coordinators are revising the prompts to encourage more open-ended responses.

There were clear benefits to engaging all stakeholders in the process. Most important among these are the on-site program directors; without their ownership of the assessment process, it would not be possible to generate reliable data. The on-site directors also need to be convinced that the purpose of the assessment is formative, not summative; the student scores do not constitute a final program evaluation. The involvement of faculty advisors as scorers of student writing likewise was essential, as the writing demonstrated learning outcomes and offered direct evidence of the value of off-campus study. An unexpected, but important, benefit of engaging faculty advisors in the assessment process was that a number of them remarked that, for the first time, they began to understand the value of good, systematic assessment of student learning. Indeed, a significant benefit of the project was the way it focused the attention of all stakeholders on student learning.

Some participants in the pilot were surprised by what they regarded as small gains in the rubric item "knowledge." These data were interpreted as students' difficulty in using their academic knowledge of culture and society to interpret what they observed on the neighborhood walks. Although this observation can be used for program improvement by identifying ways to help students develop the skills they need to transfer knowledge from one domain to another, it is also useful to point out that knowledge transfer is a challenge in all classes, not just those taught off campus. A possibility for addressing this challenge is to ask students to identify three or four connections every week between content they learn in class and what they see outside the classroom.

A description of the project and the results were presented at the annual meeting of the off-campus program directors and visiting faculty directors, in anticipation of implementing the neighborhood walk assignment and the reflection on goals at all ACM program sites in the upcoming academic year. The assignment for the neighborhood walk follows the same format, with detailed instructions that guide student observations and writing for completing the walk early in the term and repeating it at the end of the term. Some of these programs do not already include a neighborhood walk as an orientation activity, so an itinerary is being created at each program site that reflects the program goals and course content and meets the same criterion of embedded assessment that marked the initial project development. As with the pilot, the plan is for student writing to be scored by faculty program advisors, program directors, and ACM staff members, using the same set of rubrics.

One lesson on which assessment experts agree is that effective and useful assessment should tell a story, one that is clear, focused, and simple (Braskamp & Engberg, 2014). Paying attention to not only producing the assessment data but also applying these data to program development and improvement as the next step.

References

Associated Colleges of the Midwest. (2013). Expanded contexts for liberal arts learning: Designing programs to enhance liberal arts learning. In *Report on the learning from study abroad project*. Chicago, IL: Author.

Association of American Colleges and Universities. (n.d). *VALUE rubrics*. Retrieved from www.aacu.org/value-rubrics

Braskamp, L. A., & Engberg, M. E. (2014). *Guidelines for judging the effectiveness of assessing student learning*. Chicago, IL: Loyola University Chicago. Retrieved from www.liberalarts.wabash.edu/storage/Braskamp_Engberg_Assessment_Guidelines.pdf

Hammer, M. (2012). The Intercultural Development Inventory: A new frontier in assessment and development of intercultural competence. In M. Vande Berg, R. M. Paige, & K. H. Lou (Eds.), *Student learning abroad* (pp. 115–136). Sterling, VA: Stylus.

15

USING A PARTNERSHIP APPROACH IN STUDY ABROAD

Implications and Strategies for Program Design and Assessment

Mary F. Price, Julie A. Hatcher, Dawn Michele Whitehead, and Gil Latz

The steady growth of study abroad over the past 20 years in the United States, the European Union, and other regions of the world has been the result of changes in public policy (e.g., Commission on the Abraham Lincoln Study Abroad Fellowship Program in the United States, Erasmus Programme in the European Union, and Australian Education International), internationalization efforts in higher education (e.g., American Council on Education Internationalization Laboratory), and standards of best practices (e.g., Forum on Education Abroad, Institute of International Education, European Association for International Education), among other factors. In the past two decades, there has been similar growth in service-learning and community engagement in higher education in the United States. These approaches to engaged learning have become important reform movements in higher education in the United States (Boyle, 2014). As advocates of these initiatives, we can attest to the many ways that the integration of literature and best practice within service-learning and study abroad can improve each other.

This chapter seeks to push forward thinking about improved assessment and practice in study abroad by focusing on community outcomes. We argue that focusing solely on student learning outcomes reduces the potential to understand both the broader collective good that can be derived from expanding student participation in study abroad and the systemic complexities and challenges inherent in community-university engagement (Bortolin, 2011; Hartman & Kiely, 2014). In this chapter, *study abroad* is defined as credit-bearing, college- or university-facilitated programs where the credit is awarded at the home institution. This includes faculty-led, college- or university-administered, and exchange programs. Like other forms of experiential learning (e.g., community-engaged research, internships, service-learning), education abroad, and study abroad programs in particular, has a range of stakeholders that span both host and home communities. In this chapter, we draw from literature on partnerships in community engagement (Cruz & Giles, 2000; Enos & Morton, 2003; Sandy & Holland, 2006) and employ a multiconstituency assessment approach to explore the community outcomes of study abroad (Gelmon, Holland, Driscoll, Spring, & Kerrigan, 2001). Students may be perceived to be the most important stakeholder, but a partnership lens broadens the implications for practice and for assessment in study abroad to include all stakeholders, including the community.

Beyond student learning, assessment to date in study abroad has focused primarily, if not exclusively, on student learning outcomes. This should not be surprising. The *Standards of Good Practice for Education Abroad* programs focus almost entirely on student learning (Forum on Education Abroad, 2011). Guidelines on including the impact on the local host community are limited to demonstrated respect for the community and its people (Galiardi & Koehn, 2011). Likewise, the six goals identified in the "Lincoln Commission Report" make no mention of the host or home community, except for a modest reference to partnerships in goal five (Commission on the Abraham Lincoln Study Abroad Fellowship Program, 2005). A focus on student learning aligns with current best practice in study abroad and is understood as essential to garnering additional institutional and government support for study abroad programs.

Empirical evidence indicates that students report significant gains from participating in study abroad programs (Vande Berg, Connor-Linton, & Paige, 2009); indeed, it may be the most significant and long-lasting dimension of the undergraduate years (Paige, Fry, Stallman, Jon, & Josic, 2010). Others have argued that study abroad's unique value in fostering long-term impact on student learning and development has not been proven; positive outcomes attributed to study abroad may be attributable to student characteristics and other factors (Twombly, Salisbury, Tumanut, & Klute, 2012).

But students are not the only beneficiaries. An extensive study funded by the U.S. Department of Education concluded that investing in study abroad has major social and individual benefits. It contributes to the development of not only human capital but also social capital and thus contributes to the common good, above and beyond the personal private benefits (Paige et al., 2010). Beyond the impact on individual students, for the social benefit of study abroad to be realized, both host and home communities must be considered. Faculty and staff, home and host institutions, and communities supporting students are also key stakeholders in the enterprise.

Education abroad and study abroad programs are increasingly complex. Data from the Forum on Education Abroad indicate that more students have opportunities to be engaged in fieldwork, internships, or service-learning experiences in host communities. This emphasis on experiential learning is captured in the Volunteer, Internship Experience, and Work initiative of the Forum. New guidelines for credit and noncredit experiences abroad bring attention to the importance of community partnerships (Forum on Education Abroad, 2013). This heightens the importance of articulating the role of community partners and of assessing the impact in terms of benefits for the host institution and community partners.

Broadening the assessment of study abroad beyond student learning outcomes requires a multiconstituency approach. The multiconstituent approach, initiated in the United States first at Portland State University, has been replicated and modified to assess a variety of experiential learning experiences, including service-learning courses (Gelmon et al., 2001). For many years, assessment in service-learning focused solely on student learning. Similar to study abroad, there is now strong empirical evidence of the student learning outcomes associated with integrating service into academic study (Conway, Amel, & Gerwien, 2009; Finley, 2011). As the field of community engagement has grown in higher education, there is increased attention to the outcomes for community partners and organizations (Littlepage & Gazley, 2013; Reeb & Folger, 2013). The time is right to use a partnership lens when designing and assessing study abroad programs, particularly when they encourage community engagement.

Partnerships as a Framework for Study Abroad

Indiana University–Purdue University Indianapolis (IUPUI) is a metropolitan campus with a dual commitment to internationalization and community engagement. The approach to campus internationalization, as with community engagement, places an emphasis on partnerships that prioritize dialogue and collaboration. A distinctive approach to the role of partnerships can be traced over the past decade and is reflected in the campus strategic plan (IUPUI, 2014), the campus's contribution to the academic research literature (e.g., Bringle & Hatcher, 2011), and campus recognition by receipt of the 2009 Heiskell and the 2011 Simon awards for campus internationalization.

That dialogue and collaboration with community partners are essential elements of internationalization is not unique to the campus; however, the relationship between IUPUI's philosophy of and strategy for international partnerships is noteworthy in terms of a linkage to the field of service-learning and community engagement. As Sutton (2010, p. 60) observed,

> It is little surprise that many colleges and universities are working to transform traditional modes of exchange into more full-bodied relationships. In so doing, they are moving from what might be called transactional partnerships to transformational ones, terms I borrow from the service-learning work of Sandra Enos and Keith Morton.

Such an approach to transformational partnerships is embraced as a framework for the internationalization efforts of the campus. The transformational dimension of international relationships, when framed in achieving mutually identified goals, is executed strategically through agreements such as student and faculty research exchange (Halimi, Kecskes, Ingle, & Phuong, 2014; Latz, Ingle, & Fischer, 2009; Sutton, 2010). Study abroad programs represent one element of IUPUI's strategy over the past decade. Fully one third of our study abroad programs have international service-learning (ISL) components for students in the host community.

Current scholarship on ISL points to the importance of both student and faculty preparation prior to departure to improve the quality of the course or program, as well as to ensure that diverse stakeholder voices in the host country are incorporated into the planning, implementation, and assessment phases of ISL (Galiardi & Koehn, 2011; Nelson & Klak, 2012). Because ISL can be a powerful tool for relationship building between and among universities and community organizations, particularly when a clear connection between institutional partnerships and successful service-learning programs has been identified (Florman, Just, Naka, Peterson, & Seaba, 2009). New attention to faculty roles stems from claims that faculty culture in the United States tends toward isolation, privatization, and individualism. As Boyte and Fretz (2010, p. 83) note, these everyday practices work against the forms of collaboration at the heart of community-engaged scholarship. In response, new work is emerging to engage both faculty and staff in critical examination of their practices related to ISL and global community engagement more generally (e.g., Deardorff 2011; Price & Whitehead, 2013). The importance of integrating local communities into this work has also been cited as a key for successful implementation of ISL programs, yet comparatively little has been written on the impact on the community (Tomkin, 2011).

Assessing Partnerships and Community Outcomes in Study Abroad

Both service-learning and study abroad share an interest in the concept of partnerships. Well-constructed service-learning and study abroad programs are rooted in mutually beneficial, reciprocal partnerships. In study abroad, reciprocal relationships may develop among institutions, programs, or individuals. To varying degrees, each involves faculty, staff, and student interactions with local residents and organizations. Hence, using partnerships as a framework to define stakeholders, conceptualize interactions and outcomes, and organize a research or evaluation agenda is essential. Although a focus on community has been historically weak in both service-learning and study abroad, service-learning and community engagement scholars have made significant headway in expanding how higher education practitioners can utilize a partnership lens and study outcomes across multiple constituencies, including communities (Gelmon, Holland, Seifer, Shinnamon, & Connors, 1998).

As service-learning practitioners and scholars more intentionally consider the contributions of and outcomes for communities, they grapple with the complex nature of terms like *partnership*, *reciprocity*, and *community impact* and how each relates to educational practices locally and globally (Longo & Saltmarsh, 2011; Sutton, 2011). Although we do not have the space here to comprehensively review the community-university partnership literature (refer to Bringle & Clayton, 2013, for review), at least four areas are relevant to understanding partnerships and community outcomes in the study abroad context:

- the importance of gaining definitional clarity on who and what community means within a study abroad course or program,
- the value of using a partnership lens to guide program theory and logic modeling to identify and analyze stakeholder and partnership outputs and outcomes,
- the need to support instructional design practices and outcomes evaluation across multiple stakeholder groups, and
- the value of problematizing higher education institutions and their associated personnel as political and economic actors in the context of study abroad and community activities.

Assessment practices for ISL and study abroad courses are typically student centric, overlooking or, at best, only partially recognizing the effect of study abroad programs on the community, at home and abroad, or other stakeholders (e.g., faculty, NGO staff, individuals "served") (Crabtree, 2013;

Nelson & Klak, 2012; Tonkin, 2011). Traditional approaches to teaching and research tend not to recognize community members as either coeducators or coproducers of knowledge (Freire, 1986; hooks, 2003). Therefore, it is not surprising that there has been limited attention given to community outcomes in the context of study abroad, even as study abroad has increasingly emphasized the value of community engagement for student learning and development.

Although they are closely related, assessing partnerships (see table 15.1) is not the same as assessing outcomes for the host and home communities. When partnerships are the unit of analysis, analytical focus centers on study of the relationships and ties among collaborators, their distinctive attributes, and how these relationships change over time under specific conditions and across varying scales (e.g., interpersonal, organizational, interorganizational) (Bringle, Clayton, & Price, 2009; Janke, 2013). Partnership researchers argue that it is the structural and qualitative features of these relations that can significantly influence community, partnership, and student-learning outcomes (Clayton, Bringle, Senor, Huq, & Morrison, 2010).

When study abroad practitioners seek to find evidence of the outcomes for communities, to which community or whom are they referring? The term *community*, like *service*, has shifting meanings both in practice and in the academic literature (Anderson, 1983; Mac Sweeney, 2011; Macfarlane, 1977). *Community* is commonly understood both as a value and as a group that shares a sense of belonging (Stoecker, 2005). The factors generating this sense of connectedness can vary broadly by modes of affiliation, role type, interest, kinship, gender, race, and ethnicity. In addition, *community* may describe a locality in which residents' sense of connection is informed by colocation or by communion. The multiple meanings assigned to *community* make it difficult to conceptualize analytically (Stoecker, 2005; Wellman, 2001). Individuals are simultaneously members of multiple communities, socially and geospatially, a reality intensified by processes of globalization (Appadurai, 1991; Marcus, 1995) and the rise of the Internet (Wilson & Peterson, 2002).

In study abroad programs, like service-learning courses, program designers and participants may use the term *community* in multiple ways, complicating assessment of community outcomes. In the geospatial sense, study abroad programs span multiple communities. Sojourning students and faculty come from specific campus communities situated in urban or rural communities. Study abroad takes them to nested sets of place-based communities in the host country. Depending on the program design, these may include the host country campus or a village, city, or region. Host community faculty,

TABLE 15.1

Matrix for Assessing Partnerships in Study Abroad Programs

What assumptions, conceptual frameworks, and/or theories guide how we have designed this collaboration, program, or course?

What assumptions do we have about the changes this partnership has effected and on whom (e.g., students, faculty, staff, residents, community partners organizations, institutions)?

What might we want to know? (key concepts)	How would we know it? (sample indicators)	How could we measure it? (methods)	Who/what could provide the data? (sources)
Nature of formal partnership and study abroad agreements	Development of criteria to distinguish between collaborators and partners. Creation of partnerships. Memoranda of understanding. Kinds of activities conducted.	Survey Focus Group Document analysis	Faculty/Staff Administrators Organizational and Institutional partners in home and host communities Host community residents
Nature of interactions and relationships	Involvement in shared activities. Communication patterns. Shared creation of new programs. Celebration of shared accomplishments.	Survey Focus Group Document analysis Process Evaluation Network Analysis	Faculty/Staff Administrators Community Partners
Satisfaction with partnership or study abroad program	Perception of mutuality and reciprocity. Responsiveness to concerns. Willingness to provide feedback.	Survey Focus Group Interview	Faculty/Staff Administrators
Sustainability of partnership or study abroad program	Duration over time. Evidence of shared power/voice among partners. Evolution and complexity of programs. Shared external grant-funded activities.	Survey Focus Group Document analysis	Faculty/Staff Administrators
Focus area(s) that the partnership or study abroad program addresses	Host community resources and capacities. Mutually defined goals for collaboration with host community groups and organizations. Mutually defined metrics identified to demonstrate success.	Asset Mapping Needs assessment	Conducted by community/university partnership representative

Note. Adapted from *Assessing Service Learning and Civic Engagement: Principles and Techniques*, by S. Gelmon, B.A. Holland, A. Driscoll, A. Spring, and S. Kerrigan, 2001, Providence, RI: Campus Compact.

staff, NGO personnel, and residents similarly may identify with multiple communities based on their own individual and collective histories, experiences, and ties.

Those seeking to evaluate community outcome need to consider which elements (e.g., behavior, identity, structures, institutions) or modes of community partnerships organized at the course, academic program, or institutional level (e.g., physical, social, virtual) can effect change. Community outcomes evaluation can include change among any combination of the following: the physical landscape or environment, infrastructure, transportation and settlement, economic development, social structure, health, economics, language and communication, informal and formal institutions, or practices and behaviors. Community outcomes also extend beyond the host community. Educational experience abroad may prompt students to be more aware of similar dynamics in their home communities. In turn, students may be challenged to engage locally, examine similar critical issues in their home communities, and make important connections between the local and the global in their personal and professional lives.

Conceptual clarity and capacity for outcomes evaluation can guide program conceptualization and design. Articulating program theory is a valuable strategy for capturing local contexts both at home and abroad, identifying stakeholders, and surfacing tacit assumptions and epistemological frameworks that inform program design (Kellogg Foundation, 2004; Swords & Kiely, 2010). Program theory can be used at the course, program, and institutional levels of international partnership work. Useful in this context are the community capitals framework (Emery, Fey, & Flora, 2006; Emery & Flora, 2006) and the collective impact model (Hanleybrown, Kania, & Kramer, 2012). Examples of course- and program-level models include the work of Chupp and Joseph (2010), Reeb and Folger (2013), and Sandmann, Kiely, and Grenier (2009).

Developing program theory is an essential component of program planning. Unfortunately, most faculty and staff in higher education are underprepared for the task, because they lack the knowledge, skills, and experiences that would enable them to (a) design for and engage community partners in using participatory methods and (b) negotiate the complexities across stakeholder groups in terms of competing interests and power differentials (Sandmann et al., 2009). Luckily, the field of community engagement is developing a body of theory and knowledge that can explain how partnerships develop in ways that improve the quality of service-learning pedagogy and result in institutional change and community development (Bringle & Clayton, 2013; Clayton et al., 2010).

Feasibility of Evaluating Community Outcomes in Study Abroad

Thought leaders in community engagement recognize the importance of linking service-learning courses and community-based research projects to larger, mission-driven, institution-level commitments. A growing number of urban-serving institutions, for example, have taken on the role of anchor institutions in their local communities (Axelroth, Hodges, & Dubb, 2012) to support a variety of community, social, and economic development outcomes (Wittman & Crews, 2012). Organizing strategic partnership commitments at the institutional level can scaffold engagement beyond individual practitioners, where involvement and access to funding and support may be fragile over time, and individual projects may not foster broader community change (Wittman & Crews, 2012).

Analyses of anchor institution initiatives indicate that it takes anywhere from 10 to 15 years to see evidence of stated outcomes for campus-community projects (Axelroth et al., 2012). This timescale lies well outside that associated with single study abroad and service-learning courses and programs, and it questions which claims academic institutions should make regarding which community and community partner outcomes, as opposed to outputs, are achievable in a single semester or short course or program (Chupp & Joseph, 2010; Stater & Fotheringham, 2009).

Institution-level engagement does not inevitably lead to positive, sustained community impacts 30 or 40 years out (Isbell, 2009). Rather, institutional support is essential to providing core infrastructure to support communication and resourcing and building the evaluation capacity to document and analyze the multidimensional outcomes across stakeholder groups involved in study abroad programs.

Case Study of IUPUI–Moi University Partnership and Study Abroad

This case study illustrates the value of taking a partnership approach to the assessment of study abroad. IUPUI is early in this work and has not yet taken action to respond to all of the discussion in this chapter.

IUPUI's nearly 25-year involvement in Kenya is a remarkable, multifaceted collaboration between the medical schools of Indiana University in Indianapolis, Indiana, and Moi University in Eldoret, Kenya (see www.iukenya.org). The partnership has grown yearly to include wider campuses and communities at each locale, resulting in multiple points of entry for cooperation between university faculty, students, and staff, as well as organizations and residents in the communities of Eldoret and Indianapolis. Hallmarks of the partnership have been reciprocity and mutual respect based on the combined efforts of active citizens and civic-minded professionals working collectively for the common good (Quigley, 2009).

In collaboration, the two medical schools developed the Academic Model Providing Access to Healthcare (AMPATH) in western Kenya. AMPATH operates an HIV/AIDS hospital with clinical staff, laboratory support, and a strong public health infrastructure that provides high-quality treatment, testing, and counseling for more than one million people. AMPATH also operates a dozen rural clinics and a craft workshop to economically empower citizens and has been involved in the creation of a mother-baby hospital. The strength and impact of the partnership led top leaders from IUPUI and Moi University to sign a comprehensive memorandum of strategic alliance to expand the partnership across their schools and units in November 2006. A network of faculty, staff, administrators, and students at both institutions have now become connected both face-to-face and electronically, and a number of projects well beyond medicine have been developed and implemented (see table 15.2).

For this case study, we focus on an ISL study abroad program developed with faculty in the social sciences and education at Moi University and community partners in Eldoret, Kenya. This three-week credit-bearing study abroad program is designed for undergraduates in the IUPUI Honors College. In a predeparture orientation period, students attend lectures and prepare for cultural and professional differences. In Kenya, students take courses taught by Moi University faculty and Ki-Swahili lessons and also engage in service-learning at a placement site in the Eldoret area (an orphanage, an elementary school affiliated with a university, AMPATH farms, or a high school with an emphasis on mathematics and science). Students also visit key cultural sites in and around western Kenya.

Fulbright-Hays pilot funding enabled IUPUI faculty and students and Indianapolis public teachers to identify service-learning placements in spring 2009. Following the pilot, the program leaders from IUPUI and Moi assessed the community sites for suitability for undergraduate students and selected community partners; these partners have now been collaborating in the study abroad program for five years.

To assess student learning outcomes, the IUPUI program director analyzed weekly cross-cultural experience reports completed by students and an end-of-program evaluation. Students were also interviewed and/or participated in a focus group. Students worked with a supervisor at their placement sites, and the evaluations were shared with the program leader to triangulate with the other data sources.

TABLE 15.2

Sample Matrix for Assessing the IUPUI–Moi University Partnership and Community Outcomes

What Do We Want to Know? (Key Concepts)	How Will We Know It? (Sample Indicators)	How Can We Measure It? (Methods)	Who or What Will Provide the Data? (Sources)
Nature of formal partnership or study abroad agreements	Partnership between IU and Moi University schools of medicine in 1989 Memorandum of understanding between IUPUI and Moi University in 2006 Student, faculty, and staff exchange; research and teaching done at both universities	Surveys Focus groups Interviews	Faculty and staff Administrators Partners in home and host communities
Nature of interactions and relationships	Involvement in shared research projects in health care, diabetes, intergenerational relations, and education Consistent communication to continue project activity across the campuses Shared creation of new programs Joint grant-funded projects	Survey Focus group Document analysis	Faculty and staff Administrators Students Community partners
Satisfaction with partnership or study abroad program	Representation of both universities on all research projects Joint preparation for study abroad program activities Collaborative preparation for students prior to field placements	Survey Focus group Interview	Faculty and staff Administrators
Sustainability of partnership or study abroad program	Continued assessment of program activities by all involved Grant-funded activities benefit all partners	Survey Focus group Document analysis	Faculty and staff Administrators
Focus areas that the partnership or study abroad program addresses	Asset mapping of resources in Kenya and the United States Mutually defined goals for collaboration Metrics identified to demonstrate success	Needs assessment Interviews	Conducted by community-university partnership representative

To assess the community impact of the study abroad course, the program director conducted interviews with staff leaders at the community partner organizations with a primary school deputy head teacher, the founder-director of the orphanage, and the high school's science department coordinator. As the program director has remained the same since the program's founding, the relationships with the community partners involve open, honest communication. The interviews were semistructured and lasted from 30 minutes to 1 hour and were designed to examine the community partners' perceived outcomes of hosting service-learning students. The interviews focused on the overall experience, the costs and benefits, and the challenges.

Each of the three respondents shared positive experiences with the IUPUI students, with no negative experiences reported. Each focused on the positive impact of the service-learning students' ability to adapt and integrate with the staff and their positive impact on the children at the orphanage and schools. The interview data align with the distinction made between program-oriented needs and project-oriented needs. Respondents emphasized the value of incorporating students into the existing program activities of the organization rather than initiating new projects. They all reported that the additional support for staff was a major benefit of hosting service-learning students, and none cited costs as a factor in student placements. Challenges were related to communication. The American accent was an initial challenge, but this mitigated over a few days and when students slowed their speech. The orphanage cited no work-related challenges. However, there were concerns about undergraduate students' safety when going into town. The community partners' assessment confirms many of the programmatic decisions made when developing the study abroad program and will inform preparation for students going forward.

Conclusion

The concept of partnership is a foundational element of the field of service-learning and community-university engagement more broadly. This chapter argued that programs for study abroad, characterized primarily by student learning assessment, should also include evaluation of partnerships and the outcomes on communities. By examining the literature and practice of community engagement, we reconceptualized and recommended assessment strategies for study abroad, particularly for programs involving engagement with partners at study abroad sites. A multiconstituent approach was proposed to understand and assess the relationship between the home and host institutions.

The literature on service-learning and community-university partnerships is dominated by U.S.- and Western-centric models (Kahn, 2011; Sutton, 2011; Watson, Hollister, Stroud, & Babcock, 2011). In applying insights from this literature to study abroad, it is important to recognize the cultural and political economic positioning of this work. Program directors and university administrators are wise to critically examine the processes of study abroad within the context of globalization and international development. That is, benefits should not just accrue to sojourning students or their home institutions. Focusing more intentionally on community partnerships will help achieve this.

The resulting assessment matrices identify potential core concepts, indicators, methods, and sources of information to use to build evaluation capacity for community outcomes assessment (see table 15.1 and table 15.2). The brief case study of the IUPUI–Moi University partnership, including community outcomes for a study abroad program involving service-learning, illustrates how such an approach can be implemented and applied to understanding the community outcomes of campus internationalization more generally.

Universities and university agents do not engage in value-neutral activities (Lane, 2014). Study abroad and internationalization, like service-learning and civic engagement in the United States, involve educational and research practices that are subject to the individual positioning and conceptualization of faculty directors and sojourning students. Doing this work well, and in partnership with communities, is essential to maximize both the impact on student learning and the broader social benefits for communities in the United States and abroad.

References

Anderson, B. (1983). *Imagined communities: Reflections on the origin and spread of nationalism.* London, UK: Verso.

Appadurai, A. (1991). Global ethnoscapes: Notes and queries for a transnational anthropology. In R. G. Fox (Ed.), *Recapturing anthropology: Working in the present* (pp. 191–210). Santa Fe, NM: School for Advanced Research Press.

Axelroth, R., Hodges, R., & Dubb, S. (2012). *The road half traveled: University engagement at the crossroads.* East Lansing, MI: Michigan State University Press.

Bortolin, K. (2011). Serving ourselves: How the discourse on community engagement privileges the university over the community. *Michigan Journal of Community Service Learning, 18*(1), 49–58.

Boyle, N. (2014). Integrating global and local civic learning (early and often). In J. N. Reich (Ed.), *Civic engagement, civic development, and higher education: Bring-*

ing theory to practice monograph (pp. 73–75). Washington, DC: Association of American Colleges and Universities.

Boyte, H., & Fretz, E. (2010). Civic professionalism. *Journal of Higher Education Outreach and Engagement, 14*(2), 67–90.

Bringle, R. G., & Clayton, P. H. (2013). Conceptual framework for partnerships in service learning. In P. H. Clayton, R. G. Bringle, & J. A. Hatcher (Eds.), *Research on service learning: Conceptual frameworks and assessment* (pp. 539–571). Sterling, VA: Stylus.

Bringle, R. G., Clayton, P., & Price, M. (2009). Partnerships in service learning and civic engagement. *Partnerships: A Journal of Service-Learning and Civic Engagement, 1*(1), 1–20.

Bringle, R. G., & Hatcher, J. A. (2011). International service learning. In R. G. Bringle, J. A. Hatcher, & S. G. Jones (Eds.), *International service learning: Conceptual frameworks and research* (pp. 3–28). Sterling, VA: Stylus.

Chupp, M. G., & Joseph, M. L. (2010). Getting the most out of service learning: Maximizing student, university and community impact. *Journal of Community Practice, 18,* 190–212.

Clayton, P., Bringle, R., Senor, B., Huq, J., & Morrison, M. (2010). Differentiating and assessing relationships in service-learning and civic engagement: Exploitative, transactional, and transformational. *Michigan Journal of Community Service-Learning, 16*(2), 5–21. Retrieved from www.eric.ed.gov

Commission on the Abraham Lincoln Study Abroad Fellowship Program. (2005). *Global competence and national needs: One million Americans studying abroad.* Retrieved from www.nafsa.org/Resource_Library_Assets/Public_Policy/Lincoln_Commission_s_Report/

Conway, J. M., Amel, E. L., & Gerwien, D. P. (2009). Teaching and learning in the social context: A meta-analysis of service learning's effects on academic, personal, social and citizenship outcomes. *Teaching of Psychology, 36*(4), 233–245.

Crabtree, R. D. (2013). The intended and unintended consequences of international service-learning. *Journal of Higher Education Outreach and Engagement, 17*(2), 43–64.

Cruz, N., & Giles, D. (2000, Fall). Where's the community in service-learning research? *Michigan Journal of Community Service-Learning,* 28–34.

Emery, M., Fey, S., & Flora, C. B. (2006). Using community capitals to build assets for positive community change. *Community Development Practice, 13.* Retrieved from www.comm-dev.org

Emery, M., & Flora, C. B. (2006). Spiraling-up: Mapping community transformation with community capitals framework. *Community Development: Journal of the Community Development Society, 37,* 19–35. Retrieved from www.ncrcrd.iastate .edu/pubs/flora/spiralingup.html

Enos, S., & Morton, K. (2003). Developing a theory and practice of campus-community partnerships. In B. Jacoby & Associates (Eds.), *Building partnerships for service-learning* (pp. 20–41). San Francisco, CA: Jossey-Bass.

Finley, A. (2011). *Civic learning and democratic engagements: A review of the literature on civic engagement in post-secondary education*. Paper prepared for the U.S. Department of Education as part of Contract ED-OPE-10_C-0078. Retrieved from www.civiclearning.org/SupportDocs/LiteratureReview_CivicEngagement_Finley_Jul2011.pdf

Florman, J. C., Just, C., Naka, T., Peterson, J., & Seaba, H. H. (2009). Bridging the distance: Service learning in international perspective. *New Directions for Teaching and Learning, 118*, 71–84.

Forum on Education Abroad. (2011). *Standards of good practice for education abroad* (4th ed.). Carlisle, PA: Dickinson College.

Forum on Education Abroad. (2013). *Guidelines for credit and non-credit Volunteer, Internship Experience and Work (VIEW) programs abroad*. Retrieved from www.forumea.org/documents/ForumEA-VIEW-Guidelines-Dec-2013_001.pdf

Freire, P. (1986). *Pedagogy of the oppressed*. New York, NY: Continuum.

Galiardi, S., & Koehn, J. (2011). Strategies to mitigate the negative and accentuate the positive impacts of international service-learning on host communities. *Partnerships: A Journal of Service Learning and Civic Engagement, 2*(1), 1–12.

Gelmon, S., Holland, B. A., Driscoll, A., Spring, A., & Kerrigan, S. (2001). *Assessing service-learning and civic engagement: Principles and techniques*. Providence, RI: Campus Compact.

Gelmon, S., Holland, B. A., Seifer, S., Shinnamon, A., & Connors, K. (1998). Community-university partnerships for mutual learning. *Michigan Journal of Community Service Learning, 5*(1), 97–107.

Halimi, S., Kecskes, K., Ingle, M., & Phuong, P. T. (2014). Strategic international service-learning partnership: Mitigating the impact of rapid urban development in Vietnam. In P. Green & M. Johnson (Eds.), *Crossing boundaries: Tension and transformation in international service-learning* (pp. 46–67). Sterling, VA: Stylus.

Hanleybrown, F., Kania, J., & Kramer, M. (2012, January). Channeling change: Making collective impact work. *Stanford Social Innovation Review*, 1–8.

Hartmann, E., & Kiely, R. (2014). A critical global citizenship. In P. Green & M. Johnson (Eds.), *Crossing boundaries: Tension and transformation in international service-learning* (pp. 215–242). Sterling, VA: Stylus.

hooks, b. (2003). *Teaching community: A pedagogy of hope*. New York, NY: Routledge.

Indiana University–Purdue University Indianapolis. (2014). *Strategic plan*. Retrieved from http://strategicplan.iupui.edu/

Isbell, B. J. (2009). Lessons from Vicos. *Anthropology in Action, 16*(3), 41–54.

Janke, E. M. (2013). Organizational partnerships in service learning. In P. H. Clayton, R. G. Bringle, & J. H. Hatcher (Eds.), *Research on service learning: Conceptual frameworks and assessment* (pp. 573–598). Sterling, VA: Stylus.

Kahn, H. (2011). A visual approach to sharing authority, community development, and global learning. In R. G. Bringle, J. A. Hatcher, & S. G. Jones (Eds.), *International service learning: Conceptual frameworks and research* (pp. 113–124). Sterling, VA: Stylus.

Kellogg Foundation. (2004). *Using logic models to bring together planning, evaluation and action: Logic model development guide.* Retrieved from www.wkkf.org/resource-directory/resource/2006/02/wk-kellogg-foundation-logic-model-development-guide

Lane, J. E. (2014). *Higher education institutions as international actors.* Albany, NY: Nelson A. Rockefeller Institute of Government, University at Albany, SUNY. Retrieved from www.rockinst.org/pdf/public_policy_forums/2012-03-06-Lane%20International%20Actors.pdf

Latz, G., Ingle, M., & Fischer, M. (2009). Cross-border capacity building: Selected examples of Portland State University's involvement in tertiary level educational reform in Vietnam. In D. F. Kocaoglu, T. R. Anderson, T. U. Daim, A. Jetter, & C. M. Weber (Eds.), *PICMET '09: Portland international conference for management of engineering and technology: Proceedings: Technology management in the age of fundamental change.* Piscataway, NJ: IEEE.

Littlepage, L., & Gazley, B. (2013). Examining service learning from the perspective of community organization capacity. In R. G. Bringle, J. A. Hatcher, & S. G. Jones (Eds.), *International service learning: Conceptual frameworks and research* (pp. 419–440). Sterling, VA: Stylus.

Longo, N., & Saltmarsh, J. (2011). New lines of inquiry in reframing international service learning into global service learning. In R. G. Bringle, J. A. Hatcher, & S. G. Jones (Eds.), *International service learning: Conceptual frameworks and research* (pp. 69–88). Sterling, VA: Stylus.

Mac Sweeney, N. (2011). *Community identity and archaeology: Dynamic communities at Aphrodisias and Beycesultan.* Ann Arbor, MI: University of Michigan Press.

Macfarlane, A. (1977). History, anthropology and the study of communities. *Social History, 2*(5), 631–652.

Marcus, G. E. (1995). Ethnography in/of the world system: The emergence of multi-sited ethnography. *Annual Review of Anthropology, 24*, 95–117.

Nelson, E. D., & Klak, T. (2012). Equity in international experiential learning: Assessing benefits to students and host communities. *PRISM: A Journal of Regional Engagement, 1*(2), 106–129.

Paige, R. M., Fry, G. W., Stallman, E., Jon, J., & Josi, J. (2010). *Beyond immediate impact: Study abroad for global engagement (SAGE)* (Report submitted to the Title VI: International Research and Studies Program). Washington, DC: U.S. Department of Education.

Price, M. F., & Whitehead, D. M. (2013). *Motivations for service: Examining assumptions underlying instructional design and student learning for the global commons.* Paper presented at the Association of American Colleges and Universities Global Learning Summit, Providence, RI.

Quigley, F. (2009). *Walking together, walking far: How a U.S. and African medical school partnership is winning the fight against HIV/AIDS.* Bloomington, IN: Indiana University Press.

Reeb, R., & Folger, S. (2013). Community outcomes in service learning. In P. H. Clayton, R. G. Bringle, & J. A. Hatcher (Eds.), *Research on service learning: Conceptual frameworks and assessment* (pp. 389–418). Sterling, VA: Stylus.

Sandmann, L. R., Kiely, R., & Grenier, R. S. (2009). Program planning: The neglected dimension of service learning. *Michigan Journal of Community Service Learning, 15*(2), 17–33.

Sandy, M., & Holland, B. A. (2006). Different worlds and community ground: Community partner perspectives on campus-community partnerships. *Michigan Journal of Community Service Learning, 13*, 30–43.

Stater, K. J., & Fotheringham, E. (2009). Mechanisms for institutionalizing service-learning and community partner outcomes. *Journal of Higher Education Outreach and Engagement, 13*(2), 7–29.

Stoecker, R. (2005). *Research methods for community change*. Thousand Oaks, CA: Sage.

Sutton, S. (2010, January–February). Transforming internationalization through partnerships. *International Educator*, pp. 60–63.

Sutton, S. (2011). Service learning as local learning. In R. G. Bringle, J. A. Hatcher, & S. G. Jones (Eds.), *International service learning: Conceptual frameworks and research* (pp. 125–144). Sterling, VA: Stylus.

Swords, A., & Kiely, R. (2010). Beyond pedagogy: Service learning as movement building in higher education. *Journal of Community Practice, 18*, 148–170.

Tonkin, H. (2011). A research agenda for international service learning. In R. G. Bringle, J. A. Hatcher, & S. G. Jones (Eds.), *International service learning: Conceptual frameworks and research* (pp. 191–224). Sterling, VA: Stylus.

Twombly, S., Salisbury, M., Tumanut, S., & Klute, P. (2012). *Study abroad in a new global century: Renewing the promise, refining the purpose* (ASHE Higher Education Report). Hoboken, NJ: Wiley.

Vande Berg, M., Connor-Linton, J., & Paige, R. M. (2009, Fall). The Georgetown Consortium project: Intervening in student learning abroad. *Frontiers: The Interdisciplinary Journal of Study Abroad, 18*, 1–75.

Watson, D., Hollister, R. M., Stroud, S. E., & Babcock, E. (2011). *The engaged university: International perspectives on civic engagement*. New York, NY: Routledge.

Wellman, B. (2001). The persistence and transformation of community: From neighbourhood groups to social networks. *Report to the Law Commission of Canada*. Retrieved from www.chass.utoronto.ca/~wellman/publications/index.html

Wilson, S. M., & Peterson, L. C. (2002). The anthropology of online communities. *Annual Review of Anthropology, 31*, 449–467.

Wittman, A., & Crews, T. (2012). *Engaged learning economies: Aligning civic engagement and economic development in community-campus partnerships*. Boston, MA: Campus Compact.

16

CAPACITY BUILDING FOR ASSESSING STUDY ABROAD OUTCOMES

Elizabeth Brewer

I n late January–early February 2003, I attended the annual meeting of the American Council on Education's Internationalization Collaborative with a small team from Beloit College. Assessment was the topic of a Saturday morning plenary, and although the speakers, Peggy Maki (American Association for Higher Education and Accreditation) and Gloria Rogers (Rose-Hulman Institute of Technology), were enthusiastic about the value of assessment, our team was distinctly uneasy with the topic. How could we possibly assess internationalization? And why should we? Weren't grades and anecdotal information enough? Why wrestle with terms such as *direct and indirect measures* and *triangulation* and the processes linked to them?

In fact, I did know something about assessment, even if I had not been using the term. I had just spent three years as a Peace Corps volunteer in Slovakia, where I worked with my Slovak counterparts to design community development projects and secure grant funding to support them. My colleagues and I also created and facilitated workshops to enable the villagers we worked with to design, fund, and implement their own projects to address community needs. We well knew that no agencies would approve funding for projects without clear goals and objectives, feasible implementation plans that aligned with resources and needs, and measurable outcomes. We were also acutely aware of the high failure rate of community projects that did not take these into account and the disillusionment that comes with failure. People who have devoted personal time for naught and seen resources wasted understandably become skeptical. The success of our organization, therefore, rested on our ability to help rural Slovaks learn to undertake projects that improved the quality of life in their villages. The focus on outcomes and ways to achieve them are exactly what is needed for assessment.

My colleagues and I at Beloit College knew we needed to do something to strengthen students' abilities to benefit from study abroad. After all, we were counting on returned study abroad students to make contributions to the classroom. We knew that if they failed to return with new questions, perspectives, knowledge, and stronger skills, we were doing something wrong. On campus, we were also engaged in conversations about the nature of learning and how study abroad might serve as a catalyst for broader campus internationalization.

Yet despite my recent experience with project development and evaluation, and my colleagues' considerable experience building academic programs that successfully educated students, assessment seemed daunting. I believe that three fears contributed to the Beloit team's initial hesitancy. First, assessment terminology was not part of our everyday vocabularies. Nonacademics experience this with academics. What do you mean by "scaffold" an argument? Or examine "intersectionality"? Second, assessing would require stepping out of our disciplinary comfort zones to learn something that had not been part of our training. Although we expect students to do this on a regular basis, as faculty and staff we are reluctant to do so ourselves, lest we reveal our ignorance and embarrass ourselves in front of colleagues. Third, how could we come to any consensus on what we wanted students to learn abroad? If we established a set of goals, would this be divisive, given all the competing ways of knowing represented by the different departments on campus?

Getting Started: Lessons From the Case Studies

One way or another, and sooner or later, to assess you have to get started. Best practice in assessment calls for identifying desired learning outcomes in accordance with mission, aligning program elements with outcomes, using multiple measures appropriate to outcomes to be measured, and using triangulation to verify findings. It also calls for taking action on findings. Furthermore, attention must be paid to the different points in the learning cycle: what learners bring to the particular learning context (preparation), activities that enable students to acquire and construct knowledge and skills in support of the learning objectives, and opportunities for learners to take lessons from the learning (reflection, connection making).

When knowledge and resources permit, assessment can begin with the careful construction of an assessment plan, as discussed in chapter 3. Three of the case studies in this book provide examples of this approach. At Saint Mary's College, Elaine Meyer-Lee and Karen Chambers (chapter 11) were able to take a multimethod, longitudinal approach to generate rich data on student development for the purposes of program improvement and advocacy. Both are trained in psychology, and Meyer-Lee used her extensive knowledge of study abroad to investigate and experiment with different instruments. Chambers, a faculty member, is also assigned part time to Saint Mary's study abroad office to work on assessment. While a seeming luxury, Saint Mary's assessment approach and staffing have provided rich data on learning outcomes and promise to enable Meyer-Lee and Chambers to publish their findings "to contribute to the general body of empirical knowledge about growth in the context of international education for the benefit of the larger field" (Meyer-Lee, personal communication, 2014). Meyer-Lee and Chambers's chapter embodies good assessment that identifies research questions, aligns instruments and methods with the questions, and uses triangulation to make sure the findings are valid.

Duke University (chapter 8) benefited from expertise within its study abroad office and on the part of Darla Deardorff, who has studied and written extensively about intercultural development and its assessment and is based at Duke. Deardorff also recently produced a book on assessing outcomes from international education (Deardorff, 2015). Duke's assessment plan follows the assessment cycle outlined in chapter 3 and was the work of an assessment team that met regularly over several years. The team leader, Nick Gozik, has also served on and chaired the Forum on Education Abroad's Outcomes and Research Committee.

Central College's (chapter 9) study abroad assessment plan aligns with a new global perspective curricular requirement and a college decision to use the Global Perspective Inventory, developed by Larry Braskamp, a Central alumnus, to assess student success in meeting the competencies at which the requirement aims. Central invested resources to develop faculty expertise to teach toward the requirement, whereas Central's study abroad operations invested in capacity building to advance study abroad assessment around the requirement.

Other entities represented in the case studies have had to pursue more limited steps to engage with assessment. They have acquired the necessary expertise in different ways. In each case, however, it was recognized that despite limited resources, including time, doing nothing was not acceptable. Student learning was at stake, and the investments in study abroad—on the part of students and their families, institutions and organizations, and host communities—required that attempts be made to understand if the investments were yielding desired results. Although this means the individual institutions or organizations do not yet have comprehensive assessment plans and may be building expertise slowly, they are working toward building capacity and are experimenting with different methods that ultimately will provide more nuanced understandings of student learning outcomes and how this relates to study abroad programming.

In the case of Yale College (chapter 10) and the Associated Colleges of the Midwest (chapter 14), funding was available to enlist outside expertise. The ACM's assessment work began with a multi-institution collaboration that ultimately failed. Interpreting the findings proved elusive, as was connecting findings to program elements and goals. Developing an instrument to test multiple variables and outcomes is challenging indeed. After strategizing and consulting with people with expertise on study abroad and assessment, the ACM invited help from the Center of Inquiry in the Liberal Arts to understand the strengths and weaknesses of different assessment strategies and methods. Member institution faculty and staff, as well as ACM staff, were then enlisted to test a new kind of assessment that took advantage of course assignments whose assessment was easily doable by faculty and staff using a rubric after a short norming session. Rather than adopting another organization's rubric, the ACM examined several and ultimately crafted one that could serve the ACM's specific off-campus studies programs and outcomes questions.

Yale College benefited greatly from an external expert who helped it develop core values on which to base existing activities, such as advising, and add assessment activities. Like the ACM, however, Yale found itself experimenting with an instrument for which it lacked the expertise to make sense of the resulting data. On the basis of this experience and its growing knowledge of assessment practices, Yale then developed methods more appropriate to its capacities. Picking the right instrument is a matter not just of aligning the instrument with the desired learning outcome but also of aligning the instrument with organizational capacity to make sense of the data and, equally important, improve practice. When the instrument aligns with program goals and with organizational capacity, the findings can enable an institution or organization to make better use of resources and improve learning outcomes. Both the ACM and Yale were able to make small but significant change in this regard.

Western Oregon University (chapter 12) was able to draw on the expertise of an emeritus faculty member willing to volunteer time to develop both capacity and methods appropriate to the resources of a very small office. The learning outcome was clear: intercultural learning. But developing an instrument whose implementation would be efficient and not require resources beyond the study abroad office's took several tries. Beloit College (chapter 7) drew on work being undertaken by a faculty assessment committee, as well as the college's first-year program, to help it move into assessment. The process was fairly slow but began with identifying learning goals in keeping with institutional mission and then aligning elements of the study abroad office's operations with these to make sure that the goals informed advising, program selection, and study abroad applications and orientation and provided for post-study abroad opportunities for reflection. As an institution that does not offer its own programs, this is what the college could "control" and therefore assess, a criterion that also drove assessment decisions at Yale. The capacity to develop these steps was acquired through engagement with campus assessment efforts, consultations with institutional researchers, and involvement in international education organizations that allowed staff to attend workshops and conference sessions to gather ideas and test practices.

Although acquiring capacity to do assessment has been slow paced at the institutions represented in these latter case studies, and the work does not meet the traditional criteria for rigorous studies, the latter is not the point. Rather, the small-scale assessment has lent insight into student learning, led to positive changes in practice, and generated ideas for future assessment activities. Importantly, the small-scale, slow approach has helped overcome the paralysis that prevents some study abroad offices from undertaking assessment when resources are limited and there are fears about being qualified to do the work. The reality may well be that there is no one else at the institution who can take responsibility for the study abroad assessment. Small-scale assessment can build confidence without the risk of wasting valuable time and money. The Wesleyan case study (chapter 13) is an outlier in some ways. Having identified intercultural competence as a desired learning outcome, but dissatisfied with the available instruments for assessment, Steven E. Stemler and Carolyn K. Sorkin developed the Wesleyan Intercultural Competence Scale (WICS) to both better understand intercultural development in Wesleyan study abroad students and offer an assessment tool to others, which can be used at no cost and be adapted to address the specific needs of the institution or organization using the instrument. Stemler and Sorkin do not claim that the WICS is the only instrument an institution should use to assess study abroad, but they do offer it as an alternative to commercially available instruments. In addition, the Saint Mary's case (chapter 11), the Beloit case (chapter 7), and the Yale case (chapter 10) illustrate developing or adapting measures to fit the specific needs of those assessment efforts.

Mary F. Price, Julie A. Hatcher, Dawn Michele Whitehead, and Gil Latz at Indiana University–Purdue University Indianapolis (IUPUI) (see chapter

15) wanted to take into account impact on not only student learning but also community and university partners. Therefore, they looked to the literature on partnerships and community engagement to determine that costs and benefits to organizations hosting students needed to be assessed. Although IUPUI's work assessing impacts on communities is in the early stages, future work will have a strong theoretical foundation because of the IUPUI's literature review. IUPUI's capacity building around study abroad assessment also greatly benefited from IUPUI's 1998 "year of assessment," which led to the creation of a position dedicated to assessment and a culture of assessment. As faculty learned to focus on outcomes, course design improved and reflection activities were adopted to reach targeted outcomes. Finally, membership in the Forum on Education Abroad's Outcomes and Research Committee compelled several contributors to this volume to take assessment more seriously; to contribute to the committee, they became more familiar with the literature on study abroad outcomes, experimented with assessment on their campuses, and developed ways to talk about the assessment process with forum members embarking on this work. Thus, no matter your skill level, talk with others—within and outside your institution—to get going, and then refine your work. In addition, rather than undertaking assessment alone, extend invitations to others to join you. Faculty, staff, students, and of course institutional researchers are all potential partners, as are host community members, depending on the assessment question. When study abroad assessment is a shared enterprise, it can lead to shared ownership and responsibility for study abroad and also allow for multiple insights and perspectives into assessment processes and findings. Some institutions and organizations can also afford to consult outside assessment experts. Even after an assessment project is completed, the process of communicating findings and sharing revised goals can be made known to others, as described in the contextualizing chapter (chapter 4) and illustrated in the Saint Mary's example (chapter 11), the Yale case (chapter 10), and several others. Such sharing beyond the borders of the study abroad office can lead to positive outcomes in terms of visibility and credibility.

Assessment takes place in environments and under circumstances that are complicated by competing needs and limited resources. Assessment theory must inform assessment practice. However, as many of the theoretical and case study chapters demonstrate in this volume, and the voices of the volume's assessment experts and nonexpert practitioners suggest, in reality, assessing study abroad outcomes can be messy and slow paced. This volume's purpose is to inform the work of study abroad practitioners who come to study abroad assessment with a wide and varied range of skills sets. The goal is to help all determine if study abroad is helping students learn and grow. And for those beginning on study abroad assessment, we hope we have been able to help release them from the paralysis that comes from not being "qualified" by virtue of lacking specialized training and credentialing. For those more experienced, we hope the volume has reinforced assessment principles while also complicating them and provided inspiration for future assessment work.

Resources for Assessing: Publications and Organizations

Although the assessment of study abroad is a relatively recent phenomenon, the number of publications and online resources can be overwhelming for novices, if not also for those with some facility with assessment. Fortunately, a number of resources exist that provide a kind of shorthand to those seeking guidance. The list presented here is deliberately brief.

The National Institute for Learning Outcomes Assessment (NILOA), established in 2008, exists to "discover and disseminate ways that academic programs and institutions can productively use assessment data internally to inform and strengthen undergraduate education, and externally to communicate with policy makers, families and other stakeholders" (NILOA, n.d.). NILOA's website (http://learningoutcomeassessment.org) contains a number of resources on assessment in undergraduate education, and its occasional papers in particular are helpful in defining clear principles for assessment practices. Occasional Paper 1 (Ewell, 2009), for example, provides a useful distinction between assessing for accountability and assessing for improvement, whereas the authors of Occasional Paper 2 (Banta, Griffin, Flateby, & Kahn, 2019) argued that "authentic and valid assessment approaches" based in part on student work can best "capture the difficult and demanding intellectual skills that are the true aim of a college education." Occasional Paper 4 (Hutchings, 2010) discusses ways to involve faculty in assessment, and Occasional Paper 8 (Blaich & Wise, 2011) focuses on tapping existing data, enlisting students, and communicating and acting on findings. At 20–25 pages each, NILOA's occasional papers help demystify assessment principles and practices, and many of their lessons are directly applicable to the assessment of study abroad and other forms of international learning.

Mell Bolen's *A Guide to Outcomes Assessment in Education Abroad* (Bolen, 2007) emerged from the work of the Forum on Education Abroad's Outcomes Assessment Committee and remains a valuable guide. Written to fill a gap in the assessment literature, as its title suggests, the guide specifically addresses assessment within the study abroad context. Its chapters discuss the context for assessment in higher education and study abroad; research design; areas of inquiry; decision making, methods, and instruments; resources and terminology; and using results.

A 2015 volume by Darla Deardorff, who has written extensively on intercultural communication (Deardorff, 2015), serves as a primer for international educators charged with assessing learning outcomes. Deliberately repetitive and practical, the volume assumes readers have no prior knowledge of assessment, although international educators already engaged in assessing learning outcomes may find it a helpful refresher. The volume reviews assessment terminology and principles and recommends developing a plan before beginning to assess. Appendices include worksheets, advice on assessing intercultural competence, and a checklist for ensuring the quality of the assessment plan.

Study abroad practitioners are being enlisted to advance their and other study abroad practitioners' abilities to engage with assessment. Thus, at the April 2013 annual conference of the Forum on Education Abroad, members of the Outcomes Assessment and Research Committee launched the Outcomes Assessment Toolbox that is available to forum members on the forum's website (www.forumea.org/resources/outcomes). With sections on case studies, assessment texts, assessment tools, a glossary of terms, a bibliography of research, and links to useful webpages, the toolbox is intended to provide forum members with the information they need to assess study abroad outcomes. Unlike a print publication, it has the advantage of being easily updated to capture new information. However, it will also remain useful only to the extent forum members contribute to its ongoing development. They can do so by contacting forum staff or members of the committee.

The journal most closely aligned with study abroad is *Frontiers: The Interdisciplinary Journal of Study Abroad*. Since fall 2013, this online, open-access journal's current and past issues are available on its website (http://frontiersjournal.com). First published in 1995, *Frontiers* generally publishes one issue per year, and since 1998, articles related to study abroad outcomes have become a regular feature. Indeed, beginning with Volume 10 and continuing through Volume 14 in fall 2014, study abroad outcomes have several times been the major if not exclusive focus. Many contributors to *Frontiers* work in study abroad and thus offer perspectives on assessment "from the field," albeit primarily with a U.S.-centric perspective. Although its scope is broader, encompassing the internationalization of higher education, the *Journal of Studies in International Education* also publishes articles on study abroad outcomes assessment and tends to capture a wider range of perspectives, given the greater diversity of its authors, including geographic.

A review of the literature on study abroad and its outcomes (Twombly, Salisbury, Tumanut, & Klute, 2012) illuminates claims as well as questions about research on learning outcomes. Read this short volume to understand which questions seem promising and where research seems to be lacking, and, above all, to recognize that assessment efforts in study abroad offices, and other study abroad contexts, should focus on discrete questions and findings that can improve practice. Assessment should not be confused with research and should not be overcomplicated.

Finally, a number of educational associations are addressing learning outcomes related to study abroad either directly or indirectly. The Association of American Colleges and Universities (AAC&U; www.aacu.org) has been particularly effective in enlisting educators to define learning outcomes for undergraduate education and to create rubrics for analyzing the achievement of the outcomes. AAC&U rubrics for assessing intercultural knowledge and competence and for global learning may be of particular interest for assessing study abroad learning outcomes, but others may also be of interest. The AAC&U invites adaptation of its rubrics, as evidenced by more than one case study in this volume.

The American Council on Education's Center for Internationalization and Global Engagement (CIGE; www.acenet.edu/Search/Pages/results .aspx?k=CIGE) has also focused on assessment in study abroad. The council's work will be of particular interest to those interested in placing study abroad within the larger context of internationalization. CIGE's initiatives often involve working groups composed of representatives from multiple institutions; relevant to study abroad is an initiative to test the use of e-portfolios for assessing international learning. The Association of International Education Administrators (AIEA; www.aieaworld.org) also focuses on the internationalization of higher education with emphasis on the role of administrators charged with facilitating the internationalization of colleges and universities. The assessment of study abroad is increasingly featured in sessions in AIEA's annual conference.

NAFSA: Association of International Educators has also taken up outcomes assessment. Its publications on this topic are found in its section on internationalizing higher education (www.nafsa.org/Find_Resources/Inter nationalizing_Higher_Education/Comprehensive_Internationalization). New publications on assessment will continue to emerge through its professional interest groups.

The Teagle Foundation (www.teaglefoundation.org) supports projects to "improve undergraduate student learning in the arts and sciences" (Teagle Foundation, n.d.). Past grants have supported a focus on outcomes and assessment in study abroad. Project descriptions and guidelines for submitting proposals can be found on the foundation's website. The assessment work undertaken by the ACM (see chapter 14) was initially funded by the Teagle Foundation, and Beloit College (see chapter 7) has also benefited from Teagle grants. In addition, the Center of Inquiry in the Liberal Arts at

Wabash College (www.liberalarts.wabash.edu), which receives support from the Teagle Foundation, offers assistance to institutions embarking on assessment and was helpful to both the ACM's and Beloit College's study abroad assessment efforts.

Conclusion

In the foreword to *A History of U.S. Study Abroad: Beginnings to 1965*, Bill Hoffa pointed out, "Many early societies . . . concluded that people in other places, with other traditions and values, might have something to teach them" (Hoffa, 2007, p. 1). After noting intermediate steps toward contemporary study abroad (the wandering medieval scholar, the Grand Tour that arose in the seventeenth century and flourished in the nineteenth century, specialized graduate studies in Europe when those were not yet available in the United States), Hoffa located the beginnings of American study abroad as a credit-bearing component of undergraduate education in the early twentieth century, after U.S. involvement in World War I taught Americans they had "new roles to play on the world stage" (Hoffa, 2007, p. 21). Language and enrollment in university courses frequently characterized early study abroad, as did the existence of program centers, where students could study and receive advice, supervised by a faculty member from the home institution who also assigned grades and credits (pp. 72–73). Although study abroad remained associated in some people's minds with the Grand Tour, an activity for elites seeking opportunities for refinement, a counterargument is that from the start, academic rigor was expected, and study abroad was to prepare students for roles as professionals and citizens (Gore, 2005).

Study abroad's purpose remains contested. Enrollment numbers by ethnicity reveal that African American students tend to be underrepresented in study abroad, as are men. What messages are sent about study abroad that tell them that study abroad is not for them? Students of modest means may find themselves surrounded by wealthier students on some programs. When some wealthier students lunch and dine out rather than return to their host families for meals or spend weekends flying from one capital to another, the students of modest means may perceive the other students' purpose to be fun and travel rather than study and engagement with local people. It is possible, however, to reconcile these perceptions. Faculty perceptions of study abroad's purpose also vary considerably. Some want to know that academic course work abroad will meet their own high standards for instruction, content, and student work. In contrast, a faculty member recently asked students presenting in a Forum on Study Abroad why students were coming to her asking for advice on which courses to take abroad. Wasn't the point of study abroad everything except classes?

Assessment will not necessarily still such debates. However, it can help clarify for stakeholders how a program, organization, college, or university defines the purpose of study abroad and identifies desired outcomes. When purpose and desired outcomes are publicly stated, and actual outcomes are made visible, study abroad's role in undergraduate education can also be better understood. That, in turn, can help study abroad stakeholders (students and their families, faculty and staff, colleges and universities, study abroad organizations, host communities and partners) take study abroad more seriously.

As discussed repeatedly in this volume, study abroad has the potential to result in significant student learning and development. It also has the potential to strengthen undergraduate education. Indeed, study abroad is identified as a high impact educational practice, although its impact on deep learning and other gains (general, personal, practical) is less robust than, for example, faculty-student research and service-learning (Kuh, 2008). However, assessment can help tell us not only what students are learning abroad and how they are developing but also what we are doing that is helping to promote or hinder their learning and personal development. Perhaps as the assessment of study abroad continues to advance, we will learn how to strengthen study abroad as a high-impact practice, as well as to forge closer synergies with other forms of such practice, so that study abroad's promise and contributions are better realized.

References

Banta, T. W., Griffin, M., Flateby, T. L., & Kahn, S. (2009). *Three promising alternatives for assessing college students' knowledge and skills* (NILOA Occasional Paper No. 2). Urbana, IL: University of Illinois and Indiana University, National Institute for Learning Outcomes Assessment.

Blaich, C. F., & Wise, K. S. (2011). *From gathering to using assessment results: Lessons from the Wabash National Study* (NILOA Occasional Paper No. 8). Urbana, IL: University of Illinois and Indiana University, National Institute for Learning Outcomes Assessment.

Bolen, M. (Ed.). (2007). *A guide to outcomes assessment in education abroad.* Carlisle, PA: Forum on Education Abroad.

Deardorff, D. K. (2015). *Demystifying outcomes assessment for international educators: A practical approach.* Sterling, VA: Stylus.

Ewell, P. T. (2009). *Assessment, accountability, and improvement: Revisiting the tension* (NILOA Occasional Paper No. 1). Urbana, IL: University of Illinois and Indiana University, National Institute for Learning Outcomes Assessment.

Gore, J. E. (2005). *Dominant beliefs and alternative voices: Discourse, belief, and gender in American study abroad.* New York, NY: Routledge.

Hoffa, W. W. (2007). *A history of U.S. study abroad: Beginnings to 1965.* Carlisle, PA: Forum on Education Abroad.

Hutchings, P. (2010). *Opening doors to faculty involvement in assessment* (NILOA Occasional Paper No. 4). Urbana, IL: University of Illinois and Indiana University, National Institute for Learning Outcomes Assessment.

Kuh, G. D. (2008). *High-impact educational practices: What they are, who has access to them, and why they matter.* Washington, DC: Association of American Colleges and Universities. Retrieved from www.aacu.org/leap/hips

National Institute for Learning Outcomes Assessment. (n.d.). *Our mission and vision.* Retrieved from http://learningoutcomeassessment.org/AboutUs.html

Teagle Foundation. (n.d.). *Mission.* Retrieved from http://www.teaglefoundation.org/

Twombly, S., Salisbury, M., Tumanut, S., & Klute, P. (2012). *Study abroad in a new global century: Renewing the promise, refining the purpose* (ASHE Higher Education Report). Hoboken, NJ: Wiley.

ABOUT THE CONTRIBUTORS

Tasha Bleistein is a passionate intercultural educator. An assistant professor and the director of the Online TESOL program at Azusa Pacific University, she regularly teaches courses on language pedagogy and reflective teaching. Her first encounters with study abroad came as a student in Costa Rica, which lead to 11 years of teaching overseas in Honduras and China and earning a PhD in intercultural education. She has trained teachers in China, India, Thailand, and the United States, including a study abroad experience for Chinese educators in the United States. She is a qualitative researcher who also enjoys collaborating on mixed methods research projects related to novice teachers. She has coauthored two books, *One-on-One Language Teaching and Learning: Theory and Practice* (Palgrave Macmillan, 2015) and *Teaching Speaking* (TESOL Publications, 2013), as well as a number of book chapters and journal articles. She lives in Glendora with her husband, Edgar, and the local peafowl.

Elizabeth Brewer is the director of international education at Beloit College, where she is charged with facilitating campus internationalization. Central to this work have been collaborative efforts to internationalize the curriculum and to deepen the impacts of study abroad on both individual students and the larger campus. Assessment has been integral to both. Brewer's publications include *Integrating Study Abroad Into the Curriculum: Theory and Practice Across the Disciplines* (Stylus, 2009) and "Study Abroad and the City" (*Frontiers: The Interdisciplinary Journal of Study Abroad,* Vol. 20, Special Issue, 2011). A member of AIEA's executive board, she has also served as its editor and is a member of the Forum on Education Abroad's Outcomes Assessment and Research Committee. Prior to joining Beloit College, she held positions related to international education at Boston University and the University of Massachusetts at Amherst and in graduate student affairs at the New School for Social Research. Her PhD is in German literature.

Karen Chambers, PhD, is an associate professor of psychology and the faculty coordinator of international programs for Saint Mary's College. She previously served on the Global Education Advisory Committee at Saint Mary's College and is currently working on research that pertains to predictors of student success while studying abroad.

Elizabeth Ciner is a former senior program officer for faculty and staff development at the Associated Colleges of the Midwest. Prior to that she served as associate dean of the college at Carleton College, where, for almost three decades, she was involved in a wide range of faculty and program development initiatives and oversaw off-campus studies, academic advising, and the college writing program. From 2005 to 2009, she also served as principal investigator for CALL (Collaborative Assessment of Liberal Learning), a four-college consortial project, funded by the Teagle Foundation and designed to explore and evaluate a variety of value-added assessment instruments. She earned her BA with honors in English from the University of Pennsylvania and her MA and PhD in English from the University of Washington; her areas of academic specialization include rhetoric and composition and the ways writing both reflects and shapes reality.

Lisa M. Davidson is a PhD student and research assistant in Loyola University Chicago's higher education program. She earned her MA in counseling at DePaul University, where she has also served as an adjunct faculty member teaching undergraduate and graduate courses in liberal studies and college student development, respectively. Davidson's additional higher education experience spans enrollment management, career counseling, and academic advising, where she has focused on the role of academic support services in student learning. Her current research interests include examining how learning is measured in undergraduate courses that focus on race and ethnicity, with particular attention to affective dimensions of learning in this area. She is also interested in examining effective practices to recruit and retain diverse faculty and the ways in which various aspects of diversity are conceptualized and assessed in postsecondary curricula.

Dennis M. Doyle is a professor of communication studies at Central College, Pella, Iowa, where he has served as chair of the faculty advisory committee for the Central College Abroad programs. Doyle has also held the position of faculty liaison to the London program and was the 2009 recipient of Central College's Huffman Award for Outstanding Service to International Education. He is a past member of the Outcomes Assessment and Research Committee for the Forum on Education Abroad. His research investigating holistic approaches to assessing study abroad programs and their learning goals for students has appeared in *Frontiers: The Interdisciplinary Journal of Study Abroad Education*.

Mark E. Engberg is associate professor and chair of the higher education program at Loyola University Chicago. He earned his PhD in education from the University of Michigan and received his MA in counseling psychology from Northwestern University. Engberg's research investigates the educational benefits of diversity, with specific attention to how different college interventions can be used to prepare students for the diversity and global challenges of the twenty-first century. He also examines individual and organizational factors that underlie the college choice process, with a particular focus on improving access and opportunity for underserved populations. Engberg has published his work in a number of journals, including *Review of Educational Research, TC Record, The Journal of Higher Education, The Review of Higher Education,* and *Research in Higher Education.*

Joan Gillespie is vice president and director of Off-Campus Study programs at the Associated Colleges of the Midwest (ACM), a consortium of 14 liberal arts colleges in Illinois, Iowa, Minnesota, Wisconsin, and Colorado. She serves on the Forum on Education Abroad Council and is vice chair of the forum's Curriculum Development and Academic Design Committee. She was the chair of the working group of the forum's Standards Committee that developed guidelines for undergraduate research abroad. She teaches comparative higher education at Northwestern University School of Education and Social Policy graduate program in Higher Education Administration and Policy. She has authored articles and made presentations on quality standards and evaluation in international settings, assessment of student learning and development, and community-based student research. Prior to joining ACM, she served as the associate vice president for academic affairs and the assessment and program dean at IES Abroad. She holds an MA and PhD in English literature from Northwestern University and a BA in history from Vassar College.

Nick Gozik is director of the Office of International Programs and the McGillycuddy-Logue Center for Undergraduate Global Studies at Boston College. In addition, he has held positions in education abroad at Duke University, New York University, and the University of Richmond. He has served as a visiting professor at New York University, where he taught courses in research methodology, international education, and communication studies, and is currently a lecturer in Boston College's Lynch School of Education. Gozik has presented on international topics at a number of conferences. He has conducted research on education, identity, and race in the French overseas department of Martinique. He has also investigated area studies, interdisciplinarity, and the internationalization of higher education for the Social Science Research Council, with a project funded by the U.S. Department of Education. Gozik holds an MA in French language and civilization and a PhD in international education from New York University.

Julie A. Hatcher is executive director of the Center for Service and Learning and associate professor of philanthropic studies at Indiana University-Purdue University Indianapolis. She was the inaugural director of undergraduate programs in the Lilly Family School of Philanthropy, the first undergraduate degree program of its kind in the nation. Her research and scholarship focus on civic learning outcomes in higher education, the philanthropic motivations of professionals, the philosophy of John Dewey, and the public role of higher education in civil society. She serves on the National Advisory Board for the Carnegie Classification for Community Engagement and was a member of the Association of American Colleges and Universities' rubric development team for civic engagement. She consults with faculty and academic leaders on designing philanthropic studies curriculum and integrating service into academic study, and she collaborates on local and international projects to advance the public purposes of higher education.

Jen Hogan is the associate director of education abroad at Drake University in Des Moines, Iowa. She earned both her BA in anthropology and MA in interdisciplinary studies (with a concentration in international development studies) from Iowa State University. She has been in the field of international education for over 10 years and coteaches the pre- and post-study abroad courses offered through Drake's World Languages and Cultures certificate program. She has presented at various regional NAFSA conferences on topics such as quality study abroad advising and best practices for international internships. She is currently studying Arabic and is the Drake international liaison for Middle East engagement/partnerships.

Gil Latz is associate vice chancellor for international affairs and professor of geography, Indiana University-Purdue University Indianapolis, and associate vice president for international affairs and affiliated professor of philanthropy, Indiana University. From 1984 to 2012, he was affiliated with Portland State University, Oregon; over the course of his 28-year career, his appointments included geography, international studies, and vice provost for international affairs. His research on internationalization and on comparative regional development policy includes affiliation with Tokyo University and the University of Florence. He is a graduate of the University of Chicago (geography, MA, 1978; geography, PhD, 1986). Recent publications include editor of "Rediscovering Shibusawa Eiichi in the 21st Century: The Shibusawa Eiichi Memorial Foundation, 1999–2014" (*Tokyo: The Japan Journal*, 2014; Japanese edition, 2015). Current research projects include *Internationalization and the Stewardship of Urban Places* and the Global Cities Initiative, with The Brookings Institution.

Kelly McLaughlin is the assistant dean of assessment, deputy director of the Center for International and Professional Experience, and director of fellowship programs for Yale College in New Haven, Connecticut. In 2015, he began serving as Yale University's accreditation liaison officer with the New England Association of Schools and Colleges (NEASC) and will coordinate the university's 2019 report. His work in Yale College increasingly focuses on documenting students' experiential learning outcomes, work that has been positively impacted by his tenure as chair of both the Outcomes Assessment and Research Committee and the Council for the Forum on Education Abroad, which is recognized as the Standards Development Organization (SDO) for the field of education abroad. He received BA and MA degrees from UCLA in English literature before undertaking an extended period working in South Korea's higher education sector, culminating with a position at the Fulbright Commission in Seoul.

Elaine Meyer-Lee is associate vice president for global learning and leadership development at Agnes Scott College. For 13 years before that, she was the senior international officer at Saint Mary's College. Her PhD in human development and psychology is from Harvard University, where she began her studies of college student development around issues of difference and the effects of intercultural education. Besides teaching, she has conducted major research projects at the Harvard/Facing History Project, Boston College, Yale, Cambridge College, and Saint Mary's. Meyer-Lee has given numerous invited talks, consultations, and juried presentations nationally and internationally; has received grants and awards, including a Fulbright Scholarship; is the secretary of NAFSA's board of directors; and holds other national leadership positions. She wrote chapters for *The Guide to Outcomes Assessment in Education Abroad* (Forum on Education Abroad, 2007) and *Internationalizing Undergraduate Education* (University of Minnesota, 2005).

Joshua Moore has served as associate director of international education at Beloit College since 2008. Earlier, he worked in Dakar, Senegal, for four years as associate director of the ACI Baobab Center, an in-country program provider for over 20 U.S. colleges and universities. Prior to that, he was intercultural program associate at the Minnesota International Center. He holds an MA from the University of Notre Dame's Kroc Institute for International Peace Studies.

Christa Lee Olson is vice provost for international programs at Drake University in Des Moines, Iowa, and chair of the Strategic Issues Committee of the Association of International Educators. She previously held the position of associate director for international initiatives at the American Council on Education, where she directed projects on campus internationalization and communicated lessons learned through networks, publications, and presentations. Her publications include "In Quest of Meaningful Assessment of International Learning: The Development and Implementation of a Student Survey and ePortfolio Approach" (*The Journal of General Education*, 2010), *Guide for Assessing International Learning Outcomes* (2008), and *Internationalizing the Campus: A User's Guide* (American Council on Education Center for Institutional and International Initiatives, 2003). She was a Fulbright North American Senior Scholar and conducted case study research on the relationship between institutional partnerships and campus internationalization. Olson began her academic career as a professor of French and intercultural relations at New Jersey City University and holds a PhD in French from Stanford University.

Mary F. Price, PhD, currently serves as the director of faculty development at the Indiana University-Purdue University Indianapolis Center for Service and Learning (CSL). She is also an adjunct faculty member in the Department of Anthropology. Price brings a wealth of experience to her work at the center, with more than 15 years of experience working with faculty, students, and academic units in a range of domains, including undergraduate research, international study abroad, community-based learning, collaborative learning strategies, general education, and e-portfolios. As part of her scope of work, Price works directly with faculty, staff, and academic departments on course and curriculum transformation grounded using community-engaged pedagogies in the United States and abroad. Her scholarly interests include study of the processes and outcomes of community–campus partnerships, strategies and tools that cultivate critical reflection among faculty designing intercultural learning environments, and the social relations in educational production.

Michele V. Price has 34 years of experience in higher education. In 2013, she retired from Western Oregon University (WOU), where she held various positions, including serving as director of study abroad from 1999 to 2013. While at WOU, she participated in many site visits and evaluations; implemented photo-blogging and digital storytelling projects for the WOU required study abroad capstone course, which she taught; and established an ongoing research and assessment project of student reflective writing. After her retirement, she has continued research and assessment projects with a study abroad provider based in Portland, Oregon. Through her consulting work, she remains actively involved in education abroad and often serves as an on-site administrator for a London-based study abroad program. She strives to help other education abroad professionals find solutions to improve programs and to enhance student learning.

Mark Salisbury is assistant dean of academic affairs and director of institutional research and assessment at Augustana College in Rock Island, Illinois. He has published a number of research articles and essays on study abroad in both the academic and the popular press and is coauthor of the Association for the Study of Higher Education (ASHE) monograph *Study Abroad in a New Global Century*. He also publishes a weekly blog about assessing learning at a small college called Delicious Ambiguity at www.augustana.edu/blogs/ir. With a PhD in higher education and an MA in American studies, he is often drawn to the historical context of common educational practices. When Salisbury isn't engrossed in college impact work, he follows his passion for improvisational theater and applying the principles of improvisation in educational settings.

Kevin P. Saunders is the director of institutional research and assessment at Drake University. He contributed to recent books focused on applying assessment to higher education practice, including *Assessment Methods for Student Affairs* (Jossey-Bass, 2008) and *Powerful Learning Communities* (Stylus, 2013). He currently serves as a Teagle Assessment Scholar by collaborating with faculty, staff, and students to use evidence to improve student learning and by helping to facilitate multi-institution workshops. He received his PhD in higher education from Iowa State University.

Victor Savicki, professor of psychology, emeritus at Western Oregon University, received his PhD in clinical psychology and later added specialties in industrial/organizational psychology and cross-cultural psychology over his 33-year university teaching career. He has taught university students eight different times in Austria, Germany, Greece, Argentina, and the United Kingdom. Twenty-eight of his peer-reviewed publications emphasize some aspect of culture, including a six-year research study as a book, *Burnout Across Thirteen Cultures* (Praeger, 2002), and the edited book *Developing Intercultural Competence and Transformation* (Stylus, 2008). His entry in the *Encyclopedia of Intercultural Competence* (SAGE, 2015), "Stress, Coping, and Adjustment in Intercultural Competence," synthesizes his views on study abroad student development. He is a member of the Forum on Education Abroad's Outcomes Assessment and Research Committee, which amplifies his interest in evidence-based study abroad interventions and investigations.

David Schodt is professor emeritus of economics at St. Olaf College. His research interests involve Latin American economic development. He was the founding director of the college's learning and teaching center, the Center for Innovation in the Liberal Arts, a position he held from 2000 to 2011. Under his leadership, St. Olaf College was selected by the Carnegie Foundation for the Advancement of Teaching as the lead institution for an international group of eight colleges and universities exploring how the scholarship of teaching and learning can be used to examine questions about liberal learning. From 2012 to 2014, he was the senior program officer for Faculty and Staff Development Programs with the Associated Colleges of the Midwest, a consortium of 14 liberal arts colleges. He has a bachelor's degree in electrical engineering from Cornell University and an MA in public policy and a PhD in economics from the University of Wisconsin–Madison.

Rachel Shively, PhD, University of Minnesota, is an associate professor of Spanish and applied linguistics in the Department of Languages, Literatures, and Cultures at Illinois State University. Her research focuses on second-language pragmatics, discourse analysis, and language and culture learning during study abroad. Her work has been published in journals such as *The Modern Language Journal, Foreign Language Annals, System*, and the *Journal of Pragmatics*. In 2011, Shively was awarded the prestigious American Council on Teaching Foreign Languages–Modern Language Journal (ACTFL-MLJ) Pimsleur Award for Research in Foreign Language Education.

Carolyn K. Sorkin, PhD, has worked in international education for 27 years: in education abroad at Wesleyan University and the Pontificia Universidad Católica de Chile; in international admission at Brown University; in area studies, scholarly research, and public programming at New York University; and in professional training and international development through USAID-Chile. She earned her PhD in international education from NYU with a dissertation on public intellectuals in Chile's transition to democracy, a dual MA in international development education and educational administration and policy analysis from Stanford University with a thesis on Central European intellectuals and sociopolitical change, and a BA in history from Brown University. Coauthor of the Wesleyan Intercultural Competency Scale, she has served on the School for International Training's Partnership Council and Institute for Study Abroad-Butler's Executive Committee. Sorkin is now president of University Passport, LLC, a college consulting firm working primarily with international students interested in studying at U.S. universities.

Steven E. Stemler is an associate professor of psychology at Wesleyan University. He received his PhD in educational research, measurement, and evaluation from Boston College, where he worked at the Center for the Study of Testing, Evaluation, and Educational Policy and the Trends in International Mathematics and Science Study (TIMSS) International Study Center. Prior to joining the faculty at Wesleyan, Stemler spent four years at Yale

University, where he was an associate research scientist in the Department of Psychology. His area of expertise is in the assessment of noncognitive factors, with a special emphasis on the domains of social intelligence, creativity, intercultural literacy, and ethical reasoning (see http://sstemler.web .wesleyan.edu/stemlerlab and www.purposeofschool.com).

Brian Whalen is the president and CEO of The Forum on Education Abroad. Until 2010 he was also associate provost, associate professor of international studies, and executive director of the Office of Global Education at Dickinson College in Carlisle, Pennsylvania, where the Forum continues to be housed. A well-known international educator, Brian writes and speaks on a wide range of international education topics and serves on a number of boards, including the Advisory Board of the National Science Foundation Partnership for International Research and Education, NanoJapan, and the editorial board of the journal *Beliefs and Values: Understanding the Global Implications of Human Nature*. Brian is the founding editor of *Frontiers: The Interdisciplinary Journal of Study Abroad*, started in 1994 as the first academic journal devoted to study abroad, and he continues to serve as its editor and publisher. For five years he was an on-site resident director of study abroad programs in Italy, and he has developed and overseen programs in over 40 countries.

Dawn Michele Whitehead is the senior director for global learning and curricular change at the Association of American Colleges and Universities (AAC&U). Prior to her appointment at AAC&U, Whitehead served as the director of curriculum internationalization with teaching responsibilities in the global and international studies program and the Honors College at Indiana University-Purdue University Indianapolis (IUPUI). While at IUPUI, Whitehead was the program director for international service-learning programs in Costa Rica, Ghana, Kenya, and Swaziland. Her research evolved from a focus on education and educators in Ghana to the impact of service-learning on students and community partners. She also facilitated interdisciplinary campus initiatives around the assessment of global learning for students engaged with both local and international communities. In her role at AAC&U, Whitehead works with colleges and universities to integrate global learning throughout the general education curriculum. She is a graduate of Indiana University–Bloomington (PhD, 2007).

Mary Shepard Wong has three decades of teaching experience in the United States, China, Thailand, and Myanmar. Her PhD is in international and intercultural education (University of Southern California), and her MAs are in East Asian languages and cultures (UCLA) and TESOL (Azusa Pacific University). She has received two Fulbright Research Awards 2012–2013 Hong Kong, and 2015–2016 Myanmar, and served as the principal investigator of a grant commissioned by the Hong Kong Education Bureau in 2015. She has conducted over 90 presentations and has several publications, including two edited books with Routledge and one textbook with Cambridge. She has developed and led four study abroad trips in Thailand and Myanmar. Her publications and research includes internationalization of higher education, global competence, and spirituality and language teaching. She resides in Pasadena, California, with her husband and has two grown children. She directs one of the graduate TESOL programs at Azusa Pacific University, where she is a full professor.

comparative and international education, international business, intercultural relations, and service-learning that involve study abroad and that raise corresponding issues of curriculum design.

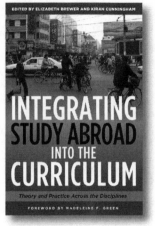

Integrating Study Abroad Into the Curriculum
Theory and Practice Across the Disciplines
Edited by Elizabeth Brewer and Kiran Cunningham
Foreword by Madeleine F. Green

"This book presents a wide range of strategies aimed at effectively integrating the benefits of time spent abroad with developments in the home campus curriculum. Drawing on a wealth of study abroad experience, this book focuses on the intentional integration of students' educational and personal experiences abroad for transformational learning and development at home."

—Comparative Education Review

22883 Quicksilver Drive
Sterling, VA 20166-2102   Subscribe to our e-mail alerts: www.Styluspub.com

Also available from Stylus

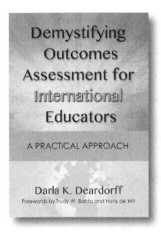

Demystifying Outcomes Assessment for International Educators
A Practical Approach
Darla K. Deardorff
Forewords by Trudy W. Banta and Hans de Wit

"This is a terrific book that will be enormously useful to international education professionals who are involved in the important work of assessing student learning outcomes."

—***Brian Whalen,*** *CEO, Forum on Education Abroad*

"This will be an enormously useful book for international educators. Thoroughly grounded in the literature and in good practice, it addresses the imperative of assessment in a clear user-friendly and practical manner."

—***Madeleine F. Green,*** *Senior Fellow, International Association of Universities and NAFSA: The Association of International Educators*

For many in international education, assessment can seem daunting and overwhelming, especially given that such efforts need to involve much more than a pre- and/or postsurvey. This book is a practical guide to learning-outcomes assessment in international education for practitioners who are starting to engage with the process, as well as for those who want to improve the quality and effectiveness of their assessment efforts.

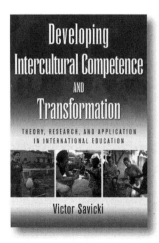

Developing Intercultural Competence and Transformation
Theory, Research, and Application in International Education
Edited by Victor Savicki

"Savicki and contributors urge educators to craft international opportunities for learning based in experiential and reflective practices. Combining educational theory, program assessment, and pedagogical design, their essays serve as a guide for educators hoping to lead students toward transformation through intercultural exchange."

—***Diversity and Democracy***

This book provides study abroad educators with a theoretical framework and examples of practice to craft more meaningful activities that will make a long-term difference in the quality of student experiences and set the stage for transformative change. It is also relevant for anyone engaged in courses in adult education, college student services,